Microwave Cooking the *Amana* Way with the *Amana* Radarange
MICROWAVE OVEN

PRECAUTIONS TO AVOID POSSIBLE EXPOSURE TO EXCESSIVE MICROWAVE ENERGY

1) Do not attempt to operate this oven with the door open since open-door operation can result in harmful exposure to microwave energy. It is important not to defeat or tamper with the safety interlocks.

2) Do not place any object between the oven front face and the door or allow soil or cleaner residue to accumulate on sealing surfaces.

3) Do not operate the oven if it is damaged. It is particularly important that the oven door close properly and that there is no damage to the: (a) door (bent), (b) hinges and latches (broken or loosened), (c) door seals and sealing surfaces.

4) The oven should not be adjusted or repaired by anyone except properly qualified service personnel.

Contents

Chapter	Page
Introduction to Radarange Oven Cooking	3
Meal Planning	20
Appetizers and Snacks	25
Beverages	32
Soups and Stews	37
Breads	43
Rice, Cereals and Pastas	50
Sandwiches	62
Eggs and Cheese	67
Fish and Seafood	74
Meats and Main Dishes	82
Poultry	106
Vegetables	115
Sauces, Jams and Relishes	128
Desserts	137
Cakes	147
Pies	155
Cookies	165
Candies	176
Radarange Oven "Extras"	182
Index	186
Reference Chart	192

This chapter contains very valuable information. You should read the "Introduction" before you begin to cook in your Radarange Oven. There is no need to memorize all of the information. You can use this chapter as a handy reference anytime you have a cooking question.

General Cookbook Format

You will find that your **Microwave Cooking the Amana Way with the Amana Radarange Microwave Oven Cookbook** is very easy to read and understand. All of the recipes in this cookbook have been tested by a staff of trained home economists.

Recipes for this cookbook were tested using 700-watt* Amana Radarange Microwave Ovens with the exclusive Rotawave® Cooking System. Ovens used had 10 power settings ("Cookmatic Levels"). This cookbook is designed for use with several different Radarange Oven models. Carefully read the "power level" section which describes your oven. Wattages for the 10 settings in this cookbook are as follows:

Settings	Cooking Power Output (Approximate Wattage)
Full Power	700 Watts
Cookmatic Level 9	630 Watts
Cookmatic Level 8	560 Watts
Cookmatic Level 7	490 Watts
Cookmatic Level 6	420 Watts
Cookmatic Level 5	350 Watts
Cookmatic Level 4	280 Watts
Cookmatic Level 3	210 Watts
Cookmatic Level 2	140 Watts
Cookmatic Level 1	70 Watts

The recipes have been selected on the basis of variety. You will find recipes that range from the gourmet type to the simple "good-home cookin'" type. Recipes from every food category are found, so you can use them as guides to adapt your own favorites.

Before reading individual recipes or beginning to cook, consult the first few pages of the particular chapter. Many hints and general instructions for preparing each food category are found at the beginning of each chapter. This information should help in answering all of your questions concerning specific types of foods. Also found at the beginning of each chapter are charts for

*Per FCC 1 liter test

convenience foods, frozen foods and others. Always look for defrosting information at the beginning of each chapter.

Whenever you can't locate a particular food item in a chapter, consult the index. The item could be located in another area.

MICRO-TIPS are found in many of the recipes throughout the cookbook. These MICRO-TIPS are helpful hints which may give you garnish suggestions, serving tips, ingredient substitutions or other information. Frequently, the MICRO-TIPS will suggest a particularly good use of a Radarange Oven feature for the particular recipe, such as the Automatic Temperature-Control feature which is present on some Radarange Oven models. You will want to quickly scan recipes and make note of any MICRO-TIP information, before cooking.

Recipe-Reading Tips for Good Food Results

Always carefully follow the recipe.

Be certain to:

- **Use the exact utensil recommended.** The size, shape and material of the utensil are all important. Large size dishes are usually recommended to avoid boil-overs. Cooking a food in a differently-shaped dish than in the one recommended could cause the amount of cooking time to vary. Utensil materials can also cause a variation in cooking results. For example, glass lids retain moisture and decrease cooking time more than do paper towels, or no cover used at all. Be sure to use exactly what is recommended.

- **Use the exact cooking time recommended.** You will notice that most recipes give ranges of cooking time. A recipe may say, for example, "Cook in Radarange Oven on Full Power for 1 to 2 minutes, or until sauce is thickened". You can check the sauce after 1 minute, since it could be thickened adequately to serve. However, it may be necessary to allow the sauce to thicken for the extra minute. Notice that the words **"or until sauce is thickened"** are included. In each recipe, there will be stated a **visual** test, whereby you can determine whether the food has actually finished cooking by knowing what it should look like.

- **Use the same type of ingredients recommended and measure**

carefully. When testing recipes for this cookbook, standard measuring utensils were used, as well as standard measuring methods. It is important in any type of cooking that measurements are accurate. Also, be careful in substituting ingredients. MICRO-TIPS often recommend substitutions which will not alter cooking times or results. Do not make a substitution which is not recommended; food product results can vary tremendously. The only **exception** in substitutions is seasonings. Salt, pepper and others can be easily added or deleted to suit personal tastes. In many recipes, you will notice in the preparation steps to "season as desired". Almost all spices can easily be substituted without affecting food results.

- **Increase the cooking time if you increase the size of a recipe.** For example, 4 potatoes require longer cooking time than does 1 potato. 6 muffins will require a longer cooking time than 3 muffins. A general rule to follow when increasing the size of a recipe is: when doubling a recipe, increase the cooking time to **slightly less** than 2 times as long. (When tripling, increase the cooking time to **slightly less** than 3 times as long, etc.) Also, be certain to change the dish size accordingly.

Don't forget to decrease the cooking time, also, when **decreasing** the size of a recipe. A general rule to follow is: when cutting a recipe in half, decrease cooking time to **slightly more** than half. Again, be certain to change the dish size accordingly. See "Adapting Conventional Recipes", on page 15.

GLOSSARY OF MICROWAVE COOKING TERMS

Before actually reading recipes, you should familiarize yourself briefly with the following microwave cooking terms. You don't have to memorize! You can always quickly check this section if you see an unfamiliar term that you don't understand. The terms are in alphabetical order, so you can easily find a particular term.

ARCING: A static discharge of electricity which causes a spark. This usually occurs between separated particles of metal, such as a metal twister for plastic bags, gold trim on a dish or a metal utensil almost touching the side wall of cooking compartment.

ARRANGING: Suggested placement of several items of the same food in the Radarange Oven to produce the most satisfactory cooking results for the particular food. Arrange foods as the recipe suggests. Example: Arrange potatoes in a circle, rather than in rows. When reheating plates of food, place dense foods near the outside of the dish where they will heat first.

AUTOMATIC TEMPERATURE CONTROL SYSTEM: See your Use and Care Manual for more information, if your oven has this feature.

BROWNING SKILLETS: Special microwave energy-absorbing dishes which, after preheating, produce heat for browning food by surface contact. See section on page 14.

BURSTING OR ERUPTING: The build-up of steam or pressure in the food product that causes the surface to split open. This may occur in foods such as apples, eggs, poultry and vegetables which are enclosed in a skin, shell or membrane. This could also occur with a plastic "membrane" such as a frozen vegetable plastic pouch. In order to prevent bursting, it is necessary to puncture or pierce the skin or membrane, or remove the shell.

CARRY-OVER COOKING TIME: Period of time during which some foods need to rest following their removal from the Radarange Oven. During this time, foods will finish cooking by themselves, without the need of extra microwave cooking time.

COOKING GRILL: Special cooking dish which consists of a plastic or glass-ceramic rack insert that fits inside of a glass or glass-ceramic dish. Particularly used for meat cookery. See "Accessories", page 10.

COOKMATIC LEVELS: Reduced cooking power levels or settings. Each power level is particularly well suited for cooking different types of foods. For instructions on how to use, see your Use and Care Manual.

COVERING OR WRAPPING: Placing a glass lid, plastic cover, paper towel or waxed paper over a dish, or around a food. Usually done to prevent spattering or to retain steam. Steam retention allows for a more even distribution of heat, more rapid cooking and prevents dehydration of the food. Heavy-duty plastic wrap should be pierced to allow some steam to escape. Do not cover dishes unless stated in the recipe. Use the type of covering the recipe recommends. Paper towels or waxed paper covering don't retain steam to the same extent as plastic and glass. See "General Utensil Tips" No. 8, on page 10.

DEFROSTING (THAWING): Method of applying microwave energy to frozen foods with short intervals of power, during which time heat is distributed throughout the entire food and ice molecules are changed into water. Food should be completely defrosted before cooking begins. See "Defrosting" section on page 13.

DELICATE INGREDIENTS: Some ingredients such as eggs, cheese, seafood, milk and others are "special" or "delicate". These foods are best prepared on a lower Cookmatic Level or setting, rather than on Full Power.

DENSITY: Foods have different densities and thus absorb microwaves in different ways. Porous foods, such as breads, allow microwaves to penetrate them instantly. Dense food items, such as meats, absorb microwaves on the exterior, while the center is heated by conduction. Thus, dense foods require a longer cooking or heating time. Foods of the same size, but having different densities, will cook at different speeds. For this reason, 2 or more foods in the raw state usually should not be cooked in the Radarange Oven at the same time, unless recommended in a recipe or menu. However, a plate containing all cooked foods can be easily reheated in the Radarange Oven. See "Reheating Cooked Foods" section on page 16. See "Meals All-At-Once", page 21.

HIGH ALTITUDE COOKING: High altitude adjustments, necessary for conventional cooking, are usually not necessary for microwave cooking. The only change required may be to slightly increase the cooking time.

HOLDING TIME: Refers to the time required for a food to "rest" before beginning to cook. For example, foods must be allowed to stand or hold after defrosting before they begin cooking, so that the food is completely defrosted. A holding time can also be used between 2 different cooking periods. During a holding time, the food is allowed to equalize in temperature. A food should be covered during the holding time for best results.

PIERCING: Breaking the skin or membrane of foods such as vegetables or eggs, which allows the steam to escape and prevents bursting. Either a knife or a fork is used to make slits or holes, depending upon the type of food. Plastic wrap or plastic cooking bags should also be pierced to allow steam to escape during cooking.

PLASTIC RACK: Insert which fits inside glass or glass-ceramic dish. Allows moisture and fat to drain off meat as it cooks. Can be used separately for heating breads, sandwiches or other foods. See "Accessories", page 10.

PREHEATING: Process of heating an empty browning skillet, without lid or oil, inside the Radarange Oven for a specified length of time, depending upon the size of skillet and type of food. The special coating on the skillet bottom will absorb microwaves and become hot. This heat is used to brown small food items, such as small cuts of meat. See "Browning", page 14.

RESTING: The amount of time suggested, after cooking or defrosting, which will allow the heat in the foods to equalize or spread to the center of the foods. Sometimes referred to as carry-over cooking. See "Carry-Over Cooking Time", page 4.

SHIELDING: Covering parts of a large food item, such as turkey, with thin strips of metal foil before cooking. This is done to shield some portions of a food product from microwave energy. Metals should not be used in small food loads, such as for T.V. dinners. Use aluminum foil strips only when recommended in recipes.

STARTING TEMPERATURE: Temperature of foods when they are first placed inside the Radarange Oven for defrosting, heating or cooking. Room temperature or warm foods heat more quickly than refrigerator temperature foods. For example, hot tap water will heat more quickly than cold.

STEAMING: Cooking in covered utensil. Steaming allows for faster cooking.

TEMPERATURE PROBE: See your Use and Care Manual for more information, if your oven has the Automatic Temperature Control System.

TURNING: Includes two different types: 1) Inverting foods or **turning foods over,** such as roasts, during the cooking cycle. 2) Rotating a dish in a clockwise manner. When using recipes in this book, turn or rotate a dish 180° or a half-turn, unless otherwise specified in the recipe. When using your Radarange Oven, little, if any, turning is required. See "Turning", page 12.

UTENSILS AND ACCESSORIES

Your Radarange Oven will make it possible to use utensils that you have never used for cooking before. You will now be able to heat food, as well as serve, on paper, plastic, glass or china plates.

There are only a few utensils, such as metal pots and pans, which should not be used in your Radarange Oven. Most utensils **can** be used. You will find that you already have many satisfactory utensils in your kitchen which can be used.

Utensils Not to Use

There are some utensils which should not be used in a microwave oven. See the photograph for examples, on page 8.

- **Metal Utensils**
  Metal utensils should not be used. This includes ceramic dishes with metal trim, foil pans and aluminum foil (except when recommended in recipes). Metals reflect microwaves. Thus, metals will keep portions of food from cooking by reflecting microwaves away from the food. The use of metal utensils can cause slower cooking, uneven cooking and can even prevent cooking. The use of metal utensils also increases the amount of energy needed for microwave cooking and can damage the utensil or parts of any microwave oven.

The only time metal should ever be used in the Radarange Oven is when it is recommended in a recipe. For example, some recipes recommend using small strips of aluminum foil when cooking large meat and poultry items. Small strips of foil can be used to "reflect" microwaves away from over-exposed areas, such as poultry wing tips or legs, which tend to dehydrate or overcook.

Foil should be used only when cooking a large food item. Metal foil strips should not touch the oven door or sides.

T.V. dinners packaged in foil trays will cook better if removed from the metal tray. Simply remove your T.V. dinner from the metal tray and place it on a ceramic or paper plate for defrosting and heating. Metal clamps or skewers should not be used. Use wooden skewers for shish kabobs and tie roasting bags with string. Remove all metal pieces from poultry, if possible, before cooking. When defrosting, remove metal parts from poultry or meats as soon as possible.

- **Centura® Dinnerware and Corelle® Livingware Cups**
  (closed-handle)
  Do not use CENTURA Dinnerware by Corning in the Radarange Oven. This dinnerware contains a glaze which absorbs microwaves, causing the dishes to heat during cooking. The dishes can become hot enough to break. CORELLE Livingware closed-handled cups should not be used in a microwave oven, since they can also heat and break during cooking. CORELLE Livingware cups having open handles may be safely used, as well as all other pieces of CORELLE Livingware.

- **Melamine Dishes**
  Melamine dishes should not be used in a microwave oven. They will become hot and may crack during cooking.

- **Lead Crystal**
  Do not use antique glassware that may contain metallic substances, such as lead crystal. Such glass could break during cooking.

- **Foil-Lined Paper**
  Foil-lined paper should not be used, due to the metallic content.

Utensils to Use

Many different utensils can be used in the Radarange Oven. See the photographs for examples, on page 9.

You may use most utensils made of non-metallic materials and utensils that do not have metal trim or hardware (handles, etc.). Recommended materials for utensils include most:

1) Paper
2) Glass
3) Glass-Ceramic
4) Plastic

Utensils made from these four material types are generally safe for use in the Radarange Oven. However, there are some exceptions. Here are specific examples of utensils made from these four materials which **are** recommended for use in the Radarange Oven.

Paper

Almost all paper products may be used. Paper plates, cups, towels and napkins are several examples. Use plain white paper products, rather than colored. Paper towels may be used to cover other cooking utensils during cooking, to help prevent the spattering of the Radarange Oven walls and interior. (Do not use paper towels which contain nylon or other synthetic fibers since the heated synthetic could cause the paper to ignite.) Paper towels or plates can also be used to absorb grease during the cooking of some foods, such as bacon. Paper products are particularly good for reheating foods. For example, breads should be wrapped in paper towels during reheating to keep them moist. Waxed paper, parchment paper or flattened brown paper bags can be used to line a high temperature plastic baking sheet for cookie baking. Paper liners can be used to line plastic muffin trays. Vegetables can be heated in cardboard (paper) boxes, if the box is pierced or slit before cooking. When using any kind of paper in the mirowave oven, follow the recipe timings carefully and don't leave the paper in the microwave oven for an extended time or it could ignite. **Newspapers** should never be placed in a microwave oven. Some types of printers' ink can absorb microwave energy and could cause the paper to ignite.

Glass

Most glassware can be used. Glass cake dishes, pie plates, measuring cups, custard cups and sauce dishes can be safely used. Fire-King® glassware by Anchor Hocking and Pyrex® by Corning are examples of glassware you can use. Do not use antique glassware or glassware having a metal trim. Be careful when using delicate glassware, because heat from the food could cause it to crack.

Glass-Ceramic and Ceramic

Most glass-ceramic utensils can also be used in the Radarange Oven. Tableware such as plates, cups or saucers made of most glass-ceramic materials can be used. Ceramic mugs, tube cake dishes, vegetable platters or other serving dishes may be used. Some specific examples of glass-ceramics which can be safely used in the Radarange Oven are as follows: CORELLE Livingware by Corning (do not use Corelle® closed-handle cups), CORNING WARE® by Corning and Cookmates® by Corning. Stoneware and china can generally be used, but it should be tested to determine whether it is Radarange Oven-safe. Some glazes used by manufacturers contain metallic substances and should not be used in a microwave oven. One example of a glass-ceramic that has a glaze not suitable for microwave oven use is CENTURA® by Corning. Many manufacturers will label packaging or the dishes themselves as being "microwave oven-safe". If you're not certain whether a dish is "microwave oven-safe" you can test your own glass-ceramic utensils by performing the utensil test. Dishes having a metal trim or metal parts should never be used in the Radarange Oven.

Utensil Test: Use this test to determine when a glass-ceramic or ceramic utensil is satisfactory to use in the Radarange Oven.

Place a glass measuring cup of water next to the empty dish to be tested in the Radarange Oven. Heat on Full Power for 1 minute, 15 seconds. At the end of this time, check the temperature of the tested dish. If the dish is cool and the water is very warm, the dish can be used. If the dish is slightly warm, it should be used for short-term cooking only. If the dish is hot and the water is cool, DO NOT USE THE DISH. (The dish will remain cool if it is not absorbing microwaves and the microwaves are then absorbed by the water. The dish will become hot if it **is** absorbing microwaves and the water will remain cool.)

Plastic

Plastic utensils (except for melamine dinnerware) can generally be used in the Radarange Oven. (See No. 1 under "General Utensil Tips", on page 10.) Examples include plastic measuring cups, plastic bowls, plastic muffin trays and other plastic containers. Heavy-duty plastic wrap, such as Saran Wrap,™ may be used to cover other utensils to prevent spattering. Some types of plastic wrap should not remain in the Radarange Oven too long because they may become sticky or shrink. Pierce a hole in plastic wrap before cooking, to allow for steam to escape during cooking. Plastic wrap having foil edges should not be used. Plastic foam cups and dishes can be used for heating foods in the Radarange Oven. Plastic freezer containers can be used for defrosting and heating foods, but remember to first remove the plastic lids. Plastic baby bottles can be placed in the Radarange Oven for quick warm-ups, but remove restrictive lids. Plastic pouches, such as "boil-in-the-bag pouches", are good to use in the Radarange Oven. Simply pierce or cut a small opening in the pouch to allow for steam to escape during cooking. Some packaged frozen vegetables-in-pouches even contain microwave cooking instructions on the packages. Plastic bags which are used with heat sealer units can also be used for cooking in the Radarange Oven. Just remember to pierce the bags before defrosting or cooking.

Use heat-set plastics or plastics that are labeled "dishwasher-safe". Avoid cooking foods having a high fat or sugar content in plastic utensils, since fat and sugar get very hot during cooking and may melt the plastic. If any **food** gets hot enough during cooking, the food itself, and not the microwaves, can melt plastics. Try to use plastic dishes for heating foods only to a serving temperature or for short-term cooking. During long-term cooking, the food can become hot enough to melt some plastics.

Other Utensils to Use

• **Wood, Straw**

Wooden spoons, straw baskets and other utensils made from these materials, can be used for quick re-heating periods, but are generally not recommended for long-term cooking. During long periods of cooking, these items may become too dry and can crack.

• **Shells**

Seafood shells, such as clam shells or escargot (snail) shells, can

be used as "utensils" in the Radarange Oven for heating seafood.

• **Natural Fiber Cloths**

Cotton or linen cloths, such as dishcloths or napkins, may be used as coverings for utensils in the Radarange Oven. Avoid using cloths made from synthetic fibers, such as nylon. Some synthetic fibers can melt in the microwave oven.

ACCESSORIES

There are some special accessories you may wish to use in your Radarange Oven. Some are briefly described here. These accessories can be ordered from your local Amana dealer.

Browning Skillets or Grills

Browning skillets or grills are ceramic utensils which contain a special coating on the bottom that helps them to brown small foods items. Browning skillets are available in several different sizes. See "Browning", page 14.

Cooking Grill: Dish & Rack

The cooking grill consists of a glass or glass-ceramic dish which is fitted with a plastic or glass-ceramic rack insert. The rack can be used separately or inside the dish. The cooking grill with the two parts used together, is good for cooking meats, heating appetizers and other uses. Calorie-watchers like the cooking grill, since fats can drip off of the rack, away from meats. The dish captures all juices, which can be saved for gravy, and can even

< **Don't use these utensils in a microwave oven:**

> metal skillets
> metal baking pans
> metal TV dinner trays
> metal twists
> dishes with metal trim
> Centura dinnerware
>   (upper left)

Use these utensils in a microwave oven

help in saving bacon grease for cooking uses. The rack can be used separately for heating sandwiches, breads and other foods.

Thermometers

No thermometer should be used **inside** the Radarange Oven while it's in operation, except the Automatic Temperature Control of your Radarange Oven, if your oven has this feature, or a specially designed microwave oven thermometer which has an all-plastic head.

General Utensil Tips

1. **All foods in this cookbook were tested using glass utensils.** If plastic utensils are used, the cooking time will need to be shortened to avoid overcooking, since foods generally cook faster in plastic utensils. If ceramic utensils are used, the cooking time will probably have to be lengthened, since most foods take longer to cook in ceramic utensils.
2. Be certain your dishes are suitable for microwave oven use.
3. Consult the recipe for the proper size utensil.
4. If you don't have the size of dish the recipe recommends, substitute a larger one. This will help to prevent "boil-overs". The amount of cooking time may be slightly less, due to the larger dish size. A larger dish will expose a greater surface area of the food to the microwaves.
5. Always select a utensil large enough to hold the food. Select a dish which has room for the food to expand during cooking. By using large dishes, you can avoid boil-overs.
6. Use round dishes whenever possible. Ring-molds are good utensils to use for baked goods. (You can invert a custard cup in an 8 or 9 x 2-inch round cake dish to create your own ring mold for breads or cakes.) See "Breads" chapter, page 43.
7. Utensils generally remain cool to the touch. However, during long-term cooking, the food may heat the dish. You may wish to keep hot pads handy to aid in removing foods which have cooked for long periods of time.
8. Always use the type of utensil **covering** recommended in the recipe. Waxed paper and paper towels don't retain moisture to the extent that heavy-duty plastic wrap and glass lids do. If a dish doesn't have a glass lid and the recipe says "cook, covered", substitute heavy-duty plastic wrap. Plastic wrap should be pierced, by making a 1-inch slit with a knife, when it's used as a covering. Paper towels or linen napkins are recommended for covering or even wrapping breads and cakes during reheating. A damp cotton cloth, such as a dishcloth, is recommended as a covering for rising breads. If a recipe does not state, "Cook in Radarange Oven, covered," then **don't** cover the food. Coverings, or lack of them, can greatly influence the amount of cooking time required.
9. Always be certain that a utensil contains food when placed in a microwave oven. Browning skillets or browning grills which are to be preheated are the **only** utensils which should be used empty in a microwave oven. See, "Browning Skillets," page 14.

RADARANGE OVEN COOKING TECHNIQUES

Radarange Oven cooking **is** slightly different from conventional cooking. Although you can apply most of your conventional cooking knowledge to microwave cooking, you should be aware of special "cooking techniques" which are unique to microwave cooking.

Cooking Variables

Microwave cooking can be directly affected by different food variables.

The **shape** of foods can greatly affect the amount of cooking time. Foods that are flat and thin heat faster than foods which are chunky. For example, a casserole will cook faster in a flat dish, rather than if heaped in a small dish. Foods cut into small pieces will cook faster than large-shaped foods. Pieces should be of a uniform size and shape for more uniform cooking, or the smaller pieces will cook faster. The greatest amount of heating takes place within 3/4 of an inch of the food's surface. The interior of large food items, or dense foods, is heated by the heat conducted from the outer food layer. For best results, cook foods together which have similar sizes and shapes.

The **quantity or volume** of a food can affect the amount of cooking time. As the volume of the food is increased, the time required to cook or heat the item increases almost proportionately. If twice the amount of food is placed in the oven, it will take almost twice as long to cook. For example, if 1 potato cooks in 4 minutes, then 2 potatoes will require about 7 to 7-1/2 minutes of cooking time, or not quite 8 minutes. Increase the amount of cooking time when you increase the amount of food to be cooked.

The **density** of foods can greatly affect the amount of cooking time. Porous foods, such as breads, cakes or pastries, will heat much more quickly than dense meats of the same size. Porous foods absorb microwaves quickly throughout. Meats absorb microwaves mostly at the exterior surface, and the interior is heated by conduction, increasing the cooking time. Meats can be cooked in a sauce, if desired. Due to the moisture content, a sauce will heat rapidly. The heat will transfer to the meat, so the meat will heat faster due to heat by conduction as well as by microwaves.

The **starting temperature** of foods affects the amount of cooking time. Each temperature degree that the food item is to raise must be supplied with a definite amount of energy. Lower initial starting temperatures require more energy and more time to cook. Therefore, refrigerator temperature foods require a longer cooking time than do room temperature foods. Foods already slightly warm will heat very quickly in the Radarange Oven.

The **moisture content** of foods affects the amount of cooking time. The higher the moisture content is in a food the longer the amount of cooking time.

The **fat and sugar content** of foods affects the amount of cooking time. Foods containing high fat and sugar levels heat very quickly and may reach much higher temperatures than foods having low fat and sugar levels. Foods having lower fat and sugar levels require longer cooking times.

The **arrangement of food** within a microwave oven cavity affects the way in which the food cooks. Arrange foods as recipe suggests. When only one food item is being cooked, place it in the center of the Radarange Oven for cooking.

Manipulation of Foods

You will find that your new Radarange Oven will require virtually no turning or rotating of cooking dishes. Some foods, such as large meats and poultry will need to be turned **over** halfway through the cooking time.

Some foods, such as sauces, gravies, soups, stews and beverages, will need to be **stirred** occasionally or halfway through cooking time because the **food** requires stirring for good results. If you prepared these foods conventionally, more constant stirring would be required.

With other foods, such as scrambled eggs, you may want to stir for a fluffier product. Some casseroles and other foods will need to be stirred halfway through the cooking time for maximum blending of food flavors.

In general, food will require little or no turning during cooking in your new Radarange Oven.

If some recipes do suggest manipulating or moving food during cooking, you should be familiar with the several forms of manipulation:

• **Stirring**
Stirring is required less often in microwave cooking than in conventional cooking. In conventional cooking, you use a spoon to move food up from the bottom of a pan to evenly distribute the heat. In microwave cooking, you still stir to redistribute the heat within some foods, but you need to stir from the outside of a dish toward the inside or center. For the recipes in this cookbook, stir only as needed. If a recipe states to stir once or twice during cooking, stir at approximately even intervals. For example, in a 12-minute cooking period, if a recipe states to stir twice, stir after 4 minutes of cooking and again, after 8 minutes of cooking. However, it is not necessary to be precise. Stir only when

necessary. When using lower Cookmatic Levels or settings, less stirring is required. Some examples of foods which may require stirring are puddings, some casseroles, some sauces, some soups and some egg dishes. Some foods can't be stirred. These foods are rearranged or turned.

• **Rearranging**

A few foods which can't be stirred should be repositioned or rearranged during cooking. One example is baked custards. Rearranging allows for the most even cooking of foods. Foods which are cooked, covered, or which are cooked using lower Cookmatic Levels, usually require very little rearranging.

• **Turning**

There are actually two types of turning. Turning is done when foods cannot be stirred. Foods which are cooked, covered, or which are cooked at lower Cookmatic Levels usually require little turning.

Turning foods over: Turning foods over is done to redistribute heat. Meat and poultry are two types of foods which are sometimes "turned over." Examples include large roasts, turkeys and whole chickens. Small meat items or poultry pieces may need to be turned over when in casseroles, or when in a browning skillet.

Rotating or turning dishes: There are a few foods which cannot be stirred, rearranged or turned over. Therefore, the actual cooking dish is turned or rotated. For the recipes in this cookbook, turn a dish one-half-turn or 180° unless otherwise stated. A half-turn means to grasp the dish and turn the portion of the dish that faces the Radarange Oven door around, until it faces the back of the oven. Examples of foods which are sometimes turned or rotated in a cooking dish include quiches and soufflés.

Power Levels

Many foods cook very well at full microwave power. However, just as some foods cook better conventionally at lower rather than higher oven temperatures, some foods cook better at lower rather than higher microwave power levels. Each power level is particularly well suited for cooking different types of foods. Each recipe in this cookbook specifies the Cookmatic Level to be used for cooking. To learn how to use the Cookmatic Power levels see your Use and Care Manual.

10 Power Levels

If your Radarange Oven has ten Cookmatic Power Levels or settings, prepare the recipes in this cookbook as indicated.

6 Power Levels

If your Radarange Oven has **only** six Cookmatic Power levels or settings, you will find that these settings are equivalent to the following Cookmatic Levels, starting with your lowest Cookmatic Level: (Cookmatic Level 1, 2, 4, 6, 8 and Full Power). For the Cookmatic Levels used in the recipes in this book, see the chart on page 3.

3 Power Levels

If your Radarange Oven has three Cookmatic Power Levels or settings, you will find that these settings are equivalent to the following Cookmatic Levels, starting with your lowest Cookmatic Level. (Cookmatic Level 4, 6 and Full Power). For the Cookmatic Levels used in the recipes in this book, see the charts on pages 3 and 18.

1 Power Level

If your Radarange Oven has one power level or setting, you will need to change some recipe times before cooking.

If your Radarange Oven is a 500-watt* microwave oven, it will cook slightly slower than a 700-watt* oven. The recipes in this cookbook are designed for 700-watt microwave ovens. However, you can easily adapt the recipe timings for your oven by consulting the "500-Watt Microwave Oven Summary Chart", on page 18. Since your oven does not have a defrost setting, make sure all foods are completely defrosted before cooking them in your Radarange Oven.

Automatic Temperature Control System

To learn to use the Automatic Temperature Control System see your Use and Care Manual, if your Radarange Oven has this feature.

Defrosting

The ability to defrost foods quickly is a major benefit of your Radarange Oven. Microwaves defrost the outer-portion of the food and the heat is carried to the center.

It's very important that most foods, especially meats, be totally defrosted before they begin to cook. If they **aren't** totally defrosted before cooking, then the cooking will be uneven.

Most defrosting in this cookbook is accomplished by using the Defrost feature, although defrosting can be accomplished by using lower Cookmatic Levels or settings. To learn how to set the oven for defrosting, see your Use and Care Manual.

Follow the defrosting instructions for each specific food type in the individual chapters of this cookbook. Defrost charts are found toward the beginning of each chapter, if applicable. (For example, there is no Defrost Chart in the "Eggs and Cheese" chapter.)

General Hints for Defrosting Foods

1. Defrosting times can vary, depending upon the sizes, shapes, weights and densities of the foods. If a food is not completely defrosted in the recommended amount of time, allow it to stand for a few minutes at room temperature to complete defrosting.
2. The amount of defrosting time can vary due to how solidly the food is frozen. (For example, a freezer in a combination refrigerator-freezer may not freeze foods as solidly as an individual freezer.)
3. Foods can be defrosted in their original wrappings. Loosen boxes or lids and pierce plastic bags. Remove all metal parts. Metal clamps holding turkey legs should be removed during defrosting as soon as possible. Remove foods from metal containers before defrosting. See the "Metal Utensils" section on page 6.
4. Some larger foods may need to be turned over during defrosting, for the best results.
5. For faster defrosting, separate foods frozen in pieces as they thaw. For example, meat patties frozen together can be separated. Hamburger can be broken apart with a fork and stirred. Thawed hamburger should be removed as it defrosts so it will not start to cook.
6. To determine whether foods such as meats are totally defrosted, insert a sharp knife in the center of the food to check for remaining ice crystals.
7. Do not completely defrost frozen fruits. Fruits taste "freshest" when served with some remaining ice crystals.
8. For best results, always bake frozen pie crusts in the Radarange Oven before adding the filling.
9. When defrosting cream pies or cakes which have frosting, turn them once or twice during the defrosting time. To avoid melting the frosting, do not completely thaw large cakes or cream pies.

• Heating Defrosted Foods

1. To avoid dehydration, don't heat porous foods such as breads or cakes after defrosting them, unless you plan to eat them immediately.
2. Frozen fried foods can be cooked, but will not be crisp when prepared in a microwave oven. Examples: fish sticks, French fries and onion rings.
3. Place uncooked cake or quick breads batter from commercial TV dinners in a 6 oz. custard cup. Cook the batter, separately, after the rest of the dinner. Also, heat any baked breads included in TV dinners, separately, after the rest of the dinner.
4. When cooking frozen pizza, use a microwave pizza crisping accessory or a preheated browning skillet for the best results. See "Appetizers and Snacks" chapter, on page 27.

Freezer to Radarange Oven

1. When freezing homemade foods, freeze them in the same dish in which they will be defrosted and heated. Use containers which can be placed directly in the Radarange Oven. If you don't wish to use a dish for freezer storage, line the dish with freezer foil. Arrange the food in the container and freeze. Once frozen, lift the food from the dish using the

foil extensions. Wrap the food tightly and return it to the freezer. When ready to use, just remove it from the foil and return it to the baking dish or casserole. When you want to store food in the serving dish, just wrap the total dish in foil or place it in a heavy plastic bag.

2. Sectional-shaped paper plates work well for freezing your own homemade TV dinners.

3. Foods can be frozen in single portions, so that a single family member can later defrost and heat them quickly.

4. Freeze your own garden vegetables after first blanching them in the Radarange Oven. Frozen vegetables can be defrosted and heated within minutes in the Radarange Oven.

5. To save food preparation time, cook extra food in the Radarange Oven for "planned-overs". Freeze these foods in Radarange-Oven-safe packaging. In the future, your food will be ready to eat in minutes, after it is quickly defrosted and heated. Pre-cooked frozen foods should be used within 2 to 3 months.

Browning

When preparing food in the Radarange Oven, you will find that some foods will not brown the same as they do in a conventional oven. This is particularly true for baked goods, such as breads and cakes. But the lack of browning can be easily "disguised."

When cooking a cake, for example, the frosting or a topping will cover the cake and the lack of browning is not noticed. Also, dark-colored ingredients can be used in bread dough and cakes to simulate browning. Some examples are whole wheat flour, rye flour, raisins, dark brown sugar or dark spices, such as cinnamon.

Browning is also easily achieved with meats. Meats which weigh 3 pounds or more will brown by themselves "naturally" in the Radarange Oven. This is because the exteriors of meats of this size become very hot during cooking. Many meats of this size have high fat content and fats also become very hot during cooking. This heat, plus the longer cooking times, are required for browning. Therefore, larger cuts of meat and poultry will brown by themselves.

For additional browning, a bottled browning sauce or soy sauce may also be used with meats. For poultry, a paste of shortening and paprika will give a golden-brown color.

Smaller cuts of meat do not require a very long cooking time. The exterior of smaller cuts will not become as hot as larger cuts during cooking, due to their short cooking time. Therefore, they will not brown to the same extent as they do when conventionally cooked. When preparing smaller cuts of meat in your Radarange Oven, a browning skillet or grill should be used in order to achieve maximum browning.

Browning Skillets

Browning skillets or grills are recommended for some foods in this cookbook.

A browning skillet or grill has a special tin oxide coating on the bottom exterior which has the ability to absorb microwaves when the skillet is preheated empty in a microwave oven. As the tin oxide coating absorbs microwaves, the skillet bottom heats.

Browning skillets or grills can be used to brown many different foods. By preheating the skillet for different amounts of time, the amount of heat for browning will vary. The type of food you wish to brown will determine the amount of preheat time. Toasted cheese sandwiches or fried eggs don't require as much heat for browning as do small meats. Therefore, preheat times for eggs or bread items are shorter than preheat times for meats. For exact preheat times, follow the manufacturer's instructions.

For more information concerning the use and care of browning skillets or grills, consult the use and care manual packaged with the browning skillet, or see the manufacturer's instructions.

Adapting Conventional Recipes

Most of your favorite conventional recipes can be easily prepared in the Radarange Oven. Since most foods cook 3 to 4 times faster in the Radarange Oven than in a conventional oven, reduce the amount of conventional cooking time to one-fourth or one-third for the Radarange Oven. For example, if a conventional recipe requires 1 hour of cooking time, reduce the cooking time to about

15 to 20 minutes for Full Power cooking in the Radarange Oven. Cook for about 15 minutes first. If necessary, add the additional few minutes. There are a few guidelines that need to be followed for converting. **Read the following tips before converting your own recipes.**

1. Use other recipes in this cookbook as guides. In this cookbook, the general hints for cooking various foods found at the beginning of each chapter will tell you how to convert your own favorite recipes. (You may wish to reduce seasonings in your conventional recipes, since almost none of their flavor will be lost during microwave cooking.) For a particular type of food, read the specific information given in the chapter. Then find a similar recipe in that chapter in terms of actual ingredients and food type. For example, if you have a favorite meatball recipe, one of the several meatball recipes in this cookbook can be used as a guide. You should choose the meatball recipe that most nearly matches your own. Then:

   a. Use the same dish and covering recommended.

   b. Use approximately the same cooking time.

   c. Use the same Cookmatic Level or setting.

   d. Test the food 1 to 2 minutes before it's supposed to be finished cooking. Your recipe could vary slightly and may not require quite as much cooking time. You can cook for the extra 2 minutes, if necessary. Your recipe might even require a slightly **longer** cooking time than the "guide" recipe.

   e. **Remember:** It's always best to slightly undercook a food and then add a few seconds or minutes to finish the cooking, if necessary. Once a food is overcooked, you can't reverse the cooking process.

   f. When you find the correct amount of cooking time required, make a note of it on your recipe. Then you will know the exact amount of cooking time required the next time you wish to prepare the same food in your Radarange Oven.

2. Most of the recipes in this cookbook have a yield of 4 to 6 servings. Whenever you wish to reduce the yield for lower-quantity cooking, remember to reduce the amount of cooking time. For example, if you decrease the quantity of a recipe by half, cut the cooking time approximately in half.

Also, remember to reduce the dish size. Try to use a dish of approximately the same shape. (For example, if the recipe requires a large round dish, use a small round dish.)

When increasing the size of a recipe or the amount of food, remember to **increase** the cooking time. For example, 4 potatoes require a longer cooking time than does 1 potato. A general rule to remember when increasing the size of a recipe is: When doubling a recipe, increase the cooking time to **slightly less** than 2 times as long. When tripling, increase the cooking time to slightly less than 3 times as long, etc. Again, be certain to change the dish size accordingly.

3. Your Radarange Oven is a 700-watt microwave oven and cooks faster than other microwave ovens on the market. When using Full Power, the Radarange Oven cooks at a very fast speed. Therefore, when using recipes other than those in your Amana cookbook, cooking times may be too long. Many newspapers, magazines and other sources print microwave oven recipes. Many convenience foods, particularly frozen convenience foods, now include microwave oven cooking times. All recipes or package directions are usually written for high or full power, which on your unit is the Full Power setting. If the recipe requires a "one-half" or 50% cycle, use the Cookmatic Level 5 setting. If the recipe requires a "one-third-power" or 30% cycle, use the Cookmatic Level 3 or Defrost setting. If the recipe requires thawing, use the Defrost pad, or on models having dial timers, use Cookmatic Level 3 for defrosting. Frequently, recipes or package instructions will have a **range** of cooking time given. For example, a recipe may state, "Cook for 4 to 7 minutes." Since your Radarange Oven cooks at a very fast speed, the recipe should require a **minimum** amount of cooking, or, in this case, only 4 minutes. Always cook for the shortest suggested amount of cooking time given in the "range". Then, check the food a short while **before** the **suggested** time is expired. Always use the Full Power setting unless otherwise stated.

Reheating Cooked Foods

When reheating **cooked** foods, you can reheat a plate containing a combination of several foods.

Reheating is a great benefit when not all family members can eat at one time. "Doggie-bag" meals can also quickly be reheated and will taste as if they've just been freshly cooked.

Also, leftovers can become "planned-overs." Extra food can be prepared in the Radarange Oven and reheated later at a minute's notice. Reheated food will always taste fresh.

There are some general guidelines to follow when reheating foods.

• General Hints for Reheating Foods

1. When reheating single dinner plates of food, place only one plate at a time inside the Radarange Oven. Cover each plate with heavy-duty plastic wrap or waxed paper to retain heat and moisture, before serving.
2. Arrange slow-to-heat foods around the outside edge of a plate. Examples include meats, poultry and potatoes.
3. Place quick-heating foods in the center of a plate. Foods having low moisture, high fat or high sugar contents heat quickly. So do foods having narrow parts or foods cut in small pieces. Examples include vegetables such as peas, fruits and some desserts.
4. Arrange irregular pieces of food with the thickest parts toward the outside edge of the plate. Examples include poultry pieces or some small cuts of meat.
5. Spread foods out or arrange them in a thin, even layer over the plate, rather than heaping them, for faster reheating. For example, spread out scalloped potatoes or mashed potatoes. Keep a food portion size small rather than large.
6. If the meat is served with a sauce or gravy, spoon some over the meat before reheating to avoid dehydration.
7. Reheat porous items such as breads and cakes for a minimum amount of time. For best results, reheat these items separately.
8. Reheat fish and seafood for a minimum amount of time.
9. Cover plates with heavy-duty plastic wrap or waxed paper, before reheating. Keep covered until ready to serve.
10. Place a plate of food directly in the center of the Radarange Oven for reheating.
11. Reheat on Full Power for about 1 to 1-1/2 minutes per plate, or until the food is warmed as desired. Reheating times can vary, depending upon the quantity and types of food being reheated. Reheat refrigerator temperature foods longer than room temperature foods. If the plate bottom feels slightly warm, then the food is probably adequately reheated, since it is conducting heat to the bottom of the plate.
12. Foods can also be reheated in serving dishes, if desired. Do not reheat foods in dishes having a metal trim.
13. Before reheating soups, sauces or beverages, stir them vigorously.
14. For reheating small quantities of food quickly, see the "Everyday Foods Heating and Reheating Chart," located for convenience at the end of this cookbook.
15. Use the Automatic Temperature Control to reheat leftover soups, casseroles, meats, vegetables, etc., to serving temperature, if your Radarange Oven has this feature. Serving temperature for most foods is 150° F.

Low Calorie Cooking

Controlling calories and cooking with microwaves are natural partners. Excessive amounts of fat, butter or margarine are not needed to prevent sticking in a microwave oven. Sauces can be eliminated or kept to a minimum and menus can be individualized to meet special diet needs.

The quick "steam-type" cooking made possible with the Radarange Oven allows foods to steam in their natural juices. Just add a touch of a favorite seasoning to enhance natural food flavors. Or, try cooking a favorite food in a little bouillon, rather than using a tempting rich sauce or butter.

Another way to reduce calories is to eat a smaller-than-normal serving. With the easy-to-reheat feature of the Radarange Oven, a single portion can be enjoyed at one meal and any remainder can be saved for reheating at another meal.

When part of the family wishes to enjoy higher calorie foods, a calorie controlled portion of the same food can be placed separately in a small dish. Heat the calorie-controlled portion separately and quickly in the Radarange Oven.

A few of the recipes in this cookbook are designed especially for calorie watchers. Look for calorie-count information in the MICRO-TIPS.

Food Precautions for Microwave Ovens

Review this list, and do not cook these items in your microwave oven.

1. **WARNING: Do not heat liquids in a microwave oven without first stirring.** Liquids must be briskly stirred or poured (to mix in air) before being heated in a microwave oven. If air is not mixed into liquid, it can erupt in the oven, or when removed from the oven.
2. **Eggs** must not be cooked or reheated in the shell. Eggs should not be cooked with an unbroken yolk. To do so may result in a pressure build-up and eruption. Pierce the yolk with a fork or knife before cooking.

   Do not reheat previously cooked eggs in the microwave oven unless finely chopped or scrambled.

3. **Potatoes, tomatoes** or **other foods with a "skin"** must only be cooked in the microwave oven after the skin has been pierced. All foods with an outer skin or membrane must be pierced to allow steam to escape during cooking.
4. **Special popcorn** in bags designed and labeled for **microwave only** may be used. Since your microwave oven cooks very fast, do **not** exceed the minimum amount of cooking time recommended on the popcorn package. Do **not** leave the oven unattended.
5. **Home canning** must not be done in a microwave oven. Home canning is generally done with metal lids. Since metal lids reflect microwaves, you cannot be assured that the food product will be heated uniformly to 212° F or above, and there is a probability of deterioration of the food product.
6. Do not leave the microwave oven unattended when drying **anything.** Foods or items being dried can become too dry and can ignite. If anything does ignite, press the STOP switch and open the oven door only after ignition ceases.
7. Do not use paper towels which contain nylon or other synthetic fibers since the heated synthetic could cause the paper to ignite.
8. **Deep fat frying** must not be done in any microwave oven. The fat could overheat and be hazardous to handle.
9. **Excess fat and drippings** from meats and poultry should be basted away during cooking to prevent spattering.
10. **Extreme overcooking,** as in conventional cooking, can cause food to smoke or possibly ignite. In the rare event this happens, close the oven door and the fire will self extinguish.
11. **We do not recommend operating the microwave power when the oven is empty.** Microwave energy can damage the magnetron tube if the oven is operated empty for an extended period of time.
12. **Metal or ceramic accessories** which have a special design to absorb microwave energy to provide heat ("active" accessories such as browning skillets) may be used with caution. Be sure to carefully read all instructions provided with the accessory. Any questions concerning these accessory products should be referred to the accessory manufacturer. Amana Refrigeration, Inc. doesn't endorse any brand of accessory. If you purchase any accessory follow the accessory manufacturer's directions. Remember that all microwave accessories are not "top quality"; some may **not** be suitable for microwave cooking. Caution must be used when purchasing microwave accessories.

Guidelines for Using an Oven with 3 Power Settings

The recipes in this Cookbook were written for Radarange Ovens with 10 cookmatic levels or power settings. If your Radarange Oven has 3 power settings, you may wish to refer to the following chart from time-to-time for guidelines on which setting to use on your oven.

3-POWER LEVEL OVEN CONVERSION CHART

Setting in Cookbook Recipe	Adaptation Instructions for 3-Power level oven
Full Power	Full Power
Cookmatic Level 9	Full Power*
Cookmatic Level 8	Full Power*
Cookmatic Level 7	Slo Cook**
Cookmatic Level 6	Slo Cook
Cookmatic Level 5	Slo Cook*
Cookmatic Level 4	Defrost
Cookmatic Level 3 or Defrost	Defrost*
Cookmatic Level 2	Defrost*
Cookmatic Level 1	Avoid recipe using this cookmatic level

*Slightly decrease the amount of cooking time given in recipe.
**Slightly increase the amount of cooking time given in recipe.

Lower Wattage Microwave Ovens

Lower wattage microwave ovens cook slower than 700-watt microwave ovens. "Full Power" on your microwave oven is not the same as "Full Power" on 700-watt microwave ovens, but is a slightly slower setting. Since all of the recipes in this cookbook were developed for 700-watt Radarange Ovens, you will need to adjust recipe times before cooking in a lower wattage microwave oven.

Guidelines for Using a 500-Watt Microwave Oven

- If your oven does not have a defrost setting, make sure fo is completely defrosted before cooking.
- Some utensils suggested in recipes may not fit in your ove Try to substitute a utensil that will hold the same amount food, and which has the same shape as the recommend utensil.
- Foods cooked in your oven will require more turning (rotati and stirring than is recommended in the recipes. You will ne to turn some foods frequently, such as cakes, pies, qui breads and other baked goods.
- Follow all instructions for preparing and covering foo exactly as stated in all recipes.
- Follow instructions given in the "500-watt Microwave Ov Summary Chart" for adjusting **all** cooking times.
- After you have cooked a food in your Radarange Oven, ma a note of the amount of cooking time **for your oven**, so you c easily cook the food again, at a future time.

500-WATT MICROWAVE OVEN SUMMARY CHART

Setting in Cookbook Recipe	Adaptation Instructions for 500-watt microwave oven
Full Power	Use the "Recipe Conversion Chart" for determining recipe times.
Cookmatic Level 9	Increase the amount of time given in the recipe by 25%.
Cookmatic Level 8	Increase the amount of time given in the recipe by 10%.
Cookmatic Level 7	Use the **same** time range given in the recipe.
Cookmatic Level 6	Decrease the amount of time given in the recipe by 15%.
Cookmatic Level 5	Decrease the amount of time given in the recipe by about 1/3.
Cookmatic Level 4	Decrease the amount of time given in the recipe by about 50%.
Cookmatic Levels 3, 2, and 1	Avoid recipes using these levels.

RECIPE CONVERSION CHART*

AMOUNT OF RECIPE TIME IN THIS COOKBOOK (For Full Power cooking)*			AMOUNT OF TIME TO USE FOR 500-WATT OVEN (For Full Power cooking)**		
Hr.	Min.	Sec.	Hr.	Min.	Sec.
		10			14
		20			28
		30			42
		40			56
		50		1	10
	1	00		1	24
	1	30		2	06
	2	00		2	48
	2	30		3	30
	3	00		4	12
	3	30		4	54
	4	00		5	36
	4	30		6	06
	5	00		7	00
	6	00		7	24
	7	00		9	48
	8	00		11	12
	9	00		12	36
	10	00		14	00
	11	00		15	24
	12	00		16	48
	13	00		18	12
	14	00		19	36
	15	00		21	00
	16	00		22	24
	17	00		23	48
	18	00		25	12
	19	00		26	36
	20	00		28	00
	25	00		35	00
	30	00		42	00
	40	00		56	00
	45	00	1	03	00
	50	00	1	10	00
1	00	00	1	24	00

*This chart should be used only for recipes which use the Full Power level or setting in the cookbook. For instructions on how to adjust recipe timings which use other settings, see the "500-Watt Microwave Oven Summary Chart" (page 18).

**The amount of Full Power cooking time in the cookbook is increased by about 40% for full power on 500-watt ovens. You may need to use slightly more cooking time for some recipes, especially for baked goods, such as cakes, pies, cookies and quick breads. All cooking times are approximate.

INSTRUCTIONS FOR USING RECIPE CONVERSION CHART

1. When a recipe in the cookbook uses the Full Power setting, you will use the "Recipe Conversion Chart" to adjust the amount of cooking time for your oven.
2. Look in the first column (or left column) for the amount of cooking time given **in the cookbook recipe.**
3. Look at the time given directly across the chart in the second column (or right column). This is the approximate amount of cooking time you will use for your oven.

Example: You may want to prepare a recipe which states, "Cook in Radarange Oven on Full Power for 2 to 3 minutes, or until warmed."

Follow these basic steps:

1. Find 2 minutes on the chart in the first column.
2. Look at the time given directly across the chart in the second column: 2 min. 48 sec.
3. Find 3 minutes on the chart in the first column.
4. Look at the time given directly across the chart in the second column: 4 min. 12 sec.
5. You have now found the range of cooking time to use for your oven. You will first cook for 2 min. 48 sec., and if the food is not "warmed" you will continue to cook up to a total of 4 min. 12 sec. This is an approximate range of cooking time. If the food is yet not "warmed" after cooking for 4 min. 12 sec. (or almost 4-1/2 minutes), you can cook for a slightly longer time, or until the food is warmed. Be careful not to overcook.

NOTE: If a recipe in this cookbook has a cooking time on Full Power that you want to adjust and it's **not** found on the chart, you can determine the amount of cooking time for your oven by adding approximately 40%.

Example: If a recipe states, "Cook in Radarange Oven on Full Power for 22 minutes," add 40% to find the cooking time for your oven.

22 minutes + 40% increase
= 30 minutes, 08 seconds

You will cook the food for 30 minutes, 08 seconds in your oven.

Once you cook a few foods in the Radarange Oven, you will soon want to combine foods to make a meal. Usually, meal preparation requires cooking food items in a sequence, one after another. However, some foods can be cooked **together** or "all-at-once" with excellent results. In this chapter, you will find meals prepared either in a sequence or cooked "all-at-once!" Both types of meal preparation can be easily accomplished in your Radarange Oven.

Until you become more familiar with microwave oven cooking, you might want to do a little extra planning when you prepare your first few microwave oven meals, just as you planned more carefully when preparing your first "conventional oven meals". In fact, planning is the key to good microwave oven meals. The extra planning will be well worth your time, because you will save a considerable amount of cooking time by using your Radarange Oven, rather than your conventional oven.

Before you prepare entire meals in your Radarange Oven, you will want to familiarize yourself with the general meal planning hints.

General Hints for Meal Planning

1. BEFORE BEGINNING

   Allow yourself plenty of time when you're planning your first few meals, so you are completely at ease and won't feel rushed.

   If you are planning a menu of your own, consider the following points as you do when cooking conventionally:

   • Contrast of color and texture of the foods

   • Nutritional balance of foods

   • Flavors of foods . . . do they blend well?

   Before starting, think through the entire meal. Assemble all of the utensils and ingredients required in the recipes. Also, **carefully read each recipe** before starting so you are familiar with all of the instructions.

2. SEQUENCING

   Sequencing is one type of meal preparation. Foods are arranged in a certain cooking **sequence**. That is, one food will be cooked first, another will be cooked second and so on. To determine in what order or sequence you should prepare foods, consider the following:

   • Can any of the foods be prepared ahead of time? Some desserts should be prepared hours ahead or even the day before, in order to cool before serving. They can generally be reheated quickly, just before serving, if desired. It is usually better to reheat these items rather than to try to completely cook them at the last minute.

   Other foods can be prepared ahead and then easily reheated. Remember, Radarange Oven reheated foods maintain a fresh flavor. Spaghetti sauce, for example, can be made the day before a big dinner and can be quickly reheated before serving time.

   • How long of a cooking time does each food require? Some foods, such as meats or main dishes, require a longer cooking time than other foods, such as vegetables. Generally, a good rule to remember when planning the sequence or order of cooking is: Cook the food having the longest cooking time first.

   Usually foods which require a longer cooking time retain or hold heat well. Some dishes, such as casseroles, will actually improve in flavor when they are allowed to stand for a few minutes. Some foods require a "carry-over" cooking time, during which the food will actually finish its cooking without microwaves. Foods which do retain heat well or which do require a "carry-over" cooking time, should be prepared first. While these foods stand, other foods can be cooked in the Radarange Oven. Therefore, proper sequencing of foods will often result in a **shorter overall cooking time** than preparing a meal "all-at-once."

   Items which are generally cooked first or sometimes hours or a day ahead, include the following:

   • Desserts (which can be reheated later or need to be served cooled or chilled)
   Examples: pies, cakes, puddings, cookies

- Sauces (which can be reheated later, if necessary)
  Examples: salad dressings, main dish sauces, dessert sauces

- Appetizers (some can be made ahead or even frozen to reheat later)
  Examples: meat balls, dips, spreads

- Long-Cooking Foods (which retain heat and may require carry-over cooking)
  Examples: large cuts of meat or poultry, meat items that require simmering, casserole mixtures

Foods which should be prepared later in a sequence include the following:

- Foods which don't reheat well
  Examples: fish and seafood, eggs, small meat items

- Foods having a shorter cooking time
  Examples: breads, fish and seafood, vegetables

- Foods which need WARMING or reheating
  Examples: rolls, sauces, beverages

Actual Meal Preparation Using Sequencing

Now that you're familiar with some of the "rules", let's consider an actual menu and how the foods should be sequenced.

A sample menu might include the following:

Meat Loaf or Roast
Baked Potatoes
Green Beans
Tossed Salad with Hot Dressing
Dinner Rolls

Chocolate Pie
Coffee

The chocolate pie should be cooked early in the day or even the day before. It can then be chilled before serving. The dinner rolls can also be cooked ahead.

The meat loaf (or roast) requires the longest amount of cooking time so it should be cooked first in the sequence. It will retain heat well, if it is covered or wrapped in aluminum foil, **after** it is removed from the Radarange Oven. Next, cook the potatoes. They, also, will retain heat well if they are wrapped in aluminum foil, **after** they are removed from the Radarange Oven. The green beans should be cooked third. Cover them with a glass lid or plastic wrap, after removing them from the Radarange Oven.

A hot salad dressing can be quickly heated fourth and the quick-heating rolls are last. Cover rolls with a linen or paper napkin during and after heating. Instant coffee can be heated while the pie is being cut for serving.

While one food is cooking, be preparing the other foods so they can be placed in the Radarange Oven immediately. Start a food cooking as quickly as possible. Remember, **always** have some food inside the Radarange Oven at all times so no cooking time is wasted. Also, while foods are cooking, the table can be set.

You will notice that foods are always **covered** after they are removed from the Radarange Oven. Foods are covered so they will stay moist and retain their heat. By covering foods, they will all be "piping hot" when served. You can also put foods in a warm place after removing them from the Radarange Oven, such as inside your insulated conventional oven. You may wish to slightly undercook some foods, such as eggs or meats so they won't overcook while covered.

Some coverings are better than others. Roasts and other meats can be wrapped with aluminum foil or they can be kept inside a baking dish, having a glass lid. Baked potatoes can be wrapped in aluminum foil. (Remember, use aluminum foil as a wrapping **only** after removing the food from the Radarange Oven.)

Glass lids or heavy-duty plastic wrap are good for covering foods, since they are water-vapor-proof. Paper towels or cotton and linen napkins are good for covering baked goods, such as breads and cakes.

3. MEALS "ALL-AT-ONCE"
   Some foods can be prepared "all-at-once" in the Radarange Oven with excellent results. Often, less-dense foods, such as dinner rolls, can be placed in the Radarange Oven during the final minute of the main dish's cooking so the rolls are hot and ready-to-serve with the rest of the meal.

Some foods which cook especially well "all-at-once" are:

    Pot roast cooked with vegetables
    Main-dish casserole cooked with a vegetable
    Main-dish casserole cooked with a dessert
    Two similar vegetables cooked together with a
        main dish

Some of the menus in this chapter, designated as "All-at-Once" Meals will give you some ideas about how to prepare meals using this method of preparation in the Radarange Oven. If you have a favorite menu which is similar to one of the "All-at-Once" Meals menus in this chapter, you can prepare your own menu, using the "All-at-Once" Meal menu as a guide.

4. QUANTITY COOKING

When preparing an extremely large meal, such as a holiday dinner, you may wish to use both the Radarange Oven and conventional oven. Foods which can be done in the Radarange Oven include the foods that take too long to cook conventionally such as a beef roast, a ham or a turkey. Foods such as rice, pasta or boiled potatoes can be prepared conventionally and reheated if necessary in the Radarange Oven. Or, these foods can be prepared a day in advance and easily reheated in the Radarange Oven before serving.

5. LATE ARRIVALS

If guests are a few minutes late, don't fret. Foods can be quickly returned to the Radarange Oven to be reheated, if necessary. A good serving temperature for most foods is 150° F. Foods can also be reheated quickly before serving second helpings. Don't reheat foods in serving dishes having a metal trim. Remember, remove aluminum foil before reheating.

6. SUMMARY

Here is a list of brief reminders to consult before preparing a Radarange Oven meal:

BEFORE MEAL PREPARATION

- Know your menu and recipes well.
- Plan a logical cooking sequence or plan to cook the meal "all-at-once."
- Prepare foods ahead, if possible.

DURING MEAL PREPARATION

- If sequencing, cook the food having the longest cooking time first. Prepare each food in sequence, ending with the food having the shortest cooking or heating time. If cooking a meal "all-at-once," place all foods together in the Radarange Oven.
- Cover foods after removing them from the Radarange Oven to keep the foods warm.
- If sequencing, always have a food ready to cook in the Radarange Oven so when one food finishes cooking, another is ready to be cooked. When you start meal preparation, begin cooking a food as quickly as possible. If preparing foods "all-at-once," you may wish to add a food such as dinner rolls in the final minutes of cooking.
- While food is cooking, set the table and do any other extra duties.
- Reheat foods, if necessary, for late arrivals just before serving.

Complete meals can be easily prepared in the Radarange Oven. Start with simple meals and think through the sequence or "all-at-once" possibilities. Always remember that no matter what unexpected interruption develops, the foods will reheat beautifully. Begin with the menu ideas on the next pages. Use these menus as a guide in cooking your own menus in the Radarange Oven. All of the menus use recipes found throughout this cookbook. For information concerning how to adapt your own favorite recipes, see page 15 in the Introduction chapter. Soon you will be preparing your own favorite meals with ease in the Radarange Oven.

Breakfast

(For 4)

Menu

Baked Grapefruit

Wake-Up Special
Cranberry Muffins

Instant Hot Chocolate

Early in the Morning or the Day Before

1. Prepare and cook the muffins. See the recipe on page 48. Store in a covered container or cover with plastic wrap, when cooled.

2. Mix together the ingredients for the hot chocolate. See the recipe on page 33. Store in a covered container, until ready to serve.

Before Serving

3. Prepare and cook the grapefruit. See the recipe on page 138. (Note: The quantity of this recipe, and therefore, also the cooking time, needs to be doubled for this menu.) Cover grapefruit loosely with waxed paper to retain the heat until ready to serve.

4. While grapefruit is cooking, prepare the eggs. See the recipe on page 71. Cook the eggs. Slightly undercook the eggs, so they won't overcook during the standing time. Keep the eggs covered with a glass lid or plastic wrap to retain the heat until ready to serve.

5. While the eggs are cooking, set the table.

6. The water for the hot chocolate can be heated while the grapefruit is being eaten.

7. The muffins may be heated, if desired. The muffins can be heated in a straw basket, wrapped with a napkin. Keep the muffins covered with the napkin to retain their heat for serving.

Brunch

(For 2)

Menu

Chilled Fruit Cup

Biscuit Breakfast Ring
Hash 'N' Egg Nests

Coffee

The Day Before

1. Prepare and cook the fruit cup. See the recipe on page 139. Chill.

Before Serving

2. Prepare and cook the bread ring. See the recipe on page 47. While bread ring is cooking, add oranges and bananas to the fruit cup, if it was prepared the day before. Place the fruit cup in individual serving dishes, if desired, and return any left-overs to the refrigerator. (Note: You may wish to divide the fruit cup recipe in half for this menu.) Invert the bread ring on a serving platter, leaving the dish on top to retain moisture and heat until ready to serve.

3. Prepare and cook the hash and eggs. See the recipe on page 73.

4. Water for instant coffee can be heated while the fruit cup is being served. (If "perking" your coffee, plug in the coffee pot just before brunch so the coffee will be ready to serve.)

"All-at-Once" Meal

"Light" Luncheon

(For 3)

Menu
Chicken 'N' Rice
Herbed Broccoli
Rolls
Coffee

Before Serving

1. Prepare Steps #1 and #2 of the chicken dish, according to the recipe on page 111.

2. Prepare the broccoli in a 9 x 5 x 2-inch loaf dish, according to the recipe on page 124, through step #1.

3. Put the chicken in the left side of the Radarange Oven and the broccoli on the right side. Cook in the Radarange Oven on Full Power for 10 minutes. Separate the broccoli. Cook in the Radarange Oven on Full Power for an additional 7 minutes.

4. Place 6 rolls in a plastic bag, leaving the bag open. Place the rolls in the Radarange Oven, on top of the chicken and broccoli dishes for the last 1 minute of cooking.

"All-at-Once" Meal

Family Dinner

(For 4)

Menu
Classic Meat Loaf
Baked Potatoes
Peas & Carrots
Tossed Salad with
Creamy French Dressing
Coffee

Early in the Morning or the Day Before
1. Prepare the salad dressing, according to the recipe on page 132. Chill.

Before Serving
2. Select 4, uniformly shaped, medium-size potatoes. Scrub and pierce each.

3. Prepare the meat loaf, according to the recipe on page 102.

4. Put the meat loaf and potatoes in the Radarange Oven. Place the 4 potatoes in a circle on the left side of the Radarange Oven. Place the meat loaf on the right side of the Radarange Oven. Cook in the Radarange Oven on Full Power for 10 minutes, or until the foods are warmed.

5. While the potatoes and meat loaf are cooking, place 1 (10 oz.) package of frozen peas and carrots in a 1-quart casserole. Add 2 tablespoons of water. Cover with a glass lid or plastic wrap. Place the frozen peas and carrots in the Radarange Oven in the middle of the circle of potatoes. Rotate the potatoes. Add sauce to meat loaf.

6. Cook all in the Radarange Oven on Full Power for an additional 10 minutes. Stir the vegetable halfway through the cooking time. When stirring the vegetable, remove the potatoes if done and wrap them in foil to keep them warm. During the final minutes of cooking, prepare the salad and add the dressing.

7. The water for instant coffee can be heated while serving the dinner. (If "perking" your coffee, plug in the coffee pot just before dinner so the coffee will be ready to serve.)

The Radarange Oven enables a host or hostess to prepare food for a party and still have time left for many last-minute details.

Some appetizers can be prepared ahead and then heated, as needed, when guests arrive. Some appetizers, such as meat balls, can be frozen ahead and then defrosted for a quick, spur-of-the-moment party.

Most appetizers can be quickly and easily heated on Full Power. Others require a lower setting for more delicate ingredients, such as cheese or mushrooms.

Read the general hints for heating appetizers and snacks before preparing them in your Radarange Oven.

General Hints for Heating Appetizers and Snacks

1. Use serving dishes for heating appetizers. Be certain dishes are Radarange Oven-safe. By using only one dish for both heating and serving, you can save precious time when entertaining.
2. Arrange appetizers in a single layer when heating, for best results. In most cases, cover with waxed paper or a paper towel to prevent spattering. Stir dips before serving.
3. Use lower settings for delicate ingredients such as cheese, mushrooms or shellfish, as recommended in the recipes. Cheese can become stringy or rubbery if heated at too high a setting. Mushrooms can "pop" if heated on Full Power. Seafood in the shell tends to become somewhat tough and it may also "pop" if heated at too high a setting.
4. Whenever possible, prepare appetizers ahead and then quickly heat when guests arrive. Freeze meatballs ahead, if desired. Quickly defrost and heat when needed.
5. Don't place spreads on crackers until ready to heat to prevent sogginess.
6. Ordinary popcorn should only be popped in the Radarange Microwave Oven Popcorn Popper. Special popcorn in bags, designed and labeled **for microwave only** may also be used.
7. Shellfish may be heated directly in the shell, since shells allow microwaves to transmit through them. Shells make attractive and unique "serving dishes".
8. Stale or soggy potato chips, crackers or other snacks can be freshened in the Radarange Oven. Heat in Radarange Oven on Full Power for about 30 seconds to 1 minute.
9. Blocks of cheese can be heated for serving. Heat for only 30 seconds to 1 minute on Cookmatic Level 5.
10. Heat most appetizers and snacks on the Full Power setting. Appetizers which include the melting of cheese, a delicate ingredient, should be heated as indicated in the recipe. Appetizers containing mushrooms can be quickly heated on Cookmatic Level 8 to avoid "popping" during heating. When heating your own favorite appetizers and snacks, select a similar recipe from this chapter as a guide. Use approximately the same amount of time recommended and use the same setting.

APPETIZERS AND SNACKS FROZEN CONVENIENCE FOOD CHART

APPETIZER OR SNACK	PKG. SIZE	DEFROSTING TIME ON DEFROST*	HOLDING TIME**	COOKING TIME ON FULL POWER
Frozen Snack Tacos	6 oz.	1 min., 30 sec.*	1 min., 30 sec.	1 min., 30 sec to 2 min.
Frozen Egg Rolls	6 oz.	3 min.*	3 min.	1 to 2 min.
Frozen Pizza Rolls	6 oz.	2 min.*	2 min.	1 to 2 min.
Frozen Snack Pizzas	7-1/4 oz.	2 min.*	2 min.	1 min., 30 sec. to 2 min.

*On models having dial timers, use Cookmatic Level 3 for defrosting.
**Allow a holding time equal to the defrosting time between defrosting and cooking.

General Instructions for Cooking Frozen Appetizers and Snacks Convenience Foods
1. Place appetizers or snacks on plastic rack over 2-quart utility dish. Cover with paper towel.
2. Defrost, hold and cook, according to timings in chart. Cook until hot.

Glazed Bacon

Yield: 14 appetizers

1/2 lb. bacon
1/2 to 1 cup brown sugar, firmly packed

1. Cut each slice bacon in half. Spread brown sugar on waxed paper or plate. Lay each piece bacon on brown sugar. Pat firmly to coat sides with sugar.
2. Arrange bacon on cooking grill. Cover with waxed paper. Cook in Radarange Oven, covered, on Full Power for 4-1/2 to 5 minutes, or until bacon is crisp, as desired. Cool on brown paper bag to absorb grease. Bacon will stick to most other types of paper.

Teriyaki Strips

Yield: 30 to 36 appetizers

1 lb. sirloin steak, 1/4 to 1/2-inch thick
1/2 teaspoon ginger
1/2 cup bottled teriyaki sauce
1/4 cup dry sherry

1. Cut beef into 30 to 36 thin strips. Spread in 2-quart utility dish.
2. Combine ginger, sauce and sherry. Pour over meat strips. Refrigerate for 1 hour, basting several times. Drain.
3. Thread meat strips on 8 wooden skewers. Arrange 4 skewers on cooking grill. Cook in Radarange Oven on Full Power for 2 minutes, or until steak is cooked, as desired. Turn skewers over halfway through cooking time. Repeat with remaining meat. Remove meat from skewers to serve.
MICRO-TIP: Serve hot with buttered slices of party rye bread.

FROZEN PIZZA CHART

PIZZA SIZE	COOKING TIME ON FULL POWER
5-1/3 oz. (Snack Size Pizza)	1 to 2 min.
9 oz. (7 to 8-inch round pizza)	1 to 2 min.
13-1/2 oz. (10-inch round pizza)	2 to 2-1/2 min.
18 oz. (7 x 8-inch Pan Style Pizza)	2-1/2 to 4 min.

*On models having dial timers, use Cookmatic Level 3 for defrosting.

General Instructions for Preparing Frozen Pizza
1. Preheat large browning skillet, or microwave pizza crisping accessory, empty, according to manufacturer's instructions. Place pizza firmly against bottom of browning skillet for maximum heat contact.
2. Heat, according to time and setting on chart.

Chinese Hors D'Oeuvres

Yield: 3 dozen appetizers

12 slices bacon
1 (8 oz.) can water chestnuts, halved
Teriyaki Sauce

1. Cut each bacon slice in thirds. Wrap each water chestnut with bacon slice. Secure each with toothpick.
2. Dip in teriyaki sauce. Arrange 12 in circle on cooking grill. Cover with paper towel.
3. Cook in Radarange Oven, covered, on Full Power for 3 to 5 minutes, or until bacon is crisp. Repeat with remaining appetizers.
   MICRO-TIP: Dip in additional teriyaki sauce or in heated "Sweet-Sour Sauce", on page 130 when serving.

Nachos

Yield: 3-1/2 dozen appetizers

1 (1 lb.) can refried beans or
1 (10-1/2 oz.) can jalapeno bean dip
1 (5-1/2 oz.) pkg. tortilla chips
4 ozs. shredded Cheddar cheese
14 pimento-stuffed olives, sliced in thirds or jalapeño peppers

1. Spread 1 teaspoon refried beans or bean dip on each tortilla chip. Top with one teaspoon cheese and one thin slice of olive. Place 8 in circle on paper plate.
2. Heat in Radarange Oven on Cookmatic Level 7 for 30 to 45 seconds, or until cheese is melted. Serve warm. Repeat with remaining appetizers.

Coquilles

Yield: 6 to 8 servings

1 lb. fresh scallops (or frozen
  and defrosted)
1 lb. fresh mushrooms
2 tablespoons butter or margarine
2 tablespoons lemon juice
1 cup dry white wine*
1/4 teaspoon savory
1 bay leaf
1/2 teaspoon salt
1/8 teaspoon pepper
3 tablespoons butter or margarine
3 tablespoons all-purpose flour
1 cup light cream
1/2 cup toasted bread crumbs
Paprika

1. If large, cut scallops into fourths. Set aside.
2. Wash, drain and slice mushrooms. Place butter in 1-1/2-quart casserol
   Heat in Radarange Oven on Full Power for 30 to 45 seconds, or until
   melted. Stir in lemon juice. Add mushrooms and toss to coat. Cook in
   Radarange Oven, covered, on Cookmatic Level 8 for 4 minutes. Stir
   halfway through cooking time. Drain.
3. Combine wine, savory, bay leaf, salt and pepper in 1-1/2-quart casserc
   Add scallops. Cook in Radarange Oven, covered, on Full Power for 3
   minutes. Remove bay leaf. Drain, reserving 1 cup of liquid.
4. Place butter in 2-quart casserole. Heat in Radarange Oven on Full Pow
   for 45 seconds, or until melted. Blend in flour until smooth. Gradually
   stir in reserved liquid and then cream. Cook in Radarange Oven on Fu
   Power for 3 to 4 minutes, or until thickened. Stir occasionally during
   cooking.
5. Stir scallops and mushrooms into sauce. Cook in Radarange Oven on
   Cookmatic Level 8 for 4 to 5 minutes, or until temperature of 150°F i
   reached.** Stir halfway through cooking time.
6. Spoon into sea shells or ramekins to serve. Garnish with sprinkling of
   bread crumbs and paprika, as desired.
   MICRO-TIPS:
   *If salted cooking wine is used, omit salt from recipe.
   **Use the Automatic Temperature Control System to maintain 150°F
     until ready to serve if your Radarange Oven has this feature. For be
     results, stir occasionally.

Escargot

Yield: 1 to 1-1/2
dozen

1/2 cup butter or margarine
1/2 teaspoon instant minced garlic
1 teaspoon parsley flakes
1 (4-1/2 oz.) can snails
White wine
Snail shells

1. Place butter in 1-cup glass measure. Heat in Radarange Oven on Full
   Power for about 1 to 1-1/2 minutes, or until melted. Add garlic and
   parsley flakes.
2. Place snails in shells. Half-fill shells with seasoned butter. Add 1/2
   teaspoon white wine to each shell. Place 6 snails on plate. Cover loose
   with plastic wrap.
3. Cook in Radarange Oven, covered, on Full Power for 30 to 45 seconds
   or until snails are heated. Be careful not to overcook. Repeat with
   remaining snails.

Clams-In-The-Shell

Yield: 4 appetizers

4 fresh clams

1. Wash and scrub clams with brush in cold water. Arrange in circle in
   9-inch glass pie plate. Cover with plastic wrap.
2. Cook in Radarange Oven, covered, on Full Power for 2-1/2 to 4 minute
   or until clams have relaxed and opened.
   MICRO-TIP: Delicious served with butter sauce.

Savory Sausage Canapes

Yield: 16 appetizers

1/2 lb. pre-cooked country-style
  pork sausage
1/4 cup dairy sour cream
1 tablespoon horseradish
2 teaspoons fresh or frozen chives
4 slices toasted pumpernickel or
  rye bread
Paprika

1. Mix together cooked sausage, sour cream, horseradish and chives.
2. Cut toast into fourths. Spread sausage mixture on toast. Sprinkle with paprika, as desired. Arrange 8 on plastic rack, over 2-quart utility dish or on plate lined with paper towel.
3. Heat in Radarange Oven on Full Power for 30 to 45 seconds, or until heated through. Repeat with remaining appetizers.

Calico Crackers

Yield: 32 to 36 appetizers

1 (3 oz.) pkg. cream cheese
1 egg
1 teaspoon lemon juice
1 teaspoon frozen chives
Dash pepper
2/3 cup shredded Cheddar cheese
1/4 cup bacon bits
32 to 36 crackers

1. Beat cream cheese, egg, lemon juice, chives and pepper until well-mixed. Stir in Cheddar cheese and bacon bits. Chill 1/2 hour.
2. Top each cracker with 1 teaspoon cheese mixture. Place 9 in circle on paper plate. Heat in Radarange Oven on Cookmatic Level 7 for 30 to 45 seconds, or until cheese is just beginning to melt. Repeat with remaining appetizers.

Prepare-Ahead Crab Balls

Yield: 18 appetizers

1 (6-1/2 or 7 oz.) can crab meat,
  drained
1 egg
1/3 cup dry bread crumbs
3 tablespoons dairy sour cream
2 tablespoons finely chopped
  onion
1 teaspoon prepared horseradish
3 tablespoons cornflake crumbs

1. Combine all ingredients except cornflake crumbs. Form mixture into 18, 1-inch diameter balls.
2. Coat each ball with crumbs. Place in single layer in shallow dish. Freeze until firm. Store in heavy plastic bag.
3. Arrange frozen balls on glass plate. Cook in Radarange Oven on Full Power for 3 to 3-1/2 minutes, or until heated through.

Hot Crab Meat Canapes

Yield: 25 canapes

6 ozs. shredded crab meat
1 cup mayonnaise
1 teaspoon lemon juice
1 egg white
Melba toast rounds

1. Combine crab meat with mayonnaise in small mixing bowl. Season with lemon juice.
2. Beat egg white until stiff but not dry. Fold into crab meat mixture.
3. Place approximately 1 teaspoon of crab mixture on each Melba toast round. Arrange 12 on serving dish.
4. Cook in Radarange Oven on Full Power for 45 to 60 seconds, or until heated through. Serve immediately. Repeat with remaining canapes.

Caramel Popcorn Balls

Yield: 12 balls

1 (14 oz.) pkg. caramels
3 tablespoons water
1 tablespoon butter or margarine
2-1/2 to 3 quarts popped popcorn,
  salted*

1. Combine caramels, water and butter in 1-quart casserole. Heat in Radarange Oven on Cookmatic Level 8 for 4 to 5 minutes, or until melted. Stir halfway through heating.
2. Pour over popcorn, tossing lightly to coat evenly. Grease or moisten hands, and form mixture into balls.

*MICRO-TIP: Ordinary popcorn must only be popped in the Radarange Microwave Oven Popcorn Popper. Special popcorn in bags, designed and labeled **for microwave only** may also be used.

Nibbles Snack

Yield: Approximately 2 to 2-1/2 quarts

3/4 cup butter or margarine
2 teaspoons garlic salt
2 teaspoons onion salt
2 teaspoons celery salt
3 tablespoons Worcestershire sauce
1 (10 oz.) box thin pretzel sticks
1 (6-3/4 oz.) can cocktail peanuts
1 (6-3/4 oz.) can mixed nuts or cashews
2 cups toasted wheat cereal squares
2 cups toasted rice cereal squares
2 cups round toasted oat cereal

1. Place butter in 5-quart casserole. Heat in Radarange Oven on Full Pow for 1 minute to 1 minute 15 seconds, or until melted. Add salts and Worcestershire sauce. Mix well.
2. Stir in remaining ingredients. Toss until well-coated.
3. Heat in Radarange Oven on Full Power for 6 to 7 minutes, or until uniformly heated. Mix thoroughly halfway through cooking time. Cool Store in airtight plastic or tin container.

Sweet-Sour Meat Balls

Yield: 20 to 24 meat balls

1 onion, finely chopped
3/4 teaspoon seasoned salt
1 (10-3/4 oz.) can tomato soup
3 tablespoons lemon juice
1/4 cup brown sugar, firmly packed
1 lb. ground beef
1 (13-1/4 oz.) can pineapple chunks, drained

1. Combine onion, salt, soup, lemon juice and brown sugar in 9 x 9 x 2-in glass dish. Cook in Radarange Oven on Full Power for 3 to 5 minutes, until simmering. Stir halfway through cooking time.
2. Roll ground beef into 1-inch diameter meat balls. Place meat balls in above sauce. Spoon some sauce over meat balls. Cook in Radarange Oven on Full Power for 6 to 7 minutes, or until meat is cooked throug
3. Stir in pineapple. Heat in Radarange Oven on Full Power for 1 minute. Serve with toothpicks.

MICRO-TIP: These meat balls are also good served as main dish. Accompany with cooked rice or whipped potatoes, as desired.

Stuffed Mushrooms

Yield: 2 to 2-1/2 dozen appetizers

1 lb. large fresh mushrooms of uniform size
1/4 lb. ground beef
1 clove garlic, minced
1/4 cup minced onion
1 tablespoon finely chopped parsley
1 teaspoon bottled browning sauce
1/2 teaspoon salt
1/4 cup dairy sour cream
2 tablespoons lemon juice

1. Remove stems from mushrooms. Chop stems.
2. Combine chopped mushroom stems, ground beef, garlic, onion, parsley bottled browning sauce and salt in 1-quart casserole.
3. Cook in Radarange Oven on Cookmatic Level 8 for 2-1/2 to 3 minutes or until beef is no longer pink. Stir halfway through cooking time. Drai Stir in sour cream.
4. Dip each mushroom cap in lemon juice and fill with meat mixture. Arrange 10 to 12 mushrooms on plate.
5. Bake in Radarange Oven on Full Power for 2 to 3 minutes, or until hot Serve immediately. Repeat with remaining mushrooms.

Oyster Cracker Snax

Yield: 6 cups

1 cup butter or margarine
1-1/2 teaspoons celery salt
1-1/2 teaspoons garlic salt
1-1/2 teaspoons onion salt
1 teaspoon paprika
1/2 cup grated Parmesan cheese
1 (10 oz.) pkg. oyster crackers
(6 cups)

1. Place butter in 2-quart utility dish. Heat in Radarange Oven on Full Power for 1 minute to 1 minute 15 seconds, or until melted. Blend in seasonings and cheese.
2. Stir in crackers. Toss until well-coated.
3. Heat in Radarange Oven on Full Power for 3 to 3-1/2 minutes, or until heated through. Stir halfway through cooking time. Cool and store in plastic bag or airtight container.

Frank Kabobs

Yield: 4 appetizers

8 cocktail frankfurters or sausages*
8 pimento-stuffed olives
8 pineapple chunks
4 teaspoons vegetable oil
2 teaspoons soy sauce
2 teaspoons pineapple juice
2 teaspoons brown sugar

1. Cut each frankfurter in half. Thread onto 4 wooden skewers, alternating with olives and pineapple.
2. Combine oil, soy sauce, pineapple juice and brown sugar. Brush mixture on appetizers.
3. Lay kabobs across 2-quart glass utility dish. Cook in Radarange Oven on Full Power for 1-1/2 to 2 minutes. Turn kabobs over. Baste with remaining sauce. Cook in Radarange Oven on Full Power for 2 minutes, or until heated as desired.

MICRO-TIPS:

* Regular-size frankfurters or sausages may be used. Cut in quarters instead of halves.

* Substitute luncheon meat for frankfurters. Cook for same amount of cooking time as for frankfurters.

Hot Cheesy Clam Dip

Yield: 2 cups dip

1/4 large green pepper, finely chopped*
1/2 bunch green onions, minced
2 (5 oz. each) jars sharp pasteurized process cheese spread
1 (7 oz.) can clams, drained, minced
2 to 4 dashes Tabasco sauce
1/8 teaspoon garlic powder

1. Combine all ingredients in 1-1/2 quart casserole.
2. Heat in Radarange Oven, uncovered, on Full Power for about 2 to 3 minutes, or until cheese is melted. Stir halfway through cooking time.

MICRO-TIPS:

• May be served very hot with crisp corn chips for dippers.

* 1/4 cup celery may be substituted for green pepper.

Pizza Fondue

Yield: 1 quart

1 lb. ground beef
2/3 cup chopped onion
3 (8 oz. each) cans pizza sauce with cheese
1 tablespoon cornstarch
3/4 teaspoon leaf oregano
1/4 teaspoon garlic powder
1 cup shredded Mozzarella cheese
2 (5 oz. each) jars sharp pasteurized process cheese spread
French bread cubes or chips

1. Place meat and onion in 2-quart casserole. Cook in Radarange Oven on Full Power for 3 to 4 minutes, or until meat is no longer pink. Break meat apart with fork during cooking time. Drain any fat.
2. Blend together sauce, cornstarch, oregano and garlic powder. Add to meat mixture. Cook in Radarange Oven on Cookmatic Level 6 for 13 to 15 minutes, or until bubbling and thickened.
3. Add cheeses by thirds, stirring well. Heat in Radarange Oven on Cookmatic Level 6 for 7 to 8 minutes, or until cheese melts and is no longer stringy. Stir occasionally. Serve hot with French bread cubes or chips.

Beverages can be quickly heated or reheated in the Radarange Oven. Individual servings can be heated directly in cups or mugs, so you avoid washing sticky pans. Handles of cups and mugs stay cool, even though the beverage gets hot. Larger quantities of a beverage can be heated in a serving pitcher, if the pitcher is not too tall and if it is Radarange Oven-safe. Check the utensil tests in the Introduction chapter to see how you can determine whether your cups, mugs or pitchers are safe for Radarange Oven use. Remember that styrofoam cups and other ''disposable'' cups can also be used. Be sure that any cups are suitable for hot beverages. Avoid using mugs or cups with glued-on handles.

Beverages can be quickly reheated. Save leftover coffee in a glass measure or serving cup and refrigerate. Later, reheat it in the Radarange Oven. The coffee will taste as if it has just been freshly brewed! There's no need to keep your coffee pot plugged in for an entire day. **Remember, however, to always vigorously stir a beverage before it is reheated.**

Many beverages are quickly prepared using Full Power. Others, however, contain ''special'' or ''delicate'' ingredients which are better heated using a lower Cookmatic Level

setting. Milk tends to boil over easily and a lower setting helps to avoid boil-overs. Since the alcohol in wine, rum or sherry will evaporate if allowed to boil, which is more likely to happen when using Full Power, most of the recipes for punches that include these ingredients require a lower setting.

Be sure to read the general hints before preparing beverages in your Radarange Oven. In this chapter, ''heating'' refers to the heating of a beverage for the first time. ''Reheating'' means to heat a beverage, **again,** after it has already been heated.

General Hints for Heating Beverages
1. If you're in a hurry, you may wish to use hot top water when heating water to make instant coffee, tea or other mixes. Hot tap water will boil faster than cold.
2. Refrigerator-temperature beverages will require a longer heating or reheating time than room-temperature beverages. Adjust times accordingly. Times for heating milk are based upon refrigerator temperature.
3. If heating 4 or more cups of a beverage at one time, you may wish to heat the beverage in a large serving bowl,

glass measure or pitcher, rather than in individual cups or mugs. Be sure that bowls or pitchers contain no metal trim. Check to see whether the container is too tall before pouring in the beverage. By using one container for a beverage, you eliminate the fuss of placing and removing several cups in and out of the Radarange Oven. Use a ladle to serve punch or other beverages from a large bowl. Try thawing frozen fruit juice in a serving pitcher.

4. To avoid boil-overs, only fill a cup 2/3 to 3/4 full. Most coffee cups are 6-ounce cups. Some larger mugs may hold 8 ounces. Be sure to alter heating times for different sizes of cups, accordingly.
5. Always stir a beverage vigorously before reheating.
6. Milk should not be allowed to boil. Heat milk until it is just warmed. Since milk will boil over easily, use the Cookmatic Level indicated in the recipe when heating milk or a beverage containing milk. Add a marshmallow to a cup of hot chocolate halfway through the heating time, if desired, and it will melt just the right amount.
7. When reheating coffee and tea, for the best taste, do not allow them to boil. Most reheated beverages taste better when reheated to **almost** boiling. When preparing a beverage and heating it for the first time, it should be heated until it is approximately 190° F or below boiling. Use the Automatic Temperature Control System to heat the beverage to 190° F, if your Radarange Oven has this feature.

8. Always add instant coffee or tea to hot water to avoid a bitter flavor and boil-overs. Water will not boil over as easily as pre-mixed coffee and tea.
9. Some persons prefer their beverage to be served at a warmer or cooler temperature. Beverages can be heated in the Radarange Oven, as desired, by increasing or decreasing heating times, accordingly.
10. When converting your own favorite beverage recipes to Radarange Oven timings, select a similar recipe from this section and use the setting and time given as a guide. Usually 1 cup of any beverage will heat in 1 to 1-1/2 minutes on Full Power, with the exception of beverages containing "special" or "delicate" ingredients, which should be heated on Cookmatic Level 8 for 1-1/2 to 2 minutes per cup.

Instant Hot Chocolate Mix

Yield: 1 gallon dry mix

1-1/2 cups (or 6 oz. jar) powdered non-dairy coffee creamer
10-2/3 cups non-fat dry milk (enough to make 8 quarts milk)
1/2 cup confectioners' sugar
1 lb. instant cocoa mix
Water

1. Combine all ingredients, except water, in large mixing bowl. (Mix may be stored in air-tight 1-gallon container.)
2. Fill serving mug half-full of mixture. Finish filling with water. Stir to blend. Heat in Radarange Oven on Full Power for 1 to 1-1/2 minutes, or until warmed, and temperature of 160° F is reached.* Do not boil.

MICRO-TIPS:
- To make a larger amount, mix one part mix to two parts water. Increase cooking time proportionately for each additional serving.
- * Use the Automatic Temperature Control System to cook to 160° F if your Radarange Oven has this feature.

Cocoa

Yield: 4 servings

1/4 cup warm water
3 tablespoons sugar
2-1/2 tablespoons cocoa
3 cups milk
Dash salt

1. Place cocoa, sugar and water in 1-1/2-quart casserole. Heat in Radarange Oven on Full Power for 30 to 60 seconds, or until mixture boils.
2. Stir in milk and salt. Heat in Radarange Oven on Cookmatic Level 8 for 6 to 8 minutes, or until warmed, and temperature of 160° F is reached.*

*MICRO-TIP: Use the Automatic Temperature Control System to cook to 160° F, if your Radarange Oven has this feature.

VARIATIONS FOR HOT CHOCOLATE CHART

HOT CHOCOLATE VARIATION	AMOUNT HOT CHOCOLATE**	ADDITIONAL INGREDIENTS	PREPARATION INSTRUCTIONS	HEATING TIME* COOKMATIC LEVEL 8
Skier's Cocoa	1 cup	1-1/2 ozs. Galliano	Stir Galliano into cocoa.	30 seconds to 1 minute, as needed.
Cocoa Grasshopper	1 cup	2 teaspoons white Creme de Menthe 1 peppermint stick or candy cane	Stir Creme de Menthe into cocoa. Use candy as stirrer.	30 seconds to 1 minute, as needed.
Hot Chocolate Schnapps	1 cup	1 tablespoon peppermint schnapps	Stir schnapps into cocoa.	30 seconds to 1 minute, as needed.
Cocoa Alexander	2 cups	1/4 cup cream 2 teaspoons brandy	Beat cream and brandy together. Stir into cocoa.	30 seconds to 1 minute, as needed.
Spicy Marshmallow Cocoa	1 cup	1 large marshmallow Dash ground cloves	Sprinkle cloves into cocoa. Add marshmallow.	30 seconds to 1 minute, as needed.
Cocoa Tahiti	1 cup	1/4 teaspoon coconut extract Toasted coconut	Stir in coconut extract. Sprinkle coconut over top.	30 seconds to 1 minute, as needed.
Cocoa Float	1 cup	1/8 teaspoon cinnamon 1 scoop vanilla ice cream	Stir cinnamon into cocoa. Top with scoop of ice cream.	30 seconds to 1 minute, as needed.

*Use Cookmatic Level 8 for heating hot chocolate beverages. Do not boil.

**Prepare amount of hot chocolate given using "Instant Hot Chocolate Mix" recipe, page 33.

French Chocolate

Yield: 4 servings

3 tablespoons chocolate syrup
2 tablespoons light corn syrup
1-1/2 tablespoons water
1/4 teaspoon vanilla
1/2 cup chilled whipping cream
2 cups milk

1. Combine syrups, water and vanilla. Heat in Radarange Oven on Full Power for 30 seconds, or until heated through.
2. In chilled bowl, beat cream until stiff. Fold in cooled chocolate mixture gradually, until evenly blended and mixture forms mounds when dropp from spoon.
3. Place milk in 1-quart glass measure. Heat in Radarange Oven on Full Power for 1-1/2 to 2 minutes, or until warmed. Do not boil. Fill serving cups half-full of cream mixture. Finish filling cups with warm milk. Sti before serving.

Hot Egg Nog

Yield: 4 servings

1 quart milk
4 egg yolks
1/3 cup sugar
1/4 teaspoon cinnamon
1/4 teaspoon nutmeg
1/4 teaspoon vanilla

1. Place milk in 2-quart casserole. Heat in Radarange Oven, covered, on Full Power for 5 to 6 minutes, or until temperature of 160° F is reached.* Do not boil.
2. Beat egg yolks lightly, with sugar, spices and vanilla. Stir one cup of hot milk into egg mixture and then gradually blend all of egg mixture into milk.
3. Heat in Radarange Oven, covered, on Full Power for 1-1/2 to 2-1/2 minutes, or until warmed. Stir halfway through cooking time.

*MICRO-TIP: Use the Automatic Temperature Control System to cook to 160° F, if your Radarange Oven has this feature.

Egg Coffee

Yield: 6 to 8 servings

6 cups water
1 egg
2 tablespoons water
3/4 cup ground coffee

1. Place water in 2-quart casserole. Heat in Radarange Oven, covered, on Full Power for 12 minutes, or until almost boiling.
2. Beat egg and 2 tablespoons water. Stir 2 tablespoons egg mixture into coffee grounds. Add enough cold water to completely moisten grounds. Pour into hot water.
3. Heat in Radarange Oven on Full Power for 4 minutes, or until almost boiling. Strain before serving.

MICRO-TIP: Because of the egg, this recipe makes very **clear** coffee.

Mexican Coffee

Yield: 4 servings

4 cups water
1/3 cup brown sugar, firmly packed
2 (3-inch each) cinnamon sticks
3 tablespoons instant coffee

1. Combine all ingredients, except coffee, in 2-quart casserole. Heat in Radarange Oven on Full Power for 8 to 10 minutes, or until almost boiling.
2. Pour over coffee. Stir. Strain before serving.

MICRO-TIP: This recipe makes a **strong** cup of coffee. The amount of coffee used can be adjusted, as desired.

Irish Coffee

Yield: 1 serving

1 cup strong hot coffee
1 jigger Irish whiskey
1 teaspoon sugar
1 tablespoon whipped cream

1. Place ingredients, except whipped cream, in large ceramic or glass mug.
2. Heat in Radarange Oven on Full Power for 1-1/2 to 2 minutes, or until warmed. Do not boil. Add whipped cream.

Moroccan Mint Tea

Yield: 4 servings

4 cups water
1/4 to 1/2 cup fresh mint leaves
1/4 cup sugar
2 teaspoons green tea

1. Place water in 1-1/2-quart casserole. Heat in Radarange Oven on Full Power for 6 to 7 minutes, or until almost boiling.
2. Add mint leaves, sugar and tea. Strain before serving.

Easy Spiced Tea

Yield: 3 servings

2 cups water
2 tablespoons sugar
1 teaspoon lemon juice
1/3 cup orange juice
2 teaspoons instant tea
4 whole cloves
Dash cinnamon (optional)

1. Combine all ingredients in 1-quart casserole or liquid measure.
2. Heat in Radarange Oven on Full Power for 4 minutes, or until warmed and temperature of 160° F is reached.* Stir well before serving.
   *MICRO-TIP: Use the Automatic Temperature Control System to cook 160° F, if your Radarange Oven has this feature.

Russian Tea

Yield: 30 to 40 servings

1 cup powdered orange flavor instant drink
1 cup sugar
1/2 cup instant tea
1 teaspoon ground cinnamon
1 teaspoon ground cloves
3/4 cup water

1. Combine all ingredients, except water, in large mixing bowl. Mix may stored in air-tight container for future use.
2. Place water in ceramic or glass mug with 2 to 3 teaspoons of tea mixture. Stir. Heat in Radarange Oven on Full Power for 1-1/2 to 2 minutes, or until warmed, and temperature of 160° F is reached.

Raspberry Cooler

Yield: 6 to 8 servings

1/4 cup sugar
1/2 cup mint leaves
1 cup water
1 (10 oz.) pkg. frozen raspberries
1 (6 oz.) can frozen limeade or lemonade concentrate
2 cups club soda

1. Combine sugar, leaves and water in 2-quart casserole. Cook in Radarar Oven on Full Power for 2-1/2 to 4 minutes, or until mixture boils. Stir halfway through cooking time. Let stand for 5 minutes.
2. Add frozen raspberries and limeade. Stir until raspberries are thawed.
3. Gradually stir in club soda, just before serving. Serve on ice.
   MICRO-TIP: Frozen strawberries may be substituted for raspberries. Water may be added instead of club soda, if the beverage will be store in the refrigerator for several days.

Hot Rum Lemonade

Yield: 1 serving

3/4 cup water
1/3 cup lemon juice
1 jigger rum
1 teaspoon honey

1. Combine all ingredients in 2-cup glass measure, or in ceramic or glass mug.
2. Heat in Radarange Oven on Full Power for 1 to 1-1/2 minutes, or until warmed. Do not boil.
   MICRO-TIP: Remember to increase each ingredient and the heating tim proportionately when increasing the number of servings.

Mulled Wine Punch

Yield: 15 to 17, 4 oz. servings

2 tablespoons whole cloves
2 tablespoons whole allspice
2 (2-inch each) cinnamon sticks
4 cups boiling water
3 to 4 tablespoons instant tea
1 (6 oz.) can frozen orange or tangerine juice concentrate
1 (6 oz.) can frozen Hawaiian Punch concentrate
2 (25 oz. each) bottles rosé wine

1. Combine all ingredients, except wine, in 3 to 3-1/2-quart casserole.
2. Heat in Radarange Oven, covered, on Cookmatic Level 3 for 20 minute or until warmed, and temperature of 160° F is reached.* Remove spice by straining. Stir in wine. Serve warm or cold.
   MICRO-TIPS:
   • Garnish with lemon or orange slices. Liquid refreshments can always reheated quickly in the Radarange Oven. Stir vigorously before reheating. Reheat in Radarange Oven on Full Power for 1 to 1-1/2 minutes per serving.
   * Use the Automatic Temperature Control System to cook to 160° F, i your Radarange Oven has this feature.

Soups and stews are quickly heated in the Radarange Oven. Soups can be heated directly in serving bowls or mugs, so there are fewer dishes to wash.

Many soups are prepared on Full Power with good results. The fast cooking speed allows soups and stews to maintain a "fresh" flavor. Other soups or stews, which contain "delicate" ingredients such as milk or cheese, should be heated at a lower power setting. Soups can be allowed to "simmer" in the Radarange Oven to blend flavors. Use the Automatic Temperature Control System feature to keep soup at 150°F to 160°F until ready for serving, if your Radarange Oven has this feature.

Read the general hints for heating soups and stews.

General Hints for Heating Soups and Stews

1. Vegetables and meat can be pre-cooked before adding to soups and stews to shorten heating time.
2. Fat may be trimmed from meat, if desired, so soup or stew is less greasy.
3. Use a container which is 2 to 3 times larger than the amount of soup or stew being heated to avoid boil-overs. Soups and stews will expand slightly during heating.
4. Soup or stew may be heated directly in serving bowls or mugs. Do not use containers having metal trim.
5. Cook soups and stews, covered, as recommended in recipes for faster, more even cooking. Cover with a glass lid or heavy-duty plastic wrap, since these types of coverings are the most water-vapor-proof. Pierce plastic wrap slightly before heating. Remove coverings from soups and stews carefully to avoid steam burns.
6. Soup may be stirred during cooking, if desired, to blend together ingredients.
7. Allow soups or stews to stand, as recommended in recipes, for "carry-over" cooking or added thickening. Stir well before serving for uniform thickening.
8. Use the Automatic Temperature Control System feature to keep a soup or stew at 150°F or 160°F, a good temperature range for serving, if your Radarange Oven has this feature.
9. When reheating soups or stews, stir the liquid vigorously or pour from a container into serving bowls or casserole before reheating.
10. Leftover soup can become "planned-over" soup. Freeze any leftover soup. It can later be prepared in the Radarange Oven. Soup can be frozen in cubes and transferred for long-term storage to plastic bags. A quick mug of soup can easily be made from 2 to 3 "soup cubes".
11. Generally, less liquid is required in "Radarange Oven stews" than in conventionally-prepared stews. Adjust your own favorite stew recipes, accordingly.
12. Most soups and stews are cooked on Full Power. Some

soups and stews contain delicate ingredients, such as mushrooms or cheese, and are best prepared using a lower power setting. When preparing your own favorite homemade soups or stews, heat, covered, on the same setting and for about the same amount of time as a similar recipe in this chapter. If you wish to let a soup or stew "slow cook" to blend flavors, cook on Cookmatic Level 5. Cut the amount of time required for a **conventional** recipe in half. If using a **microwave** recipe, use **slightly less** than double the amount of **microwave** cooking time required for Full Power cooking.

CANNED SOUPS AND STEWS HEATING CHART

SOUP OR STEW	YIELD	SIZE CAN	HEATING TIME	COOKMATIC LEVEL	SPECIAL INSTRUCTIONS
Beef Stew	2 to 3 servings	15 oz.	2-1/2 to 3 min.	Full Power	— — —
	4 to 5 servings	24 oz.	4-1/2 to 5 min.	Full Power	— — —
Chili with Beans	2 servings	15 oz.	2 to 2-1/2 min.	Full Power	— — —
Condensed Soup (add water)	2 servings	10 to 11 oz.	3 to 4 min.	Full Power	Combine 1 soup can of water with soup in casserole before heating. Stir halfway through cooking time.
(add milk)	2 servings	10 to 11 oz.	4 to 5 min.	Cookmatic Level 8	Combine 1 soup can of milk with soup in casserole before heating. Stir halfway through cooking time.

General Instructions for Heating Canned Soups and Stews

1. Place soup or stew in 1 to 1-1/2-quart casserole.
2. Read "Special Instructions" before heating. Heat, on recommended Cookmatic Level, according to recommended time, or until heated through.
3. Stir halfway through cooking time, or as needed.

French Onion Soup

Yield: 4 servings

2 medium onions, thinly sliced
2 tablespoons butter or margarine
2 (14 oz. each) cans beef broth
1/2 cup water
1 teaspoon Worcestershire sauce
4 slices toasted French bread
Grated Parmesan cheese
4 slices Mozzarella cheese, halved or shredded

1. Place onion and butter in 3-quart casserole. Cook in Radarange Oven, covered, on Full Power for 8 to 10 minutes, or until onion is tender.
2. Add beef broth, water and Worcestershire sauce. Cook in Radarange Oven, covered, on Full Power for 5 to 7 minutes, or until mixture boils.
3. Toast French bread. Place on paper towels or plastic rack. Sprinkle with Parmesan cheese. Top with Mozzarella cheese. Heat in Radarange Oven on Full Power for 15 to 30 seconds, or until cheese is softened.
4. Place one slice of bread in each serving bowl. Pour soup over bread.

Cream of Tomato and Rice Soup

Yield: 6 to 8 servings

1 medium onion, thinly sliced
1/4 cup butter or margarine
1 small carrot, grated
3 tablespoons all-purpose flour
2 cups pureed tomatoes
2 cups milk
3/4 cup evaporated milk
1 cup cooked rice
1 teaspoon salt
1/8 teaspoon pepper

1. Place onion and butter in 3-quart casserole. Cook in Radarange Oven on Full Power for 3 minutes, or until onion is tender.
2. Add carrot. Cook in Radarange Oven on Full Power for 1-1/2 minutes, or until carrot is tender.
3. Blend in flour. Add tomato puree gradually. Cook in Radarange Oven on Full Power for 4 minutes, or until thickened.
4. Slowly add milks, rice and seasonings. Cook in Radarange Oven on Cookmatic Level 5 for 6 to 8 minutes, or until heated through. Stir halfway through cooking time.

Hearty Hamburger Soup

Yield: 10 to 12 servings

1 lb. ground beef
3 medium onions, sliced
3 medium carrots, sliced
3 medium stalks celery, sliced
1/4 cup water
7 cups water
1 (16 oz.) can stewed tomatoes
1/2 cup quick-cooking barley
1/4 cup quick-cooking rice
1 tablespoon instant beef bouillon
1 tablespoon salt
1 teaspoon monosodium glutamate

1. Crumble beef in 1-1/2 quart casserole. Cook in Radarange Oven on Full Power for 3 to 4 minutes, or until beef is no longer pink. Stir halfway through cooking time. Drain.
2. Combine onions, carrots, celery and 1/4 cup water in 4-quart casserole. Cook in Radarange Oven, covered, on Full Power for 9 to 12 minutes, or until vegetables are tender. Stir halfway through cooking time.
3. Mix in remaining ingredients. Cook in Radarange Oven, covered, on Full Power for 30 to 35 minutes, or until temperature of 160°F is reached.* Let stand, covered, 5 minutes before serving.

   *MICRO-TIP: Use the Automatic Temperature Control System to cook to 160°F, if your Radarange has this feature.

Shrimp and Crab Gumbo

Yield: 6 servings

1 (10 oz.) pkg. frozen okra
1/2 cup chopped celery
1/3 cup chopped green onion
1/4 cup water
1 teaspoon salt
1/4 teaspoon instant minced garlic
1/4 teaspoon leaf oregano
1/4 teaspoon pepper
1 bay leaf
4 to 5 drops Tabasco sauce
2 (1 lb. each) can tomato wedges, with liquid
12 ozs. shrimp, cleaned
6 to 8 ozs. crab meat
1-1/2 cups cooked rice

1. Place frozen okra, in opened package, in Radarange Oven. Cook in Radarange Oven on Full Power for 1 minute, or until pieces can be separated. Slice while still slightly frozen. Place slices in 3-quart casserole.
2. Add celery, green onion, water and seasonings to okra. Blend well. Cook in Radarange Oven, covered, on Full Power for 5 to 6 minutes, or until vegetables are tender.
3. Add tomatoes with liquid, shrimp and crab meat. Cook in Radarange Oven, covered, on Full Power for about 13 to 15 minutes, or until shrimp is cooked and temperature of 160°F is reached.* Remove bay leaf. Place 1/4 cup rice in each of 6 individual serving bowls. Fill each bowl with gumbo mixture.

   *MICRO-TIP: Use the Automatic Temperature Control System to maintain 160°F, if your Radarange Oven has this feature, until ready to pour over rice and serve.

Minestrone Soup

Yield: 8 to 10 servings

1/2 cup thinly sliced carrots
1-1/2 cups thinly sliced celery
1 tablespoon water
1 lb. country style pork sausage
1/2 medium onion, chopped
1 (28 oz.) can tomatoes, undrained
1 cup kidney beans
1 teaspoon garlic salt
1/4 teaspoon salt
Dash pepper
2 tablespoons chopped parsley
1 bay leaf
1/4 teaspoon basil leaves
3 cups hot water
6 ozs. cooked spaghetti rings
1/2 cup coarsely chopped spinach
  or celery tops
Grated Parmesan cheese

1. Combine carrots, celery and water in 4-quart casserole. Cook in Radarange Oven, covered, on Full Power for 6 to 7 minutes, or until vegetables are tender.

2. Add sausage and onion. Cook in Radarange Oven on Cookmatic Level for 8 to 10 minutes, or until sausage is no longer pink and thoroughly cooked, and onion is tender. Stir halfway through cooking time. Drain.

3. Add tomatoes, beans, salts, pepper, parsley, bay leaf, basil leaves and water. Cook in Radarange Oven on Full Power for 15 minutes. Stir halfway through cooking time.

4. Add spaghetti and spinach. Cook in Radarange Oven on Full Power for minutes, or until temperature of 160° F is reached.* Remove bay leaf before serving. Sprinkle servings with Parmesan cheese, as desired.

   *MICRO-TIP: Use the Automatic Temperature Control System to cook 160° F, if your Radarange Oven has this feature.

Chili Con Carne

Yield: 4 to 6 servings

1 cup chopped onion
1/2 cup chopped green pepper
1 tablespoon vegetable oil
1 lb. ground beef
1 (1 lb.) can tomatoes
1 (8 oz.) can tomato sauce
1/3 cup catsup
1 (1 lb.) can chili beans,
  drained
1/2 teaspoon chili powder*
Dash cayenne pepper
1 bay leaf
1/4 teaspoon oregano
1 teaspoon salt

1. Place onion, green pepper and oil in 2-quart casserole. Cook in Radarange Oven on Full Power for 4 to 5 minutes, or until onion and green pepper are tender.

2. Add ground beef. Cook in Radarange Oven on Full Power for 4 to 5 minutes, or until beef is no longer pink. Stir halfway through cooking time. Drain.

3. Blend in remaining ingredients. Cook in Radarange Oven on Full Power for 10 minutes, or until heated through. Stir halfway through cooking time. Remove bay leaf.

   *MICRO-TIP: The amount of chili powder can be increased or decrease as desired.

Easy New England Clam Chowder

Yield: 8 servings

1 cup chopped onion
1/4 cup butter or margarine
1 (10 oz.) can clams, with liquid
2 (10-3/4 oz. each) cans New
  England-Style clam chowder
2 (10-3/4 oz. each) cans cream
  of potato soup
2-2/3 cups milk
1 (13 oz.) can evaporated milk
Salt
Pepper

1. Place onion and butter in 4-quart casserole. Cook in Radarange Oven o Full Power for 3 to 4 minutes, or until onion is tender.

2. Stir in remaining ingredients. Season with salt and pepper, as desired. Cook in Radarange Oven on Full Power for 15 minutes, or until heated through, and temperature of 160°F is reached.* Stir halfway through cooking time.

   *MICRO-TIP: Use Automatic Temperature Control System to cook to 160°F, if your Radarange Oven has this feature.

Corn and Potato Chowder

Yield: 8 to 10 servings

1/2 lb. bacon
1 cup chopped onion
5 cups peeled and cubed potatoes
1/4 cup water
1 (1 lb.) can whole corn, drained
2-1/2 cups milk
1 cup water
1 teaspoon salt
1/4 teaspoon pepper

1. Cut bacon into small pieces. Combine bacon and onion in 4-quart casserole. Cook in Radarange Oven on Full Power for 9 to 11 minutes, or until bacon is cooked and onion is tender. Stir halfway through cooking time. Drain.
2. Add potatoes and 1/4 cup water. Stir. Cook in Radarange Oven, covered, on Full Power for 10 to 12 minutes, or until potatoes are tender. Stir halfway through cooking time.
3. Add remaining ingredients. Cook in Radarange Oven, covered, on Cookmatic Level 8 for 9 to 11 minutes, or until heated through, and temperature of 160°F is reached.* Do not boil. Stir halfway through cooking time.

   *MICRO-TIP: Use the Automatic Temperature Control System to cook to 160°F, if your Radarange Oven has this feature.

Flounder Stew

Yield: 4 to 6 servings

1 cup coarsely chopped onion
1 cup celery, sliced in 1/2-inch pieces
1 cup carrots, sliced in 1/2-inch pieces
2 medium potatoes, pared and diced
1/4 cup water
1 (1 lb.) can tomatoes
1 lb. flounder fillets, cut in bite-size pieces
1 teaspoon salt
1/2 teaspoon thyme
1 tablespoon parsley flakes
Dash pepper

1. Combine onion, celery, carrots, potatoes and water in 3-quart casserole. Cook in Radarange Oven, covered, on Full Power for 8 to 10 minutes, or until vegetables are tender.
2. Add remaining ingredients. Cook in Radarange Oven, covered, on Full Power for 4 to 6 minutes, or until fish flakes easily with fork.

Irish Lamb Stew

Yield: 6 to 8 servings

2 tablespoons butter or margarine
2-1/2 to 3 lbs. lamb stewing meat or neck slices
2 cups water
2 teaspoons seasoned salt
1/4 teaspoon pepper
1/4 teaspoon dried thyme
1 teaspoon dried parsley
1 large onion, chopped
3 medium potatoes, peeled and chopped
1 (17 oz.) can green peas, drained
1 (5-1/3 oz.) can evaporated milk
1/4 cup cornstarch
2 tablespoons bottled browning sauce

1. Place butter in 3-quart casserole. Heat in Radarange Oven on Full Power for 30 to 45 seconds, or until melted. Add lamb pieces. Cook in Radarange Oven on Full Power for 6 minutes, or until lamb is no longer pink.
2. Stir in water, salt, pepper, thyme, parsley, onion and potatoes. Cook in Radarange Oven, covered, on Cookmatic Level 5 for 45 to 60 minutes, or until meat is tender.
3. Stir in peas. Cook in Radarange Oven, covered, on Cookmatic Level 5 for 15 minutes.
4. Blend together evaporated milk, cornstarch and browning sauce in small bowl. Stir into stew. Cook in Radarange Oven on Full Power for 5 to 8 minutes, or until thickened. Stir halfway through cooking time.

Russian Borscht

Yield: 4 servings

1/2 cup finely chopped onion
2 tablespoons butter or margarine
1 (16 oz.) can diced beets, drained
2 cups hot water
3 teaspoons instant beef bouillon
1/2 teaspoon salt
Dash Tabasco sauce
1 tablespoon lemon juice
Dairy sour cream

1. Place onion and butter in 3-quart casserole. Cook in Radarange Oven on Full Power for 3 minutes, or until onion is tender.
2. Place beets and onion in blender. Process until smooth. Return mixture to casserole. Mix in water, instant bouillon, salt and Tabasco sauce. Heat in Radarange Oven on Full Power for 5 minutes, or until temperature of 160° F is reached.* Stir in lemon juice. Pour into individual serving bowls. Add sour cream to each serving, as desired.

*MICRO-TIP: Use the Automatic Temperature Control System to cook to 160° F, if your Radarange Oven has this feature.

Old-Fashioned Beef Stew

Yield: 6 to 8 servings

1 lb. stew beef
4 medium carrots, sliced in 1/2-inch pieces
4 medium potatoes, cut in eighths
1 cup water
1 (8 oz.) can tomato sauce
3/4 cup dry red wine or 3/4 cup beef broth
1 bay leaf
1 clove garlic, minced
1/2 teaspoon monosodium glutamate
1/2 teaspoon salt
1/2 teaspoon pepper
Dash thyme
1 (16 oz.) jar boiled whole onions, drained
2 tablespoons cornstarch
2 tablespoons water

1. Place beef in 4-quart casserole. Cook in Radarange Oven on Full Power for 5 minutes, or until beef is no longer pink.
2. Stir in remaining ingredients, except onions, cornstarch and water. Cook in Radarange Oven, covered, on Cookmatic Level 5 for 60 minutes.
3. Stir in onions. Cook in Radarange Oven on Cookmatic Level 5 for 10 minutes, or until vegetables and meat are tender.
4. Combine cornstarch and water. Stir into stew. Cook in Radarange Oven on Full Power for 2 to 3 minutes, or until thickened. Remove bay leaf and stir before serving.

Meat Ball Stew

Yield: 6 servings

2 lbs. ground beef
2/3 cup applesauce
2 eggs
1 cup bread crumbs
1 green pepper, chopped
1/2 cup chopped celery
1/2 cup chopped carrots
1 onion, chopped
1/4 cup tomato juice
2-3/4 cups tomato juice
2 teaspoons instant beef bouillon
1 tablespoon cornstarch
Salt
Pepper

1. Combine beef, applesauce, eggs and bread crumbs. Form into medium-size meat balls. Place in 2-quart utility dish. Cover with waxed paper. Cook in Radarange Oven, covered, on Full Power for 10 to 12 minutes, or until beef is no longer pink.
2. Combine green pepper, celery, carrots, onion and 1/4 cup tomato juice in 4-quart casserole. Cook in Radarange Oven, covered, on Full Power for 8 to 10 minutes, or until vegetables are tender.
3. Add remaining tomato juice, bouillon, cornstarch and meat balls. Season with salt and pepper, as desired. Cook in Radarange Oven, covered, on Full Power for 12 minutes, or until temperature of 160°F is reached.* Stir halfway through cooking time.

*MICRO-TIP: Use the Automatic Temperature Control System to cook to 160°F, if your Radarange Oven has this feature.

Breads are easily prepared in the Radarange Oven with good results. Yeast breads cooked at lower power settings are evenly cooked and very tender. In yeast breads, lower settings allow the yeast to stay alive and active long enough to make breads light. Quick breads are cooked with good results on Full Power.

Breads cooked in the Radarange Oven are very moist and have a good eating quality. Due to short cooking times, you can cook a "spur-of-the-moment" coffee cake for a coffee break with a neighbor. When overnight guests arrive unexpectedly, surprise them with fresh hot muffins in the morning. Breads cooked in the Radarange Oven are great for toast, too.

Before getting started, review the general hints for cooking breads.

General Hints for Cooking Breads

1. UTENSILS & COVERINGS

   All testing for breads in this chapter was done using glass utensils. When a plastic or ceramic utensil is used, cooking times may need to be shortened or lengthened, respectively.

   Plastic or glass dishes can be used when cooking or proofing (rising) breads. In most cases, dishes should be greased before cooking. During **rising** of yeast breads, cover the bread dough with a damp cotton cloth, such as a dishcloth or plastic wrap. Breads are generally cooked, uncovered.

Several recipes in this chapter require an 8-1/2-inch glass ring mold. You can create your own "ring mold" by simply placing a 6 oz. custard cup in an 8 or 9 x 2-inch round glass dish. For easy removal of bread from a bread ring, run a knife along the edge of the dish. Place a serving platter over the top of the dish and invert. Usually the custard cup is removed more easily **after** inverting the bread ring on the serving platter. Some recipes require a larger 10-cup ring mold. You can place a 2 to 3-inch diameter drinking glass in a 3 or 4-quart glass casserole. The glass should be the same height as the casserole dish used. Usually it is easier to remove the glass **before** inverting the bread ring on the serving platter. When a plastic or ceramic utensil is used, cooking times may need to be shortened or lengthened, respectively.

2. BROWNING

   Breads won't brown in a microwave oven as they do in a conventional oven. For color, use toppings or ingredients which supply color. Some examples include rye flour, whole wheat flour, brown sugar or dark spices, such as cinnamon. In some recipes, there may seem to be extra topping ingredients leftover. Use all ingredients, since the bread will expand during cooking. All ingredients will be needed.

3. RISING OR PROOFING

   The process of rising yeast breads is delicate. But this process can be quickly and easily accomplished by using the Cookmatic Level 1 setting. Use the rising (proofing) instructions in the recipes as a guide for proofing your own favorites.

4. MUFFINS

When cooking muffins, use 6 oz. glass custard cups or a 6-cupcake capacity plastic tray. When a plastic or ceramic utensil is used, cooking times may need to be shortened or lengthened, respectively. Line custard cups or plastic tray compartments with paper liners. Fill liners half-full of batter to avoid having the muffins rise over the edges. Arrange custard cups in a circle, rather than in rows, according to the recipe. Remove muffins from custard cups and plastic tray, immediately, to avoid soggy "bottoms". Most plastic cupcake trays have holes in the compartment bottoms which allow moisture to escape and help to eliminate sogginess.

5. AFTER COOKING

Breads are usually fully cooked when:

a. A toothpick inserted in the center comes out clean (generally recommended for quick breads).

b. The top springs back when lightly pressed with a finger (generally recommended for yeast breads). Recipe instructions in this chapter will indicate the recommended test for the particular recipe.

Some breads will look slightly moist when first removed from the Radarange Oven. Look through bottom of glass dish to see if bread is fully cooked. Breads should be allowed to stand for a few minutes after cooking. During this time the breads will "carry-over" cook. After 3 to 5 minutes, remove the bread from the glass dish so the bottom won't become soggy. Invert the bread on a serving platter or turn it out on a cooling rack.

If the bottom of the bread is slightly underdone, return the bread to the Radarange Oven, upside-down, on Full Power for 30 seconds to 1 minute, to allow the bottom to dry.

6. WRAPPING BREADS

After cooking or reheating, breads should be covered tightly with plastic wrap or stored in an air-tight container to keep them moist and fresh. Keep warm breads on a serving table covered with a cloth, napkin or paper towel to keep them warm and moist.

Warm bread is very delicate when fresh and should be handled carefully. An electric knife will help to prevent tearing when cutting. When bread is cooled, it cuts more easily and can be cut with a regular, serrated knife.

7. REHEATING BREADS

When reheating baked bread, heat for only a **few** seconds. Over-heated bread will become tough, rubbery and hard. As a general rule, reheat only as much bread as is needed for each meal. Wrap the bread in a paper towel or napkin when reheating to capture steam and help keep the bread moist. You may heat bread in a straw basket, if desired, as long as there is no metal trim. Bread should still be covered by a linen napkin, cotton cloth or paper towel to retain moisture. Bread can also be reheated, wrapped in a paper towel and placed on a plastic rack. Breads can be reheated in a plastic wrapper or plastic bag. Loosen the end of the wrapper or bag and remove any metal fasteners before heating.

Moist fillings inside coffee cakes or rolls, as well as frostings, will reheat more rapidly and to higher temperatures than the dough part of the bread. Be certain the entire bread is warmed before serving.

When reheating a group of rolls or muffins, either heat in a basket or place them in a circle in the Radarange Oven, rather than in rows. Left-over breads can be freshened, if stale. Reheat them, covered, for only a few seconds. Eat them immediately.

8. EXTRAS

Bread crumbs and croutons can be made quickly and economically in the Radarange Oven. See the chapter, "Radarange Oven Extras".

9. ADAPTING RECIPES

When converting your own favorite bread recipes, select a similar recipe from this chapter and use it as a guide. Yeast breads are cooked on Cookmatic Level 7. Quick breads are cooked on Full Power. Use the same recommended setting and approximately the same amount of time for cooking your own favorite breads. When you find the correct amount of time for your recipe, jot it down for future use.

FROZEN CONVENIENCE BREADS DEFROST CHART

BREAD TYPE	PKG. SIZE	DEFROST TIME	SETTING	SPECIAL INSTRUCTIONS
Frozen Bread Dough	1 lb. loaf	4 to 6 min.	Defrost*	Wrap dough loosely in waxed paper or keep in plastic wrapper. Bake frozen bread dough conventionally.
Frozen Donuts	2 donuts	1 min. to 1 min., 15 sec.	Defrost*	Place donuts on plastic rack or paper plate. Cover with paper towel. Jelly donuts take slightly longer defrost times.
Frozen Bread	1 lb. loaf 1-1/2 lb. loaf	3 to 4 min. 5 to 6 min.	Defrost* Defrost*	Defrost in plastic wrapper.
Frozen Pancake Batter	17 oz. carton	3 to 6 min.	Defrost*	Open carton before defrosting. Defrost in carton. Stir occasionally during defrosting. Grill pancakes conventionally or on browning grill.
Frozen Sweet Rolls	2 individual rolls	2 to 2-1/2 min.	Defrost*	Remove rolls from metal container. Place on plastic rack or paper plate. Cover with paper towel.

*On models having dial timers, use Cookmatic Level 3 for defrosting.

General Instructions for Defrosting Frozen Convenience Breads
1. Read the "Special Instructions" before defrosting the frozen convenience bread.
2. A bread may be defrosted in the plastic wrapper. Loosen the end of the wrapper before defrosting.

Quick Corn Bread Ring

Yield: 1 ring

1 (8-1/2 oz.) pkg. corn muffin mix
2/3 cup biscuit baking mix
2/3 cup milk
1 egg
Spray-on vegetable coating
3 tablespoons cornflake crumbs

1. Mix together corn muffin mix and biscuit baking mix in large mixing bowl. Blend in milk and egg.
2. Spray inside of 9 x 2-inch round glass dish and outside of 6 oz. glass custard cup with spray-on vegetable coating. Coat both with cornflake crumbs. Invert custard cup in center of dish to form ring mold. Pour batter into dish.
3. Cook in Radarange Oven on Full Power for 3 to 4 minutes, or until toothpick inserted in center comes out clean.* Let stand 10 minutes. Invert ring on serving platter and remove custard cup.

   *MICRO-TIP: You may want to turn dish halfway through cooking time.

Pumpkin Bread Ring

Yield: 1 ring

1/2 cup butter or margarine
3/4 cup sugar
3/4 cup brown sugar, firmly packed
1/2 cup water
2 eggs
1 cup canned pumpkin
2 cups all-purpose flour
1/2 cup raisins (optional)
2 teaspoons pumpkin pie spice
1 teaspoon baking powder
3/4 teaspoon salt

1. Cream butter and sugars in large mixing bowl. Add water, eggs and pumpkin.
2. Combine dry ingredients. Add to liquid ingredients. Mix until smooth.
3. Place 2-inch diameter glass in center of waxed paper-lined 2-quart glass casserole to form ring mold.* Pour batter into dish.
4. Cook in Radarange Oven on Full Power for 8 to 9 minutes, or until top springs back when lightly pressed with finger.** Let stand 10 minutes. Remove glass and invert ring on serving platter.

   MICRO-TIPS:
   *Be sure waxed paper remains flat in dish.
   **You may want to turn dish halfway through cooking time.
   • Glaze with a cream cheese frosting.

CONVENIENCE BREAD MIX BAKING CHART

BREAD MIX	PKG. SIZE	QUANTITY	COOKING TIME ON FULL POWER
Coffee Cake Mix	14 to 16 ozs.	8 x 8 x 2-inch or 9-inch round	3-1/2 to 4 min.*
	17 to 19 ozs.	8 x 8 x 2-inch or 9-inch round	4 to 5 min.*
Corn Bread Muffin Mix	8 to 9 oz.	6 muffins	1 min. to 1 min., 15 sec.
		4 muffins	45 sec. to 55 sec.
Blueberry Muffin Mix	12 to 14 oz.	6 muffins	1 min., 15 sec. to 1 min., 30 sec.
		2 muffins	20 to 30 sec.
Quick Bread Mix	16 to 17 oz.	1, 9 x 5 x 2-inch loaf	3 min., 45 sec. to 4 min., 15 sec.
Gingerbread Mix	14 to 15 oz.	1, 8 x 8 x 2-inch or 1, 9-inch round loaf	5 min., 30 sec. to 6 min.

*You may want to turn dish halfway through cooking time.

General Instructions for Cooking Convenience Bread Mixes

1. Follow the package instructions for mixing specific breads. Use the recommended utensil size. Use a glass, ceramic or plastic utensil. (If a plastic or ceramic utensil is used, cooking times may need to be shortened or lengthened, respectively.) For muffins, use 2 tablespoons of batter per muffin.

2. Breads are done when a toothpick inserted in the center comes out clean or when the top springs back when pressed lightly with a finger. Some breads may look slightly moist on the surface. Look at bottoms when possible.

Cherry Crumb Coffee Cake

Yield: 2, 9-inch round coffee cakes

1/4 cup butter or margarine
1 cup sugar
2 eggs
1 cup dairy sour cream
2 cups all-purpose flour
1-1/2 teaspoons baking powder
1/2 teaspoon baking soda
1/2 teaspoon salt
1/4 teaspoon vanilla extract
1/4 teaspoon almond extract
1 (21 oz.) can cherry pie filling
TOPPING
1/2 cup all-purpose flour
1/4 cup dark brown sugar, firmly
    packed
1 teaspoon cinnamon
2 tablespoons butter or margarine
1/2 cup chopped nuts

1. Cream butter and sugar in large mixing bowl. Add eggs one at a time. Mix well.
2. Add remaining ingredients except pie filling. Beat well.
3. Spread 1/4 of batter in each of 2, greased 9 x 2-inch round glass dish. Spread 1/2 can of cherry pie filling in each dish over batter. Spread each with remaining batter.
4. For topping, combine all ingredients, except butter and nuts in small mixing bowl. Cut in butter. Stir in nuts. Sprinkle topping over batter in both dishes. Cook each coffee cake separately.
5. Cook in Radarange Oven on Full Power for 6 to 7 minutes, or until top springs back when lightly pressed with finger.* Repeat with remaining coffee cake.

MICRO-TIPS:
• Eat one coffee cake now and freeze the other.
* You may want to turn dish halfway through cooking time.

Biscuit Breakfast Ring

Yield: 1 ring

1/3 cup brown sugar, firmly packed
3 tablespoons butter or margarine
1 tablespoon water
1/3 cup chopped nuts
10 refrigerated biscuits

1. Place sugar, butter and water in 1-cup glass measure. Heat in Radarange Oven on Full Power for 1 minute. Stir until butter is melted.
2. Invert 6 oz. glass custard cup in center of 9 x 2-inch round glass dish to form ring mold, or use 8-1/2-inch glass ring mold.
3. Sprinkle nuts evenly around custard cup. Cut each biscuit into halves. Stir into sugar mixture, coating each piece. Arrange around custard cup.
4. Cook in Radarange Oven on Full Power for 2-1/2 to 3 minutes, or until top springs back when lightly pressed with finger.* Let stand 2 minutes. Invert ring on serving platter and remove custard cup. Serve immediately.

*MICRO-TIP: You may want to turn dish halfway through cooking time.

Banana Nut Bread

Yield: 1 loaf

3/4 cup brown sugar, firmly packed
1/3 cup vegetable oil
2 eggs
1 teaspoon vanilla
3 bananas, mashed (1-1/2 cups)
1/3 cup chopped walnuts
1-1/4 cups all-purpose flour
1/3 cup all-bran cereal
3/4 teaspoon baking soda
1/2 teaspoon salt

1. Combine sugar, oil, eggs and vanilla in large mixing bowl.
2. Stir in bananas, nuts and then remaining ingredients. Pour into greased 9 x 5 x 2-inch loaf glass dish.
3. Cook in Radarange Oven on Full Power for 6 to 7 minutes, or until toothpick inserted in center comes out clean.* Let stand 5 minutes. Turn out onto cooling rack.

*MICRO-TIP: You may want to turn dish halfway through cooking time.

Toffee Coffee Cake

Yield: 1, 9-inch round coffee cake

1/3 cup flaked coconut
1/4 cup chopped nuts
1/3 cup semi-sweet chocolate morsels
1/4 cup brown sugar, firmly packed
1 tablespoon butter or margarine, melted
2 cups biscuit baking mix
1/4 cup brown sugar, firmly packed
1 egg
2/3 cup milk
2 tablespoons vegetable oil

1. Combine coconut, nuts, chocolate morsels, brown sugar and butter in greased 9 x 2-inch round glass dish. Mix well.
2. Combine remaining ingredients. Pour over nut mixture.
3. Cook in Radarange Oven on Full Power for 4 to 4-1/2 minutes, or until top springs back when lightly pressed with finger.* Invert on serving platter immediately.

MICRO-TIPS:

• This cake makes a good dessert when served with vanilla ice cream.

* You may want to turn dish halfway through cooking time.

Cheese Spoon Bread

Yield: 1 round loaf

1 cup yellow cornmeal
1/2 teaspoon salt
1 tablespoon brown sugar
1-1/2 cups milk
1/4 cup vegetable oil
1-1/2 cups shredded sharp Cheddar cheese
4 eggs, separated
1 teaspoon baking powder
Butter or margarine

1. Combine cornmeal, salt and sugar in large mixing bowl.
2. Place milk and oil in 1-quart glass measure. Heat in Radarange Oven on Cookmatic Level 8 for 4 to 6 minutes, or until warmed. Stir once during cooking. Add cheese. Stir until cheese is melted. Stir into cornmeal mixture.
3. Beat egg whites until stiff peaks form. Beat yolks until thick and lemon colored.
4. Fold yolks, whites and baking powder into cornmeal mixture. Pour into greased 2-quart glass casserole.
5. Cook in Radarange Oven on Cookmatic Level 6 for 8 to 10 minutes, or until toothpick inserted in center comes out clean. Serve immediately with butter, as desired.

Cranberry Muffins

Yield: about 2 dozen muffins

2 cups all-purpose flour
1/2 cup sugar
1 tablespoon baking powder
1/2 teaspoon salt
1 cup milk
1/4 cup vegetable oil
1 egg, beaten
1 cup coarsely chopped cranberries
1/2 cup chopped nuts
1 tablespoon grated orange peel
2 tablespoons sugar
1 teaspoon cinnamon
2 tablespoons chopped nuts

1. Combine flour, sugar, baking powder and salt in large mixing bowl. Combine milk, oil and egg. Add to combined dry ingredients. Mix until just blended.
2. Fold in cranberries, nuts and 2 teaspoons orange peel. Spoon 2 tablespoons of batter into plastic muffin tray (or 6, 6 oz. glass custard cups) lined with paper liners.* Combine remaining ingredients and sprinkle over muffins. Arrange 6 muffins in circle in Radarange Oven using custard cups.
3. Cook half-dozen in Radarange Oven on Full Power for 1 minute, 10 seconds to 1 minute, 20 seconds, or until tops spring back when lightly pressed with finger. Remove muffins from tray or custard cups and place on cooling rack immediately. Repeat with remaining muffins.
    *MICRO-TIP: If a plastic tray is used, the cooking time may need to be shortened.

Blueberry Muffins

Yield: about 1-1/2 to 2 dozen muffins

2 cups all-purpose flour
1/2 cup sugar
1 tablespoon baking powder
1/2 teaspoon salt
1 cup milk
1/4 cup vegetable oil
1 egg
1 cup fresh blueberries, washed and drained*
CRUMB TOPPING
3 tablespoons all-purpose flour
3 tablespoons sugar
1 teaspoon cinnamon
3 tablespoons butter or margarine

1. Combine flour, sugar, baking powder and salt in large mixing bowl. Combine milk, oil and egg. Add to combined dry ingredients. Mix until just blended.
2. Fold in blueberries. Spoon 2 tablespoons of batter into plastic muffin tray (or 6, 6 oz. glass custard cups) lined with paper liners.**
3. For crumb topping, cut butter into dry ingredients. Sprinkle over muffin batter. Arrange 6 muffins in circle in Radarange Oven if using custard cups.
4. Cook half-dozen in Radarange Oven on Full Power for 1 minute, 10 seconds to 1 minute, 20 seconds, or until tops spring back when lightly pressed with finger. Remove muffins from tray or custard cups and place on cooling rack immediately. Repeat with remaining muffins.

MICRO-TIPS:
    *Canned or frozen and defrosted blueberries may be used.
    **If a plastic tray is used, the cooking time may need to be shortened.

Perpetual Muffins

Yield: 6 dozen muffins

2 cups boiling water
4 cups all-bran cereal
2 cups 100% Bran Flakes
1 quart buttermilk
3 cups sugar
4 eggs, beaten
1 cup soft shortening or vegetable oil
5 cups all-purpose flour
5 teaspoons baking soda
1 teaspoon salt

1. Pour hot water over cereals in large mixing bowl. Stir in buttermilk, sugar, eggs, shortening, flour, baking soda and salt. Mix until just blended.
2. Spoon 2 tablespoons of batter into plastic muffin tray (or 6, 6 oz. glass custard cups) lined with paper liners* Arrange 6 muffins in circle in Radarange Oven if using custard cups.
3. Cook half-dozen in Radarange Oven on Full Power for 1 minute, 10 seconds to 1 minute, 20 seconds, or until tops spring back when lightly pressed with finger. Remove muffins from tray or custard cups and place on cooling rack immediately. Repeat with remaining muffins.

MICRO-TIPS:
    *If a plastic tray is used, the cooking time may need to be shortened.
• To cook 4 muffins, cook in Radarange Oven on Full Power for 40 to 5 seconds. To cook 2 muffins, cook in Radarange Oven on Full Power 25 seconds to 35 seconds.
• This batter can be refrigerated for up to 3 to 4 weeks. Refrigerator temperature batter requires slightly longer baking time.

Quick Sweet Rolls

Yield: 3 batches of about 1 dozen rolls each

2 cups warm water
2 (1/4 oz. each) pkgs. active dry yeast
1/3 cup sugar
1 tablespoon salt
1/3 cup vegetable oil
2 eggs, beaten
6 to 6-1/2 cups all-purpose flour
Butter or margarine, softened
1/2 cup sugar
1 tablespoon cinnamon
1/3 cup raisins (optional)
ICING**
3 tablespoons butter or margarine, melted
1 tablespoon milk
1/2 teaspoon vanilla
1 cup confectioners' sugar

1. Place water in 1-quart mixing bowl. Heat in Radarange Oven on Full Power for 1-1/2 to 2 minutes, or until warmed, and temperature of 105° F to 115° F is reached.* Dissolve yeast in water. Stir in sugar and salt.

2. Blend in oil and eggs. Mix in flour, 2 cups at a time. Scrape dough from sides of bowl to center. Cover. Let stand for 20 minutes. Knead dough until smooth and elastic, or about 5 minutes.

3. Turn dough out onto lightly floured board. Divide dough into thirds. Roll each third into 1/4-inch thick rectangle. Spread each with butter, as desired. Sprinkle each with mixture of sugar and cinnamon. Sprinkle raisins on each, if desired. Roll each starting with narrow sides. Cut rolls into 3/4-inch slices. Evenly distribute slices among 3, greased 9 x 2-inch round glass dishes. Let each dish of rolls rise and cook separately. Let rise in Radarange Oven on Cookmatic Level 1 for 10 minutes. Let stand 10 minutes, or until doubled.

4. Cook in Radarange Oven, uncovered, on Cookmatic Level 7 for 3 to 4 minutes, or until tops spring back when lightly pressed with finger.*** Invert on serving platter. Repeat with remaining rolls.

5. For icing**, add butter, milk and vanilla to confectioners' sugar. Stir until smooth. Drizzle over rolls.

MICRO-TIPS:

*Use the Automatic Temperature Control System to cook to 110° F, if your Radarange Oven has this feature.

**This icing will cover 1, 9-inch round glass dish of sweet rolls. Triple recipe to make icing for 3 dishes.

***You may want to turn dish halfway through cooking time.

Rye Bread

Yield: 1 round loaf

1 cup water
1 (1/4 oz.) pkg. active dry yeast
2 tablespoons molasses
2 tablespoons brown sugar
1/2 teaspoon salt
1 tablespoon butter or margarine, melted
1-1/2 teaspoons caraway seed
3/4 cup rye flour
1-3/4 to 2 cups all-purpose flour
Cornmeal

1. Place water in 2-quart glass measure or large mixing bowl. Heat in Radarange Oven on Full Power for about 1 minute, or until temperature of 105° F to 115° F is reached.* Dissolve yeast in water. Stir in molasses.

2. Dissolve brown sugar and salt in yeast mixture. Add butter, caraway seeds and rye flour. Mix well. Stir in enough flour to make moderately stiff dough.

3. Turn dough out onto floured board. Let stand 5 to 10 minutes. Knead dough until smooth and elastic or about 5 minutes. Place in greased bowl. Grease top of dough. Cover with damp cotton cloth, such as dishcloth. Let rise in Radarange Oven on Cookmatic Level 1 for 10 to 15 minutes, or until almost doubled.

4. Punch down dough and shape into round loaf. Place dough on high temperature plastic baking sheet sprinkled with cornmeal. Let rise in Radarange Oven on Cookmatic Level 1 for 10 to 15 minutes, or until doubled.

5. Cook in Radarange Oven, uncovered, on Cookmatic Level 7 for 3-1/2 to 4 minutes, or until top springs back when lightly pressed with finger. Remove from waxed paper onto cooling rack.

*MICRO-TIP: Use the Automatic Temperature Control System to cook to 110° F, if your Radarange Oven has this feature.

Rice, cereals and pastas are easy to prepare. These foods can be cooked directly in serving dishes when cooked in the Radarange Oven, avoiding hard-to-clean pans. Also, cooking can be done without scorching.

Before preparing these three foods in the Radarange Oven, note the few basic hints that are given. Consult the charts in this section for accurate cooking instructions.

General Hints for Cooking Rice

1. When preparing rice in the Radarange Oven, the size of the dish is important to consider. If too small a dish is used for the amount of rice, water will boil over slightly due to the expansion of the rice as it cooks. Choose a glass cooking dish which is of an adequate size to allow water to boil vigorously. The addition of oil will help to prevent boil-overs.

2. It's very important to cook rice in a covered dish. This allows for faster cooking. Glass lids or heavy-duty plastic wrap are the best coverings to use since they are the most water-vapor-proof. After rice is added to boiling water, the lid may be left slightly off-center to avoid boil-overs. You may wish to stir rice halfway through the cooking time to avoid boil-overs. You may wish to use hot pads when removing rice from the Radarange Oven.

3. Rice should require virtually no stirring during cooking. In fact, less stirring is better since over-stirring can cause a "mushy" texture. Even after rice is cooked, avoid too much tossing.

4. The standing time, after cooking, allows the rice to finish its own cooking and to absorb all of the moisture.

5. Long grain white rice begins cooking at Full Power but finishes cooking at a lower setting. This slower cooking

helps to give the rice a fluffier texture.

6. Quick-cooking rice can be simply rehydrated. Bring the required amount of water to a boil in the serving dish. Stir in quick-cooking rice, cover with glass lid or heavy-duty plastic wrap, and let stand according to the amount of time required on the package. (See the "Rice Cooking and Convenience Food Chart" on pages 52 and 53.)

7. Wild rice is actually not a cereal grain, but is a grass seed. Wild rice cooking instructions are, however, included in the "Rice Cooking and Convenience Food Chart" on pages 52 and 53. If wild rice is presoaked before cooking, it will be more tender.

8. Rice can be reheated quickly in the Radarange Oven. Rice should be reheated on Full Power in a covered casserole, until it is steaming hot. Again, a glass lid or heavy-duty plastic wrap covering is best. It is not necessary to add liquid for reheating. However, for a large quantity you may wish to add 1 to 2 tablespoons of water. If rice has been refrigerated, stir once or twice during reheating. Since rice is easily reheated, rice can be cooked ahead and later reheated quickly for casserole dishes requiring rice.

RICE YIELD CHART

UNCOOKED RICE	COOKED RICE
1 cup raw, long grain white rice	3 to 3-1/2 cups
1 cup raw, brown rice	4 cups
1 cup raw, wild rice	3-1/2 cups
1 cup quick-cooking rice	2 cups

Rice and Spinach Deluxe

Yield: 6 servings

2 tablespoons butter or margarine
1 cup chopped onion
1-1/2 cups quick-cooking rice
1/2 teaspoon salt
1-1/2 cups water
1 (10 oz.) pkg. frozen chopped spinach
1 (5 oz.) jar sharp process cheese spread
1 (10-3/4 oz.) can cream of mushroom soup
1/8 teaspoon nutmeg (optional)

1. Place butter in 1-1/2-quart casserole. Heat in Radarange Oven on Full Power for 20 to 30 seconds, or until melted. Stir in onion. Cook in Radarange Oven on Full Power for 3 to 4 minutes, or until onion is tender.
2. Add rice, salt and water. Cook in Radarange Oven, covered, on Full Power for 2 to 3 minutes, or until boiling. Let stand, covered, until moisture is absorbed.
3. Place frozen spinach in 1-quart casserole. Cook, covered, in Radarange Oven on Full Power for 2-1/2 to 3 minutes, or until thawed. Drain and add to rice along with cheese spread. Stir until cheese spread melts.
4. Stir in soup. Add nutmeg, if desired. Cook in Radarange Oven on Full Power for about 7 to 9 minutes, or until heated through.

Wild Rice and Mushrooms

Yield: 4 to 5 servings

1 (6-3/4 oz.) pkg. long grain and wild rice mix
1 (4 oz.) can sliced mushrooms, drained
1 tablespoon fresh or frozen chives
1/4 cup dairy sour cream or
    1/4 cup Cheddar cheese soup

1. Prepare rice according to package directions or according to chart on pages 52 to 53. Place in 3-quart casserole. Cook in Radarange Oven, covered, on Full Power for 15 to 20 minutes, or until all water is absorbed.
2. Add mushrooms, chives and sour cream. Heat in Radarange Oven on Full Power for 1 minute, or until heated through.

Orange Rice

Yield: 4 servings

1/4 cup chopped onion
1 cup chopped celery
2 tablespoons vegetable oil
1-1/4 cups water
2 tablespoons undiluted orange juice concentrate
1/2 teaspoon salt
1-1/3 cups quick-cooking rice

1. Combine onion, celery and oil in 2-quart casserole. Cook in Radarange Oven on Full Power for 3 to 4 minutes, or until onion and celery are tender.
2. Stir in water, orange juice concentrate and salt. Cook in Radarange Oven, covered, on Full Power for 3 to 4 minutes, or until mixture boils. Mix in rice. Cover and let stand 5 minutes, or until water is absorbed. Stir and serve.

Quick Fried Rice

Yield: 4 to 5 servings

2 tablespoons butter or margarine
2 tablespoons chopped onion
2 cups quick-cooking rice
1-2/3 cups water
2 teaspoons instant beef bouillon
1/2 teaspoon salt
Dash pepper
2 eggs, slightly-beaten
1/4 cup sliced green onion
2 teaspoons soy sauce

1. Place butter in 2-quart casserole. Heat in Radarange Oven on Full Power for 20 to 30 seconds, or until melted. Add onion. Cook in Radarange Oven on Full Power for 1 to 2 minutes, or until onion is tender.
2. Stir in rice, water, instant bouillon, salt and pepper. Cook in Radarange Oven, covered, on Full Power for about 3 to 4 minutes, or until rice is tender. Stir halfway through cooking time. Stir and let stand, covered, until water is absorbed, or about 4 to 5 minutes.
3. Mix in eggs, green onion and soy sauce. Cook in Radarange Oven on Full Power for 2 to 3 minutes, or until eggs are set. Stir halfway through cooking time. Stir in soy sauce.

RICE COOKING A|

RICE TYPE	AMOUNT OR PKG. SIZE	DISH SIZE	AMOUNT HOT TAP WATER	AMOUNT OIL, BUTTER OR MARGARINE	AMOUNT SALT	EXTRA INGRED.
Brown Rice	1 cup rice	3-quart casserole	3 cups	1 teaspoon oil	1 teaspoon	—
Long Grain White Rice	1 cup rice	3-quart casserole	2 cups**	1 teaspoon oil	1 teaspoon	—
Quick Brown Rice	1 cup rice	3-quart casserole	1-1/2 cups	1 teaspoon oil	1/2 teaspoon	—
Quick-Cooking Rice	Amount rice equal to amt. water	Twice as large as amt. water	Equal to amt. rice	1/2 teaspoon butter or margarine per serving	1/8 teaspoon per serving	—
Long Grain White and Wild Rice Mix	6-3/4 oz. pkg.	3-quart casserole	2-1/2 cups*	1 tablespoon oil	1 teaspoon	—
Wild Rice**	4 oz. pkg.	3-quart casserole	2-1/2 cups	1 teaspoon oil	1 teaspoon	—

*Use amount of ingredients recommended on package instructions.

**Pre-soak wild rice before cooking, for a more tender product.

General Instructions for Cooking Rice and Rice Convenience Foods

1. Read the "Special Instructions" in the chart before cooking.
2. When water is used, be certain to use hot tap water, since it will boil faster than cold. Water also boils faster in a covered utensil.
3. Be sure to cook, covered, if the "Special Instructions" state to do so. Cooking is accomplished faster in a covered utensil. Let stand for 5 minutes, covered, in most cases, before serving. Fluff with fork.

NVENIENCE FOOD CHART*

1ST COOKING TIME ON FULL POWER	2ND COOKING TIME ON FULL POWER	3RD COOKING TIME ON COOKMATIC LEVEL 3	SPECIAL INSTRUCTIONS
5 to 7 min.	25 to 30 min.	—	Stir salt and oil into hot tap water. Heat, covered, according to 1st time and setting, or until water boils. Stir in rice. Cook, covered, according to 2nd time and setting, or until rice is tender. Allow a 5-minute standing time, if necessary, after the rice finishes cooking.
4 to 5 min.	1-1/2 to 2-1/2 min.	12 to 14 min.	Stir salt and oil into hot tap water. Heat, covered, according to 1st time and setting, or until water boils. Stir in rice. Cook, covered, according to 2nd time and setting, or until water boils. Cook, covered, according to 3rd time and setting or until rice is tender. Allow a 5-minute standing time, if necessary, after the rice finishes cooking.
3 to 5 min.	10 to 12 min.	—	Stir salt and oil into hot tap water. Heat, covered, according to 1st time and setting, or until water boils. Stir in rice. Cook, covered, according to 2nd time and setting, or until rice is tender. Allow a 5-minute standing time, if necessary, after the rice finishes cooking.
1 cup water — 1 to 1-1/2 min. 2 cups water — 4 to 5 min.	—	—	Heat water, salt and butter according to 1st time and setting, or until water boils. (Use equal measures of rice and water.) Stir in rice. Let stand, covered, for amount time recommended on package. Fluff with fork to serve. For firmer rice, use 1 tablespoon less water per serving.
15 to 20 min.		—	Stir butter into hot tap water. Add packaged ingredients. Cook, according to 1st time and setting, or until rice is tender and water is absorbed. Allow a 5-minute standing time, if necessary, after the rice finishes cooking.
5 to 6 min.	20 to 25 min.		Stir salt and oil into hot tap water. Heat, covered, according to 1st time and setting, or until water boils. Stir in rice. Cook, covered, according to 2nd time and setting, or until rice is tender. Allow a 5-minute standing time, if necessary, after the rice finishes cooking.

Apple 'N' Rice Casserole

Yield: 4 servings

2 tablespoons butter or margarine

2 cups cooked rice
2 cups pared, cored and thinly sliced apples
1 tablespoon lemon juice
1/4 cup sugar
1 teaspoon cinnamon
2 tablespoons dairy sour cream

1. Place butter in 1-quart casserole. Heat in Radarange Oven on Full Power for 20 to 30 seconds, or until melted.
2. Stir in rice, apples, lemon juice, sugar, cinnamon and sour cream.
3. Cook in Radarange Oven, covered, on Full Power for about 4-1/2 to 5 minutes, or until apples are tender.

MICRO-TIP: Add 1/2 cup raisins, if desired. Great to serve with pork.

General Hints for Cooking Cereals

1. Cereals can be simply prepared in the Radarange Oven. Each family member, even each child, can fix his or her own cereal directly in the serving bowl, with no worry of scorching. Clean-up following breakfast is easy, too, since there is no sticky pan to wash.

2. Large cereal bowls or casserole dishes are best-suited for cooking cereals in the Radarange Oven. With large bowls, there is less chance for cereals to spill over into the Radarange Oven cavity. Stirring during the cooking time will help to prevent boil-overs and lumping.

CEREAL COOKIN

CEREAL TYPE & SERVINGS	UTENSIL	AMOUNT HOT TAP WATER	AMOUNT SALT	AMOUNT CEREAL	1ST COOKING TIME	1ST SETTING
Grits (Instant) (1 serving)	1-cup glass measure	1/2 cup	—	8 oz. pkg.	1 min.	Full Power
Hot Malted Wheat Cereal (4 servings)	1-quart casserole	2-1/2 cups	1/2 teaspoon	1/2 cup hot malted wheat cereal	5 to 6 min.	Full Power
Oatmeal (Quick-Cooking Oats) (1 serving)	Serving bowl	1/2 cup	1/8 teaspoon	1/4 cup quick-cooking rolled oats	1 min.	Full Power
(4 to 6 servings)	2-quart casserole	3 cups	3/4 teaspoon	1-1/2 cups quick-cooking rolled oats	5 to 7 min.	Full Power
Oatmeal (Old-Fashioned Oats) (4 to 6 servings)	3-quart casserole	4 cups	1 teaspoon	2 cups old-fashioned rolled oats	7 to 8 min.	Full Power

General Instructions for Cooking Cereals

1. Read the "Special Instructions" in the chart before cooking each cereal.
2. Use hot tap water, since it boils faster than cold.
3. Let each cereal stand, covered, about 5 minutes before serving if necessary, for all water to be absorbed. Stir before serving.

Bran-Oatmeal

Yield: 1 serving

3/4 cup water
1/8 teaspoon salt
1/4 cup quick-cooking rolled oats
2 tablespoons all-bran cereal
1/8 teaspoon cinnamon

1. Combine water and salt in 1-quart casserole. Heat in Radarange Oven on Full Power for 1 to 1-1/2 minutes, or until boiling.
2. Stir in remaining ingredients. Cook in Radarange Oven on Full Power for 30 to 60 seconds, or until cereal is thickened, as desired.

ART

2ND COOKING TIME	2ND SETTING	SPECIAL INSTRUCTIONS
—	—	Place water in utensil. Heat, according to 1st time and setting, or until water boils. Stir into instant grits.
1 min.	Full Power	Place water and salt in casserole. Heat, according to 1st time and setting, or until water boils. Stir in cereal. Cook, according to 2nd time and setting, or until cereal is cooked, as desired. Stir as needed to prevent boiling over. 1/2 cup raisins may be added to cereal before serving. May be served with brown sugar and milk.
15 sec.	Full Power	Place water and salt in utensil. Heat in Radarange Oven, according to 1st time and setting, or until water boils. Stir in cereal. Cook, according to 2nd time and setting, or until cereal is cooked, as desired. Be careful not to boil over. (Alternate method: Place cereal, water and salt in utensil. Cook, according to 1st cooking time and setting, or until cereal is cooked as desired. This method makes a thicker cereal.)
—	—	Place oats, water and salt in casserole. Cook, according to 1st time and setting, or until cereal is cooked, as desired.
4 min.	Cookmatic Level 5	Place water and salt in casserole. Heat, according to 1st time and setting, or until water boils. Stir in oats. Cook, according to 2nd time and setting. Stir often during cooking time to prevent boiling over. Let stand, covered, until thickened.

Granola

Yield: 6 cups

3 cups quick-cooking or old-fashioned rolled oats
1/3 cup wheat germ
1/3 cup shredded coconut
1/3 cup sesame seeds
1/3 cup chopped nuts
1/3 cup brown sugar, firmly packed
1/2 teaspoon cinnamon
1/3 cup vegetable oil or
   1/3 cup butter or margarine, melted
1/4 cup honey
1 teaspoon vanilla
1/2 cup raisins

1. Place oats in ungreased 2-quart utility dish. Heat in Radarange Oven on Full Power for 2-1/2 minutes.
2. Add wheat germ, coconut, sesame seeds, nuts, brown sugar and cinnamon to oats. Stir to blend.
3. Add oil, honey and vanilla to dry ingredients. Toss lightly, until coated. Cook in Radarange Oven on Cookmatic Level 7 for about 6 minutes, or until heated through. Stir twice during cooking.
4. Add raisins. Cook in Radarange Oven on Full Power for 1 to 2 minutes, or until ingredients are heated through. Press granola firmly against bottom of dish. Cool. Break into pieces and store in tightly-covered container in refrigerator.

Saucy Chops and Rice

Yield: 4 servings

1 tablespoon vegetable oil
4 (8 oz. each) pork chops
2 (8 oz. each) cans tomato sauce
1 cup long-grain rice
1-1/2 cups water
1/2 cup chopped onion
1 teaspoon salt

1. Preheat large browning skillet for maximum amount of time, accordin to manufacturer's instructions. Place oil and pork chops in skillet. Coc in Radarange Oven on Full Power for 5 minutes. Turn chops over halfway through cooking time.
2. Add remaining ingredients. Cook in Radarange Oven, covered, on Cookmatic Level 3 for 32 to 45 minutes, or until no longer pink, and thoroughly cooked. Turn chops over and stir sauce halfway through cooking time.

Swedish Rice Pudding

Yield: 5 to 6 servings

1-1/2 cups cooked rice
3 cups milk
3 eggs, beaten
3/4 cup sugar
1 teaspoon vanilla
1/2 teaspoon ground cardamon
1/4 teaspoon salt
2 tablespoons sugar
1 teaspoon cinnamon

1. Combine rice and milk in 1-1/2-quart casserole.
2. Combine eggs, sugar, vanilla, cardamon and salt. Add to rice mixture.
3. Cook in Radarange Oven, covered, on Cookmatic Level 4 for 30 to 35 minutes, or until knife inserted in center comes out clean. Sprinkle wi sugar and cinnamon.

MICRO-TIPS:
- This is a good way to use left-over rice.
- Serve hot. Sprinkle individual servings with additional sugar and cinnamon, if desired.

Jambalaya

Yield: 4 to 6 servings

1/2 cup chopped onion
1/3 cup chopped green pepper
1/8 teaspoon instant minced garlic
1 tablespoon vegetable oil
1 teaspoon instant chicken bouillon
1/2 cup boiling water
1 (12 oz.) pkg. frozen shrimp*
1 (8 oz.) can stewed tomatoes
1 cup cubed pre-cooked ham
1/2 teaspoon salt
1/8 teaspoon pepper
1-1/2 cups cooked rice

1. Place onion, green pepper, garlic and oil in 2-quart casserole. Cook in Radarange Oven on Full Power for 2 to 3 minutes, or until onion and green pepper are tender.
2. Dissolve bouillon in water. Add to onion and green pepper.
3. Add remaining ingredients, except rice. Cook in Radarange Oven, covered, on Full Power for 7 to 8 minutes, or until hot. Stir halfway through cooking time.
4. Add rice. Cook in Radarange Oven on Full Power for 3 to 5 minutes, c until heated through. Stir before serving.

*MICRO-TIP: When substituting fresh shrimp for frozen, slightly decrea cooking time in step #3.

Fiesta Rice

Yield: 6 to 8 servings

1 tablespoon butter or margarine
2 cups chopped celery
1 cup chopped green pepper
1 cup chopped onion
1 lb. ground beef
3 cups cooked rice
1 (8 oz.) can tomato sauce
1 teaspoon garlic salt
1/2 to 1 teaspoon chili powder
1/2 teaspoon cumin powder
1/2 teaspoon leaf oregano

1. Place butter and vegetables in 2-quart casserole. Cook in Radarange Oven, covered, on Full Power for 4 to 6 minutes, or until vegetables a almost tender.
2. Add beef. Cook in Radarange Oven on Full Power for 4 to 5 minutes, c until beef is no longer pink. Stir halfway through cooking time. Drain.
3. Add remaining ingredients. Cook in Radarange Oven on Full Power for to 6 minutes, or until heated through.

General Hints for Cooking Pastas

1. The amount of oil in the water is important when cooking pasta, as it helps to keep the water from boiling over.

2. It's very important to cook pasta in a covered dish. This allows for faster cooking. Glass lids or heavy-duty plastic wrap are the best coverings to use since they are the most water-vapor-proof.

3. Use a large enough dish so that water can completely cover pasta. Pasta can be more completely tenderized when covered with water.

4. Pasta can be reheated quickly in the Radarange Oven. Pasta should be reheated on Full Power in a covered casserole until it is steaming hot. Again, a glass lid or plastic wrap covering is best. For a large quantity, you may wish to add 1 to 2 tablespoons of liquid before reheating. If pasta has been refrigerated, stir once or twice during reheating.

PASTA YIELD CHART

UNCOOKED PASTA	COOKED PASTA
1 (7 oz.) pkg. macaroni	4 cups
1 (7 oz.) pkg. spaghetti	4 cups
1 cup egg noodles	1 to 1-1/2 cups

PASTA COOKING CHART*

PASTA TYPE	DISH SIZE	AMOUNT HOT TAP WATER	AMOUNT SALT	AMOUNT PASTA	AMOUNT OIL	1ST COOKING TIME	1ST SETTING	2ND COOKING TIME	2ND SETTING
Egg Noodles	3-quart casserole	4 cups	1 teaspoon	2 cups	2 tablespoons	5 to 7 min.	Full Power	—	—
Lasagna Noodles	5-quart casserole	6 cups	1 teaspoon	8 oz.	2 tablespoons	6 min.	Full Power	4 to 7 min.	Cookmatic Level 5
Macaroni	4-quart casserole	4 cups	1 teaspoon	2 cups	2 tablespoons	3 min.	Full Power	2 to 4 min.	Cookmatic Level 3
Spaghetti	4-quart casserole	4 cups	1 teaspoon	8 ozs.	2 tablespoons	3 min.	Full Power	2 to 4 min.	Cookmatic Level 3

*For Touchmatic models having automatic programming ability, see the Use and Care Manual for information about programmed cooking.

General Instructions for Cooking Pasta

1. Place water and salt in a covered casserole. Be certain to cover the casserole so the water will boil faster. Cook in Radarange Oven on Full Power for 7 to 9 minutes, or until water boils. Hot tap water will boil faster than cold.

2. Stir in the pasta and oil. Cover. Be certain to cover so the pasta will cook faster. Cook, according to 1st and 2nd cooking times and settings recommended on the chart.

3. Cook all pasta until it reaches the desired tenderness. Allow a 5 minute, covered, standing time, if necessary, after the pasta finishes cooking. (Pastas can vary slightly in the amount cooking time they require.)

4. Sample the pasta before draining the liquid. If it is not tender, it can be quickly returned to the Radarange Oven for 1 to 2 additional minutes of cooking. Drain after the pasta has reached the desired tenderness. Rinse with hot tap water before serving.

CONVENIENCE FOOD TYPE & PKG. SIZE	DISH SIZE AND YIELD	AMOUNT HOT TAP WATER	AMOUNT SALT	1ST COOKING TIME (TO BOIL WATER)	1ST SETTING	2ND COOKING TIME	2ND SETTING	3RD COOKIN TIME
Macaroni and Cheese Dinner Mix (7-1/4 oz. pkg.)	3 to 4-quart casserole (4 to 6 servings)	6 cups	1 teaspoon	8 to 10 min.	Full Power	1-1/2 to 2 min.	Full Power	3 to 5 min.
Noodles Romanoff (5.5 oz. pkg.) OR Noodles Stroganoff (5.25 oz. pkg.)	2-quart casserole (5 servings)	3 cups	1/2 teaspoon	6 to 7 min.	Full Power	5 to 7 min.	Full Power	—
Lasagna Dinner Mix (23-7/8 oz. pkg.)	3 to 4-quart casserole (6 servings)	1-1/2 quarts	2 teaspoons	8 to 10 min.	Full Power	15 to 17 min.	Full Power	8 to 10 min.
Spaghetti and Sauce Dinner Mix (8 oz. pkg.)	4-quart casserole (4 servings)	2-1/2 cups	2 teaspoons	5 to 6 min.	Full Power	7 to 8 min.	Full Power	4 to 5 min.

General Instructions For Cooking Pasta Convenience Foods
1. Read package instructions and add any extra ingredients not suggested in chart.
2. Read the "Special Instructions" in the chart before cooking each convenience food.
3. Use hot tap water since it boils faster than cold. Water will boil faster if the dish is covered.

Macaroni and Cheese

Yield: 6 servings

2 tablespoons butter or margarine
2 tablespoons all-purpose flour
1/2 teaspoon salt
1/4 teaspoon pepper
1-1/2 cups milk
1-1/2 cups shredded sharp Cheddar cheese
3 cups cooked macaroni
1/4 cup bread crumbs
1/2 teaspoon paprika

1. Place butter in 1-quart glass measure. Heat in Radarange Oven on Fu Power for 20 to 30 seconds, or until melted. Stir in flour, salt and pepper.
2. Add milk slowly. Cook in Radarange Oven on Cookmatic Level 8 for 8 minutes, or until thickened. Stir in cheese, stirring until melted.
3. Stir sauce into cooked macaroni in 1-1/2-quart casserole. Top with mixture of bread crumbs and paprika. Heat in Radarange Oven on Fu Power for 2 to 3 minutes, or until bubbling.

ODS CHART

3RD SETTING	EXTRA INGREDIENTS	AMOUNT OIL	SPECIAL INSTRUCTIONS
Cookmatic Level 3	1/4 cup butter or margarine 1/4 cup milk	—	Combine water and salt in casserole. Heat, covered, according to 1st time and setting, or until water boils. Stir in macaroni. Cook, covered, according to 2nd time and setting, or until water boils. Cook, covered, according to 3rd time and setting, or until macaroni is tender. Stir halfway through cooking time. Drain. Add butter. Stir until melted. Add milk and cheese mix. Blend well.
—	2 tablespoons butter or margarine 1/3 cup milk (2/3 cup milk for Noodles Stroganoff)	—	Combine water and salt in casserole. Heat, covered, according to 1st time and setting, or until water boils. Add noodles. Cook, uncovered, according to 2nd time and setting, or until noodles are tender. Stir halfway through cooking time. Drain. Stir in sauce mix and extra ingredients. Blend well.
Full Power	—	1 tablespoon	Combine water and salt in casserole. Heat, covered, according to 1st time and setting, or until water boils. Add oil and lasagna noodles. Cook, covered, according to 2nd time and setting, or until noodles are tender. Stir halfway through cooking time. Follow package instructions and assemble dinner mix in 1-1/2-quart utility dish. Cook, according to 3rd time and setting, or until heated through.
Full Power	1 (6 oz.) can tomato paste 2 cans water 1 tablespoon butter or margarine	1 tablespoon	Combine water and salt in casserole. Heat, covered, according to 1st time and setting, or until water boils. Add spaghetti noodles. Cook, covered, according to 2nd time and setting, or until noodles are tender. Stir occasionally. Allow to stand in hot water. Combine sauce mix, tomato paste, water and margarine in 1-quart casserole. Cook, according to 3rd time and setting. Stir occasionally. Drain spaghetti noodles. Toss lightly with oil. Pour sauce over and serve.

Lasagna

Yield: 10 to 12 servings

1 lb. ground beef or Italian sausage
1 clove garlic, minced
1 (1-1/2 oz.) pkg. dry onion soup mix (optional)
1-1/2 cups water
1 (6 oz.) can tomato paste
1 (8 oz.) can tomato sauce
1/2 teaspoon salt
1/4 teaspoon pepper
1/2 teaspoon sugar
1 teaspoon leaf oregano
1/2 teaspoon basil
1/2 lb. cooked lasagna noodles
1/2 lb. shredded Mozzarella cheese
1 lb. cottage cheese or ricotta cheese
Grated Parmesan cheese

1. Combine meat and garlic in 2-quart casserole. Cook in Radarange Oven on Full Power for 3 to 4 minutes. Stir 1 to 2 times during cooking time. Drain.

2. Blend in onion soup, water, tomato paste, tomato sauce, salt, pepper, sugar, oregano and basil. Cook in Radarange Oven, covered, on Full Power for 10 minutes. Stir halfway through cooking time.

3. Layer meat mixture, noodles, Mozzarella cheese and cottage cheese in 2-quart utility dish. Repeat layers, ending with meat sauce. Sprinkle top generously with Parmesan cheese, as desired.

4. Cover loosely with plastic wrap. Cook in Radarange Oven, covered, on Full Power for 12 to 14 minutes, or until heated through.

Beef-Noodle Casserole

Yield: 8 to 10 servings

1/2 cup chopped onion
1/2 cup chopped celery
1/4 cup diced green pepper
1 tablespoon vegetable oil
1-1/2 lbs. ground beef
10 to 12 ozs. cooked noodles
1 (10-3/4 oz.) can cream of mushroom soup
1 (10-3/4 oz.) can cream of chicken soup
1 (4 oz.) can mushrooms, drained (optional)
1/2 cup milk
1/2 cup cashews (optional)
1-1/2 teaspoons salt
1/4 teaspoon pepper

1. Combine onion, celery, green pepper and oil in 3-quart casserole. Coo Radarange Oven on Full Power for 4 minutes, or until vegetables are tender.
2. Add beef. Cook in Radarange Oven on Full Power for 7 minutes, or u beef is no longer pink. Stir halfway through cooking time. Drain.
3. Blend in remaining ingredients. Cook in Radarange Oven on Full Pow for 10 to 12 minutes, or until heated through, and temperature of 15C is reached.* Stir halfway through cooking time.

*MICRO-TIP: Use the Automatic Temperature Control System to maintain 150° F until ready to serve, if your Radarange Oven has this feature.

Goulash

Yield: 4 to 6 servings

1 medium onion, chopped
1 tablespoon butter or margarine
1 lb. ground beef
1 (15 oz.) can stewed tomatoes
1 cup cooked elbow macaroni
1 teaspoon salt
1/4 teaspoon pepper
1 tablespoon cornstarch
1 tablespoon water

1. Combine onion and butter in 1-1/2-quart casserole. Cook in Radarang Oven on Full Power for 2 minutes, or until onion is tender.
2. Add beef. Cook in Radarange Oven on Full Power for 3 to 4 minutes, until beef is no longer pink. Stir halfway through cooking time. Drain
3. Add tomatoes, noodles, salt and pepper. Cook in Radarange Oven on Full Power for 4 to 5 minutes, or until bubbling. Stir halfway through cooking time.
4. Blend together cornstarch and water. Add to casserole. Cook in Radarange Oven on Full Power for 1 minute, or until thickened, and temperature of 150° F is reached.*

*MICRO-TIP: Use the Automatic Temperature Control Sytem to main 150° F until ready to serve, if your Radarange Oven has this feature

Beef Corkscrew Bake

Yield: 4 to 6 servings

1/2 cup chopped green onion
1 tablespoon butter or margarine
1 lb. ground beef
1 (10-3/4 oz.) can golden cream of mushroom soup
1/2 cup catsup
4 ozs. cooked corkscrew macaroni
1/2 cup shredded Cheddar cheese

1. Place onion and butter in 1-1/2-quart casserole. Heat in Radarange O on Full Power for 1-1/2 minutes, or until onion is tender.
2. Add beef. Cook in Radarange Oven on Full Power for 3 to 4 minutes, until beef is no longer pink. Stir halfway through cooking time. Drain
3. Add remaining ingredients, except cheese. Cook in Radarange Oven Full Power for 4 to 5 minutes, or until heated through, and temperatu of 150° F is reached.* Stir halfway through cooking time.
4. Mix in cheese before serving.

*MICRO-TIP: Use the Automatic Temperature Control System to maintain 150° F until ready to serve, if your Radarange Oven has th feature.

Italian Spaghetti

Yield: 8 servings

1 cup chopped onion
1/2 cup chopped celery
1 clove garlic, minced
1 tablespoon vegetable oil
1-1/2 lbs. ground chuck
1 (28 oz.) can tomatoes, with liquid
1 (10-3/4 oz.) can tomato soup
1 (8 oz.) can tomato sauce
1 (6 oz.) can tomato paste
1 (4 oz.) can mushrooms, drained
1 tablespoon sugar
1 bay leaf
1 teaspoon salt
1/4 teaspoon pepper
1/4 teaspoon oregano
1/2 teaspoon basil
1 lb. cooked spaghetti
Grated Parmesan cheese

1. Mix together onion, celery, garlic and oil in 4-quart casserole. Cook in Radarange Oven on Full Power for 4 to 5 minutes, or until onion and celery are tender.
2. Add beef. Cook in Radarange Oven on Full Power for 4 to 5 minutes, or until beef is no longer pink. Drain.
3. Add remaining ingredients, except spaghetti and cheese.
4. Cook in Radarange Oven on Full Power for 15 minutes. Then, cook in Radarange Oven on Cookmatic Level 5 for 45 minutes. (For best results, stir every 20 minutes and remove lid for last 20 minutes.) Serve over cooked spaghetti. Sprinkle with Parmesan cheese, as desired.

MICRO-TIPS:
- For extra flavor, refrigerate overnight and reheat next day in Radarange Oven on Full Power for 10 to 15 minutes.
- Prepare the spaghetti after cooking the sauce. Keep the sauce covered, while the spaghetti is cooking, to keep it warm.

All-At-Once Spaghetti

Yield: 6 servings

1 tablespoon butter or margarine
1 cup chopped onion
1 lb. ground beef
1 teaspoon salt
1/4 teaspoon pepper
2 (8 oz. each) cans tomato sauce
1-1/2 cups water
1/2 teaspoon ground oregano
1/2 teaspoon basil
1/4 lb. uncooked spaghetti
Grated Parmesan cheese

1. Place butter and onion in 2-quart casserole. Heat in Radarange Oven on Full Power for about 3 to 4 minutes, or until onion is tender.
2. Add beef. Cook in Radarange Oven on Full Power for 3 to 4 minutes, or until beef is no longer pink. Stir halfway through cooking time. Drain.
3. Add salt, pepper, tomato sauce, water, oregano and basil. Cook in Radarange Oven, covered, on Full Power for 4 minutes.
4. Break spaghetti in half and stir into sauce. Cook in Radarange Oven, covered, on Full Power for 18 to 20 minutes, or until spaghetti is tender. Stir twice during cooking time. Sprinkle with Parmesan cheese, as desired.

Roman Noodles

Yield: 4 to 5 servings

1/2 cup chopped onion
1 green pepper, chopped
2 tablespoons vegetable oil
1 (4 oz.) can sliced mushrooms, with liquid
2 (8 oz. each) cans tomato sauce
1/4 teaspoon powdered thyme
1/2 teaspoon salt
1/8 teaspoon pepper
8 ozs. uncooked medium noodles
3/4 cup water
1 (8 oz.) can peas, drained
1/4 cup grated Parmesan cheese

1. Combine onion, green pepper and oil in 2-quart casserole. Cook in Radarange Oven on Full Power for 2 to 3 minutes, or until onion and green pepper are tender.
2. Stir in mushrooms with liquid, tomato sauce and seasonings. Cook in Radarange Oven, covered, on Full Power for 3 minutes, or until heated through.
3. Stir in noodles and water. Cook in Radarange Oven, covered, on Full Power for 9 to 12 minutes, or until noodles are tender. Stir halfway through cooking time.
4. Stir in peas. Sprinkle with Parmesan cheese before serving.

Sandwiches can be heated instantly in the Radarange Oven for a quick lunch. You can be creative in making sandwich fillings; some leftover casseroles or salads often make great fillings. Clean-up is easy, too, since sandwiches can be heated in paper towels, which are disposable.

Most sandwiches can be heated in the Radarange Oven on Full Power. Sandwiches having fillings which contain cheese, however, should be heated as indicated in the recipe. Cheese is a "special" or "delicate" ingredient which can tend to become tough and "rubbery" when heated using too high a setting.

Read the general tips before heating sandwiches in your Radarange Oven.

General Hints for Heating Sandwiches

1. Sandwiches should be covered with a paper towel when heated in buns or bread, to prevent the buns or bread from losing moisture and becoming too dry. Sandwiches should be placed on a paper towel or a plastic or ceramic rack during heating to prevent the bottoms from becoming soggy.

2. Whenever possible, heat the sandwich filling before spreading it inside the bun. Then heat the entire sandwich, just until the bun is warmed. Again, this will prevent moisture loss in the bun. Also, the shorter amount of time a filling is inside a bun, the less chance there is for sogginess to occur.

3. Toasted bread or day-old bread make great bases for Radarange Oven sandwiches, since they do not tend to become soggy as readily as fresh bread or buns. Also, day-old bread will tend to "freshen" during the heating time.

4. Heat sandwiches just until the bread is warmed, or until cheese, a "delicate" ingredient, is melted.

5. Sandwiches spread with a "thin" layer of filling will heat faster than sandwiches with thicker fillings. When heating meat sandwiches, use thin, rather than thick, slices of meat.

6. For heating your own favorite sandwich "creations," use Full Power. Heat 1 sandwich, inside a bun or bread, for approximately 1 to 2 minutes, or until warmed, depending upon the size of the sandwich. If the sandwich filling includes cheese as a main ingredient, heat as indicated in recipe until the cheese is melted.

French Dip Sandwiches

Yield: 4 servings

2 cups water
2 teaspoons instant beef bouillon
2 tablespoons dry onion soup mix
3/4 to 1 lb. roast beef, cooked and thinly sliced
4 French rolls

1. Combine water, instant bouillon and soup mix in 1-quart casserole or glass measure. Cook in Radarange Oven on Full Power for 4 to 6 minutes, or until mixture boils and bouillon is dissolved.
2. Place meat on plate. Cover with paper towel. Heat in Radarange Oven, covered, on Full Power for 3 to 5 minutes, or until hot.
3. Place roast beef in rolls. Serve with hot beef broth dip.

CONVENIENCE SANDWICH FILLING SEASONING MIX COOKING CHART

MIX TYPE	1ST COOKING TIME ON FULL POWER*	2ND COOKING TIME ON FULL POWER**	ADDITIONAL INGREDIENTS	SPECIAL INSTRUCTIONS
Sloppy Joe Seasoning Mix (1-1/2 oz.) (8 servings)	3 to 4 min.	3 to 4 min.	1 lb. ground beef 1 (6 oz.) can tomato paste 1-1/4 cups water 8 hamburger buns	Crumble beef in 1-1/2-quart casserole. Cook, according to 1st cooking time and setting. Drain. Blend in remaining ingredients. Cook, according to 2nd cooking time and setting. Spoon 1/4 cup mixture into each hamburger bun.
Taco Seasoning Mix (1-3/4 oz.) (4 to 6 servings)	4 to 5 min.	7 to 8 min.	1 lb. ground beef 1 cup water	Crumble beef in 1-1/2-quart casserole. Cook, according to 1st cooking time and setting. Drain. Blend in remaining ingredients. Cook, according to 2nd cooking time and setting. Follow package instructions for serving.

*Stir halfway through cooking time.
**Stir 1 to 2 times during cooking time.

Barbecued Hamburgers

Yield: 4 servings

1/2 cup chopped onion
1 tablespoon vegetable oil
1 lb. ground beef
1/3 cup catsup
1 tablespoon brown sugar
2 teaspoons vinegar
1 teaspoon prepared mustard
1/2 teaspoon Worcestershire sauce
1/2 teaspoon salt
4 hamburger buns

1. Combine onion and oil in 2-quart casserole. Cook in Radarange Oven on Full Power for 3 to 4 minutes, or until onion is tender.
2. Add crumbled beef to onion. Cook in Radarange Oven on Full Power for 3 to 4 minutes, or until beef is no longer pink. Stir halfway through cooking time. Drain.
3. Add remaining ingredients, except buns. Blend well. Heat in Radarange Oven on Full Power for 3 minutes, or until heated through, and temperature of 150° F is reached.* Spoon into hamburger buns and serve.

   *MICRO-TIP: Use the Automatic Temperature Control System to cook to 150° F, if your Radarange Oven has this feature.

Surf and Turfwiches

Yield: 6 servings

1 (6 oz.) can flaked crab meat
1 cup diced cooked chicken
1/3 cup finely diced celery
1/3 cup mayonnaise
1 teaspoon prepared mustard
6 split and toasted English muffins
6 slices bacon, cooked and crumbled
6 slices Swiss cheese, halved

1. Mix together crab meat, chicken, celery, mayonnaise and mustard.
2. Spread mixture on muffin halves. Place 6 halves on plastic rack or on paper towels.
3. Heat in Radarange Oven on Full Power for 1-1/2 to 2 minutes, or until hot. Top each half with bacon and one slice cheese.
4. Heat in Radarange Oven on Full Power for 1 to 3 minutes, or until cheese is almost completely melted. Repeat with remaining 6 halves.

Pizzawiches

Yield: 8 sandwiches

1 cup chopped onion
1 tablespoon vegetable oil
1 lb. ground beef
1 (8 oz.) can tomato sauce
1 (2-1/2 oz.) jar sliced mushrooms, drained
1/2 teaspoon oregano
1/2 teaspoon basil
1/2 teaspoon salt
1/8 teaspoon pepper
4 split and toasted English muffins
4 ozs. (1 cup) shredded Mozzarella cheese

1. Place onion in oil in 1-1/2-quart casserole. Cook in Radarange Oven on Full Power for 2 minutes, or until onion is tender.
2. Add meat. Cook in Radarange Oven on Full Power for 3 to 4 minutes, until beef is no longer pink. Stir halfway through cooking time. Drain.
3. Blend in remaining ingredients except muffins and cheese. Cook in Radarange Oven on Full Power for 4 to 6 minutes, or until heated through. Stir 2 to 3 times during cooking time.
4. Spoon 1/4 cup hot mixture on each muffin half. Top with cheese. Place 4 muffin halves on plastic rack or paper towels. Heat in Radarange Oven on Full Power for 1 to 2 minutes, or until cheese is melted. For one muffin half, heat on Full Power for 15 to 30 seconds. For two, heat on Full Power for 30 to 60 seconds.

MICRO-TIPS:
- Sliced French bread may be used instead of muffins. May be topped with green pepper, crumbled bacon or olives, as desired.
- If meat mixture is chilled before using, remember to allow slightly longer cooking time.

Made-Right Mushroom Burgers

Yield: 6 to 8 servings

1 cup chopped celery
1 cup chopped onion
1 tablespoon vegetable oil
1 lb. ground beef
1 (10-3/4 oz.) can cream of onion soup
1 (4 oz.) can sliced mushrooms, drained
3/4 cup catsup
1 teaspoon chili powder
1 teaspoon salt
6 to 8 hamburger buns

1. Combine celery, onion and oil in 1-1/2-quart casserole. Cook in Radarange Oven on Full Power for 3 to 4 minutes, or until celery and onion are tender.
2. Add beef. Cook in Radarange Oven on Full Power for 3 to 4 minutes, or until beef is no longer pink. Stir halfway through cooking time. Drain.
3. Combine remaining ingredients, except buns, and add to meat. Heat in Radarange Oven on Full Power for 7 to 8 minutes, or until heated through, and temperature of 150° F is reached.* Spoon into split hamburger buns.

*MICRO-TIP: Use the Automatic Temperature Control System to cook 150° F, if your Radarange Oven has this feature.

Hot Swiss Chicken Salad Sandwiches

Yield: 8 sandwiches

1 cup diced cooked chicken
2/3 cup diced celery
1/2 cup cubed Swiss cheese
1/4 teaspoon salt
1/4 cup mayonnaise
1/2 teaspoon lemon juice
8 hamburger buns

1. Combine all ingredients, except buns. Fill each bun with 1/4 cup mixture. Place 4 sandwiches on plastic rack.
2. Heat in Radarange Oven on Full Power for 45 seconds to 1-1/2 minutes, or until heated through.

MICRO-TIPS:
- Heat 1 sandwich in Radarange Oven on Full Power for 15 to 30 seconds. For 2 sandwiches, heat in Radarange Oven on Full Power for 30 to 60 seconds.
- 1 (6-1/2 oz.) can tuna, drained, may be substituted for chicken, if desired.
- 4 split and toasted English muffins may be substituted for buns, if desired.

Taco Heroes

Yield: 6 servings

1/2 cup finely chopped onion
1/4 cup finely chopped celery
1 tablespoon vegetable oil
1-1/2 lbs. ground beef
1 (1-3/4 oz.) pkg. taco seasoning mix
1 (8 oz.) can tomato sauce
6 split and toasted English muffins or hamburger buns
12 slices tomato
1 cup shredded Cheddar cheese
3/4 cup shredded lettuce (optional)
12 ripe olives chopped (optional)

1. Place onion, celery and oil in 1-1/2-quart casserole. Cook in Radarange Oven on Full Power for 2 to 3 minutes, or until onion and celery are tender.
2. Add beef. Cook in Radarange Oven on Full Power for 4 to 5 minutes, or until beef is no longer pink. Stir halfway through cooking time. Drain.
3. Add taco mix and tomato sauce. Heat in Radarange Oven on Full Power for 4 minutes, or until heated through, stirring halfway through cooking time.
4. Spread 1/2 cup of meat mixture on each muffin half. Top each with tomato slice and sprinkle with cheese. Place 6 halves on cooking grill.
5. Heat in Radarange Oven on Full Power for 2 to 3 minutes, or until cheese is melted. Top with lettuce and olives, if desired.

Hot Crab Meat Sandwiches

Yield: 6 sandwiches

1 cup flaked crab meat
3 hard-cooked eggs, chopped*
1/4 cup mayonnaise
1 teaspoon instant minced onion
1 teaspoon Worcestershire sauce
1/4 teaspoon lemon juice
3/4 teaspoon salt
1/8 teaspoon pepper
6 slices bread or 3 English muffins, split
1/4 cup shredded Cheddar cheese
Paprika

1. Mix together crab meat, eggs, mayonnaise, onion, Worcestershire sauce, lemon juice, salt and pepper.
2. Toast bread or muffins. Spread crab meat mixture on toast. Sprinkle with cheese and then paprika, as desired. Place 6 sandwiches on plastic rack or paper towels. Heat in Radarange Oven on Full Power for 2 to 3 minutes, or until cheese is melted. Serve immediately.

*MICRO-TIP: Remember, do not hard-cook eggs in the Radarange Oven.

Reuben Sandwich

Yield: 1 serving

1 slice cooked corned beef
2 slices toasted rye bread
2 tablespoons sauerkraut
1 slice Swiss cheese
1 teaspoon thousand island dressing

1. Place corned beef slice on one slice of bread. Drain sauerkraut well. Place sauerkraut and Swiss cheese on corned beef.
2. Spread second piece of bread with dressing and place on top. Place sandwich on paper plate. Cover with paper towel.
3. Heat in Radarange Oven, covered, on Full Power for 30 to 45 seconds, or until cheese is melted.

Ham Salad Sandwiches

Yield: 4 sandwiches

1 cup pre-cooked ground ham
1/2 cup finely chopped celery
2 tablespoons pickle relish, drained
1/4 cup mayonnaise
4 hamburger buns

1. Combine all ingredients, except buns. Divide ham mixture and spread in 4 buns. Place 4 sandwiches on plastic rack or paper towels.
2. Heat in Radarange Oven on Full Power for 1-1/2 to 2 minutes, or until heated through.

MICRO-TIP: Sandwiches can be made on toasted rye bread or English muffins, if desired.

Turkey, Bacon and Tomato Sandwiches

Yield: 6 servings

6 slices bacon
1/4 cup mayonnaise
1/4 cup dairy sour cream
1 tablespoon lemon juice
Dash cayenne pepper
6 split and toasted English muffins
12 slices cooked turkey
12 slices tomato
6 slices American process cheese

1. Place bacon on plastic rack or paper plate. Cover with paper towel. Cook in Radarange Oven, covered, on Full Power for 4 to 5 minutes, or until crisp. Crumble.
2. Blend together mayonnaise, sour cream, lemon juice and cayenne pepper. Spread mixture on each muffin half.
3. Place one slice turkey and then one slice tomato on each muffin half. Sprinkle with bacon.
4. Cut each slice cheese in 4 strips. Crisscross 2 strips over each sandwich. Place 6 muffin halves on plastic rack or paper towels.
5. Heat in Radarange Oven on Full Power for 1-1/2 to 3 minutes, or until cheese is melted. Repeat with remaining muffin halves.

"Left-Over" Turkey In Buns

Yield: 4 servings

4 toasted hamburger buns
1 cup chopped cooked turkey*
1 tablespoon instant minced onion
1 teaspoon parsley flakes
1/4 cup chopped salted peanuts (optional)
1 egg, hard-cooked and chopped**
1/2 cup mayonnaise
1/3 cup shredded sharp Cheddar cheese
Salt
Pepper

1. Place bottom halves of buns on paper towel-lined plate. Combine remaining ingredients. Season with salt and pepper, as desired. Spread filling on buns. Add bun tops to make 4 "bunwiches."
2. Heat in Radarange Oven on Full Power for 2 to 3 minutes, or until heated through.
MICRO-TIPS:
   *Any leftover cooked poultry or meat may be used.
   **Remember, do not hard-cook eggs in the Radarange Oven.

Eggs and Hamwich

Yield: 4 sandwiches

2 hard-cooked eggs, chopped*
1/2 cup cubed pre-cooked ham
1/4 cup mayonnaise
8 slices toasted bread
4 slices process cheese

1. Blend together eggs, ham and mayonnaise. Spread mixture on 4 slices toasted bread. Place one slice cheese over each. Top with second slice bread. Place all sandwiches on plastic rack on paper towels. Cover with paper towel.
2. Heat in Radarange Oven, covered, on Full Power for 1 to 2 minutes, or until cheese is melted.
   *MICRO-TIP: Remember, do not hard-cook eggs in the Radarange Oven.

Egg Salad Sandwiches

Yield: 4 to 5 servings

4 hard-cooked eggs, chopped*
2 tablespoons chopped pimento-stuffed olives
3 tablespoons mayonnaise
2 teaspoons prepared mustard
1/4 teaspoon salt
Dash pepper
2 to 3 split and toasted English muffins
Paprika

1. Blend together eggs, olives, mayonnaise and mustard. Season with salt and pepper, as desired.
2. Spread 1/4 cup mixture on each muffin half. Sprinkle with paprika, as desired. Place 4 halves on plastic rack or paper towels. Heat in Radarange Oven on Full Power for 1-1/2 to 2 minutes, or until heated through.
MICRO-TIPS:
   • To heat 1 muffin half, heat in Radarange Oven on Full Power for 30 to 45 seconds.
   • Substitute 4 to 5 hamburger buns for muffins.
   * Remember, do not hard-cook eggs in the Radarange Oven.

Les Oeufs (eggs) can be prepared in endless ways. In this chapter we'll show you how the Radarange Oven can make fluffy scrambled eggs in seconds. Breakfast will never be dull again after using this variety of scrambled egg recipes. Also, there will never be any "hard-to-wash" pans or skillets.

In this chapter, you will find omelets, soufflés and many other "Eggs and Cheese" dishes. Be sure to try one of the quiche recipes. A quiche (pronounced keesh) is a savory, rather than sweet, custard pie. It is served as an hors d'oeuvre in a French meal, but it can be used as a brunch or supper dish. If you are proud of your custard-baking ability, this is a great way to "show it off." Dessert custards are found in the Desserts chapter.

When using one of the charts in this chapter be sure to read the general cooking instructions for valuable cooking information. Be certain to read all of the general hints for cooking eggs and cheese before preparing them in your Radarange Oven. Fondue recipes are found in the "Appetizers and Snacks" chapter. Since eggs and cheese both cook best on lower Cookmatic Levels, these two food items can be easily combined in recipes.

General Hints for Cooking Eggs

1. **Do not** hard-cook eggs or boil eggs in the shell in a microwave oven. Yolks cook faster than whites and the rapid heat generated through microwave cooking expands the air inside the shell, causing it to burst. **Do not** reheat eggs which have been prepared conventionally or in the Radarange Oven unless they are finely chopped or scrambled before heating. Pressure can build up in reheated eggs and cause them to burst.

2. The size, temperature and age of the eggs can affect cooking times. Large eggs require a slightly longer cooking time than small eggs. Large-size eggs were used in developing the recipes in this chapter. Room temperature eggs cook faster than refrigerator temperature eggs. Recipes in this chapter are based upon refrigerator-temperature eggs. Older eggs should be used for scrambling, rather than for poaching or frying. Yolk membranes become weak in older eggs and tend to break during cooking when fried or poached. Use fresh eggs for frying and poaching.

3. Egg yolks and whites cook at different rates of speed. Egg yolks cook faster than egg whites due to the fat content. Egg dishes which require the mixing of egg whites and yolks, such as omelets or scrambled eggs, cook evenly and easily. Fried eggs and poached eggs require special handling. Read the tips on pages 68, 69 and 70, for preparing scrambled, fried and poached eggs.

4. Use the exact utensils recommended for cooking eggs in the recipes. Cooking times can vary due to the types and shapes of utensils.

5. Eggs can be prepared in individual serving dishes. Remember, do not use dishes which have a metal trim.

6. Before frying or poaching eggs, gently pierce or puncture the yolk membrane with a knife or the tines of a fork. This will slightly break the membrane and prevent the yolk from erupting during cooking.

7. Cook eggs covered. Glass lids or heavy-duty plastic wrap are the best coverings to use since they are the most water-vapor-proof of all coverings. Since egg yolks cook faster than egg whites, a yolk can become tough or may "pop," while the white is still undercooked, if cooked uncovered. A lid will retain steam which cooks the egg white. Steam will also help keep the yolk tender.

8. Remove eggs and egg dishes while they are still slightly moist and slightly underdone. Let them stand a few minutes, covered, to complete the cooking process, as recommended in the recipes. Eggs may be stirred during or after cooking for a fluffier texture.

9. Be careful not to overcook eggs. Overcooking can cause eggs to become tough and "rubbery." Check eggs at the minimum amount of cooking time recommended in the recipe to see if they are done.

10. Use the Cookmatic Level indicated in the recipe when preparing egg dishes. When converting your own favorite egg recipes, use a lower Cookmatic Level. Select a similar recipe in this chapter and use approximately the same amount of cooking time. Check eggs early during cooking to see if they are done. If not, cook slightly longer. Be careful not to overcook. Make a note of the correct time for your recipe for future reference.

General Hints for Cooking Cheese

1. Use the type of cheese that is recommended in the recipe. If you wish to substitute cheeses, substitute another cheese of the same general type. Example: substitute a hard cheese, for another hard cheese, and not with a soft cheese.

2. When recipes require a covering, use a glass lid or heavy-duty plastic wrap, since they are the most water-vapor-proof of all coverings.

3. Cheese can be easily and rapidly softened or melted, due to its fat content. Melt cheese using Cookmatic Level 5. Soften cheese using Cookmatic Level 3.

4. Cheese should be cooked using Cookmatic Level 8 or Full Power as indicated in the recipe so it will cook quickly, but below the boiling point to avoid a tough "rubbery" product. Prepare your own favorite recipes using these settings. Select a similar recipe in this chapter and use approximately the same amount of cooking time.

SCRAMBLED EGGS CHART

NO. OF EGGS	BOWL SIZE	AMOUNT OF BUTTER*	AMOUNT OF MILK** OR WATER (OPTIONAL)	COOKING TIME	COOKMATIC LEVEL
1	1-pt. bowl	1 teaspoon	2 teaspoons	45 sec. to 1 min.	Full Power
2	1-pt. bowl	1 teaspoon	1 tablespoon	1 min., 15 sec. to 1 min., 30 sec.	Full Power
4	1-qt. bowl	2 teaspoons	1-1/2 tablespoons	2 min. to 2 min., 15 sec.	Full Power
6	1-1/2-qt. bowl	1 tablespoon	2 tablespoons	3 min. to 3 min., 30 sec.	Full Power

*Spray-on vegetable coating may be used instead of butter. Spray to cover entire dish.

**When using milk, increase cooking time about 10 to 15 seconds.

General Instructions for Cooking Scrambled Eggs

1. Melt butter in bottom of bowl (see chart for bowl size) in Radarange Oven on Full Power for 20 to 30 seconds. Swirl bowl so melted butter covers entire dish bottom. Butter will help to keep eggs from sticking to bowl and thus aids in clean-up.

2. Stir eggs vigorously with fork in butter-coated bowl. Add milk or water if desired, for a smooth texture.

3. Cook in Radarange Oven, covered, on Full Power for the time specified in the "Scrambled Eggs Chart," depending upon the quantity of eggs used. Eggs may be covered loosely with waxed paper. For fluffier eggs, stir halfway through cooking time or several times during cooking.

4. Eggs are cooked when they look done, but are still slightly moist. Stir or fluff with fork before serving. Be careful not to overcook. Season with salt and pepper, as desired.

FRIED EGGS CHART

NO. OF EGGS	AMOUNT OF BUTTER OR MARGARINE*	COOKING TIME**	COOKMATIC LEVEL
1	2 teaspoons	30 to 45 sec.	Full Power
2	2 teaspoons	45 sec. to 1 min., 5 sec.	Full Power
4	1 tablespoon	1 min. to 1 min., 15 sec.	Full Power
6	1 tablespoon	1 min., 15 sec. to 1 min., 30 sec.	Full Power

*Spray-on vegetable coating may be used instead of butter or margarine.

**Cooking times for these eggs are based upon refrigerator temperatures.

Fried Eggs

Fried Eggs should be cooked in a browning skillet for best results. Without a browning skillet, eggs are really "baked", rather than fried. See the section on browning, page 14, for hints on using browning skillets.

General Instructions for Cooking Fried Eggs

1. Preheat the browning skillet for the proper amount of time according to manufacturer's instructions. Always preheat the skillet **completely** empty. Skillet should have a slight "yellow" color when eggs are added.
2. Melt butter in browning skillet before adding egg(s), according to the amount required as indicated on the "Fried Eggs Chart".
3. Add eggs quickly to browning skillet to avoid scorching butter. Pierce yolk(s) with knife or tines of fork. For more tender eggs, 1 to 2 teaspoons of water can be added with eggs.
4. **Cover** eggs with glass lid, so the eggs will cook evenly. (The glass lid will retain steam for even cooking.)
5. Cook eggs in the Radarange Oven for the amount of time indicated in the "Fried Eggs Chart." The shorter cooking time will produce soft-cooked yolks. The longer cooking time in the chart is for more hard-cooked yolk(s). If eggs have been standing at room temperature, decrease cooking time slightly since cooking times are based upon refrigerator-temperature eggs.
6. Let eggs stand, covered, 1 minute before serving. Season with salt and pepper, as desired.
7. When frying 4 to 6 eggs, slightly undercook. Let stand, covered, for about 5 minutes. The egg whites will finish cooking without overcooking the yolks.
8. **We do not recommend reheating leftover fried eggs in a microwave oven.**

Eggs Benedict

Yield: 2 servings

4 eggs, poached
1/2 cup Hollandaise sauce*
4 thin slices pre-cooked Canadian bacon or ham
2 English muffins, split

1. Poach eggs according to timing in above chart. Let stand in water, covered. Prepare Hollandaise sauce according to recipe on page 131. Let stand, covered. Place Canadian bacon on plate. Heat in Radarange Oven on Full Power for 45 seconds.
2. Arrange 2 muffin halves, cut-side up, on each serving plate. Top each half with slice of Canadian bacon or ham. Remove eggs from water, using slotted spoon. Place eggs on bacon. Spoon sauce over eggs. Heat one plate at a time. Heat in Radarange Oven on Full Power for 15 seconds, or until heated through.

*MICRO-TIP: See Hollandaise Sauce recipe, page 131.

POACHED EGGS CHART

NO. OF EGGS	UTENSIL	AMOUNT OF WATER	COOKING TIME*	COOKMATIC LEVEL
1	1 pt. bowl	1 cup	20 sec. to 45 sec.	Full Power
2	1 qt. bowl	1 cup	45 sec. to 1 min., 30 sec.	Full Power
4	1-1/2-qt. bowl	1-1/2 cups	1 min., 30 sec. to 2 min.	Full Power
6	1-1/2-qt. bowl	1-1/2 cups	2 min., 15 sec. to 2 min., 45 sec.	Full Power

*Cooking times for these eggs are based upon refrigerator temperatures.

Poached Eggs

Poached eggs cook beautifully in the Radarange Oven. Consult the "Poached Eggs Chart" for specific cooking instructions.

General Instructions for Cooking Poached Eggs

1. Bring the required amount of water to a boil in a glass measure in the Radarange Oven on Full Power.
2. Break egg(s) into size of utensil indicated on "Poached Eggs Chart". Be sure to use a bowl having rather steep sides so water won't "spread out" too much in dish.
3. Pierce yolk(s) with knife or tines of fork.
4. Pour boiling water **slowly over** eggs. Be sure that water covers eggs. If more water is needed to cover eggs, slightly increase cooking time. 1 tablespoon of vinegar can be added to the water to help egg(s) hold its (their) shape.
5. Cook egg(s) according to time on "Poached Egg Chart". Egg(s) may be covered loosely with plastic wrap. The shorter cooking time in the chart will produce soft-cooked yolks. The longer cooking time in the chart is for more hard-cooked yolk(s). For soft yolks, eggs can be removed from Radarange Oven while slightly undercooked. Allow to stand, covered. Whites will finish cooking without over-cooking yolks. If eggs have been standing at room temperature, decrease cooking time slightly since cooking times are based upon refrigerator-temperature eggs. Remove eggs after cooking with slotted spoon. Season with salt and pepper, as desired.
6. **We do not recommend reheating leftover poached eggs in a microwave oven.**

Egg and Sausage Scramble

Yield: 4 to 6 servings

6 eggs, slightly-beaten
6 slices bread, cubed
1 cup shredded Cheddar cheese
1 teaspoon salt
1 teaspoon dry mustard
12 ozs. pork sausage (or smokies), fully cooked and cut into pieces
2 cups milk

1. Mix all ingredients together in 1-1/2-quart casserole. Refrigerate 4 to 6 hours or overnight.
2. Cook in Radarange Oven, covered, on Cookmatic Level 8 for 12 to 14 minutes, or until knife inserted in center comes out clean. Serve immediately.

Wake-Up Special

Yield: 4 to 6 servings

6 slices bacon
1/4 cup chopped green pepper
4 eggs
1/2 (10-3/4 oz.) can cream of chicken soup
Salt
Pepper

1. Place bacon slices side by side in 1-quart casserole. Cover with paper towel. Cook in Radarange Oven, covered, on Full Power for 4 to 5 minutes, or until crisp. Remove bacon and crumble. Reserve 1 tablespoon of grease.
2. Add green pepper to bacon grease. Cook in Radarange Oven on Full Power for 60 seconds, or until green pepper is tender.
3. Combine eggs and soup. Pour into casserole with green pepper. Cook in Radarange Oven, covered, on Cookmatic Level 8 for 3-1/2 to 4 minutes, or until eggs are cooked as desired. Stir halfway through cooking time for fluffier eggs.
4. Sprinkle crumbled bacon over top. Season with salt and pepper, as desired.

MICRO-TIP: If desired, mix remaining soup with 1/2 cup milk. Heat in Radarange Oven on Full Power for 2 to 3 minutes, or until warmed. Use as sauce for eggs.

Fancy Scrambled Eggs

Yield: 6 to 8 servings

3 tablespoons butter or margarine
8 eggs
1/2 cup milk
1 teaspoon chopped chives
1/2 teaspoon salt
1/4 teaspoon dry mustard

1. Place butter in 1-quart casserole. Heat in Radarange Oven on Full Power for 30 to 40 seconds, or until melted. Add remaining ingredients. Beat vigorously with fork until well-mixed.
2. Cook in Radarange Oven, covered, on Cookmatic Level 8 for 6 to 7 minutes, or until eggs are cooked as desired. Stir halfway through cooking time for fluffier eggs.

Wheat Crusted Quiche

Yield: 6 servings

3/4 cup wheat germ
3/4 cup all-purpose flour
1/4 teaspoon salt
1/2 cup shortening
2 to 3 tablespoons cold water
9 to 10 slices (1/2 lb.) bacon, cooked and crumbled
3/4 cup shredded Swiss cheese
1/4 cup minced onion
3 eggs
1/2 cup evaporated milk
1/2 teaspoon salt
1/8 teaspoon cayenne pepper

1. Combine wheat germ, flour and salt. Cut in shortening. Stir in water. Press dough firmly against bottom and sides of 9-inch glass pie plate. Prick bottom and sides with tines of fork. Cook in Radarange Oven on Full Power for 1-1/2 to 2 minutes, or until cooked but slightly moist.
2. Sprinkle bacon, cheese and onion on crust.
3. Beat together eggs, evaporated milk and seasonings until well-blended. Pour into shell. Cook on Cookmatic Level 8 for 6 to 8 minutes, or until knife inserted near center comes out clean.*

*MICRO-TIP: You may want to turn dish halfway through cooking time.

Toast-Framed Egg

Yield: 1 serving

1 slice toasted bread, buttered
1 egg

1. Cut 3-inch diameter circle in toast with biscuit cutter or knife. Place toast on plate. Break egg into hole. Pierce yolk with knife or tines of fork. Cover with plastic wrap.
2. Cook in Radarange Oven, covered, on Full Power for 20 to 45 seconds, or until egg is cooked as desired.

Crustless Quiche Lorraine

Yield: 4 servings

9 to 10 slices (1/2 lb.) bacon, cooked and crumbled*
1 cup shredded Swiss cheese
1/4 cup minced onion
4 eggs
1 cup evaporated milk
3/4 teaspoon salt
1/4 teaspoon sugar
1/8 teaspoon cayenne pepper

1. Sprinkle bacon, cheese and onion into 9-inch glass pie plate.
2. Beat eggs, milk and seasonings in large mixing bowl with rotary beater until well-blended. Pour over bacon mixture.
3. Cook in Radarange Oven on Cookmatic Level 8 for 9-1/2 to 11 minutes or until knife inserted near center comes out clean.** Let stand, 1 minute, before serving.

MICRO-TIPS:

*Prepare bacon, according to instructions, on page 94.
**You may want to turn dish halfway through cooking time.

Savory Bacon Omelet

Yield: 4 servings

9 to 10 slices (1/2 lb.) bacon
1/2 cup thinly sliced green onions
8 eggs, beaten
1/4 cup heavy cream
2 teaspoons prepared mustard
1/4 teaspoon pepper
Salt

1. Place bacon slices in 10-inch glass pie plate side by side. Cover with paper towel. Cook in Radarange Oven, covered, on Full Power for 8 to minutes, or until crisp.
2. Remove bacon and crumble. Remove all of grease, reserving 1 tablespoon. Add green onions to grease. Cook in Radarange Oven on Power for 1 minute, or until green onions are almost tender.
3. Mix together eggs, bacon, green onions, cream and seasonings. Season with salt, as desired. Pour into pie plate. Cook in Radarange Oven on Cookmatic Level 8 for 6 to 7 minutes, or until firm but moist. Lift out edge once or twice during cooking to allow uncooked portion to touch outside of dish. Serve immediately.

Puffy Omelet

Yield: 2 to 3 servings

4 egg whites
3 tablespoons water
1/4 teaspoon cream of tartar
1/4 teaspoon salt
4 egg yolks
1/8 teaspoon pepper
Spray-on vegetable coating

FRUIT FILLED DESSERT OMELET VARIATION:
1/4 cup sugar
1/2 cup sliced strawberries or other fruit
1/2 cup whipped cream

1. Beat egg whites, water, cream of tartar and salt until egg whites are s but not dry.
2. Beat together yolks and pepper until yolks are thick and lemon-colored Fold into egg whites.
3. Preheat large browning skillet in Radarange Oven, according to manufacturer's instructions. Spray with vegetable coating. Pour omele mixture into skillet. Cook in Radarange Oven on Cookmatic Level 8 fo to 6 minutes, or until knife inserted in center comes out clean. To ser make cut across middle of omelet but don't cut completely through. Fold omelet over and slide out of dish onto warm platter.

MICRO-TIPS:

• Sprinkle center of omelet with shredded cheese before folding, if desired.
• For Fruit-filled Dessert Omelet Variation, follow original "Puffy Omel recipe except the following:
1. Omit pepper in Step #2. Add sugar to egg yolks before beating.
2. Blend together strawberries and whipped cream. Spread half on omele before folding. Spread remaining mixture over top before serving.

 Eggs Delicious

Yield: 4 servings

1/2 cup milk
1 (3 oz.) pkg. cream cheese
6 medium eggs
1 cup diced pre-cooked ham
1 large ripe tomato, cut in wedges
Salt
Pepper
2 tablespoons butter or margarine

1. Place milk in 1-cup glass measure. Heat in Radarange Oven on Full Power for 45 seconds to 1 minute, or until warmed.
2. Beat cream cheese until fluffy in large mixing bowl. Beat in milk and eggs.
3. Stir in ham and tomato. Season with salt and pepper, as desired.
4. Place butter in 10-inch glass pie plate. Heat in Radarange Oven on Full Power for 20 to 30 seconds, or until melted. Pour egg mixture into pie plate. Cook in Radarange Oven, covered, on Cookmatic Level 8 for 8 to 10 minutes, or until firm, but moist. Stir 2 to 3 times during cooking time.

Hash 'N' Egg Nests

Yield: 2 to 4 servings

1 (15-1/2 oz.) can hash*
4 eggs

1. Divide hash evenly among 4, 6-oz. custard cups, spreading hash up the sides of cups.
2. Break egg into each hash-lined cup and pierce each yolk with knife or tines of fork. Place cups on plate. Cover with plastic wrap.
3. Cook in Radarange Oven, covered, on Cookmatic Level 8 for 4-1/2 to 5 minutes, or until eggs are cooked as desired.**
MICRO-TIPS:
   - You can cook one at a time to achieve either soft or hard-cooked egg yolks for different personal preferences. Increase or decrease cooking time, accordingly.
   *Any type of hash may be used.
   **You may want to turn plate halfway through cooking time.

Cheese Soufflé

Yield: 4 to 6 servings

2 tablespoons butter or margarine
2 tablespoons all-purpose flour
1/2 teaspoon salt
1/2 teaspoon dry mustard
1/8 teaspoon paprika
1 cup evaporated milk
1-1/2 cups shredded sharp Cheddar cheese
4 eggs, separated
1/4 teaspoon cream of tartar

1. Place butter in 1 to 1-1/2-quart casserole. Heat in Radarange Oven on Full Power for 20 to 30 seconds, or until melted. Stir in flour, salt, mustard and paprika. Gradually add evaporated milk.
2. Cook in Radarange Oven on Cookmatic Level 8 for 2-1/2 to 3 minutes, or until thickened. Stir with wire whip until smooth. Stir in cheese until melted. If necessary, heat in Radarange Oven on Full Power for 1 to 2 minutes, or until cheese is completely melted.
3. Beat egg whites with cream of tartar until stiff, but not dry.
4. Beat egg yolks until thick and lemon-colored. Beat cheese mixture slowly into egg yolks, beating until well-blended. Fold cheese mixture into egg whites thoroughly, but gently. Turn into 1-quart soufflé dish.
5. Cook in Radarange Oven on Cookmatic Level 8 for 6-1/2 to 7-1/2 minutes, or until top seems dry.* Serve immediately.
   *MICRO-TIP: You may want to turn dish halfway through cooking time.

Whether you're fishing for flattery, or just preparing fish, a few guidelines will help you catch compliments. This chapter includes instructions and recipes for cooking a variety of fish and seafood which can be prepared in your Radarange Oven. You can serve the seafood with one of the sauces found in the "Sauces, Jams, and Relishes" chapter.

Fish and seafood are delicate food items to prepare, so follow recipe instructions carefully. Fish and seafood are more flaky and moist when prepared in a Radarange Oven instead of in a conventional oven. Since fish is delicate and has no tough tissues, the cooking time will be short. Weight-watchers will love Radarange Oven-prepared fish and seafood since oils and fats can be eliminated. Shellfish are easily prepared, since the huge quantities of water necessary in conventional cooking of shellfish are not required. The "Appetizers and Snacks" chapter includes several seafood appetizers. Read the following tips before preparing fish and seafood.

General Hints for Cooking Fish and Seafood

1. In most cases, fish should be defrosted, before cooking, unless otherwise specified in a recipe. Consult the "Fish and Seafood Defrosting Chart" for complete instructions. When fish is not completely thawed after defrosting, rinse with cold running water to complete the defrosting process.

2. Most fish and seafood require a cooking time of 3 to 4 minutes per pound on Full Power. When "delicate" ingredients, such as cheese, are cooked with seafood, sometimes a recipe will suggest cooking at a lower power setting. A lower setting, for example, will prevent such ingredients as cheese from becoming "rubbery."

3. Always cook fish and seafood in a covered utensil, so steam and moisture will be retained. The use of coverings also decreases the cooking time as well as prevents dehydration. Glass lids or heavy-duty plastic wrap are the best coverings to use since they retain more moisture than other types of coverings. If a dish doesn't have a glass lid, plastic wrap can easily be substituted. Plastic wrap should be pierced, by making a 1-inch slit with a knife.

4. Place larger and thicker pieces of fish and seafood near the edge of the dish for more even cooking.

5. Cook fish only until it may be easily flaked with a fork. Make certain that the center of large fish flakes easily as well as the edges. Shellfish meat will look opaque, and the shell will have a pink color when it is completely cooked. The flesh of all seafood, such as shrimp, crab and lobster, will look opaque and firm. Always try to cook fish and seafood for the minimum amount of time, since it is easily overcooked. Be careful not to overcook. Cover all fish and seafood during the standing time to:
   a) Keep it hot.
   b) Keep it moist and prevent dehydration.
   c) Finish its cooking process. (For example, the center may need to finish cooking.)

6. Always cook fish last when preparing an entire meal. Fish and seafood won't reheat as well as some foods, and overcooking can occur during reheating. Other foods, such as vegetables, will keep a better texture longer after cooking and can be reheated more easily. If necessary, however, fish and seafood can be quickly reheated before

serving. Be certain to cover during reheating.

7. One kind of fish required in a recipe can easily be substituted for another. For example, snapper, flounder, perch, halibut and sole can be used interchangeably in the following recipes. Fish steaks can also be substituted for fillets, but they may require slightly longer cooking and defrosting times.

8. Shellfish can be prepared right in the shell. Shells make very attractive and unusual serving "dishes." Shellfish cooked in the shell will have the same cooking time as fish cooked out of the shell since shells do not absorb microwaves.

9. Seafood can be attractively garnished by using lemon slices, parsley, almonds, tomato slices or spices. Consult the MICRO-TIPS for other serving hints.

10. Most seafood casserole recipes can be prepared ahead of time and refrigerated. Remember to allow 4 to 7 minutes of extra cooking time, due to the refrigerator temperature. The cooking time of a refrigerated casserole will vary slightly, depending upon the size and ingredients of the casserole.

11. You can convert your own favorite seafood recipes to Radarange Oven cooking times. Use the timings of the recipes in this chapter as a general guide. Find a recipe that is approximately the same size and includes the same type of seafood. Cook most casseroles covered on Full Power. Follow the other cooking tips found in this section.

FISH AND SEAFOOD DEFROSTING CHART

TYPE	PKG. SIZE	PREPARATION INSTRUCTIONS	DEFROSTING TIME	SETTING
Crab Claws	12 oz.	Make 1-inch slit in pkg. Turn and rearrange claws halfway through cooking time.	6 to 8 min.	Defrost*
Crab Meat	6 oz.	Make 1-inch slit in pkg. Turn halfway through cooking time.	3-1/2 to 4-1/2 min.	Defrost*
Fillets, Flounder, Cod, Sole, Haddock etc.	16 oz.	Unwrap pkg. and open. Turn fillets over halfway through cooking time.	8 to 12 min.	Defrost*
Lobster Tail	16 oz.	Wrap in plastic wrap or waxed paper.	7-1/2 to 9-1/2 min.	Defrost*
Shrimp	12 oz.	Make 1-inch slit in pkg. Turn halfway through cooking time.	7 to 9 min.	Defrost*

*On models having dial timer, use Cookmatic Level 3 for defrosting.

General Instructions for Defrosting Fish and Seafood

1. Frozen seafood may be thawed in its original package. Open the package slightly, or pierce it by making a 1-inch slit with a knife. Place it directly on the Radarange Oven glass tray or on a plastic rack. Consult the "Fish and Seafood Defrosting Chart" for complete instructions.

2. Be sure to use the Defrost cycle or Cookmatic Level 3 for thawing. This cycle operates at a low enough power to prevent cooking from starting at the outer edges.

3. Allow thawed seafood to stand for a short period of time before cooking to be certain the seafood is totally defrosted. Larger seafood pieces can be held under cold running water, if necessary, to finish the defrosting process, or to allow still-frozen fillets to be separated. Fish and seafood should be totally defrosted before cooking, so that cooking will be done evenly.

FISH AND SEAFOOD CONVENIENCE FOOD CHART

TYPE OF SEAFOOD	PKG. SIZE	COOKING TIME ON DEFROST*	HOLDING TIME**	COOKING TIME ON FULL POWER
Frozen Fish Sticks	8 oz.	3 min., 30 sec.*	3 min., 30 sec.	2 min to 3 min., 30 sec.
Frozen Fried Fish Fillets	2 oz. (1 fillet)	1 min., 30 sec.*	1 min., 30 sec.	30 sec. to 1 min.
Frozen Fried Fish Fillets	4 oz. (2 fillets — 2 ozs. each)	2 min., 30 sec.*	2 min., 30 sec.	1 to 2 min.
Frozen Fried Fish Fillets	8 oz. (4 fillets — 2 ozs. each)	3 min.*	3 min.	2 min., 30 sec. to 3 min., 30 sec.

*On models having dial timers, use Cookmatic Level 3 for defrosting.
**Allow a holding time equal to the defrosting time between defrosting and cooking.

General Instructions for Fish and Seafood Convenience Food Chart
1. Place the frozen seafood on a cooking grill or paper plate. Cover with a paper towel, waxed paper or plastic wrap.
2. Defrost, hold and cook, according to the instructions in the chart. The Hold period is necessary before cooking to be certain the seafood is totally defrosted.

Fresh Crab Claws

Yield: 2 to 3 servings

12 fresh crab claws

1. Place crab claws in circle in pie plate or au gratin dish with claws toward center. Cover with plastic wrap.
2. Cook in Radarange Oven, covered, on Full Power for 1-1/2 to 2 minut or until hot.

Crunchy Crab Bake

Yield: 4 to 6 servings

1 (4 oz.) can mushrooms, drained
1/2 cup mayonnaise
1/3 cup shredded Cheddar cheese
1 (10-3/4 oz.) can cream of shrimp soup
1 (6-1/2 oz.) can crab meat, drained
1 (8 oz.) can water chestnuts, drained and sliced
2 hard-cooked eggs, chopped*
1 (3 oz.) can French fried onion rings

1. Blend together mushrooms, mayonnaise, cheese and soup in 1-1/2-qu casserole.
2. Gently fold in crab meat, water chestnuts and eggs. Cook in Radaran Oven on Full Power for 5 minutes. Stir halfway through cooking time and at end of cooking time.
3. Sprinkle onion rings over casserole. Cook in Radarange Oven on Full Power for 2-1/2 to 3 minutes, or until heated through and temperature 150°F is reached.**

MICRO-TIPS:
  *Remember, do not hard-cook eggs in the Radarange Oven.
  **Use the Automatic Temperature Control System to cook to 150°F, your Radarange Oven has this feature.

Fish For One

Yield: 1 serving

1/4 lb. fish fillet
1/2 tablespoon butter or margarine
1 teaspoon lemon juice
Salt
Pepper

1. Arrange fish on glass serving plate. Dot with butter. Sprinkle with lemon juice. Season with salt and pepper, as desired. Cover with plastic wrap.
2. Cook in Radarange Oven, covered, on Full Power for 1 to 2 minutes, or until fish flakes easily with fork. Remove excess liquid, using paper towels, before serving.

French Fish Fillets

Yield: 4 servings

1 lb. fish fillets
1/4 cup French dressing
1/2 cup cracker crumbs
Paprika

1. Dip fillets in dressing. Coat with crumbs. Place fillets in greased 1-1/2-quart utility dish. Sprinkle with paprika, as desired. Cover with plastic wrap.
2. Cook in Radarange Oven, covered, on Full Power for 3-1/2 to 5 minutes, or until fish flakes easily with fork.

Colorful Fillets

Yield: 4 servings

1 lb. haddock fillets, cut into serving pieces
3 green onions, sliced
1 cup sliced fresh mushrooms
1 cup chopped tomato
1/8 teaspoon basil
3/4 teaspoon salt
Dash pepper

1. Arrange fillets in 8 x 8 x 2-inch glass baking dish. Top with vegetables. Sprinkle with seasonings. Cover with plastic wrap.
2. Cook in Radarange Oven, covered, on Full Power for 3 to 4 minutes, or until fish flakes easily with fork.

MICRO-TIP: This is a good fish recipe for weight watchers. There are approximately 136 calories per serving!

Springtime Sole

Yield: 4 servings

1 lb. sole fillets
1 (10 oz.) pkg. frozen asparagus or 3/4 lb. fresh asparagus, cooked
1/2 teaspoon salt
1/4 teaspoon leaf thyme
1/2 cup plain yogurt
1 teaspoon buttermilk salad dressing mix

1. Arrange fillets evenly in 1-1/2-quart utility dish. Layer asparagus over fillets. Sprinkle with salt and thyme. Cover loosely with plastic wrap. Cook in Radarange Oven, covered, on Full Power for 3-1/2 to 4-1/2 minutes, or until fish flakes easily with fork.
2. Combine yogurt and dressing mix. Spoon evenly over asparagus. Cook in Radarange Oven on Full Power for 1 to 2 minutes, or until sauce is heated through.

MICRO-TIP: This low-calorie recipe has only about 138 calories per serving.

Fillet of Sole with Oyster Sauce

Yield: 4 servings

1 (16 oz.) pkg. fillet of sole, defrosted
1 (10-3/4 oz.) can oyster stew
1 (4 oz.) can mushrooms, drained
1/2 teaspoon salt
Paprika

1. Separate fillets and arrange in 1-1/2-quart utility dish.
2. Blend together oyster stew, mushrooms and salt. Pour over fillets. Sprinkle with paprika, as desired. Cover with plastic wrap.
3. Cook in Radarange Oven, covered, on Full Power for 5 to 7 minutes, or until fish flakes easily with fork.

MICRO-TIP: For tartness, add sprinkling of lemon juice. Fresh fillet of sole may be substituted for frozen.

Savory Salmon Steaks

Yield: 4 servings

1 egg
1 tablespoon milk
1 tablespoon lemon juice
1/2 teaspoon salt
4 (3/4 to 1-inch thick each) salmon steaks
1/2 cup cornflake or bread crumbs
2 tablespoons butter or margarine

1. In shallow bowl, combine eggs, milk, lemon juice and salt. Beat well.
2. Dip each steak in egg mixture and then into cornflake crumbs.
3. Place butter in 2-quart utility dish. Heat in Radarange Oven on Full Power for 20 to 30 seconds, or until melted. Arrange steaks in dish. Cover with plastic wrap. Cook in Radarange Oven, covered, on Full Power for 6 to 8 minutes, or until fish flakes easily with fork.

Salmon Quiche

Yield: 6 servings

1, 9-inch baked pastry shell
2 cups cooked and boned salmon chunks, or 1 (1 lb.) can salmon, drained
1/2 cup sliced ripe olives
1 tablespoon snipped parsley
1 cup shredded Cheddar cheese
3 eggs
3/4 cup light cream or 3/4 cup evaporated milk
1/4 teaspoon salt
1/4 teaspoon onion powder

1. Bake pastry shell, as desired. Set aside.
2. Lightly mix salmon, olives and parsley. Place in pastry shell. Top with cheese.
3. Combine eggs with light cream, salt and onion powder. Pour over salmon.
4. Cook in Radarange Oven on Cookmatic Level 5 for 12 to 14 minutes, until knife inserted in center comes out clean.*
   *MICRO-TIP: You may want to turn dish halfway through cooking time.

Creole Halibut

Yield: 4 servings

1-1/2 lbs. halibut steaks
1 cup chopped onion
1/2 cup chopped green pepper
1/4 cup finely chopped celery
1 clove garlic, minced
1/4 cup butter or margarine
1 (1 lb.) can stewed tomatoes
1 (4 oz.) can mushrooms, drained
1 teaspoon salt
1/2 teaspoon sugar
Dash Tabasco sauce

1. Arrange halibut in greased 2-quart utility dish. Set aside.
2. Combine onion, green pepper, celery, garlic and butter in 1-quart casserole. Cook in Radarange Oven on Full Power for 3 to 4 minutes, until green pepper and celery are tender. Stir halfway through cooking time.
3. Blend in tomatoes, mushrooms and seasonings. Pour over fish. Cook in Radarange Oven on Full Power for 6-1/2 to 8 minutes, or until fish flakes easily with fork.
   MICRO-TIP: May be garnished with parsley and lemon wedges.

Halibut Teriyaki

Yield: 4 to 6 servings

1/4 cup soy sauce
1/4 cup dry white wine
1-1/2 tablespoons vegetable oil
1 tablespoon thinly sliced green onion
2 teaspoons sugar
1/8 teaspoon garlic powder
1-1/2 lbs. halibut fillets

1. Blend together all ingredients, except halibut, in 1-cup jar. Cover with Shake vigorously.
2. Arrange fish in single layer in 2-quart utility dish. Pour liquid over fish. Cover with plastic wrap and refrigerate for 30 minutes. Drain all but 2 tablespoons liquid from dish.
3. Cook in Radarange Oven, covered, on Full Power for 4-1/2 to 6 minutes, or until fish flakes easily with fork.

Baked Stuffed Whole Fish

Yield: 4 servings

1-1/2 lb. whole fish
1/4 cup butter or margarine, melted
1/2 teaspoon salt
2 cups bread cubes
1/4 cup boiling water
1/4 cup finely chopped celery
1/4 teaspoon poultry seasoning
2 tablespoons minced onion
Paprika

1. Wash dressed whole fish and wipe dry with paper towel. Brush interior of fish with half of butter. Sprinkle with salt.
2. Toss remaining ingredients together lightly for stuffing. Loosely fill cavity. Fasten with toothpicks.
3. Place stuffed fish on cooking grill. Sprinkle with paprika, as desired. Cover with plastic wrap. Cook in Radarange Oven, covered, on Full Power for 4-1/2 to 6 minutes, or until fish flakes easily with fork.
MICRO-TIP: Several different types of fish can be used in this recipe: lake trout, white fish and red snapper are some examples.

Stuffed Red Snapper

Yield: 6 servings

1 (2-1/2 to 3 lb.) whole red snapper
Salt
Pepper
1 egg
1/4 cup evaporated milk
2 tablespoons butter or margarine, melted
1-1/2 cups soft bread crumbs
1/2 cup minced celery leaves
1/4 cup chopped onion
1/4 cup minced parsley
1 teaspoon salt
1/8 teaspoon seasoned pepper
Pinch dill weed

1. Rinse prepared whole fish and pat dry. Sprinkle interior cavity with salt and pepper, as desired.
2. Mix together egg, milk, butter, bread crumbs, celery leaves, onion, parsley, salt, pepper and dill weed to make stuffing.
3. Stuff fish. Skewer with wooden picks. Lace with string to close. Make 3 small slashes in top of fish skin. Place fish on cooking grill or place on greased heavy brown paper or parchment paper. Fold over parchment and if necessary secure ends with rubber bands. If using cooking grill, cover with plastic wrap.
4. Cook in Radarange Oven, covered, on Full Power for 8 to 10 minutes, or until fish flakes easily with fork. Turn fish over halfway through cooking time.
MICRO-TIP: May be garnished with lemon wedges and watercress.

Curried Scallops

Yield: 3 to 4 servings

1 tablespoon butter or margarine
1 lb. scallops, rinsed and drained
1/4 cup sliced green onions
1-1/2 teaspoons cornstarch
1/2 teaspoon curry powder
1/4 teaspoon salt

1. Place butter in 9-inch glass pie plate. Heat in Radarange Oven on Full Power for 20 seconds, or until melted.
2. Add scallops and onions. Cover with plastic wrap. Cook in Radarange Oven, covered, on Full Power for 2-1/2 to 3-1/2 minutes, or until scallops are almost opaque. Stir halfway through cooking time. Reserve 2 tablespoons liquid.
3. Combine cornstarch, curry powder and salt with 2 tablespoons reserved liquid. Stir into scallops. Cover with plastic wrap.
4. Cook in Radarange Oven, covered, on Full Power for 2 minutes, or until sauce is thickened and smooth. Scallops should be opaque.
MICRO-TIP: Serve scallops over rice. Garnish with tomatoes and watercress.

Cooked Shrimp

Yield: 1/2 to 3/4 lb. cooked shrimp, approx. 4 servings

1 lb. shrimp, shelled and cleaned
1/4 cup hot water
2 teaspoons lemon juice
1/4 teaspoon salt
1/8 teaspoon thyme

1. Place shrimp in 1 to 1-1/2-quart casserole. Add water, lemon juice, salt and thyme.
2. Cook in Radarange Oven, covered, on Full Power for 2 to 3 minutes, or until shrimp is opaque and firm. Drain shrimp. Cover and chill.
MICRO-TIP: Use this shrimp for cocktails or salads.

Shrimp Creole

Yield: 4 to 5 servings

2 tablespoons butter or margarine
3/4 cup chopped green pepper
1 cup chopped onion
1 cup chopped celery
2 tablespoons all-purpose flour
1 (14-1/2 oz.) can tomatoes
1 teaspoon sugar
5 to 6 drops Tabasco sauce
1 bay leaf
1 teaspoon salt
1/8 teaspoon pepper
1 lb. shrimp, shelled and cleaned

1. Place butter in 2-1/2 to 3-quart casserole. Heat in Radarange Oven on Full Power for 20 to 30 seconds, or until melted.
2. Stir in green pepper, onion and celery. Cook in Radarange Oven on Full Power for 6 to 8 minutes, or until vegetables are tender. Stir halfway through cooking time.
3. Sprinkle vegetables with flour and stir to blend. Mix in tomatoes. Cook Radarange Oven on Full Power for 4 to 6 minutes, or until heated through. Stir halfway through cooking time.
4. Blend in remaining ingredients. Cook in Radarange Oven on Full Power for 6 minutes, or until shrimp are fully cooked. Stir twice during cooking time. Remove bay leaf before serving.
   MICRO-TIP: May be served over cooked rice.

Curried Shrimp and Broccoli

Yield: 6 to 8 servings

1 (10-3/4 oz.) can cream of celery soup
1 to 2 teaspoons curry powder
2 teaspoons Worcestershire sauce
1/2 cup finely chopped onion
1/2 cup milk
2 lbs. shrimp, shelled and cleaned
1 (10 oz.) pkg. frozen chopped broccoli, cooked
4 cups (8 ozs.) cooked fine egg noodles
Salt
1 tablespoon grated Parmesan cheese

1. Combine soup, curry powder, Worcestershire sauce and onion in 3-quart casserole. Stir in milk. Cook in Radarange Oven, covered, on Full Power for 4 to 5 minutes, or until onion is slightly tender. Stir halfway through cooking time.
2. Stir in shrimp and broccoli. Cook in Radarange Oven, covered, on Full Power for 4 to 5 minutes, or until shrimp is cooked and temperature of 160° F is reached.* Stir halfway through cooking time.
3. Gently combine soup mixture with noodles. Salt, as desired, and toss. Sprinkle with cheese before serving.
   *MICRO-TIP: Use the Automatic Temperature Control System to maintain 160° F until ready to serve, if your Radarange Oven has this feature. Toss with noodles just before serving.

Scalloped Oysters

Yield: 4 to 6 servings

1/4 cup butter or margarine
1/4 cup chopped onion
1/4 cup chopped celery
1 tablespoon parsley flakes
1 teaspoon lemon juice
1 teaspoon salt
1/8 teaspoon pepper
1/8 teaspoon instant minced garlic
1 pint oysters, drained
2 cups butter flavor cracker crumbs
1 cup milk
1/2 cup shredded Cheddar cheese

1. Combine butter, onion, celery, parsley flakes, lemon juice, salt, pepper and garlic in 1-1/2-quart casserole. Cook in Radarange Oven on Full Power for 3 to 4 minutes, or until onion and celery are tender.
2. Place oysters in 1-quart casserole. Cook in Radarange Oven, covered, on Full Power for 2 to 3 minutes, or until edges of oysters curl.
3. Blend oysters, 1-1/2 cups crumbs and milk into onion and celery mixture.
4. Sprinkle remaining crumbs and then cheese over casserole. Cook in Radarange Oven on Full Power for 3 to 4 minutes, or until temperature of 150° F is reached.*
   *MICRO-TIP: Use Automatic Temperature Control System to maintain 150° F until ready to serve, if your Radarange Oven has this feature.

Tuna Tot Casserole

Yield: 6 to 8 servings

1/3 cup chopped green pepper
1/2 cup chopped onion
1 tablespoon vegetable oil
1 (10-3/4 oz.) can cream of mushroom soup
2 tablespoons milk
1 (2-1/2 oz.) can sliced mushrooms, drained (optional)
2 (6-1/2 or 7 oz. each) cans tuna, drained
1 (8-1/2 oz.) can peas, drained
1/2 lb. Tater Tots®

1. Combine green pepper, onion and oil in 1-1/2-quart casserole. Cook in Radarange Oven on Full Power for 2 minutes, or until green pepper and onion are tender.
2. Blend in soup, milk, mushrooms, tuna and peas. Top with Tater Tots.®
3. Cook in Radarange Oven on Full Power for 10 to 12 minutes, or until temperature of 150° F is reached.*

*MICRO-TIP: Use the Automatic Temperature Control System to maintain 150° F until ready to serve, if your Radarange Oven has this feature.

Tuna Divan

Yield: 6 to 8 servings

2 (10 oz. each) pkgs. frozen broccoli cuts
1/4 cup water
2 (6-1/2 to 7 oz. each) cans tuna, drained
1 (10-3/4 oz.) can cream of onion soup
1/3 cup grated Parmesan cheese
1/3 cup milk
1 (2-1/2 oz.) jar sliced mushrooms, drained
1 tablespoon lemon juice
Dash cayenne pepper
Paprika

1. Place broccoli in 2-quart utility dish. Pour water over broccoli. Cover with plastic wrap. Cook in Radarange Oven, covered, on Full Power for 9 to 11 minutes, or until broccoli is cooked as desired. Stir to break apart after 5 minutes. Drain.
2. Spread tuna evenly over broccoli.
3. Blend together soup, cheese, milk, mushrooms, lemon juice and cayenne pepper. Pour evenly over tuna. Sprinkle with paprika, as desired. Cover with plastic wrap.
4. Cook in Radarange Oven, covered, on Full Power for 4-1/2 to 5-1/2 minutes, or until heated through.

Shoestring Tuna Casserole

Yield: 4 to 5 servings

1 (4 oz.) can cheese flavor shoestring potatoes
1 (10-3/4 oz.) can golden cream of mushroom soup
1 (6-1/2 or 7 oz.) can tuna, drained
1 (5.3 oz.) can evaporated milk
1 (3 oz.) can sliced mushrooms, drained
1/4 cup chopped pimento

1. Combine all ingredients in 1-1/2-quart casserole, reserving 1 cup of shoestring potatoes. Sprinkle reserved potatoes over top.
2. Cook in Radarange Oven on Full Power for 10 minutes, or until temperature of 150° F is reached.*

*MICRO-TIP: Use the Automatic Temperature Control System to cook to 150° F, if your Radarange Oven has this feature.

Tuna Stroganoff

Yield: 4 servings

2 (6-1/2 to 7 oz. each) cans tuna
1 (10-3/4 oz.) can cream of mushroom soup
1 (3 or 4 oz.) can sliced mushrooms, with liquid
1/2 cup dairy sour cream
1 tablespoon chopped parsley (optional)

1. Combine tuna, soup and mushrooms in 1-1/2-quart casserole.
2. Cook in Radarange Oven on Full Power for 4 to 5 minutes, or until mixture begins to boil. Stir twice during cooking time. Stir in sour cream. Garnish with parsley, as desired.

Meats can be prepared in your Radarange Oven with excellent results. This chapter will tell you exactly how to prepare and cook meats to achieve the best results. This chapter includes many recipes which are main dishes that include meat as the basic ingredient.

Throughout this section, all cooking times given for meats are based upon completely defrosted meat items of refrigerator temperature. To determine whether a meat item is completely defrosted, insert a sharp knife in the meat. Do not cook meat before it is completely thawed.

Before cooking meats in your Radarange Oven, be sure to read this chapter introduction carefully.

General Hints for Defrosting Meats

1. Meats should be removed from their original coverings during defrosting. Any metal wrapping, should especially be removed.
2. Defrosting time depends upon the **shape** of the meat, such as the meat's thickness, irregular areas, etc. For example, thinner cuts defrost more quickly than thicker cuts. Rolled roasts require longer defrosting times than flat-shaped roasts.
3. Defrosting time also depends upon how solidly a piece of meat is frozen. For example, a freezer in a combination refrigerator-freezer may not freeze meat as solidly as an individual freezer. If meat is frozen in an individual freezer, slightly increase the defrosting time.
4. The cooking grill is ideal for defrosting since juices can drain away from the meat into the 2-quart utility dish.
5. Cover meats with heavy-duty plastic wrap during defrosting to speed the defrosting process and to defrost more evenly.
6. Large cuts of meat may need to be turned over during defrosting to ensure even defrosting.
7. If a meat is frozen in pieces, such as individual steaks, chops, hamburgers, etc., the pieces should be separated before the last half or last quarter of the defrosting time. This will allow for faster more even defrosting.
8. Allow a holding time equal to the defrosting time between the defrosting and the cooking times to allow meat to finish defrosting. Remember, meats should be totally defrosted before cooking begins. You can determine whether a meat is completely defrosted by inserting a sharp knife in the center of the meat to check for ice crystals, if you are in doubt.

SMALL SIZE MEATS DEFROSTING CHART

MEAT TYPE	WEIGHT	DEFROSTING TIME ON DEFROST*	SPECIAL INSTRUCTIONS
Bacon	16 ozs.	3 to 5 min.	Remove from package.
Frankfurters	12 ozs.	4 to 6 min.	Remove from package.
	16 ozs.	3 to 6 min.	Remove from package.
Ground Beef	16 ozs.	10 to 13 min.	Remove from plastic wrap. Remove outside meat as it defrosts. Break apart with fork.
Bulk			
Patties	16 ozs.	7 to 10 min.	Remove from plastic wrap. Arrange in circle.
Sausage	12 ozs.	4 to 6 min.	Remove from package.
Steaks (beef)	16 ozs.	5 to 9 min.	Remove from plastic wrap.

*On models having dial timers, use Cookmatic Level 3 for defrosting.

General Instructions for Defrosting Small Size Meats
1. Read the "Special Instructions" on the chart before defrosting small meat items.
2. Defrost the meat, according to the time on the chart. Use the Defrost setting.

ROAST DEFROSTING CHART*

WEIGHT	MINUTES PER POUND ON DEFROST**
Under 3 lbs.	8 min./lb.
3 to 6 lbs.	10 min./lb.
Over 6 lbs.	12 min./lb.

*This chart is designed for defrosting large cuts of meat.
**On models having dial timers, use Cookmatic Level 3 for defrosting.

General Instructions for Defrosting Roasts or Large Cuts of Meat
1. Place meat on cooking grill and cover with plastic wrap or place in heavy-duty plastic roasting bag in 2-quart utility dish.
2. Defrost according to the amount of time on the chart. For example, if a roast weighs 4 pounds, defrost it for 10 minutes per pound, or 40 minutes on the Defrost setting.

$$4 \text{ lbs.} \times 10 \text{ min./lb.} = 40 \text{ minutes}$$

3. Thicker cuts of meat weighing between 2 and 3 pounds should be defrosted for 10 minutes per pound, rather than 8 minutes per pound.
4. Roasts should be given a standing time equal to the defrosting time before cooking to allow completion of the defrosting process.

General Hints for Cooking Meats

1. Meats weighing 3 pounds or more will brown by themselves "naturally" in the Radarange Oven. The exterior of a meat this size becomes very hot during cooking, and it requires a longer cooking time than do smaller cuts. The long cooking time and the heat are required for browning.

2. For more browning of small cuts of meat such as steaks, chops and hamburgers, a browning skillet or a bottled browning sauce may be used. See "Browning", on page 14.

3. Most meats are best prepared by using a cooking grill. (See the "Glossary of Microwave Cooking Terms", page 5.) A heavy duty plastic roasting bag is recommended for some meats.

4. Do not salt meats, until after cooking or just before serving. This is especially important when cooking solid cuts of meat. Do not salt the raw meat surface. If, however, the meat is just one ingredient in a main dish, or if the meat is covered by a sauce, then you may add salt to the sauce or the main dish. When a raw meat surface is salted in microwave or conventional cooking, the meat surface will become dehydrated and tough, since salt draws out the meat moisture.

5. Excess fat may be trimmed from meat before cooking to decrease the amount of accumulated meat juices and to prevent spattering within the Radarange Oven.

6. Aged or ripened meat will tend to cook more quickly than fresh meat. If you are cooking an aged piece of meat, decrease the cooking time slightly.

7. Tender meat can be cooked quickly in the Radarange Oven on higher Cookmatic Levels with good results. For less tender cuts of meat, use lower Cookmatic Levels for the best results. Less tender meat needs a longer cooking in order to tenderize. Moist cooking methods are recommended for less tender cuts of meat. Tenderizing agents can also be used. For less tender cuts of meat (particularly flat cuts), such as blade steak, chuck roast, pot roast, shoulder cuts, arm cuts or ribs, you may wish to use a tenderizing agent. Less tender cuts can also be marinated or mechanically tenderized by pounding with a meat mallet before cooking.

8. When cooking medium tender or less tender cuts of meat, you may wish to use Temperature-Hold to hold the meat at the final temperature, to tenderize, with the Automatic Temperature Control System feature, if your Radarange Oven has this feature. If you are not in the kitchen to remove the meat when the Temperature-Hold time is finished, the Radarange Oven will continue to hold the meat at the desired temperature. The meat will be warm when ready to serve.

9. For the best cooking results, turn most large meats over approximately halfway through the cooking time, in order to achieve even cooking throughout the meat.

10. When barbecuing meats on an outdoor grill, barbecue a few "extras", and freeze them. Later, these meats can be defrosted and reheated quickly in the Radarange Oven.

METHODS FOR COOKING BEEF, LAMB AND VEAL

In this cookbook, there are 3 basic methods in which beef, lamb and veal should be cooked. These methods are easy to follow and they are based upon whether a cut of meat is tender, medium tender or less tender. The method for cooking pork is described on page 88.

On the cooking charts on pages 90 and 91, the recommended method for cooking each particular cut of meat is listed. You can check on pages 84 to 88 to see how the recommended methods are accomplished. Soon, you will automatically remember these methods. You can use the cooking method instructions in this chapter only as a handy reference.

Before cooking a meat, check the charts on pages 90 and 91 to be sure you have selected the proper cooking method. These charts indicate which cooking method should be used for each individual meat cut. The charts list the different sections of beef, lamb, pork and veal. The charts further indicate from which section the individual cuts of meat are taken. In general, the section of the animal from which individual cuts are taken determines whether the cut is tender cut or less tender cut.

Notice that on the charts on pages 92 to 96 meats are generally cooked by the minutes per pound method.

However, if your Radarange Oven has the Automatic Temperature Control feature, meats may be cooked to a desired temperature. The three cooking methods also describe how cooking is accomplished with the Automatic Temperature Control System feature. Basically, cooking is done exactly the same as in the minutes per pound method. However, in the 2nd and final cooking time, the Automatic Temperature Control System determines when the meat is done, rather than an amount of time.

If your Radarange Oven does not have the Automatic Temperature Control feature, you can determine when your meat is fully cooked by using a regular meat thermometer or a microwave oven thermometer which has an all-plastic head. If a regular meat thermometer is used, do not leave the thermometer inside the Radarange Oven while it's operating.

The Automatic Temperature Control System feature can also be used to maintain a meat temperature for a desired length of time for tenderizing. The amounts of time required for tenderizing are described in the three recommended cooking methods. This tenderizing time is not required in Cooking Method #1. If your Radarange Oven doesn't have the Automatic Temperature Control System feature, change the Cookmatic Level setting to 1 after cooking and continue to cook the meat until it is tender, as desired. If your Radarange Oven does not have a Cookmatic Level 1, you can continue to cook the meat on the lowest setting your oven has. However, you will need to frequently check the temperature of the meat. The meat temperature should **not** be allowed to exceed the desired end temperature. (See the "Recommended End Temperature Chart", on page 90.)

Cooking Method #1: Tender Beef, Lamb and Veal

1. Place the meat fat-side-down on the cooking grill.
2. Cover the meat with heavy-duty plastic wrap. Tuck the plastic wrap beneath the edges of the plastic rack.
3. Cook in the Radarange Oven on Cookmatic Level 9 for 3 minutes per pound. Then, cook in the Radarange Oven on Cookmatic Level 6, according to the time per pound on the Beef, Lamb and Veal Cooking Charts on pages 90 and 91. The time per pound for the 2nd cooking time will vary, depending upon the weight of the meat and whether the meat is cooked to the rare, medium or well-done stage. You may wish to turn large cuts of meat over halfway through the cooking time for best results.

NOTE: **If your Radarange Oven has the Automatic Temperature Control System feature, you can cook meats using this system, rather than by using the minutes per pound method.** Follow steps #1 and #2 in Cooking Method #1. Replace step

#3 with the following procedure:
- If the meat is frozen, defrost before cooking, according to the "Roast Defrosting Chart," on page 83. Insert a sharp knife in the meat to determine whether the meat is totally defrosted, before cooking. Defrost the meat completely before inserting the temperature probe.
- Insert the temperature probe halfway between the center and outside edge of the meat, through the plastic wrap. Be sure the probe is inserted in the largest lean area of the meat. Avoid touching fat or bone with the probe. Be sure the plastic has been pierced well, either by inserting the probe through it or by slitting it with a knife. If the probe is inserted directly in the center of a meat cut, it is possible for the meat to overcook during "carry-over" cooking time.
- Cook in the Radarange Oven on Cookmatic Level 9 for 3 minutes per pound. Then, cook in the Radarange Oven on Cookmatic Level 6 until a temperature of 140° F, 150° F, 160° F or 170° F is reached, as desired. (See the "Recommended End Temperature Chart" on page 90.) Use the Automatic Temperature Control System to maintain a temperature until ready to serve, if desired. However, holding is not necessary for good results with tender meats. You may wish to turn large cuts of meat over halfway through the cooking time, for best results.

EXAMPLE: **Frozen** Standing Rib Roast (Beef) weighing 2 lbs. (under 3 lbs. category on chart) prepared to the Rare degree. See the "Beef Cooking Chart," page 90. (Note: If your microwave oven does not have a defrost setting, make sure the meat is completely defrosted before cooking.)

1. Prepare the meat, according to Cooking Method #1, as just described.
2. In this example, you will use 2 different charts for defrosting and cooking. First, see the "Roast Defrosting Chart," on page 83. Since the roast in this example weighs 2 lbs., then the 1 to 3 lbs. category on the chart is used.

   For defrosting, as shown in the "Roast Defrosting Chart," a 1 to 3 lb. roast should be defrosted for 8 minutes per pound. Therefore, a 2 pound roast should be defrosted for

8 minutes.

2 lbs. × 8 min./lb. = 16 minutes

Also for defrosting, as shown in the "Roast Defrosting Chart," roasts should be given a standing time equal to the defrosting time before cooking to allow completion of the defrosting process.

2 lbs. × 8 min./lb. = 16 minutes standing time

For cooking, the meat should be cooked on Cookmatic Level 9 for 3 minutes per pound, according to the "Beef Cooking Chart," on page 90. Therefore, a 2 pound roast should be cooked for 6 minutes.

2 lbs. × 3 min./ lb. = 6 minutes

Also for cooking, the meat should be cooked on Cookmatic Level 6 for 4 to 5 minutes per pound, or until the rare degree (as stated in the example), according to the "Beef Cooking Chart," on page 90. Therefore, a 2 pound roast should be cooked for an additional 10 to 12 minutes.

2 lbs. × 4 to 5 min./lb. = 8 to 10 minutes

NOTE: **If your Radarange Oven has the Automatic Temperature Control System feature, defrost as described in this example.** Insert a sharp knife in the meat to determine whether the meat is totally defrosted, before cooking. Then, insert the temperature probe in the meat before cooking, as described in Cooking Method #1. Cook on Cookmatic Level 9 for 3 minutes per pound, as already described in this example, according to 1st setting on the "Beef Cooking Chart," page 90. Then, cook on Cookmatic Level 6 to 140° F, or until the rare degree (as stated in the example), according to the 2nd setting on the "Beef Cooking Chart," on page 90. This second cooking step will require about 4 to 5 minutes per pound, according to the 2nd cooking time for the rare degree for this particular cut and weight of meat. Since the Automatic Temperature Control System feature is used, there is no need to set the 2nd cooking time. The Automatic Temperature Control System will determine when the meat has finished cooking.

Cooking Method #2: Medium Tender Beef, Lamb and Veal

1. Place the meat fat-side-down on the cooking grill. One of the sauces for meats on page 88 may be used, if desired.
2. Cover the meat with heavy-duty plastic wrap. Tuck the plastic wrap beneath the edges of the plastic rack.
3. Cook in the Radarange Oven, on Cookmatic Level 8 for 3 minutes per pound. Then, cook in the Radarange Oven on Cookmatic Level 5 according to the time per pound on the Beef, Lamb and Veal Cooking Charts on pages 90 and 91. The time per pound for the second cooking time will vary depending upon the weight of the meat, and whether the meat is cooked to the rare, medium or well-done stage. You may wish to turn large cuts of meat over halfway through the cooking time, for best results.

NOTE: **If your Radarange Oven has the Automatic Temperature Control System, you can cook meats using this system, rather than by using the minutes per pound method.** Follow steps #1, #2 and #3 in Cooking Method #2. Replace step #4 with the following procedure:

- If the meat is frozen, defrost before cooking, according to the "Roast Defrosting Chart," on page 83. Insert a sharp knife in the meat to determine whether the meat is totally defrosted before cooking. Defrost the meat completely before inserting the temperature probe.
- Insert the temperature probe halfway between the center and the outside edge of the meat, through the plastic wrap. Be sure the probe is inserted in the largest lean area of the meat. Avoid touching fat or bone with the probe. Be sure the plastic has been pierced well, either by inserting the probe through it or by slitting it with a knife. If the probe is inserted directly in the center of a meat cut, it is possible for the meat to overcook during "carry-over" cooking time.
- Cook in the Radarange Oven on Cookmatic Level 8 for 3 minutes per pound. Then, cook in the Radarange Oven on Cookmatic Level 5 until a temperature of 160° F or 170° F is reached, as desired. (See the "Recommended End Temperature Chart", on page 90.) Use the

Automatic Temperature Control System to maintain the desired temperature for at least 15 to 30 minutes for good product results. You may wish to turn large cuts of meat over halfway through the cooking time, for best results.

EXAMPLE: **Refrigerator Temperature** Round (Rolled) Rump Roast (Beef) weighing 4 lbs. (3 to 6 lb. category on the chart) prepared to the Medium degree. See the "Beef Cooking Chart," page 90.

1. Prepare the meat, according to Cooking Method #2, as just described.
2. For cooking, the meat should be cooked on Cookmatic Level 8 for 3 minutes per pound, according to the "Beef Cooking Chart" on page 90. Therefore, a 4 pound roast should be cooked for 12 minutes.

$$4 \text{ lbs.} \times 3 \text{ min./lb.} = 12 \text{ minutes}$$

Also for cooking, the meat should be cooked on Cookmatic Level 5 for 9 to 11 minutes per pound, or until the medium degree (as stated in the example), according to the "Beef Cooking Chart", on page 90. Therefore, a 4 pound roast should be cooked for an additional 36 to 44 minutes.

$$4 \text{ lbs.} \times 9 \text{ to } 11 \text{ min./lb.} = 36 \text{ to } 44 \text{ minutes}$$

NOTE: **If your Radarange Oven has the Automatic Temperature Control System feature, insert the temperature probe in the meat before cooking, as described in Cooking Method #2.** Cook on Cookmatic Level 8 for 3 minutes per pound, as already described in this example, according to the 1st setting on the "Beef Cooking Chart" page 90. Then, cook on Cookmatic Level 5 to 160° F or until the medium degree (as stated in the example), according to the 2nd setting on the "Beef Cooking Chart," on page 90. This second cooking step will require about 9 to 11 minutes per pound, according to the 2nd cooking time for the medium degree for this particular cut and weight of meat. Since the Automatic Temperature Control System feature is used, there is no need to set the 2nd cooking time. The Automatic Temperature Control System will determine when the meat has finished cooking.

Cooking Method #3: Less Tender Beef and Veal

1. Place the meat inside a heavy-duty plastic roasting bag.
2. Pierce the plastic bag. Tuck the end of the plastic bag securely beneath the meat.
3. Cook in the Radarange Oven on Cookmatic Level 7 for 3 minutes per pound. Then, cook in the Radarange Oven on Cookmatic Level 4, according to the time per pound on the Beef, Lamb, and Veal Cooking Charts on pages 90 and 91. The time per pound for the 2nd cooking time will vary depending upon the weight of the meat and whether the meat is cooked to the rare, medium or well-done stage. You may wish to turn large cuts of meat over halfway through the cooking time, for best results.

NOTE: If you wish to cook vegetables with a pot roast, you may put them in the cooking bag when cooking the meat. Onions, potatoes or carrots may be added. If vegetables are large, slice them into smaller pieces before cooking.

NOTE: **If your Radarange Oven has the Automatic Temperature Control System, you can cook meats using this system, rather than by using the minutes per pound method.** Follow steps #1 and #2 in Cooking Method #3. Replace step #3 with the following procedure:

- If the meat is frozen, defrost before cooking, according to the "Roast Defrosting Chart", on page 83. Insert a sharp knife in the meat to determine whether the meat is totally defrosted, before cooking. Defrost the meat completely before inserting the temperature probe.
- Insert the temperature probe halfway between the center and the outside edge of the meat, through the plastic bag. Be sure the probe is inserted in the largest lean area of the meat. Avoid touching fat or bone with the probe. Inserting the probe, or "poking" it through the plastic bag, will also "pierce" the bag. Tuck the end of the plastic bag securely beneath the meat. If the probe is inserted directly in the center of a meat cut, it is possible for the meat to overcook during "carry-over" cooking time.

- Cook in the Radarange Oven on Cookmatic Level 7 for 3 minutes per pound. Then, cook in the Radarange Oven on Cookmatic Level 4 until a temperature of 170° F is reached. (Usually 170° F is the desired end temperature for less tender cuts of meat. See the "Recommended End Temperature Chart" on page 90.) Use the Automatic Temperature Control System to maintain 170° F for at least 30 to 60 minutes for good product results. You may wish to turn large cuts of meat over halfway through the cooking time, for best results.

EXAMPLE:　Refrigerator Temperature Round Pot Roast (Beef) weighing 2-1/2 lbs. (1 to 3 lb. category on chart) prepared to the well-done degree. See the "Beef Cooking Chart," page 90.

1. Prepare the meat, according to Cooking Method #3, as just described.
2. For cooking, the meat should be cooked on Cookmatic Level 7 for 3 minutes per pound, according to the "Beef Cooking Chart," on page 90. Therefore, a 2-1/2 pound roast should be cooked for 7-1/2 minutes.

$$2\text{-}1/2 \text{ lbs.} \times 3 \text{ min./lb.}$$
$$= 7\text{-}1/2 \text{ minutes}$$

Also for cooking, the meat should be cooked on Cookmatic Level 4 for 7 to 9 minutes per pound, or until the well-done degree (as stated in the example), according to the "Beef Cooking Chart," on page 90. Therefore, a 2-1/2 pound roast should be cooked for an additional 17-1/2 to 20 minutes.

$$2\text{-}1/2 \text{ lbs.} \times 7 \text{ to } 8 \text{ min./lb.}$$
$$= 17\text{-}1/2 \text{ to } 20 \text{ minutes}$$

NOTE:　**If your Radarange Oven has the Automatic Temperature Control System feature, insert the temperature probe in the meat, before cooking, as described in Cooking Method #3.** Cook on Cookmatic Level 7 for 3 minutes per pound, as already described in this example, according to the 1st setting on the "Beef Cooking Chart," page 90. Then, cook on Cookmatic Level 4 to 170° F, or until the well-done degree (as stated in the example), according to the 2nd setting on the "Beef

Cooking Chart," on page 90. This second cooking step will require about 7 to 8 minutes per pound according to the 2nd cooking time for the well-done degree for this particular cut and weight of meat. Since the Automatic Temperature Control System feature is used, there is no need to set the 2nd cooking time. The Automatic Temperature Control System will determine when the meat has finished cooking.

METHOD FOR COOKING PORK

1. Place the meat fat-side-down on the cooking grill.
2. Cover the meat with heavy-duty plastic wrap. Tuck the plastic wrap beneath the edges of the plastic rack.
3. Cook in Radarange Oven on Cookmatic Level 3 for 19 to 21 minutes per pound, or until no longer pink, thoroughly cooked, and a temperature of 170° F is reached. Turn pork over and turn dish halfway through cooking time. Let stand, covered, 15 to 30 minutes before serving.

NOTE:　Fresh pork should be slowly cooked, covered, to an internal, uniform temperature of 170° F for maximum juiciness and flavor. Cook pork until no trace of pink color remains. If your Radarange Oven has the Automatic Temperature Control System feature, you can cook meats using this system, rather than by the minutes per pound method.

SAUCES FOR MEATS

For some cuts of meat such as blade steak, chuck roast, pot roast, shoulder cuts, arm cuts or ribs, you may wish to use one of these sauces or one of your own favorites, to add flavor.

Baste the meat with the desired sauce, and cook, covered, with heavy-duty plastic wrap. Notice there are no cooking times for these sauces, since they are cooked with the meat. One of these sauces may be used in Cooking Method #2 or in the cooking bag in Cooking Method #3.

a. Spicy Sauce
　1/2 cup vinegar
　1/2 cup water
　1 bay leaf
　1 medium onion, sliced
　10 whole cloves
　　1 teaspoon Worcestershire
　　　sauce
　　1 bay leaf
　　2 teaspoons seasoned salt
　　1 tablespoon bottled
　　　browning sauce

b. Wine Sauce
　1/2 cup wine
　1/2 cup bouillon or
　　consomme
　(See next column)

c. Sweet-Sour Sauce
　1/3 cup sherry
　1/3 cup soy sauce
　2 tablespoons honey
　(See next page)

1 clove garlic
1 tablespoon sugar
2 teaspoons salt
1/2 teaspoon pepper
d. Tangy Tomato Sauce
3/4 cup tomato sauce
1/4 cup vinegar or lemon juice
1 small onion, minced
1 bay leaf
1/2 teaspoon oregano
2 tablespoons brown sugar
1 teaspoon prepared mustard
(See next column)

2 teaspoons salt
1/2 teaspoon pepper
1/8 teaspoon instant, minced garlic
(1 (1lb.) jar meatless spaghetti sauce can be substituted for the Tangy Tomato Sauce)
e. Barbecue Sauce
3/4 cup barbecue sauce
1/4 cup water
1 teaspoon salt
1 teaspoon liquid smoke

NOTE: Tougher cuts of meat may require a commercial or mechanical tenderizing agent. Follow the instructions on the jar label. Mechanically tenderize meat by using a meat mallet.

NOTE: If your microwave oven is a 500-watt oven, do not use the "Beef, Pork, Lamb and Veal Charts" on pages 90 and 91. Do not use the "Meat Summary Chart" on this page. When cooking meats, use the "500-watt microwave oven Meat Cooking Chart" on page 90.

EXPLANATION OF CHARTS

The charts on the following pages give directions for cooking many types of meats. The "Beef Cooking Chart", "Lamb Cooking Chart", "Veal Cooking Chart" and "Pork Cooking Chart" all recommend one of the three major cooking methods:

Cooking Method #1: Tender Meats
Cooking Method #2: Medium Tender Meats
Cooking Method #3: Less Tender Meats

The chart below includes a summary of cooking instructions for the three cooking methods. Use this chart as a handy reference guide.

MEAT COOKING METHODS: SUMMARY CHART*

COOKING METHOD	SPECIAL INSTRUCTIONS	1ST COOKING TIME	1ST COOKMATIC LEVEL	COOK TO FINAL TEMP.	2ND COOKMATIC LEVEL	2ND COOKING TIME	RECOMMENDED TEMP.-HOLD TIME
Cooking Method #1: Tender Meats	Cover the meat with heavy-duty plastic wrap.	3 min./lb.	9	140°, 150°, or 160° F	6	**	not necessary
Cooking Method #2: Medium-Tender Meats	Cover meat with heavy-duty plastic wrap.	3 min./lb.	8	160° or 170° F	5	**	15 to 30 min.
Cooking Method #3: Less Tender Meats	Place meat in roasting bag.	3 min./lb.	7	160° or 170°F	4	**	30 to 60 min.
Method For Cooking Pork	Cover meat with heavy-duty plastic wrap.	19 to 21 min./lb.	3	170° F	—	—	—

*Detailed instructions for these cooking methods are found on pages 84 to 88 of this cookbook.

**See the "Beef, Lamb, and Veal Cooking Charts" on pages 90 and 91 for the amount of cooking time for the 2nd cooking time. The time per pound for the 2nd cooking time will vary, depending upon the weight of the meat and whether the meat is cooked to the rare, medium or well-done stage. On models having the Automatic Temperature Control System feature, the meat can be cooked to a desired temperature using this feature. See the "Methods for Cooking Meats" pages 84 to 89 for further instructions.

There are some meats which are exceptions and do not "fit" into the categories for the three major methods. Therefore, these meats have separate charts of cooking instructions.

Most of the meats which don't use one of the three major methods are items which are smaller meat cuts, pre-cooked or require the use of a browning skillet.

500-WATT MICROWAVE OVEN MEAT COOKING CHART

(Beef, Pork, Lamb, Veal)

MEAT TYPE (3 lbs.)*	COOKING TIME—MINUTES PER POUND		
	Rare	Med.	Well
Beef**	8 to 9 min./lb.	9 to 11 min./lb.	11 to 12 min./lb.***
Pork**	—	—	10 to 12 min./lb.***
Lamb**	—	—	8 to 11 min./lb.***
Veal**	—	—	9 to 11 min./lb.***

*Testing for cooking times on this chart was done for 3 pound meats. Cooking times for larger or smaller meats should be lengthened or shortened, accordingly.

**Prepare meats for cooking, according to the directions in the "Methods for Cooking Meats" section, pages 84 to 88.

***Cooking times are approximate. Meat should be cooked until done, as desired. You may want to turn meats over 2 to 3 times during cooking time.

RECOMMENDED END TEMPERATURE CHART

MEAT TYPE	COOKED DEGREE	END TEMPERATURE
Beef	Rare	140°F
	Medium	160°F
	Well-Done	170°F
Lamb	Well-Done	170°F
Pork*	Well-Done	170°F
Fresh		170° F
Smoked		170° F
Pre-cooked		140° F
Veal	Well-Done	170°F

*Pork must always be cooked until it is no longer pink, well done and a temperature of 170°F is reached.

BEEF COOKING CHART

SECTION	CUT	WEIGHT	COOKING METHOD	1ST SETTING COOKMATIC LEVEL	1ST COOKING TIME	2ND SETTING COOKMATIC LEVEL	COOK TO FINAL TEMP.*	2ND COOKING TIME* MINUTES PER POUND			RECOMMENDED TEMP.— HOLD TIME
								RARE	MED	WELL	
Rib	Standing	Under 3 lbs.	#1	9	3 min./lb.	6	140°, 150° or 160°F	4 to 5	5 to 6	7 to 8	—
		3 to 6 lbs.						5 to 6	6 to 7	8 to 9	
		Over 6 lbs.						6 to 7	7 to 8	9 to 10	
Rib	Rolled	Under 3 lbs.	#1	9	3 min./lb.	6	140°, 150° or 160°F	5 to 6	6 to 8	8 to 10	—
		3 to 6 lbs.						7 to 8	8 to 9	9 to 11	
		Over 6 lbs.						8 to 9	9 to 10	10 to 12	
Sirloin	Tip Roast	Under 3 lbs.	#1	9	3 min./lb.	6	140°, 150° or 160°F	5 to 6	6 to 7	8 to 10	—
		3 to 6 lbs.						6 to 7	7 to 8	8 to 10	
		Over 6 lbs.						8 to 9	9 to 10	10 to 12	
Round	Rump Roast (Rolled)	Under 3 lbs.	#2	8	3 min./lb.	5	160° or 170°F	—	8 to 9	9 to 11	15 to 30 min.
		3 to 6 lbs.						—	9 to 11	11 to 13	
		Over 6 lbs.						—	11 to 12	12 to 14	
Round	Pot Roast (Arm)	Under 3 lbs.	#3	7	3 min./lb.	4	160° or 170°F	—	—	7 to 8	30 to 60 min.
		3 to 6 lbs.						—	—	8 to 10	
Chuck	Blade Steak or Roast	2 to 3 lbs.	#3	7	3 min./lb.	4	160° or 170°F	—	—	8 to 10	30 to 60 min.
		3 to 6 lbs.						—	—	10 to 12	

*On models having the Automatic Temperature Control System feature, the meat can be cooked to a desired temperature using this feature. See the "Methods for Cooking Meats," pages 84 to 89 for further instructions.

LAMB COOKING CHART

CTION	CUT	WEIGHT	COOKING METHOD	1ST SETTING COOKMATIC LEVEL	1ST COOKING TIME	2ND SETTING COOKMATIC LEVEL	COOK TO FINAL TEMPERATURE**	2ND COOKING TIME MINUTES PER POUND
oulder	Shoulder Roast	2 to 5 lbs.	#2	8	3 min./lb.	5	170°F	9 to 11*
g	Leg	3 to 5 lbs. 5 to 8 lbs.	#1	9	3 min./lb.	6	170°F	8 to 10* 10 to 12*

*The lamb in this chart is cooked to the well-done degree. If cooking to the medium degree, decrease cooking time, accordingly. See the ''Recommended End Temperature Chart'' page 90.

**On models having the Automatic Temperature Control System feature, the meat can be cooked to a desired temperature using this feature. See the ''Methods for Cooking Meats'' pages 84 to 89 for further instructions.

VEAL COOKING CHART

CTION	CUT	WEIGHT	COOKING METHOD	1ST SETTING COOKMATIC LEVEL	1ST COOKING TIME	2ND SETTING COOKMATIC LEVEL	COOK TO FINAL TEMPERATURE**	2ND COOKING TIME MINUTES PER POUND
east uffed & led)	Brisket	1 to 3 lbs.	#3	7	3 min./lb.	4	170°F	13 to 15*
oulder	Roast	2 to 5 lbs.	#2	8	3 min./lb.	5	170°F	11 to 13*

*The veal in this chart is cooked to the well-done degree. If cooking to the medium degree, decrease cooking time, accordingly. See the ''Recommended End Temperature Chart'' page 90.

**On models having the Automatic Temperature Control System feature, the meat can be cooked to a desired temperature using this feature. See the ''Methods for Cooking Meats'' pages 84 to 89 for further instructions.

PORK COOKING CHART

CTION	CUT	WEIGHT	COOKMATIC LEVEL	COOKING TIME	COOK TO FINAL TEMPERATURE**	STANDING TIME, COVERED, AFTER COOKING TIME
in	Loin Roast	2 to 5 lbs. 5 to 8 lbs.	3 3	19 to 21 min./lb.* 19 to 21 min./lb.*	170° F 170° F	15 to 30 min. 15 to 30 min.
oston utt	Butt Roast	2 to 5 lbs. 5 to 8 lbs.	3 3	19 to 21 min./lb.* 19 to 21 min./lb.*	170° F 170° F	15 to 30 min. 15 to 30 min.

*Pork is cooked until it is no longer pink, thoroughly cooked, and a temperature of 170° F is reached.

**On models having the Automatic Temperature Control System feature, the meat can be cooked to a desired end temperature using this feature.

PRE-COOKED HAM CHART

SECTION	CUT	WEIGHT	COOKING TIME ON COOKMATIC LEVEL 5	APPROXIMATE TOTAL COOKING TIME*
Boneless	Ham	2 to 5 lbs.	10 to 12 min./lb.	30 to 60 min.
		5 to 8 lbs.	12 to 14 min./lb.	1-1/2 to 2 hrs.
Ham w/Bone	Ham	2 to 5 lbs.	12 to 14 min./lb.	45 min. to 1-1/4 hrs.
		5 to 8 lbs.	14 to 16 min./lb.	1-1/4 to 1-3/4 hrs.
Picnic	Ham	2 to 5 lbs.	9 to 11 min./lb.	25 to 40 min.
		5 to 8 lbs.	11 to 13 min./lb.	40 to 90 min.
		8 to 12 lbs.	13 to 14 min./lb.	1-3/4 to 2-1/2 hrs.
Canned	Ham	2 to 5 lbs.	8 to 10 min./lb.	30 to 45 min.

*On models having the Automatic Temperature Control System feature, insert the temperature probe and use the Automatic Temperature Control System to cook to 140°F, the serving temperature for pre-cooked ham.

PRE-COOKED HAM

General Instructions for Cooking Pre-Cooked Ham

Pre-cooked ham should be cooked by the following method, instead of by one of the major cooking methods previously described.

1. Place the ham fat-side-down on a cooking grill. Cover the ham with heavy-duty plastic wrap.
2. Cook in Radarange Oven on Cookmatic Level 5, until the temperature of 140° F is reached. Consult the "Pre-Cooked Ham Chart" for an estimate of the total cooking time required. For the best results, you may wish to turn the ham over halfway through the cooking time. (You may want to turn larger hams over 2 to 3 times during cooking time.) A basting sauce may be used as desired.

Suggested Basting Sauces
a. Fruit Glaze
   1 cup brown sugar, firmly packed
   1/2 cup fruit juice
   (Ham may be decorated with fruit such as pineapple or oranges. The fruit should be added to the ham during the last 1/2 hour of cooking time.)

b. Sweet-Sour Mustard Sauce
   1/2 cup vinegar
   1/2 cup water
   2 teaspoons prepared mustard
   1/4 cup brown sugar, firmly packed
   Whole cloves (insert directly into ham)

c. Cranberry Sauce
   1-1/2 cups halved raw cranberries
   1 cup honey
   1/2 teaspoon ground cloves

SAUSAGE COOKING CHART

SAUSAGE TYPE	WEIGHT	COOKMATIC LEVEL	COOKING TIME	COOK TO FINAL TEMPERATURE
atwurst*	16 ozs.	3	19 to 21 min.	170° F
esh Sausage Patties*	4 ozs.	4	5-1/2 to 6-1/2 min.	170° F
	8 ozs.	4	6 to 7 min.	170° F
	12 ozs.	4	7-1/2 to 8 min.	170° F
e-Cooked Polish Sausage	16 ozs.	3	3-1/2 to 4-1/2 min.	140° F
e-Cooked Sausage Links	8 ozs.	3	2-1/2 to 3-1/2 min.	140° F
	2 links	3	2 to 3 min.	140° F
e-Cooked Cocktail Sausages	4 ozs.	3	45 sec. to 1-1/2 min.	140° F
	8 ozs.	3	1 to 2 min.	140° F

*Cook fresh sausage until no longer pink, thoroughly cooked, and a temperature of 170° F is reached.

CURED BREAKFAST MEATS COOKING CHART

PE	WEIGHT	COOKING TIME ON COOKMATIC LEVEL 3	COOK TO FINAL TEMPERATURE
e-Cooked Canadian Bacon	2 ozs.	45 sec. to 1 min.	140° F
d Ham Slices	4 ozs.	1 to 1-1/2 min.	140° F
	8 ozs.	1-1/2 to 2 min.	140° F
noked Pork Chops	1 (6 oz.) chop	7-1/2 to 8-1/2 min.	170° F
	2 (6 oz. each) chops	13 to 17 min.	170° F

General Instructions for Cooking Sausage or Cured Breakfast Meats

1. Preheat a browning skillet or grill for the maximum amount of time, according to the manufacturer's instructions. Place the meat in the skillet. Press the meat firmly against the skillet for good heat contact.
2. Cook on Cookmatic Level 3. Do not cook covered with the glass lid, since meat will develop a "steamed" flavor. A paper towel may be used to prevent spattering. Do not allow a paper towel to touch the hot skillet bottom. Turn the meat over after 45 to 60 seconds of cooking.

BACON COOKING CHART

NO. OF SLICES	COOKING TIME ON FULL POWER
2	1 min., 30 sec.
4	2 min., 45 sec. to 3 min.
12	6 to 7 min.

BACON

Bacon should be cooked by the following method, instead of by one of the three major cooking methods previously described.

General Instructions for Cooking Bacon

1. Arrange bacon slices on a cooking grill. Cover the bacon with a paper towel.

OR

Arrange bacon slices on a paper towel, cover with another paper towel and repeat the process of layering the bacon slices between paper towels.

2. Cook in the Radarange Oven, until browned, crisp and thoroughly cooked, according to the directions on the chart.

PORK, LAMB AND VEAL CHOPS— LAMB AND VEAL SHOULDER STEAKS

Pork, lamb and veal chops, as well as lamb and veal shoulder steaks should be cooked by the following method, instead of by one of the three major cooking methods previously described.

1. Preheat browning skillet or grill for the maximum amount of time, according to the manufacturer's instructions. Add chops or steaks. Cook in Radarange Oven on Full Power for 1 minute per side.

FRANKFURTER COOKING CHART

NO. OF FRANKFURTERS	COOKING TIME ON FULL POWER
2	45 sec.
4	1 min., 15 sec. to 1 min., 30 sec.
6	1 min., 45 sec. to 2 min., 15 sec.

FRANKFURTERS

Frankfurters should be cooked by the following method, inste[ad] by one of the three major cooking methods previously descri[bed].

General Instructions for Cooking Frankfurters

1. Place the frankfurters on a cooking grill. Pierce the skins w[ith] fork or a knife. Cover with a paper towel, if desired, to [avoid] spatters.

2. Cook in the Radarange Oven, covered, on Full Power [until] steaming hot.

   MICRO-TIP: Frankfurters can also be heated in buns. Wrap [in] paper towel and heat for approximately the same amount of [time] on the chart.

2. Add a sauce. Select from one of the 5 sauces suggested on page 88. One tablespoon of wine, vermouth or water may be substituted for the sauce. Season to taste omitting salt until just before serving.

3. **For Lamb and Veal:**
Cook in Radarange Oven, covered, on Cookmatic Level 5 for 8 to 12 minutes per pound, or until meat is tender.
For Pork:
Cook in Radarange Oven, covered, on Cookmatic Level 3 for 16 to 18 minutes per pound, or until no longer pink, thoroughly cooked and a temperature of 170° F is reached.

TENDER BEEF STEAK COOKING CHART*

SIZE AND COOKED DEGREE	COOKING TIME ON FULL POWER
14 to 16 oz. (.88 to 1.0 lb.) (approx. 3/4" thick)**	
Rare	2 min., 15 sec. to 2 min., 45 sec.
Medium	3 min. to 3 min., 30 sec.
Well-Done	3 min., 45 sec. to 4 min., 45 sec.
12 to 14 oz. (.75 to .87 lb.) (approx. 3/4" thick)**	
Rare	2 min. to 2 min., 45 sec.
Medium	3 min. to 3 min., 15 sec.
Well-Done	3 min., 30 sec. to 4 min.
10 to 12 oz. (.63 to .74 lb.) (approx. 3/4" thick)**	
Rare	1 min., 45 sec. to 2 min., 15 sec.
Medium	2 min., 30 sec. to 3 min.
Well-Done	3 min., 15 sec. to 3 min., 45 sec.
8 to 10 oz. (.50 to .62 lb.) (approx. 3/4" thick)**	
Rare	1 min., 15 sec. to 1 min., 45 sec.
Medium	2 min. to 2 min., 45 sec.
Well-Done	2 min., 45 sec. to 3 min., 15 sec.

*Follow this procedure to cook rib, rib eye (Delmonico), club, sirloin, porterhouse, filet, tenderloin, cube steak, minute steak, T-bone, strip steak and filet mignon.

**Thicker steaks may require slightly longer cooking times; thinner steaks may require slightly shorter cooking times.

BEEF STEAKS

Because of their relatively small size and short cooking times, steaks do not brown when cooked in a microwave oven. Therefore, it is recommended that steaks be cooked in a browning skillet or grill.

General Instructions for Cooking Beef Steaks

1. Preheat the browning skillet or grill for the maximum amount of time, according to the manufacturer's instructions. Add the steak(s). Press the steak(s) firmly against the bottom of the skillet for good heat contact. See "Browning", page 14.
2. Cook the steak(s), according to the directions on the chart. Turn the steak(s) over after 45 to 60 seconds of cooking.
3. Do not cook steak(s) which is (are) not completely thawed. See the "Small Size Meats Defrosting Chart" on page 83.

GROUND BEEF, LAMB AND VEAL PATTY COOKING CHART

TYPE OF MEAT AND WEIGHT	COOKING TIME ON FULL POWER FOR COOKED DEGREE		
	RARE	MEDIUM	WELL
Beef			
1/4 lb.	45 sec. to 1 min.	1 to 1-1/2 min.	1-1/2 to 2 min.
1/2 lb.	1-1/2 to 2 min.	2 to 2-1/2 min.	2-1/2 to 3 min.
1 lb.	2-1/2 to 3 min.	3 to 3-1/2 min.	3-1/2 to 4 min.
Lamb or Veal			
1/4 lb.	—	—	1 min., 45 sec. to 2 min., 15 sec.
1/2 lb.	—	—	2 min., 45 sec. to 3 min.
1 lb.	—	—	3 min., 15 sec. to 3 min., 45 sec.

GROUND BEEF, LAMB AND VEAL PATTIES

Because of their relatively small size and short cooking times, ground meat patties will not brown when cooked in a microwave oven. Therefore, it is recommended that ground meat patties be cooked in a browning skillet or grill, unless they will be used in sandwiches where a lack of browning is not noticed.

General Instructions for Cooking Ground Beef, Lamb and Veal Patties

1. Preheat the browning skillet or grill for the maximum amount of time, according to manufacturer's instructions. Add patties. Press patties firmly against the bottom of the skillet for good heat contact. See "Browning" page 14.
2. Cover patties with a paper towel or waxed paper to reduce spattering inside the Radarange Oven. If covered with the glass lid, patties will develop a "steamed" flavor.
3. Cook in the Radarange Oven on Full Power, according to the directions on the chart. Turn the patties over after 45 to 60 seconds of cooking.
4. Do not cook patties which are not completely thawed. See "Small Size Meats Defrosting Chart" on page 83.
5. Ground beef which has been "extended" with soy or another vegetable protein cooks more quickly than 100% ground meat. To cook ground meat with an "extender" reduce the cooking time by approximately 1/3.

BULK GROUND BEEF, LAMB AND VEAL

To prepare ground meat cooked "loosely", place in a 1-1/2-quart casserole. Break meat apart with a fork. Cover with waxed paper or a paper towel, if desired, to prevent spattering. Cook in the Radarange Oven on Full Power for 3 to 4 minutes per pound, or until meat is no longer pink. Stir halfway through cooking time. Drain.

FROZEN MAIN DISH DEFROSTING CHART

DISH SIZE	DEFROSTING TIME ON DEFROST*	HOLDING TIME**	COOKING TIME***	COOKMATIC LEVEL	TOTAL APPROXIMATE RADARANGE OVEN TIME
-quart	15 min.*	15 min.	10 to 15 min.	8	40 to 45 min.
-1/2 quart	20 min.*	20 min.	5 to 15 min.	8	45 to 55 min.
-quart	25 min.*	25 min.	10 to 30 min.	7	1 hr. to 1 hr., 20 min.
-quart	40 min.*	40 min.	15 to 30 min.	7	1 hr., 35 min. to 1 hr., 55 min.
Meat Loaf (9 x 5 x 2-inch)	25 min.*	25 min.	15 to 20 min.	7	1 hr., 5 min. to 1 hr., 10 min.

n models having dial timers, use Cookmatic Level 3 for defrosting.
llow a holding time equal to defrosting time between defrosting and cooking.
stead of cooking by time, insert probe into defrosted casserole and program Radarange Oven to cook main dish to 150° F., if your Radarange Oven
as this feature.

General Instructions for Defrosting, Cooking Frozen Main Dishes

1. Select the defrosting and cooking instructions, according to the size of dish in which your frozen main dish is being cooked. Insert the temperature probe in the food. Cover the dish with a glass lid or plastic wrap.
2. Defrost, hold and cook, according to the directions in the chart.

General Hints for Defrosting, Reheating or Cooking Frozen Main Dishes.

1. Hints for Foods
   Baked beans, lima bean casseroles and cooked vegetables in sauces will all freeze well.

   Eggs in casseroles freeze well, but only use eggs that have been finely chopped.

Rice, macaroni and noodles will freeze very well in casseroles. Be sure to undercook casseroles slightly for freezing because as the food is reheated, it will continue to cook.

Season prepared foods lightly. Add any additional seasoning, if needed, during reheating or at serving time. Some seasonings increase in strength during a long freezing time.

FROZEN CONVENIENCE MEAT AND MAIN DISH CHART

FROZEN FOOD	QUANTITY OR PKG. SIZE	DEFROSTING TIME ON DEFROST**	HOLDING TIME***	COOKING TIME ON FULL POWER	SPECIAL INSTRUCTIONS
Buffet Supper	32 ozs.	10 min.	10 min.	10 to 14 min.	Remove from metal contain Place in 2-quart utility dish. Cover with plastic wrap.
Dinners	7 to 9 ozs.	4 min.	4 min.	2 to 4 min.	Remove from metal contain Place on dish.* Cover with plastic wrap.
Dinners	9 to 12 ozs.	4 min.	4 min.	2 to 3 min.	Remove from metal contain Place on dish.* Cover with plastic wrap.
Dinners	12 to 15 ozs.	5 min.	5 min.	3 to 4 min.	Remove from metal contain Place on dish.* Cover with plastic wrap.
Dinners	15 to 18 ozs.	5 min.	5 min.	5 to 6 min.	Remove from metal contain Place on dish.* Cover with plastic wrap.
Dinners in Cooking Bags	5 to 6-1/2 ozs.	—	—	3 to 4 min.	Slit bag before cooking.
Entrees	5 to 7 ozs.	4 min.	4 min.	2 to 4 min.	Remove from metal contain Place on dish. Cover with plastic wrap.
Pot Pies	8 ozs.	4 min.	4 min.	2 to 4 min.	Remove from metal contain Place in dish of same appro imate size and shape.

*Sectioned paper plates also work well.

**On models having dial timers, use Cookmatic Level 3 for defrosting.

***Allow a holding time equal to defrosting time between defrosting and cooking.

General Instructions for Frozen Convenience Meats and Main Dishes

1. Read the "Special Instructions" on the chart before defrosting and cooking. Then, defrost, hold and cook, according to the instructions on the chart.
2. The holding time allows for the food to equalize in temperature and finish defrosting.
3. The final setting is Full Power. This provides full power for heating quickly. However, if a dinner or entree includes a food which has a "delicate" ingredient, a lower Cookmatic Level may be used, if desired. If a lower Cookmatic Level is used, slightly increase the amount of cooking time.

General Hints for Cooking Meat Main Dishes

1. Prepare ingredients, such as chopped meat and vegetables, in uniform sizes and shapes whenever possible. Main dishes will cook more evenly when the ingredients have similar sizes and shapes.

2. Since casseroles cook more rapidly in the Radarange Oven than in a conventional oven, you may wish to use less liquid in your own favorite recipes. Liquid will not evaporate to the extent that it does in conventional cooking.

3. When preparing purchased frozen convenience main dishes, remove all metal parts including containers, before cooking in the Radarange Oven.

4. Cover main dishes as recommended in the recipes. Use a glass lid or heavy-duty plastic wrap since these coverings are the most water-vapor-proof. Usually, by covering a main dish, the cooking time is shortened.

5. Most main dishes are cooked on Full Power. However, main dishes containing "delicate" or "special" ingredients may require a lower Cookmatic Level or setting. When melting shredded cheese on top of a main dish during the last 1 to 1-1/2 minutes of cooking, use Cookmatic Level 8.

6. Casseroles may require occasional stirring during cooking.

7. Most main dishes should be served at a temperature of 150° F. Use the Automatic Temperature Control System to cook to one of these temperatures, if your Radarange Oven has this feature. The Automatic Temperature Control System feature can be used to maintain 150° F until ready to serve, if desired.

8. Main dishes will not have "crisp" exteriors as they often do when conventionally cooked. The amount of cooking time in a microwave oven is not long enough for crisping to occur.

9. Whenever possible, stir main dishes before serving to equalize food temperature. Keep casseroles covered before serving to keep them hot and to equalize temperatures.

10. By making main dishes, you can save on your food budget. Extenders, such as rice, pasta, potatoes or vegetables may be used with meat. Other main dishes in addition to the ones in this chapter can be found in the "Rice, Cereals and Pastas," "Fish and Seafood," and "Poultry" chapters.

11. You can prepare frozen main dishes ahead and later defrost and reheat them quickly in the Radarange Oven.

12. Many of the main dishes in this chapter give you the opportunity to use leftover meats. Leftovers can become "planned-overs". Prepare extra meat, use the extra to make a casserole and freeze the casserole for future use.

13. When cooking your own favorite main dishes (or freezing your own favorite dishes for later use), use a similar recipe in this cookbook as a guide. Use the same setting and same approximate amount of cooking time.

CONVENIENCE MAIN DISH MIX COOKING CHART

CONVENIENCE MIX TYPE AND PKG. SIZE	AMOUNT OF GROUND BEEF	1ST COOKING TIME ON FULL POWER	AMOUNT OF HOT WATER	2ND COOKING TIME ON FULL POWER
Chili-Tomato Mix (7.25 oz.)	1 lb.	4 to 5 min.	4 cups	12 to 14 min.
Hamburger Hash Mix (6 oz.)	1 lb.	4 to 5 min.	3 cups	14 to 15 min.
Hamburger Stew Mix (5.5 oz.)	1 lb.	4 to 5 min.	4 cups	14 to 15 min.

General Instructions for Cooking Convenience Main Dish Mixes

1. Crumble the ground beef in a 3-quart casserole. Cook in the Radarange Oven on Full Power, according to the 1st cooking time on the chart. Stir halfway through the cooking time. Drain.

2. Stir in the mix and the hot water. Cook in the Radarange Oven on Full Power, according to the 2nd cooking time on the chart, or until all ingredients are tender and the sauce is thickened.

Slow Cook Pot Roast

Yield: 1, 2 to 5 lb. roast

1 (2 to 5 lb.) pot roast
2 tablespoons seasoning mix
1 medium onion, sliced
1/4 cup water

1. Sprinkle 1 tablespoon seasoning mix on each side of roast. Rub in gently.
2. Place pot roast, sliced onion and water in plastic roasting bag. Place in 2-quart utility dish. Tuck end of bag loosely under roast.
3. Cook in Radarange Oven on Cookmatic Level 3 for 36 to 39 minutes pound, or until tender. Turn roast over 2 to 3 times during cooking ti Let stand, covered, 10 to 15 minutes before serving.

Sukiyaki

Yield: 4 servings

1 lb. round or sirloin steak
1 tablespoon vegetable oil
1 (8 oz.) can bamboo shoots, drained
1 (8 oz.) can water chestnuts, drained
1 (16 oz.) can bean sprouts, drained
1/2 lb. fresh mushrooms, sliced
1 medium onion, sliced
3 stalks celery, sliced diagonally in 1/2-inch pieces
3 tablespoons sugar
1/3 cup soy sauce
1/2 cup beef bouillon

1. Slice steak very thin, diagonally across grain. Place beef and oil in 2-quart casserole. Cook in Radarange Oven on Full Power for 5 to 6 minutes, or until meat is no longer pink.
2. Add vegetables to skillet. Combine sugar, soy sauce and bouillon. Po over vegetables.
3. Cook in Radarange Oven, covered, on Full Power for 6 to 8 minutes. not overcook. Vegetables should be quite crisp.

MICRO-TIP: If desired, thicken sauce with mixture of 1 tablespoon cornstarch and 2 tablespoons water. Cook in Radarange Oven, uncovered, for 1 minute, or until thickened.

Steak Teriyaki

Yield: 2 servings

1/2 cup soy sauce
1/4 cup dry white wine
1 clove garlic, minced
2 tablespoons sugar
1/2 teaspoon ginger
1-1/2 lb. sirloin steak or rib steak

1. Combine soy sauce, wine, garlic, sugar and ginger in small bowl or g measure. Let stand for 5 minutes to dissolve sugar.
2. Place steak in heavy duty plastic bag. Pour marinade over steak. Sec bag, making sure marinade surrounds meat. Refrigerate for 4 to 24 hours.
3. Preheat large browning skillet or grill for maximum amount of time, according to manufacturer's instructions. Remove steak from marina and place in skillet. Cook in Radarange Oven on Full Power for 6 to 8 minutes, or until steak is cooked to desired degree. Turn steak over a first minute of cooking.

Beef Strips with Tomatoes

Yield: 5 servings

1 (1 lb.) flank steak
1/3 cup soy sauce
1/3 cup dry white wine
1 teaspoon sugar
2 tablespoons cornstarch
1 medium onion, sliced
2 cups sliced fresh mushrooms
1/2 green pepper, sliced
1 pint cherry tomatoes

1. Slice steak very thin, diagonally across grain. Place in 2-quart casser Combine soy sauce, wine and sugar. Pour over meat. Mix lightly to c evenly. Marinate for 1 to 2 hours in refrigerator.
2. Stir in cornstarch, onion, mushrooms and green pepper.
3. Cook in Radarange Oven, covered, on Full Power for 7 to 9 minutes, until sauce is thickened. Stir halfway through cooking time. Add tomatoes. Pierce skin of tomatoes slightly.
4. Cook in Radarange Oven, covered, on Full Power for 1 minute, or un tomatoes are heated.

MICRO-TIP: This recipe is excellent for calorie watchers. There are o 232 calories per serving.

Beef Stroganoff
Yield: 4 servings

1 lb. sirloin steak, 1/2-inch thick
2 tablespoons all-purpose flour
1 teaspoon salt
1/4 teaspoon pepper
2 tablespoons butter or margarine
1/3 cup finely chopped onion
1 clove garlic, minced
1 (10-3/4 oz.) can cream of mushroom soup or cream of chicken soup
1 (4 oz.) can sliced mushrooms, drained
1/4 cup water
2 tablespoons tomato paste
1 cup dairy sour cream

1. Trim excess fat from meat. Combine flour, salt and pepper. Pound into both sides of meat. Cut beef into thin strips.
2. Place butter in 2-quart casserole. Cook in Radarange Oven on Full Power for 30 seconds, or until melted. Add meat. Cook in Radarange Oven on Full Power for 5 to 6 minutes, or until meat is no longer pink.
3. Stir in onion and garlic. Cook in Radarange Oven on Full Power for 2 to 3 minutes, or until onion and garlic are tender.
4. Stir in soup, mushrooms, water and tomato paste. Cook in Radarange Oven on Full Power for 8 to 10 minutes, or until meat is tender.
5. Stir in sour cream. Heat in Radarange Oven on Full Power for 1 minute.
MICRO-TIP: May be served over cooked noodles or rice.

Stuffed Peppers
Yield: 4 servings

4 medium green peppers
3 cups boiling water
1 cup finely diced cooked roast beef
1 (7-1/2 to 8 oz.) can tomato sauce
1 cup cooked rice
1/4 cup finely chopped celery
1 tablespoon instant minced onion
1/2 teaspoon seasoned salt

1. Cut off tops of each pepper. Remove seed and inner membrane from each. Place peppers in water. Cook in Radarange Oven on Full Power for 4 to 5 minutes, or until partially cooked. Drain.
2. Combine remaining ingredients and fill peppers. Place peppers in 9 x 2-inch round dish. Cook in Radarange Oven on Full Power for 8 to 10 minutes, or until filling is heated through.
MICRO-TIP: Peppers may be prepared ahead and refrigerated. Increase cooking time slightly if peppers are of refrigerator temperature.

Beef 'N' Tater Casserole
Yield: 6 servings

1 lb. ground beef
1 (1 lb.) pkg. frozen Tater Tots®
2 teaspoons instant minced onion
1 (10-3/4 oz.) can cream of celery soup
1 (10-3/4 oz.) can golden cream of mushroom soup

1. Crumble meat in 2-quart casserole. Cook in Radarange Oven on Full Power for 3 to 4 minutes, or until beef is no longer pink. Stir halfway through cooking time. Drain.
2. Top with Tater Tots® and onion. Mix soups together and pour over Tater Tots®.
3. Cook in Radarange Oven on Full Power for 12 to 14 minutes, or until heated through, and temperature of 150° F is reached.*
   *MICRO-TIP: Use the Automatic Temperature Control System to cook to 150° F, if your Radarange Oven has this feature.

Basic Meat Balls
Yield: 4 servings

1 lb. ground beef
1 small onion, finely chopped
1/3 cup dry bread crumbs
1/4 cup milk
1 egg
3/4 teaspoon salt
1/8 teaspoon pepper

1. Combine all ingredients in large mixing bowl. Mix well. Form into about 18 meat balls, 1-1/2 inches each in diameter. Arrange in 8 x 2-inch round dish. Cover with waxed paper.
2. Cook in Radarange Oven, covered, on Full Power for 4 to 6 minutes, or until meat is cooked as desired. Drain.

Classic Meat Loaf

Yield: 6 to 8 servings

1-1/2 lbs. ground beef
1 (8 oz.) can tomato sauce
1 egg, slightly-beaten
1 cup quick-cooking rolled oats
1 tablespoon instant, minced onion
1/8 teaspoon instant, minced garlic
1-1/2 teaspoons salt
1/4 teaspoon pepper
SAUCE (Optional)
1/3 cup catsup
1 teaspoon Worcestershire sauce
1 tablespoon dark brown sugar
1 tablespoon prepared mustard

1. Combine all ingredients. Pat into 9 x 5 x 2-inch loaf dish.
2. Cook in Radarange Oven on Full Power for 8 to 10 minutes, or until temperature of 160° F is reached.*   13
3. For sauce, blend ingredients well. Pour over meat loaf halfway throug cooking time.

MICRO-TIPS:

- For a firmer meat loaf, decrease tomato sauce to 3/4 cup.
- * Use the Automatic Temperature Control System to cook to 160° F, your Radarange Oven has this feature.

Taco Casserole

Yield: 4 to 6 servings

1 lb. ground beef
1 (15 oz.) can tomato sauce
1 (1-3/4 oz.) envelope taco seasoning mix
1 (16 oz.) can refried beans
1/4 cup chopped pimento-stuffed olives
2-1/2 cups corn chips
1/2 cup shredded Cheddar cheese

1. Place meat in 1-1/2-quart casserole. Cook in Radarange Oven on Full Power for 3 to 4 minutes, or until beef is no longer pink. Stir halfway through cooking time. Drain.
2. Combine with remaining ingredients, except corn chips and cheese.
3. Spoon meat mixture over 2 cups of corn chips in 1-1/2-quart cassero Cook in Radarange Oven on Full Power for 5 minutes, or until heated through.
4. Crush remaining corn chips. Sprinkle casserole with corn chips and cheese. Heat in Radarange Oven on Full Power for 30 seconds to 1-1/ minutes, or until cheese is melted.

Hamburger Stroganoff

Yield: 4 to 6 servings

1/2 cup chopped onion
1 tablespoon vegetable oil
1 lb. ground beef

1 (4 oz.) can mushrooms, drained
2 tablespoons all-purpose flour
1 teaspoon salt
1/2 teaspoon paprika
1 (10-3/4 oz.) can cream of chicken soup
1 cup dairy sour cream

1. Place onion and oil in 2-quart casserole. Cook in Radarange Oven on Power for 2 minutes, or until onion is tender.
2. Add meat. Cook in Radarange Oven on Full Power for 3 to 4 minutes until beef is no longer pink. Stir halfway through cooking time. Drain.
3. Add mushrooms, flour, salt and paprika. Blend well. Stir in soup.
4. Cook in Radarange Oven, covered, on Full Power for 5 minutes. Stir halfway through cooking time.
5. Blend in sour cream. Cook in Radarange Oven on Full Power for 1 to minutes, or until heated through. Stir halfway through cooking time.

MICRO-TIP: May be served over cooked noodles or rice.

Salisbury Steak

Yield: 6 servings

1/2 cup chopped onion
1 teaspoon vegetable oil
1-1/2 lbs. ground beef
1 (10-3/4 oz.) can golden cream of mushroom soup
1/2 cup bread crumbs
1 egg, slightly-beaten
Dash pepper
1/4 cup water

1. Place onion and oil in 1-1/2-quart casserole. Cook in Radarange Oven Full Power for 1-1/2 to 2 minutes, or until onion is tender.
2. Add ground beef, 1/4 cup soup, bread crumbs, egg and pepper. Mix and shape into 6 patties. Arrange in 2-quart utility dish. Cover with waxed paper. Cook in Radarange Oven, covered, on Full Power for 6 7 minutes. Turn patties over halfway through cooking time. Drain.
3. Blend remaining soup with water. Pour over meat. Cook in Radarange Oven, covered, on Full Power for 2 to 4 minutes, or until meat is coo as desired.

MICRO-TIP: For a zestier flavor, use Italian seasoned bread crumbs.

Veal Parmigiana

Yield: 4 servings

1 egg, slightly-beaten
2 tablespoons milk
1 teaspoon salt
3/4 to 1 lb. veal cutlets
1/2 cup dry bread crumbs
1/4 cup grated Parmesan cheese
2 tablespoons butter or margarine
1 (8 oz.) can tomato sauce
1/4 teaspoon Italian seasoning
1/8 teaspoon instant, minced garlic
4 ozs. Mozzarella cheese, sliced

1. Combine egg, milk and salt in small bowl. Dip veal first in egg mixture, and then in mixture of bread crumbs and cheese.
2. Preheat large browning skillet for maximum amount of time, according to manufacturer's instructions. Add half of butter and half of meat. Cook in Radarange Oven on Full Power for 2 to 2-1/2 minutes, or until cooked. Turn meat over after 1 minute of cooking. Wipe out skillet with paper towel. Re-preheat browning skillet, according to manufacturer's instructions. Repeat cooking time with remaining butter and meat. Return all meat to skillet.
3. Combine tomato sauce, seasoning and garlic. Pour over meat. Cook in Radarange Oven, covered, on Full Power for 6 minutes, or until meat is tender.
4. Top with cheese. Cook in Radarange Oven, covered, on Full Power for 1 to 2 minutes, or until cheese is melted.

Veal Scallopini

Yield: 4 servings

1/4 cup vegetable oil
1 lb. veal, thinly sliced
1 clove garlic, minced
3/4 cup sliced onion
1 (4 oz.) can mushrooms, drained
2 tablespoons all-purpose flour
1 teaspoon salt
1/8 teaspoon pepper
1 (8 oz.) can tomato sauce
1/2 cup water

1. Preheat large browning skillet for maximum amount of time, according to manufacturer's instructions. Add oil, veal and garlic. Cook in Radarange Oven on Full Power for 2 minutes, or until browned. Turn meat over halfway through cooking time. Remove garlic and veal from skillet.
2. Stir onion and mushrooms into hot oil. Cook in Radarange Oven on Full Power for 3 minutes. Stir in flour, salt and pepper until well-blended. Gradually stir in tomato sauce and water. Cook in Radarange Oven on Full Power for 5 minutes. Stir halfway through cooking time.
3. Arrange veal in skillet. Cook in Radarange Oven, covered, on Full Power for 5 to 6 minutes, or until veal is tender.

Spiced Cider Baked Ham

Yield: 4 to 6 servings

2 slices (1 to 1-1/2 lbs. each) pre-cooked ham steak, center cut
1 large onion, thinly sliced
1 cup sweet cider or apple juice
3 tablespoons brown sugar
1 teaspoon cloves (optional)
SAUCE
1/2 cup seedless raisins
2 tablespoons cornstarch
2 tablespoons water
1/4 teaspoon cinnamon
1/8 teaspoon nutmeg

1. Place both steaks in 2-quart utility dish. Arrange onion over steaks. Mix together cider and sugar. Pour over onion. Place cloves in fat along edges of ham, if desired. Cook in Radarange Oven, covered, on Full Power for 8 to 10 minutes. Turn ham over halfway through cooking time.
2. Remove ham from juice. Add raisins to juice. Combine cornstarch, water, cinnamon and nutmeg. Add to juice.
3. Cook in Radarange Oven on Full Power for 3 to 4 minutes, or until thickened. Stir occasionally. Serve sauce over ham.

Baked Canadian Bacon

Yield: 8 servings

2 lbs. pre-cooked Canadian bacon
1/2 cup brown sugar, firmly packed
1/2 cup unsweetened pineapple juice
1/2 teaspoon dry mustard

1. Place Canadian bacon in 1-1/2-quart casserole.
2. Combine brown sugar, pineapple juice and mustard. Pour over Canadian bacon.
3. Cook in Radarange Oven, covered, on Cookmatic Level 5 for 25 to 30 minutes, or until temperature of 130° F is reached.* Turn meat over halfway through cooking time.

   *MICRO-TIP: Use the Automatic Temperature Control System to cook to 130° F, if your Radarange Oven has this feature.

Pork-Vegetable Roast

Yield: 6 to 8 servings

2-1/2 to 3 lb. boneless pork roast
Garlic salt
Pepper
3 medium potatoes, peeled and cut in eighths
1 medium onion, sliced
1/2 teaspoon oregano
1 (14-1/2 oz.) can tomatoes

1. Place pork roast in 3-quart casserole. Sprinkle with garlic salt and pepper, as desired. Add remaining ingredients.
2. Cook in Radarange Oven, covered, on Cookmatic Level 3 for 1 to 1-1/ hours, or until no longer pink, thoroughly cooked and temperature of 170° F is reached.* Let stand, covered, 15 to 30 minutes before servir
   *MICRO-TIP: Use the Automatic Temperature Control System to cook 170° F, if your Radarange Oven has this feature.

Stuffed Pork Chops

Yield: 4 servings

4 pork chops, 1-inch thick each
1 cup stuffing croutons
2 tablespoons butter or margarine, melted
1 tablespoon instant, minced onion
1 teaspoon parsley flakes
1/4 teaspoon salt
Dash pepper
Dash poultry seasoning
1 tablespoon hot water
Spray-on vegetable coating
4 slices apple
1/4 cup honey
Nutmeg

1. Cut large gash or pocket in side of each chop.
2. Mix together stuffing croutons, butter, onion and seasonings in large mixing bowl. Gradually add hot water until stuffing is just moistened.
3. Divide stuffing, fill each chop.
4. Preheat large browning skillet for maximum amount of time, according to manufacturer's instructions. Spray with vegetable coating. Place chops in skillet. Cook in Radarange Oven on Cookmatic Level 5 for 5 minutes, or until partially cooked. Turn chops over after 1 minute of cooking time.
5. Place apple slice on each chop. Brush generously with honey. Sprinkle with nutmeg, as desired.
6. Cook in Radarange Oven, covered, on Cookmatic Level 3 for 20 to 23 minutes, or until chops are no longer pink, thoroughly cooked and temperature of 170° F is reached.

Pork Chops Maui

Yield: 4 servings

4 pork chops (about 1-1/2 lbs.)
1/2 cup canned, crushed pineapple, drained
1/4 cup chopped onion
1/4 cup brown sugar, firmly packed
3 tablespoons cider vinegar
1 clove garlic, minced
1 teaspoon salt
1/2 teaspoon grated orange peel (optional)
1/2 teaspoon ground ginger
1/4 teaspoon seasoned pepper
Dash Tabasco sauce

1. Preheat large browning skillet for maximum amount of time, according to manufacturer's instructions. Place chops in skillet. Cook in Radaran Oven on Cookmatic Level 5 for 5 minutes, or until partially cooked. Turn chops over halfway through cooking time. Drain.
2. Combine remaining ingredients. Pour over chops.
3. Cook in Radarange Oven, covered, on Cookmatic Level 3 for 20 to 23 minutes, or until chops are no longer pink, thoroughly cooked and temperature of 170° F is reached. Turn chops over halfway through cooking time.

Cantonese Ribs

Yield: 6 servings

4 lbs. country style pork ribs
1/2 cup soy sauce
1/2 cup dry sherry
1/2 cup lemon juice
1-1/2 tablespoons brown sugar
1 teaspoon grated lemon peel
1/2 teaspoon garlic powder
1/4 teaspoon ginger
1 cup orange marmalade

1. Separate ribs. Place in 2-quart utility dish.
2. Combine remaining ingredients, except orange marmalade, in 2-cup gla measure. Pour over ribs. Cover with plastic wrap. Let marinate in refrigerator for 2 hours. Baste frequently. Drain, reserving 1/3 cup marinade.
3. Mix together marmalade and reserved marinade. Pour over ribs. Cook Radarange Oven, covered, on Cookmatic Level 3 for 1-1/2 to 1-3/4 hours, or until meat is no longer pink, thoroughly cooked and temperature of 170° F is reached.

Oriental Pork

Yield: 4 to 6 servings

1 (1 lb.) pork tenderloin
3 tablespoons soy sauce
1 tablespoon cornstarch
1 teaspoon instant chicken bouillon
1 (6 oz.) pkg. frozen pea pods
1 (8 oz.) can bamboo shoots, drained
1 (8 oz.) can water chestnuts, drained and sliced
1/2 cup sliced green onion
1/2 cup sliced onion
1/2 cup water

1. Trim fat from pork. Cut pork into bite-size pieces. Combine pork, soy sauce, cornstarch and bouillon in 2-quart casserole.
2. Cook in Radarange Oven, covered, on Cookmatic Level 3 for 15 to 18 minutes, or until pork is no longer pink and thoroughly cooked. Add remaining ingredients.
3. Cook in Radarange Oven, covered, on Cookmatic Level 5 for 10 to 12 minutes, or until meat and vegetables are cooked as desired. Stir halfway through cooking time.

MICRO-TIP: This dish may be served over cooked rice, if desired.

Sweet-Sour Pork

Yield: 4 servings

1-1/2 lbs. boneless pork loin, cubed
1 (1 lb., 4 oz.) can pineapple chunks, with liquid
1/2 cup water
1/4 cup brown sugar, firmly packed
3 tablespoons vinegar
2 tablespoons cornstarch
1 tablespoon soy sauce
1/2 teaspoon salt

1. Place pork in 1-1/2-quart casserole. Cook in Radarange Oven, covered, on Cookmatic Level 3 for 16 to 18 minutes, or until meat is no longer pink and thoroughly cooked. Stir halfway through cooking time.
2. Combine liquid from pineapple, water, brown sugar, vinegar, cornstarch, soy sauce and salt in 2-cup glass measure or small bowl. Cook in Radarange Oven on Full Power for 3 to 5 minutes, or until thickened. Stir halfway through cooking time.
3. Pour sauce over pork. Add pineapple. Cook in Radarange Oven on Full Power for 2 to 3 minutes, or until heated through.

Tangy Ham Loaf

Yield: 4 to 5 servings

1 lb. pre-cooked ground ham
1/3 cup milk
1 egg, slightly-beaten
1/2 cup graham cracker crumbs
1/4 cup finely chopped onion
Dash pepper
1/4 cup dark brown sugar, firmly packed
1/4 cup tomato juice
1 teaspoon dry mustard
1 teaspoon vinegar

1. Blend together ham, milk, egg, crumbs, onion and pepper. Pat into 9 x 5 x 2-inch loaf dish.
2. Combine sugar, tomato juice, mustard and vinegar. Pour over meat loaf.
3. Cook in Radarange Oven on Full Power for 9 to 11 minutes, or until temperature of 160° F is reached.*

*MICRO-TIP: Use the Automatic Temperature Control System to cook to 160° F, if your Radarange Oven has this feature.

Spanish Lamb Chops

Yield: 4 servings

1 tablespoon vegetable oil
4 (1/2 lb. each) shoulder lamb chops
1 (16 oz.) can stewed tomatoes
1 small green pepper, sliced
1/2 cup chopped onion
4 slices lemon
1 teaspoon salt
1/4 teaspoon pepper

1. Preheat large browning skillet for maximum amount of time, according to manufacturer's instructions. Place oil and then chops in skillet. Cook in Radarange Oven on Full Power for 4 minutes. Turn meat over halfway through cooking time.
2. Mix in tomatoes, green pepper, onion, lemon, salt and pepper. Cook in Radarange Oven, covered, on Cookmatic Level 5 for 25 to 35 minutes, or until meat is tender.

In this chapter, you will find poultry prepared in a variety of ways in the Radarange Oven. You'll find that poultry will be more moist when prepared in the Radarange Oven than when prepared in a conventional oven.

Herbs such as tarragon, curry, saffron and sage complement poultry. The next time you have leftover chicken or make a chicken salad, look for an appropriate recipe in this chapter. Many recipes are well-suited to using leftover chicken or turkey and the poultry will taste freshly cooked when reheated in the Radarange Oven.

Before preparing poultry, read the general defrosting and cooking hints.

General Hints for Defrosting Poultry

1. Poultry may remain in its original wrappings for defrosting. Pierce the plastic wrap or bag before defrosting. Remove metal clamps from poultry as soon as possible during, or after defrosting.
2. When defrosting whole poultry, large poultry may need to be turned over occasionally for even defrosting. Remove loosened giblets as soon as possible and set them aside for gravy, soup or dressing.
3. When defrosting poultry pieces, turn the pieces over, separate, and rearrange them during defrosting. Cover pieces with heavy-duty plastic wrap to hasten defrosting.

4. If poultry begins to feel warm or starts to cook during defrosting, remove it from the Radarange Oven and let stand, covered, or place it in cold water to finish defrosting.
5. Since poultry is such an irregularly-shaped food, it may need to be defrosted partially on Cookmatic Level 1 prevent cooking around the leg and wing areas. Large poultry weighing over 5 pounds requires a soaking period in cold water to complete the defrosting process.

General Hints for Cooking Poultry

1. Remove metal clamps from poultry and tie the legs and wings with string, if desired, before cooking.
2. Small poultry items can be cooked on the cooking grill The 2-quart utility dish will catch the drippings.
3. The Radarange Oven will hold a family-size turkey. You may prefer to cook your turkey in a roasting bag. Choose a heavy-duty roasting bag. Pierce the bag before cooking Secure the bag with string. Do not secure the bag with metal twist.
4. Poultry weighing 3 pounds or more will brown by itself "naturally" in the Radarange Oven.
5. For some poultry items, you may wish to add additional color. Seasoned coating mixes and paprika will improve the color of poultry. Try making a paste of 1 tablespoon of paprika and 2 tablespoons of shortening. Rub this paste over poultry for a nice reddish-brown color.

6. A non-salted vegetable oil is best for basting poultry. Do not salt poultry until just before serving, since salt will dehydrate the surface of poultry, making it tough. Salt may be added before cooking to a sauce that covers the poultry.

7. Begin cooking chicken pieces skin-side-down. Turn the pieces over halfway through the cooking time in most recipes.

8. When cooking whole poultry, begin by cooking breast-side-down. When the poultry is turned over, cooking can be completed breast-side-up for a nicer, browned, finished appearance.

9. Pierce the skin of poultry before placing it in the Radarange Oven, to prevent popping.

10. Cook poultry, covered. Use a glass lid or heavy-duty plastic wrap since they are more water-vapor-proof than other types of coverings. Poultry pieces cooked in a sauce should be cooked, covered, to blend flavors.

11. When browning chicken in a browning skillet, do not cover the skillet with the glass lid, since a "steamed" flavor will develop. A paper towel covering may be used to prevent spattering. Do not allow a paper towel to touch the bottom of the hot browning skillet.

12. Poultry should be cooked on Full Power for approximately 5 to 6 minutes per pound. Since poultry is a tender food, a lower Cookmatic Cycle or setting is not necessary for cooking. Poultry pieces will cook slightly faster per pound than whole poultry. Poultry cooked in a sauce which includes a "special" or "delicate" ingredient may be cooked at a lower Cookmatic Level or setting.

13. You may wish to stuff poultry with a dressing. The addition of dressing should not alter the cooking time.

14. After the poultry has started to brown, you may wish to cover the wing tips, the narrow part of the legs and the high point of the breast bone with small thin strips of foil. This process is called shielding. The small amount of foil will slow the cooking of these areas and prevent them from dehydrating and overcooking.

15. Large poultry items, such as large turkeys, may need to be turned over several times during cooking, for more even cooking.

16. When cooking large poultry items, you may wish to "baste off" the juices as they accumulate. The microwaves will be attracted to the liquid, thus keeping the energy away from the poultry and resulting in a longer cooking time. By "basting off," spattering is also reduced.

17. Poultry is done when it is fork tender and the thickest part of the thigh or "dark meat" has a temperature of 170° F. Also, the flesh and juices should no longer be pink. Juices should be clear. Slice the poultry between the leg and body to see if it is done. On whole poultry, the joints of the legs should move easily when done. The thick meat on the leg should feel soft. The "white meat" pieces, such as the breast, should register 180° F when done. Since poultry contains many bones and since large poultry items need to be turned over 2 to 3 times during cooking for good results, cook poultry for the 5 to 6 minutes per pound, rather than using the Automatic Temperature Control for cooking, if your Radarange Oven has this feature. The Automatic Temperature Control may be used, however, when the cooking process is finished, if your Radarange Oven has this feature. Check the temperature of both the "dark" and "white" meat areas, before serving.

18. A 10 to 15 minute standing time before carving will help the juices to set in the meat, keep the meat more moist and make the poultry easier to carve. The poultry will continue to cook if it stands, covered. Poultry should be completely defrosted before cooking.

19. When preparing your own favorite poultry recipes, use a recipe in this chapter as a guide. Use Full Power for most poultry cooking, unless the dish includes a "delicate" ingredient. Then, select a lower Cookmatic Level or setting.

Roasting Directions for Whole Poultry

(Including: Chicken, Turkey, Duckling or Cornish Hens)

1. Wash body cavity of poultry with water, after removing giblets and neck from poultry.* Pat dry with paper towels.

2. Sprinkle poultry cavity with salt. If dressing is used, stuff just before roasting. Allow 3/4 cup stuffing per pound of ready-to-cook weight. Fill main cavity and neck cavity with dressing. Close neck and body cavity openings with wooden picks or skewers. Pierce skin of poultry with tines of fork to prevent popping.

3. Tie legs together and wings to body, loosely, with string. Place poultry in 2-quart utility dish or directly on Radarange Oven glass tray, breast-side-down. Brush exterior with melted butter or margarine or use 2 to 1 ratio mixture of melted butter or margarine and paprika. Cover with heavy-duty plastic wrap. (Poultry may also be cooked in heavy-duty plastic roasting bag, if desired.)

4. Cook in Radarange Oven, covered, on Full Power for 5 to 6 minutes per pound, or until temperature of 165° F to 170° F is reached in thigh and 175° F is reached in breast meat. (Use the Automatic Temperature Control System to check the temperatures in these areas, after cooking, if your Radarange Oven has this feature.) Turn poultry over 2 to 3 times during roasting to ensure even cooking of entire poultry. For large poultry items, baste off excess accumulated juices when turning. Baste the poultry, if desired. If tips of legs, wings or other areas become too brown, use thin strips of aluminum foil to cover these areas. Finish cooking breast-side-up.

5. Let stand, covered, with aluminum foil, for 10 to 15 minutes before serving. Temperature will increase 10° F to 15° F during this time.

Other tests for determining when whole poultry is fully cooked are:

Pierce inside thigh muscle deeply with tines of fork. If juices are clear without tinge of pink, poultry is done.

Press thickest part of drumstick between fingers. It should feel very soft when done. Move drumstick. Leg joint should move freely or break when poultry is done.

*MICRO-TIP: Use giblets for dressing, if desired. The "Poultry Dress recipe on this page or your own favorite dressing recipe, may be Save drippings to use for gravy.

Poultry Dressing

Yield: Stuffing for a 12 to 16 lb. turkey

1 lb. pork sausage
1/2 cup butter or margarine
1 cup chopped onion
1 cup chopped celery
1 medium apple, chopped
1 tablespoon parsley flakes
1 teaspoon poultry seasoning
1 teaspoon ground sage
1/2 teaspoon salt
1/2 teaspoon pepper
1 egg, slightly-beaten
10 cups dry whole wheat or white bread cubes (about 1, 1 lb. loaf)
3/4 cup chicken broth or bouillon

1. Crumble sausage in 1-1/2-quart casserole. Cook in Radarange Oven o Cookmatic Level 4 for 8 to 10 minutes, or until sausage is no longer pink and thoroughly cooked. Stir halfway through cooking time. Drai

2. Place butter in 3 to 4-quart casserole. Heat in Radarange Oven on Ful Power for 1 minute, or until melted.

3. Add onion, celery and apple. Stir to coat with butter. Cook in Radara Oven, covered, on Full Power for 5 to 7 minutes, or until tender.

4. Stir in sausage and seasonings. When slightly cooled, stir in egg.

5. Gradually stir in bread cubes. Pour chicken broth over all and toss to moisten. Stuff bird.

Variations: Add: 1 to 2 cups chopped, cooked neck and giblets or 2 (6 oz. each) cans sliced mushrooms, drained.

MICRO-TIPS:

• To dry the bread in the Radarange Oven, spread half of the slices, o or two deep, on a plastic rack. Heat in Radarange Oven on Full Pow for 1 to 3 minutes, or until hot. Spread out on paper towels to cool. Repeat with remaining bread. Allow to stand 30 to 60 minutes.

• To cook dressing separately, add 1/4 to 1/2 cup more broth. Cook Radarange Oven, covered, on Full Power for 6 to 8 minutes, or until heated through. Let stand, covered, for 5 to 10 minutes.

POULTRY DEFROSTING CHART*

WEIGHT & SIZE OF POULTRY	1ST DEFROSTING TIME ON DEFROST**	2ND DEFROSTING TIME ON COOKMATIC LEVEL 1	SPECIAL INSTRUCTIONS
2 lbs. or less; package is less than 2-1/2-inches thick.	6 to 7 min./lb.	—	—
2 lbs. or less; package is 2-1/2-inches thick or greater.	7-1/2 to 8 min./lb.	—	—
2 to 5 lbs.	5-1/2 min./lb.	5 min./lb.	—
5 to 10 lbs.	4 min./lb.	2-1/2 min./lb.	Soak in cool water if not completely defrosted.
10 to 15 lbs.	3 min./lb.	2 min./lb.	Soak in cool water if not completely defrosted.
Over 15 lbs.	2 min./lb.	2 min./lb.	Soak in cool water for 30 to 60 minutes to finish defrosting.

*The "Poultry Defrosting Chart" lists defrosting times for all types of poultry, in terms of minutes-per-pound. The chart applies to Cornish hens, capon, duck and individual poultry pieces, as well as the whole chicken and turkey. For best results when defrosting, be sure to consider the general hints.

**On models having dial timers, use Cookmatic Level 3 for defrosting.

General Instructions for Defrosting Poultry

1. Place the frozen poultry on a plate or cooking grill. Cover with plastic wrap. Remove all metal pieces, if possible.
2. Defrost, according to the instructions on the chart. Turn large poultry over halfway through the defrosting time for best results. Soak large poultry in cool water, if necessary, to finish defrosting.

FROZEN FRIED CHICKEN COOKING CHART

PKG. SIZE	DEFROSTING TIME ON DEFROST*	HOLDING TIME**	COOKING TIME ON FULL POWER
16 oz.	4-1/2 min.*	4-1/2 min.	3 to 4 min.
28 oz.	6 min.*	6 min.	4 to 6 min.
32 oz.	8 min.*	8 min.	5 to 7 min.

*On models having dial timers, use Cookmatic Level 3 for defrosting.

**Allow a holding time equal to defrosting time between defrosting and cooking.

General Instructions for Defrosting and Cooking Frozen Fried Chicken

1. Spread chicken pieces in 2-quart utility dish. Arrange the chicken pieces with the large, thicker pieces, such as thighs and breasts, at the corners of the dish. Place the smaller pieces, such as legs and wings, at the center of the dish.
2. Defrost, Hold, and Cook, according to the directions on the chart.

FROZEN TURKEY ROAST COOKING CHART

ROAST SIZE	UTENSIL	DEFROSTING TIME ON DEFROST*	HOLDING TIME**	COOKING TIME ON COOKMATIC LEVEL 8***
2 lb.	9 x 5 x 2-inch utility dish	25 min.	25 min.	15 to 20 min.
3 lb.	2-quart utility dish	30 min.	30 min.	20 to 30 min.

*On models having dial timers, use Cookmatic Level 3 for defrosting.

**Allow a holding time equal to defrosting time between defrosting and cooking.

***Use the Automatic Temperature Control System to cook to 170° F, rather than cooking for the amount of time given on the chart, if your Radarange Oven has this feature. Turn roast over halfway through cooking time.

General Instructions for Defrosting and Cooking Frozen Turkey Roasts

1. Remove the frozen roast from the metal container. Place it in the glass utensil listed on chart. Cover loosely with plastic wrap.
2. Defrost, Hold and Cook, according to the times on the chart. Remember to allow a holding time equal to the defrosting time between defrosting and cooking.
3. After defrosting and holding, you might want to cook the roast to 170° F using the Automatic Temperature Control System, if your Radarange Oven has this feature. You will not need to set an amount of cooking time since the Automatic Temperature Control System will determine when the roast has finished cooking. Insert the temperature probe into the center of the roast through the plastic wrap, thereby piercing the plastic wrap. Cook in the Radarange Oven on Cookmatic Level 8 to the final temperature of 170° F. Turn roast over halfway through cooking time. For more information about the Automatic Temperature Control System, see your Use and Care Manual, if your Radarange Oven has this feature.

Easy Barbecued Chicken

Yield: 4 to 6 servings

3 lb. broiler-fryer, cut-up
3/4 cup bottled barbecue sauce
1 teaspoon liquid smoke (optional)
1 teaspoon instant minced onion (optional)

1. Arrange chicken in 2-quart utility dish with larger pieces, such as thigh and breasts, at corners, skin-side-down. Place small pieces such as legs and wings at center. Mix sauce, liquid smoke and onion together. Pour over chicken. Cover with waxed paper or plastic wrap.
2. Cook in Radarange Oven, covered, on Full Power for 12 to 15 minutes or until chicken is tender. Turn chicken pieces over halfway through cooking time.

   MICRO-TIP: Try using hickory smoke flavor barbecue sauce or barbec sauce with onion bits.

Apricot-Baked Chicken

Yield: 4 to 6 servings

2-1/2 lb. broiler-fryer, cut-up
2 tablespoons mayonnaise
1/2 (1-1/2 oz.) pkg. dry onion soup mix
1/4 cup bottled Russian salad dressing
1 cup apricot preserves

1. Arrange chicken in 2-quart utility dish with larger pieces, such as thigh and breasts, at corners, skin-side-down. Place small pieces, such as leg and wings, at center.
2. Combine remaining ingredients. Spread over chicken. Cover with wax paper or plastic wrap.
3. Cook in Radarange Oven, covered, on Full Power for 12 to 14 minutes or until chicken is tender. Turn chicken pieces over halfway through cooking time.

Speedy Baked Chicken

Yield: 4 servings

2 tablespoons butter or margarine
3 lb. broiler-fryer, cut-up
Pepper
Paprika
Salt

1. Preheat large browning skillet for maximum amount of time, according to manufacturer's instructions. Add butter. Arrange chicken with larger pieces, such as thighs and breasts, at corners, skin-side-down. Place small pieces, such as legs and wings, at center. Season with pepper and paprika, as desired. Cover with waxed paper or plastic wrap.
2. Cook in Radarange Oven, covered, on Full Power for 12 to 15 minutes, or until chicken is tender. Turn chicken pieces over halfway through cooking time. Drain. Salt before serving, as desired.
MICRO-TIP: Gravy may be made from drippings, if desired.

Shake and Bake Chicken

Yield: 6 servings

2 lb. broiler-fryer, cut-up
1 (1-1/4 oz.) pkg. seasoned coating mix for chicken*
Spray-on vegetable coating

1. Coat chicken with seasoned mix by shaking in bag, according to directions on package.
2. Preheat large browning skillet or grill for maximum amount of time, according to manufacturer's instructions. Spray skillet with vegetable coating.
3. Arrange chicken with larger pieces, such as thighs and breasts, at corners, skin-side-down. Place small pieces such as legs and wings at center.
4. Cook in Radarange Oven on Full Power for 8 to 10 minutes, or until chicken is tender. Turn chicken pieces over after 1 minute of cooking. Turn chicken pieces over again halfway through cooking time.
*MICRO-TIP: You may use your own favorite coating for the chicken in this recipe.

Chicken 'N' Rice

Yield: 2 to 4 servings

1 (10-3/4 oz.) can golden cream of mushroom soup
1 (5.3 oz.) can evaporated milk
1/2 cup milk
3/4 cup quick-cooking rice
1 (2-1/2 oz.) can mushrooms, with liquid
1/2 (1-1/2 oz.) pkg. onion soup mix
2 tablespoons chopped pimentos (optional)
2 chicken breasts, halved

1. Mix together soup and milks. Reserve 1/2 cup of mixture.
2. Mix remaining soup mixture with rice, mushrooms, 1/4 pkg. of onion soup mix and pimento. Pour into 8 x 8 x 2-inch glass dish. Cover with waxed paper or plastic wrap. Cook in Radarange Oven, covered, on Full Power for 4 minutes.
3. Place chicken breasts on rice mixture. Pour reserved soup mixture over chicken. Sprinkle with remaining 1/4 pkg. onion soup mix. Cover with waxed paper or plastic wrap. Cook in Radarange Oven, covered, on Full Power for 15 to 18 minutes, or until chicken is tender. Turn chicken over 1 to 2 times during cooking time.

Chicken Teriyaki

Yield: 4 to 6 servings

1/2 cup soy sauce
1/4 cup dry white wine
1 clove garlic, minced
2 tablespoons sugar
1/2 teaspoon ginger
3 lb. broiler-fryer, cut-up

1. Combine soy sauce, wine, garlic, sugar and ginger. Stir well.
2. Place chicken in heavy-duty plastic bag. Pour marinade sauce over chicken. Tie securely with string. Refrigerate for 1 to 2 hours.
3. Arrange chicken pieces in 10-inch ceramic skillet or 2-quart utility dish with larger pieces, such as thighs and breasts, at corners, skin-side-down. Place small pieces such as legs and wings towards center. Cover with waxed paper, plastic wrap or glass lid. Cook in Radarange Oven, covered, on Full Power for 12 to 15 minutes, or until chicken is tender. Turn chicken pieces over halfway through cooking time.

Chicken Parmesan

Yield: 4 to 6 servings

3 lb. broiler-fryer, cut-up
1 egg, beaten
1/2 cup cornflake crumbs
1/2 cup grated Parmesan cheese
1/4 teaspoon ground oregano
Dash ground thyme
Dash garlic salt
Dash pepper
1 (10-3/4 oz.) can golden cream
   of mushroom soup
1/3 cup milk
2 tablespoons snipped parsley

1. Dip chicken in egg. Roll in mixture of crumbs, cheese and spices. Coat thoroughly.
2. Arrange chicken in 10-inch ceramic skillet or 2-quart utility dish with larger pieces, such as thighs and breasts, at corners, skin-side-down. Place small pieces such as legs and wings at center. Cook in Radarange Oven, covered, on Full Power for 10 minutes. Turn chicken pieces over halfway through cooking time.
3. Combine soup and milk. Pour over chicken. Cook in Radarange Oven, covered, on Full Power for 4 to 6 minutes, or until chicken is tender. Garnish with any remaining cheese mixture and parsley.

Chicken 'N' Dumplings

Yield: 4 to 6 servings

3 lb. broiler-fryer, cut-up
3 small onions, quartered
4 medium carrots, cut in 1-inch
   pieces, and then halved
4 parsley sprigs
1 (13-3/4 oz) can chicken broth
2 cups water
2 bay leaves
2-1/2 teaspoons salt
1/4 teaspoon thyme
1/4 teaspoon poultry seasoning
1/8 teaspoon pepper

3 tablespoons cornstarch
1/3 cup water
DUMPLINGS
1 cup biscuit baking mix
1/3 cup milk
1/4 teaspoon poultry seasoning

1. Combine chicken, vegetables, parsley, broth, water and seasonings in 4-quart casserole. Cook in Radarange Oven, covered, on Full Power for 25 minutes, or until vegetables are tender.
2. Remove chicken. Add mixture of cornstarch and 1/3 cup water. Blend well. Cook in Radarange Oven on Full Power for 3 minutes, or until thickened. Return chicken to casserole.
3. Mix together biscuit mix, milk and seasoning until moistened. Spoon mixture over casserole. Cook in Radarange Oven, covered, on Full Power for 3 to 4-1/2 minutes, or until dumplings are done.

Chicken Cacciatore

Yield: 4 to 6 servings

1/4 cup all-purpose flour
1 teaspoon salt
1/2 teaspoon pepper
3 lb. broiler-fryer, cut-up
1/3 cup vegetable oil
4 parsley sprigs
2 medium onions, sliced
2 cloves garlic, minced
1 bay leaf
1/4 teaspoon leaf basil
1/4 teaspoon oregano
1/4 teaspoon saffron (optional)
2 pimentos, diced (optional)
1 (20 oz.) can Italian tomatoes,
   drained
1 teaspoon salt

1. Combine flour, salt and pepper. Coat chicken pieces with seasoned mixture.
2. Preheat large browning skillet for maximum amount of time, according to manufacturer's instructions. Place oil and chicken in skillet. Cook in Radarange Oven on Full Power for 1-1/2 minutes, or until chicken is lightly browned. Turn chicken pieces over after 45 seconds of cooking.
3. Remove chicken. Combine remaining ingredients, except tomatoes and salt, in browning skillet. Cook in Radarange Oven, covered, on Full Power for 5 minutes.
4. Return chicken to skillet. Pour tomatoes over chicken. Blend in salt. Cook in Radarange Oven, covered, on Full Power for 20 to 24 minutes, or until chicken is tender. Turn chicken pieces over halfway through cooking time. Remove bay leaf before serving.

Swiss Turkey and Ham Bake

Yield: 6 servings

2 tablespoons butter or margarine
1/2 cup cornflake, cracker or bread crumbs
2 cups cubed cooked turkey
1 cup cubed cooked ham
1 (8 oz.) can water chestnuts, drained and sliced
1 (4 oz.) can sliced mushrooms, drained
1-1/2 teaspoons parsley flakes
1 (10-3/4 oz.) can cream of onion soup
1/4 teaspoon salt
1/8 teaspoon pepper
1/2 cup shredded Swiss cheese
Paprika

1. Place butter in small bowl. Heat in Radarange Oven on Full Power for 20 to 30 seconds, or until melted. Mix in crumbs. Set aside.
2. Combine turkey, ham, water chestnuts, mushrooms, parsley, soup and seasonings in 2-quart casserole. Cook in Radarange Oven on Full Power for 7 to 9 minutes, or until heated through, and temperature of 150° F is reached.* Stir halfway through cooking time.
3. Top with cheese and sprinkle with buttered crumbs. Sprinkle with paprika, as desired. Cook in Radarange Oven on Full Power for 45 seconds to 1-1/2 minutes, or until cheese is melted.

*MICRO-TIP: Use the Automatic Temperature Control System to cook to 150°F, if your Radarange Oven has this feature.

Chicken Livers Chablis

Yield: 4 to 6 servings

2 tablespoons butter or margarine
1-1/2 lbs. chicken livers (about 16 to 20)
2-1/2 tablespoons all-purpose flour
3/4 cup white wine
1/4 cup minced onion
2 tablespoon catsup
Salt
Pepper

1. Place butter in 10-inch ceramic skillet or 2-quart casserole. Heat in Radarange Oven on Full Power for 30 to 45 seconds, or until melted.
2. Dredge livers in flour. Arrange in melted butter. Cook in Radarange Oven on Full Power for 5-1/2 to 6-1/2 minutes, or until livers are no longer pink. Turn livers over halfway through cooking time.
3. Lightly stir in wine, onion and catsup. Cook in Radarange Oven on Full Power for 2 to 3 minutes, or until heated through. Season with salt and pepper, as desired.

MICRO-TIP: May be served over cooked rice or noodles.

Chicken Liver Stroganoff

Yield: 4 servings

2 tablespoons butter or margarine
1 medium onion, sliced
3/4 lb. chicken livers (about 8)
1-1/2 cups sliced fresh mushrooms*
1 teaspoon paprika
1/2 teaspoon salt
Dash pepper
1 tablespoon all-purpose flour
3/4 cup dairy sour cream

1. Place butter and onion in 10-inch ceramic skillet or 2-quart utility dish. Cook in Radarange Oven on Full Power for 2 to 3 minutes, or until onion is tender.
2. Cut each chicken liver in half. Add livers and mushrooms to onion mixture. Sprinkle with paprika, salt and pepper. Cook in Radarange Oven, covered, on Full Power for 8 to 9 minutes, or until livers are cooked. Stir halfway through cooking time.
3. Stir flour into sour cream. Spoon over chicken livers. Cook in Radarange Oven on Full Power for 1 minute, or until heated through.

MICRO-TIPS:
* 1 (4 oz.) can sliced mushrooms, drained, may be substituted for fresh mushrooms.
• This dish may be served over cooked rice or noodles.

Barbecued Chicken Thighs

Yield: 6 to 8 servings

2 lbs. chicken thighs (about 8)
  or 2 lb. broiler-fryer, cut-up
3/4 cup cola
Salt
1 cup catsup

1. When using broiler-fryer, cut up, arrange chicken in ceramic skillet wi larger pieces, such as thighs and breasts, at corners, skin-side-down. Place smaller pieces, such as legs and wings, at center. Pour cola ove chicken. Cook in Radarange Oven, covered, on Full Power for 10 minutes. Turn chicken pieces over halfway through cooking time.
2. Drain off about 1/4 cup cola. Sprinkle chicken with salt, as desired. Pour catsup over chicken. Cook in Radarange Oven on Full Power for to 7 minutes, or until chicken is tender. Turn chicken pieces over halfway through cooking time.

Duckling Bordeaux

Yield: 4 servings

4 to 5 lb. duckling
2 tablespoons vegetable oil
1/2 cup marmalade
1 tablespoon soy sauce
SAUCE
1 tablespoon butter or margarine
1 tablespoon all-purpose flour
3/4 cup white wine
1/3 cup chicken broth
1 tablespoon vinegar
1/4 teaspoon pepper

1. Quarter duckling. Preheat large browning skillet for maximum amoun time, according to manufacturer's instructions. Add 1 tablespoon of o Place two pieces of duckling skin-side-down in skillet. Cook in Radara Oven on Full Power for 5 minutes. Turn duckling halfway through cooking time. Drain.
2. Wipe out skillet with paper towel. Re-preheat browning skillet, accordi to manufacturer's instructions. Add 1 tablespoon of oil. Repeat cookir time with remaining duckling.
3. Mix together marmalade and soy sauce. Reserve 1/4 cup of mixture. Use remainder to baste duckling. Arrange all duckling quarters in skil with thicker portions toward outside. Cook in Radarange Oven, covere on Full Power for 8 to 10 minutes. Turn duckling pieces over halfway through cooking time. Cover and let stand while preparing sauce.
4. Place butter in 1-quart mixing bowl. Heat in Radarange Oven on Full Power for 20 to 30 seconds, or until melted. Stir in flour. Add remaini ingredients.
5. Cook in Radarange Oven on Full Power for 1 minute. Add reserved marmalade mixture. Cook in Radarange Oven on Full Power for 1 to 1-1/2 minutes, or until smooth. Spoon over duckling.

Stuffed Duckling L'Orange

Yield: 4 to 6 servings

4 to 5 lb. duckling with giblets
1 cup water
12 ozs. pork sausage
1/2 cup chopped celery
1/2 cup chopped onion
2 cups peeled and chopped apples
2 cups croutons
1/2 cup chopped walnuts
1 teaspoon salt
1/2 teaspoon thyme
1/2 teaspoon poultry seasoning
1/4 teaspoon pepper
1/2 cup marmalade
2 tablespoons white wine
1 tablespoon butter or margarine,
  melted
1 tablespoon soy sauce
1/2 teaspoon thyme
1/8 teaspoon dry mustard
1/8 teaspoon salt

1. Place giblets and water in 1-quart casserole. Cook in Radarange Oven, covered, on Full Power for 10 to 15 minutes, or until tender. Chop giblets.
2. Place sausage in 1-quart casserole. Cook in Radarange Oven on Cookmatic Level 4 for 6 to 9 minutes, or until meat is no longer pink and thoroughly cooked. Remove sausage. Add celery and onion. Cook Radarange Oven on Full Power for 3 to 4 minutes, or until celery and onion are almost tender.
3. Combine sausage, celery, onion, giblets, apples, croutons, walnuts and seasonings. Stuff cleaned duckling. Secure openings with wooden pick and tie with string, if desired. Pierce skin of duckling near thighs.
4. Combine remaining ingredients. Baste duckling. Cook in Radarange Oven, covered, on Full Power for 20 to 25 minutes. Turn duckling ove and baste 3 to 4 times during cooking time.

You'll be "cooking in color" when you prepare vegetables in the Radarange Oven. Vegetables require very little liquid to cook and thus they retain their bright colors as well as good texture. Vitamin retention is another plus when cooking vegetables in the Radarange Oven, due to the small amount of liquid used and the short amount of cooking time.

Be sure to read the general hints before cooking vegetables.

General Hints for Cooking Vegetables

1. Vegetables can vary in the amount of cooking time they require. The age, freshness, size, shape, temperature and variety can all affect cooking times. You may need to adjust cooking times slightly.

2. Prepare vegetables for cooking as you normally would for conventional cooking, but don't add salt until just before serving. Salt will dehydrate vegetables making them tough, if added before cooking.

3. For preparing fresh, canned or frozen vegetables, see the individual charts for cooking instructions.

4. Many vegetable recipes in this chapter can use fresh, frozen or canned vegetables. For recipes requiring canned vegetables, either cooked fresh vegetables or thawed frozen vegetables may be used. When substituting a canned vegetable for frozen, the cooking time may have to be decreased slightly.

5. Arrange the "toughest" thickest parts of a vegetable toward the outside of the dish where they will cook faster. Broccoli stalks, for example, should be placed toward the dish edge and the more delicate heads placed toward the dish center.

6. Pierce the skins of vegetables such as squash, potatoes or sweet potatoes before cooking. Piercing will allow steam to escape during cooking, and will avoid bursting.

7. Always cook vegetables, especially fresh vegetables, covered. Use a glass lid or heavy-duty plastic wrap since these coverings are the most water-vapor-proof. By covering vegetables, they will cook faster and more evenly. Pierce plastic wrap coverings before cooking. Unwrap plastic wrap and remove glass lids carefully after cooking to avoid steam burns.

8. When cooking vegetables such as baked potatoes or individual squashes, leave a space of about 1-inch between each. You may want to turn individual vegetables over halfway through the cooking time.

9. Fresh vegetables should be eaten soon after they are harvested or purchased for maximum retention of vitamins. Fresh vegetables should be cooked covered. Between 2 to 4 tablespoons water should be added for steaming. Some of the water may be substituted with butter or oil, if desired. Calorie-watchers will prefer to use water.

10. When cooking a quantity of vegetables, note that as with any food cooked in the Radarange Oven, the amount of cooking time will increase almost proportionately to a weight change. Use **slightly less** than double the amount of cooking time when doubling a quantity.

11. Cook vegetables on Full Power, unless they are cooked with a sauce which contains a "delicate" or "special" ingredient.

12. Whole vegetables will require a slightly longer cooking time than vegetables cut in pieces. For fast even cooking,

cut vegetables into small uniformly-shaped pieces.

13. You may want to stir some vegetables halfway through the cooking time to redistribute heat and moisture.

14. Recipes in this cookbook give cooking times for vegetables to be cooked to the "barely tender" stage. If a softer vegetable texture is desired, add slightly more liquid, cook covered and slightly increase the amount of cooking time.

15. Be careful not to overcook vegetables. Vegetables will continue to cook slightly after removed from the Radarange Oven. If vegetables will be standing for several minutes before serving, slightly undercook them and they will finish cooking by themselves. Keep vegetables covered to retain heat before serving. Baked potatoes can be wrapped in aluminum foil **after** cooking to keep them "piping" hot until served.

16. Home canning should not be done in a microwave oven. Home canning is generally done with metal lids. Since metal lids reflect microwaves, you cannot be assured that the food product will be heated uniformly to 212° F or above, and there is a probability of deterioration of the food product. Vegetables may be blanched in the Radarange Oven with good results. See the chart on page 117.

17. Grated or shredded cheese may be added to vegetables. Top vegetables with cheese just before serving. Heat in Radarange Oven on Cookmatic Level 5 for 1 to 1-1/2 minutes, or until cheese is melted.

18. Fresh vegetable dishes can be prepared in "planned-over" quantities. Prepare a large quantity and freeze the extra or planned-over for future use.

19. For vegetable sauces and salad dressings, see the "Sauces, Jams and Relishes" chapter on page 128.

20. Fruits are prepared similarly to vegetables. Information about fruits is found in the "Desserts" chapter on page 137.

21. When preparing your own vegetable recipes, select a recipe in this chapter as a guide. Then, use about the same amount of time and cook, covered, on Full Power.

Blanching and Freezing Vegetables

Select only the best vegetables for freezing. They should be slightly immature by table or canning standards. vegetables which are the most brightly colored and have best texture.

To preserve their fresh qualities, almost all vegetables sh be blanched before freezing. Blanching slows and checks plant enzyme activity responsible for losses in qua Blanching maintains color, making vegetables m attractive. It softens vegetables, making packaging ea Blanching also cleans the vegetable and destroys harmful undesirable bacteria.

Blanching may be done more easily and quickly in Radarange Oven than conventionally. Follow the spe instructions and timings on the "Blanching Vegetables Ch for each specific vegetable. For any vegetable not liste general rule to follow is: blanching time is approxima equal to half of the regular microwave cooking time. See "Fresh Vegetable Cooking Chart," on pages 118 to 11S cooking times. Always blanch on Full Power. Stir or rearra the vegetables halfway through blanching to assure distribution of heat.

General Instructions for Blanching Vegetables

1. Prepare the vegetables, according to the "Preparat described in the chart. Use only the amount of vegeta recommended and use the size of utensil stated in chart. When increasing or decreasing the amount vegetables listed, adjust the blanching accordingly.

2. Add the amount of water suggested in the chart. Do salt the vegetables.

3. Heat in the Radarange Oven, covered, on Full Power. and rearrange the vegetables halfway through cooking time.

4. Plunge the vegetables into ice water immediately a blanching so cooking will cease. Remove excess mois from vegetables with paper towels.

5. Package the vegetables for the freezer in airt containers, using proper freezing methods. Label vegetable with its name and the date.

BLANCHING VEGETABLES CHART

VEGETABLE	PREPARATION	AMOUNT OF VEGETABLE	CASSEROLE SIZE	AMOUNT OF WATER	BLANCHING TIME ON FULL POWER
Asparagus	Wash and trim as for table use (do not use woody portions). Cut in 1-inch pieces. (Less desirable pieces may be completely cooked and frozen for use in soups.)	1 lb.	2-quart	1/4 cup	2-1/2 to 3-1/2 min.
Beans, Yellow, Snap Green	Select tender pods with beans slightly under-mature. Wash thoroughly. Remove ends and cut into desired lengths, leave whole or French cut.	1 lb. or 3 cups	1-1/2-quart	1/3 cup	4 to 5 min.
Broccoli	Use compact heads of uniform green color. (Soak first in salt solution for 1/2 hour to remove insects). Rinse. Remove woody portions, cut into pieces not more than 1" across and 5-6" long.	1 lb.	2-quart	1/3 cup	3-1/2 to 4-1/2 min.
Carrots	Select young tender carrots. Remove tops, wash and scrape. Small carrots may be frozen whole. Others may be sliced, diced or Frenched.	1 lb.	1-1/2-quart	1/4 cup	3-1/2 to 4-1/2 min.
Cauliflower	Use compact tender white heads. Wash. Break into flowerets. (Soak in salt solution if desired — see Broccoli.)	1 head	2-quart	1/3 cup	4 to 5 min.
Corn on the Cob	Select tender ripe ears, in full milk stage. Remove husks and silk. Wash and trim ears.	4 ears	2-quart	none	3-1/2 to 4-1/2 min.
Corn, Whole Kernel	Same as corn on the cob.	4 cups	1-1/2-quart	none	3-1/2 to 4-1/2 min.
Peas	Select tender peas, not fully mature. Shell. (If hard to shell, plunge pods in boiling water for 1 min. Cool quickly.) Do not wash after shelling.	4 cups	1-1/2-quart	1/4 cup	4 to 5 min.
Spinach	Pick young tender leaves. Discard tough, large stems. Wash very thoroughly. Blanch only a small amount at one time.	1/2 lb.	2-quart	none	1-1/2 to 2 min.
Squash, Summer, Zucchini	Pick squash while rind is still tender and seeds small. Wash, then peel, if desired, or leave unpeeled. Cut in 1/4-inch slices.	1 lb.	1-1/2-quart	1/4 cup	2 to 3 min.

Vegetables

FRESH VEGETABLE COOKING CHART

VEGETABLE	AMOUNT	UTENSIL	COOKING TIME ON FULL POWER
Asparagus	1 lb.	1-1/2 quart casserole	6 min.
Beans, Green (Pole Beans)	3 cups	1-1/2-quart casserole	10 to 12 min.
Beans, Green	1 lb.	2-quart casserole	10 to 12 min.
Beans, Yellow Wax	1 lb.	2-quart casserole	10 to 12 min.
Beets	1 lb., thinly sliced	1-1/2-quart casserole	8 min.
Broccoli	1-1/2 lbs.	3-quart casserole	10 to 11 min.
Brussels Sprouts	1-1/2 lbs.	1-1/2-quart casserole	7 to 8 min.
Cabbage, Red or Green	2-1/2 to 3 lbs., quartered (medium head)	3-quart casserole	13 to 15 min.
Cabbage, Chinese Celery	1 lb.	1-1/2-quart casserole	8 min.
Carrots	1 lb. whole, sliced 1/2-inch pieces	2-quart casserole	6 to 8 min.
Cauliflower	1-1/2-lb. whole 1 lb. flowerets	1-1/2 to 2-quart casserole 1-1/2-quart casserole	8 to 10 min. 8 min.
Celery	4 cups, diced	1-1/2-quart casserole	7 to 8 min.
Corn on the Cob	4 ears	2-quart utility dish, waxed paper or the husk	6 to 8 min.
Eggplant	4 cups, diced	10-inch ceramic skillet	3 to 4 min.
Mushrooms	1/2 lb.	1-1/2-quart casserole	2-1/2 to 3-1/2 min.
Okra	1 lb.	1-1/2-quart casserole	5 min.
Parsnips	1 lb., sliced in 1/2-inch pieces	2-quart casserole	6 to 8 min.
Peas, Green	2 lbs. (2 cups) 4 lbs. (4 cups)	1-1/2-quart casserole 1-1/2-quart casserole	6 min. 9 to 10 min.
Pea Pods (Chinese)	1 lb.	2-quart casserole	10 min.
Potatoes, Baked	2 medium	paper towels	5 to 6 min.
Potatoes, Red Boiled	2 lbs. (4 large), in 1/4-cup water	2-quart casserole	10 to 12 min.
Potatoes, New Boiled in Jackets	6, 2-inch diameter, in 1/4-cup water	2-quart casserole	8 to 10 min.
Potatoes, Sweet	2 medium 4 medium	paper towels paper towels	4-1/2 to 5-1/2 min. 7 to 9 min.

FRESH VEGETABLE COOKING CHART (Continued)

VEGETABLE	AMOUNT	UTENSIL	COOKING TIME ON FULL POWER
Rutabaga	3 cups, cubed	1-1/2-quart casserole	8 to 10 min.
Spinach	10 ozs.	3-quart casserole	3 to 4 min.
Squash, Acorn	1-1/2 lbs., split and remove seeds	Shallow baking dish	6 to 8 min.
Squash, Butternut	3 lbs., pared and cut into 1-inch slices	2-quart casserole	8 to 10 min.
Squash, Summer Yellow Crookneck	1 lb. (5 small)	Shallow baking dish	4 to 6 min.
Swiss Chard	3/4 lb., with 1/4 cup water	1-1/2-quart casserole	6 to 7 min.
Tomatoes, Baked	1 lb. (2 medium)	1-1/2-quart casserole	3 to 4 min.
Turnips	3 cups, cubed	1-1/2-quart casserole	7 to 9 min.
Zucchini	2 medium (3 cups), sliced in 1/4-inch slices	1-1/2-quart casserole	4 to 6 min.

General Instructions for Cooking Fresh Vegetables
1. Place the prepared vegetable in the utensil recommended on the chart.
2. Add 2 to 4 tablespoons of water when cooking most vegetables. Cream, melted butter or oil may also be used for moisture, if desired. Use a larger quantity of liquid for larger quantities of vegetables and for fibrous vegetables such as green beans and broccoli.
3. The cooking times in the chart are only guidelines. Cook vegetables until tender, as desired. To prepare a smaller quantity of vegetables than the amount on the chart, decrease the cooking time. See page 15 for instructions on increasing or decreasing a recipe size.
4. Cook in the Radarange Oven, covered, on Full Power, according to the time on the chart. Stir or rearrange the vegetable halfway through the cooking time, if necessary. Keep the vegetable covered until ready to serve.

Acorn Squash
Yield: 2 servings

1 acorn squash
1 tablespoon brown sugar
1/4 teaspoon cinnamon
1 tablespoon butter or margarine

1. Cut squash in half lengthwise. Remove seeds. Combine brown sugar and cinnamon. Sprinkle half of mixture in each squash half. Dot with butter. Place in shallow dish. Cover loosely with plastic wrap.
2. Cook in Radarange Oven, covered, on Full Power for 6 to 8 minutes, or until tender.

Cranberry Squash
Yield: 2 servings

1 acorn squash
1/4 cup cranberries
1/4 cup brown sugar, firmly packed
1/4 teaspoon cinnamon
1 tablespoon butter or margarine

1. Cut squash in half lengthwise. Remove seeds. Combine cranberries, brown sugar and cinnamon. Sprinkle half of mixture in each squash half. Dot with butter. Place in shallow dish. Cover loosely with plastic wrap.
2. Cook in Radarange Oven, covered, on Full Power for 7 to 9 minutes, or until tender.
   MICRO-TIP: Substitute orange marmalade or whole berry cranberry sauce for cranberries and sugar, if desired.

Vegetables

FROZEN VEGETABLE COOKING CHART

FROZEN VEGETABLE	PACKAGE SIZE OR AMOUNT	AMOUNT OF WATER, BUTTER OR MARGARINE	COOKING TIME ON FULL POWER
Artichoke Hearts	9 oz.	1 tablespoon water	4 to 5 min.
Asparagus Cuts	10 oz.	2 tablespoons water	5 to 6 min.
Asparagus Spears	10 oz.	2 tablespoons water	6 to 8 min.
Baked Potato	12 oz.	—	4 to 5 min.
Broccoli Cuts	10 oz.	2 tablespoons water	5 to 7 min.
Broccoli Spears	8 oz.	2 tablespoons water	5 to 7 min.
Broccoli in Cheese Sauce	10 oz.	—	6-1/2 to 7-1/2 min.
Brussels Sprouts	8 oz.	1 tablespoon water	5 to 6 min.
Carrots	10 oz.	2 tablespoons water	5 to 7 min.
Cauliflower	10 oz.	2 tablespoons water	4 to 5 min.
Cauliflower in Cheese Sauce	10 oz.	—	6 to 7 min.
Corn, Cream Style	10 oz.	—	4-1/2 to 5-1/2 min.
Corn on the Cob**	1 ear 2 ears 4 ears	— — —	3-1/2 to 4-1/2 min. 5 to 6 min. 10 to 11 min.
Corn, Whole Kernel	10 oz.	2 tablespoons water	4 to 5 min.
Green Beans, Cut	10 oz.	2 tablespoons water	5 to 7 min.
Green Beans, French Cut	9 oz.	1 tablespoon water	5-1/2 to 6-1/2 min.
Green Beans, French Cut with Almonds	9 oz.	1 tablespoon water	5-1/2 to 6-1/2 min.
Green Beans, Italian	10 oz.	2 tablespoons water	5 to 7 min.
Green Beans, Whole	9 oz.	1 tablespoon water	6 to 7 min.
Lima Beans, Baby	10 oz.	2 tablespoons water	4-1/2 to 6 min.
Lima Beans, Fordhook	10 oz.	2 tablespoons water	7-1/2 to 8-1/2 min.
Mixed Vegetables	10 oz.	2 tablespoons water	4-1/2 to 5-1/2 min.
Onion Rings, Fried*	7 oz. 9 oz.	— —	2 to 2-1/2 min. 2-1/2 to 3 min.
Pea Pods	6 oz.	1 tablespoon water	2 to 3 min.
Peas	10 oz.	2 tablespoons water	5 to 6 min.
Peas, Baby Early	10 oz.	2 tablespoons water	3 to 3-1/2 min.
Peas and Carrots	10 oz.	2 tablespoons water	4 to 5 min.

*Place on paper plate or towels. Cover with paper towels. These will not be crisp when cooked in a microwave oven.
**Place in covered casserole or wrap in plastic wrap or waxed paper.

FROZEN VEGETABLE COOKING CHART (Continued)

FROZEN VEGETABLE	PACKAGE SIZE OR AMOUNT	AMOUNT OF WATER, BUTTER OR MARGARINE	COOKING TIME ON FULL POWER
Peas, Green with Cream Sauce	8 oz.	2/3 cup water	5 to 6 min.
Peas, Green and Pearl Onions	10 oz.	1 teaspoon water	3 to 4 min.
Peas, Green and Potatoes	8 oz.	3/4 cup water	5 to 6 min.
Spinach, Chopped	10 oz.	1 tablespoon water	4-1/2 to 5-1/2 min.
Spinach, Leaf	10 oz.	2 tablespoons water	4-1/2 to 5-1/2 min.
Squash	12 oz.	2 tablespoons butter or margarine	3-1/2 to 4-1/2 min.
Succotash	10 oz.	1 tablespoon water	4 to 5 min.
Sweet Potatoes, Candied	12 oz.	1 tablespoon butter or margarine	4 to 4-1/2 min.
Tater Tots*	16 oz.	—	3-1/2 to 4-1/2 min.
Vegetable Combinations (Green Beans and Spaetzle, etc.)	10 oz.	2 tablespoons water	4 to 5 min.

*Place on plastic rack or paper plate. Cover with paper towels. These will not be crisp when cooked in a microwave oven.

General Instructions for Cooking Frozen Vegetables

1. Place the frozen vegetable in a 1 to 1-1/2-quart casserole unless another utensil is recommended. Add water or butter as needed. Cook in Radarange Oven, covered, on Full Power for the amount of time given for the specific vegetable on the chart.
2. When cooking a vegetable frozen in a plastic cooking pouch, make one or two 1-inch slits on the top of the pouch to allow for steam to escape. Place the pouch directly on the Radarange Oven glass tray to cook.
3. There is no need to defrost frozen vegetables before cooking.
4. Always keep vegetable covered to hold in steam after cooking.
5. With vegetables frozen in a solid block, stir to break them apart halfway through the cooking time.
6. If the amount or package size is doubled, the cooking time will be slightly less than two times as long.

Artichoke

Yield: 1 artichoke

2 tablespoons water
1 teaspoon vinegar
4 drops olive oil
1 medium artichoke

1. Combine water, vinegar and olive oil in 4-cup glass measure. Trim sharp ends of artichoke leaves with kitchen shears. Invert artichoke in glass measure. Cover with waxed paper.
2. Cook in Radarange Oven, covered, on Full Power for 4 to 6 minutes, or until barely tender.

DRIED LEGUME COOKING CHART

LEGUME TYPE	1st COOKING TIME ON FULL POWER*	2nd COOKING TIME	2nd SETTING
Baby Lima Beans	8 min.	12 to 15 min.	Cookmatic Level 4
Black-Eyed Beans	9 min.	8 to 12 min.	Cookmatic Level 5
Black Turtle Beans	9 min.	17 to 19 min.	Cookmatic Level 4
Garbanzos (Chick Peas)	9 min.	10 to 15 min.	Cookmatic Level 3
Lentils	9 min.	5 to 7 min.	Cookmatic Level 5
Lima Beans	7 min.	14 to 18 min.	Cookmatic Level 4
Navy (Pea) Beans	7 min.	15 to 20 min.	Cookmatic Level 5
Pinto Beans	9 min.	14 to 18 min.	Cookmatic Level 5
Red Kidney Beans	9 min.	15 to 20 min.	Cookmatic Level 5
Split Peas	6 min.	5 to 7 min.	Cookmatic Level 3
Whole Yellow Peas	9 min.	8 to 12 min.	Cookmatic Level 5

*For Touchmatic models having automatic programming ability, see the Use and Care Manual for information about programmed cooking.

General Instructions for Cooking Dried Legumes

1 cup dried legumes
3 cups water

1 teaspoon salt
1/8 teaspoon baking soda
2 tablespoons vegetable oil

1. Soak legumes in water overnight in 3 to 4-quart casserole.

2. Add salt, baking soda and oil. Cover. Cook in Radarange Oven, cover according to directions in chart, or until legumes are tender, as desire Stir occasionally during cooking time.

Asparagus Royale

Yield: 6 servings

1/2 small onion, chopped
1/3 cup chopped green pepper
2 tablespoons water
2 (10 oz. each) pkgs. frozen asparagus spears
1 tablespoon diced pimento
1 tablespoon parsley flakes
Salt
Pepper

1. Combine onion, green pepper and water in 2-quart casserole. Cook in Radarange Oven, covered, on Full Power for 2 to 3 minutes, or until onion and green pepper are tender.

2. Add remaining ingredients. Season with salt and pepper, as desired. N well. Cover with plastic wrap. Cook in Radarange Oven, covered, on Power for 8 to 10 minutes, or until asparagus is tender. Stir halfway through cooking time.

MICRO-TIP: This is a colorful recipe for weight watchers.

Asparagus Sea Shore Style

Yield: 6 servings

2 (10 oz. each) pkgs. frozen asparagus pieces
1/4 cup water
1 (10-3/4 oz.) can cream of shrimp soup
1 (3 oz.) pkg. cream cheese, softened
Dash cayenne pepper
1 (4-1/2 oz.) can small shrimp, drained
1/2 cup buttered bread crumbs
Paprika

1. Place asparagus and water in 2-quart glass casserole. Cook in Radarange Oven, covered, on Full Power for 8 to 10 minutes. Drain.
2. Blend together soup, cream cheese and pepper. Stir in shrimp. Pour over asparagus. Top with buttered crumbs. Sprinkle with paprika, as desired.
3. Cook in Radarange Oven on Full Power for 4 to 5 minutes, or until tender.

Toll House Baked Beans

Yield: 6 to 8 servings

2 (1 lb. 2 oz. each) cans New England Style baked beans
1 (1 lb.) can solid packed tomatoes
1/4 lb. bacon, cooked and crumbled
1/2 cup minced onion
2 tablespoons dark molasses
1 tablespoon sugar
2 teaspoons dry mustard

1. Pour beans into 3-quart casserole or bean pot. Break up tomatoes and combine with remaining ingredients. Mix into beans.
2. Cook in Radarange Oven, covered, on Full Power for 10 to 12 minutes, or until temperature of 150° F is reached.* Stir halfway through cooking time.

   *MICRO-TIP: Use the Automatic Temperature Control System to cook to 150° F, if your Radarange Oven has this feature.

Calico Bean Pot

Yield: 12 servings

8 slices bacon, cut in small pieces
1 cup chopped onion
1 (1 lb.) can green beans, drained
1 (1 lb.) can lima beans, drained
1 (1 lb. 15 oz.) can pork and beans
1 (1 lb.) can kidney beans, drained
3/4 cup brown sugar, firmly packed
1/2 cup vinegar
1/2 teaspoon garlic salt
1/2 teaspoon dry mustard
1/8 teaspoon pepper

1. Place bacon in 4-quart casserole. Cook in Radarange Oven on Full Power for 6 to 7 minutes, or until crisp. Remove bacon and reserve.
2. Place onion in bacon fat. Cook in Radarange Oven on Full Power for 2 to 3 minutes, or until onion is tender.
3. Add remaining ingredients and bacon. Mix lightly. Cook in Radarange Oven on Full Power for 12 to 15 minutes, or until heated through, and temperature of 150°F is reached.* Stir halfway through cooking time.

   *MICRO-TIP: For extra rich flavor, use the Automatic Temperature Control System to cook to 150° F on Cookmatic Level 5, if your Radarange Oven has this feature. This method should take about twice as long but will slow cook for maximum blending of flavors.

Honeyed Beets

Yield: 6 servings

1 tablespoon cornstarch
1/2 teaspoon salt
1 tablespoon water or beet juice
2 tablespoons vinegar
1/4 cup honey
1 tablespoon butter or margarine
2 cups diced or sliced cooked beets

1. Combine cornstarch and salt in small glass bowl or measure. Blend in water. Stir in vinegar, honey and butter. Cook in Radarange Oven on Full Power for 45 seconds to 1 minute, or until thickened. Stir occasionally during cooking time.
2. Place beets in 1-1/2-quart casserole. Pour sauce over beets. Heat in Radarange Oven, covered, on Full Power for 1 to 1-1/2 minutes, or until heated through.

   MICRO-TIP: For maximum blending of flavors, let stand 10 minutes covered. Reheat in Radarange Oven on Full Power for 1 minute.

Herbed Broccoli

Yield: 3 to 4 servings

3 tablespoons water
1 teaspoon instant chicken bouillon
1 teaspoon Italian seasoning
1/4 teaspoon onion powder
1 (10 oz.) pkg. frozen broccoli

1. Combine water and instant bouillon in 1-1/2-quart casserole. Cook in Radarange Oven on Full Power for 30 seconds, or until boiling. Stir in seasonings. Add broccoli.
2. Cook in Radarange Oven, covered, on Full Power for 5 to 7 minutes, or until tender. Break apart and stir halfway through cooking time.

Broccoli-Onion Casserole

Yield: 6 to 8 servings

2 (10 oz. each) pkgs. frozen broccoli cuts
2 tablespoons water
1 (8 oz.) can pearl onions, drained
1 (10-3/4 oz.) can cream of celery or cream of mushroom soup
1/4 cup cracker crumbs
1/2 cup shredded Cheddar cheese

1. Place frozen broccoli and water in 2-quart casserole. Cook in Radarange Oven, covered, on Full Power for 10 to 11 minutes, or until tender. Drain. Stir to break up. Stir in onions and soup. Top with cracker crumbs.
2. Cook in Radarange Oven on Full Power for 5 to 7 minutes, or until heated through. Sprinkle with cheese. Cook in Radarange Oven on Full Power for 45 seconds to 1-1/2 minutes, or until cheese is melted.

Sweet-Sour Red Cabbage

Yield: 6 servings

1 medium head red cabbage, shredded
2 tart apples, peeled and chopped
1 cup boiling water
1/2 cup apple cider vinegar
3 tablespoons butter or margarine
3 tablespoons sugar
1/2 teaspoon salt
1 stick cinnamon

1. Combine all ingredients in 3-quart casserole.
2. Cook in Radarange Oven, covered, on Full Power for 10 to 12 minutes, or until cabbage is barely tender. Stir halfway through cooking time.

Parsley Buttered Carrots

Yield: 3 to 4 servings

2 tablespoons butter or margarine
2 cups carrots, sliced into 1/3 to 1/2-inch pieces
1 tablespoon parsley flakes

1. Place butter in 1-quart casserole. Heat in Radarange Oven on Full Power for 20 to 30 seconds, or until melted. Stir in carrots and parsley flakes. Mix well.
2. Cook in Radarange Oven, covered, on Full Power for 4 to 5 minutes, or until tender.
   MICRO-TIP: Calorie watchers may substitute 2 tablespoons of water for butter.

Mandarin Carrots

Yield: 6 servings

4 cups carrots, cut into 2-inch slices
2 tablespoons butter or margarine
1 (11 oz.) can mandarin orange sections, drained
1/2 teaspoon salt
1/8 teaspoon ginger

1. Place carrots and butter in 1-1/2-quart casserole. Cook in Radarange Oven, covered, on Full Power for 7 to 9 minutes. Stir halfway through cooking time. Add mandarin oranges, salt and ginger.
2. Cook in Radarange Oven, covered, on Full Power for 2 minutes, or until heated through.

Cauliflower Oriental

Yield: 6 servings

1 medium head cauliflower, broken into pieces
2 tablespoons water
1/2 onion, chopped
1/2 cup diced celery
1 tablespoon chopped parsley
1 tablespoon butter or margarine
1 teaspoon instant chicken bouillon
1 cup boiling water
1 tablespoon cornstarch
1 tablespoon soy sauce
Dash pepper

1. Place cauliflower and water in 2-quart casserole. Cook in Radarange Oven, covered, on Full Power for 8 to 10 minutes, or until tender. Let stand, covered.
2. Combine onion, celery, parsley and butter in 1-quart casserole. Cook in Radarange Oven on Full Power for 3 to 4 minutes, or until vegetables are tender. Stir halfway through cooking time.
3. Dissolve bouillon in water. Blend in cornstarch, soy sauce and pepper. Pour into onion mixture. Cook in Radarange Oven on Full Power for 2 minutes, or until thickened. Stir halfway through cooking time.
4. Drain cauliflower. Place in serving dish if other than casserole. Spoon sauce over.

MICRO-TIP: 2 (10 oz. each) pkgs. frozen cauliflower may be used instead of fresh.

Corn-in-the-Husk

Yield: 3 to 5 servings

5 ears corn
Butter or margarine (optional)

1. Remove outer husks, but leave inner husk on corn. Carefully remove silk. Spread butter on corn, if desired. Replace husks and fasten with string or rubber band. Place corn on plastic rack or directly on Radarange Oven glass tray.
2. Cook in Radarange Oven on Full Power for 8 to 9 minutes, or until steaming hot. Turn corn over halfway through cooking time.

MICRO-TIPS:
• If husks are removed, wrap corn in waxed paper.
• To cook a smaller quantity of corn, cook 1 ear in Radarange Oven on Full Power for 1-1/2 to 2 minutes, or until steaming hot.

Scalloped Corn

Yield: 4 to 6 servings

1 (17 oz.) can cream-style corn
1/2 cup milk
1 egg
1/2 teaspoon onion salt
1/4 cup cornflake crumbs
1/4 cup shredded Cheddar cheese

1. Combine corn, milk, egg and onion salt in 1-quart casserole. Combine cornflake crumbs and cheese. Spread over corn mixture.
2. Cook in Radarange Oven on Cookmatic Level 5 for 15 to 18 minutes, or until knife inserted near center comes out clean.*

*MICRO-TIP: You may want to turn dish halfway through cooking time.

Ratatouille

Yield: 4 to 6 servings

1-1/2 cups peeled and diced eggplant
1/2 cup thinly sliced onion
1 clove garlic, minced
3 tablespoons olive oil or vegetable oil
1 medium green pepper, cut in 1/2-inch strips
1-1/2 cups sliced zucchini
1 (16 oz.) can stewed tomatoes
1 teaspoon salt
1/4 teaspoon Italian seasoning
Dash pepper

1. Place eggplant, onion, garlic and oil in 2-quart casserole. Cook in Radarange Oven on Full Power for 5 minutes. Stir halfway through cooking time.
2. Layer peppers and zucchini over eggplant mixture. Add seasonings to tomatoes. Pour over vegetables.
3. Cook in Radarange Oven, covered, on Full Power for 8 to 10 minutes, or until vegetables are tender. Let stand 5 minutes, covered, before serving.

Classic Green Bean Treat

Yield: 4 to 6 servings

2 (10 oz. each) pkgs. frozen green beans, regular or French-cut
1/2 teaspoon salt
1 (10-3/4 oz.) can cream of celery soup
1 (2 oz.) can sliced mushrooms, drained (optional)

1 (3 oz.) can French fried onion rings

1. Place beans in 1-1/2-quart casserole. Sprinkle with salt. Spread soup, mushrooms over beans.
2. Cook in Radarange Oven, covered, on Full Power for 7 to 10 minutes until warmed. Stir.
3. Sprinkle onion rings over top. Cook in Radarange Oven on Full Power 6 to 7 minutes, or until heated through, and temperature of 150° F is reached.*

MICRO-TIPS:

* Use the Automatic Temperature Control System to cook to 150° F, your Radarange Oven has this feature.
• 2 (1 lb. each) cans of green beans may be substituted for the frozen green beans. Combine all ingredients and cook in Radarange Oven on Full Power for 5 to 7 minutes, or until temperature of 150° F is reached. Use the Automatic Temperature Control System to cook to 150° F, if your Radarange Oven has this feature.

Baked Potatoes

Select uniform, medium-size baking potatoes about 7-ozs. each. Scrub potatoes well. Prick each potato through the skin with the tines of a fork in several places. Arrange potatoes on a paper towel in the Radarange Oven. Leave about 1-inch space between potatoes and avoid placing one potato in the center surrounded by other potatoes. Cook in Radarange Oven on Full Power for the times indicated below. These times are approximate and will vary, according to the size and variety of the potatoes being cooked. Turn the potatoes over halfway through the cooking time.

QUANTITY	TIME	SETTING
1 potato	3 to 5 min.	Full Power
2 potatoes	5 to 6 min.	Full Power
4 potatoes	9 to 11 min.	Full Power

MICRO-TIP: If the potatoes are still slightly undercooked or if you want to keep them warm for several minutes before serving, wrap the potatoes in foil **after** their removal from the Radarange Oven.

Party Potatoes

Yield: 8 servings

8 to 10 medium potatoes, peeled and cut into eighths
1/2 cup water
1 (8 oz.) pkg. cream cheese
1 (8 oz.) carton French onion dip
1/2 teaspoon salt
1/8 teaspoon pepper
1/2 teaspoon garlic salt (optional)
Butter or margarine
Paprika

1. Place potatoes in 3-quart casserole. Add water. Cook in Radarange Oven, covered, on Full Power for 12 to 14 minutes, or until potatoes are tender. Stir halfway through cooking time. Drain.
2. Beat together cream cheese, onion dip, salt, pepper and garlic salt in large mixing bowl, until well-blended. Add hot potatoes, one at a time, beating until light and fluffy. Spoon into 2-quart casserole. Dot with butter, as desired.
3. Cook in Radarange Oven, covered, on Cookmatic Level 8 for 5 to 7 minutes, or until heated through, and temperature of 150° F is reached. Sprinkle with paprika as desired before serving.

*MICRO-TIP: Use the Automatic Temperature Control System to cook 150° F, if your Radarange Oven has this feature.

Twice-Baked Potatoes

Yield: 4 servings

4 medium (7 oz. each) baking potatoes
1/2 cup dairy sour cream
1 (3 oz.) pkg. cream cheese, softened
2 tablespoons butter or margarine
1 teaspoon onion salt
1 teaspoon frozen chives
1/8 teaspoon pepper
Paprika
Parsley flakes

1. Pierce skins of potatoes with tines of fork. Arrange potatoes on Radarange Oven glass tray. Cook in Radarange Oven on Full Power for 9 to 11 minutes, or until potatoes are done.
2. Cut slice from top of each potato and scoop out insides into mixing bowl. Add remaining ingredients, except paprika and parsley flakes. Beat until smooth. Spoon back into potato shells. Garnish with paprika and parsley flakes, as desired.
3. Heat in Radarange Oven on Full Power for 2-1/2 to 3 minutes, or until heated through.

MICRO-TIP: Potatoes may be topped with shredded Cheddar cheese. Heat in Radarange Oven on Full Power for 30 seconds to 1 minute, or until cheese is melted.

Scalloped Tomato Potatoes

Yield: 6 to 8 servings

1/2 cup chopped onion
2 tablespoons butter or margarine
2 tablespoons all-purpose flour
1/2 teaspoon salt
1/8 teaspoon pepper
1 cup water
1 (8 oz.) can stewed tomatoes
2 teaspoons instant chicken bouillon
5 cups peeled and thinly sliced potatoes
Grated Parmesan cheese

1. Place onion and butter in 1-1/2-quart casserole. Cook in Radarange Oven on Full Power for 1-1/2 minutes, or until onion is tender.
2. Blend in flour, seasonings, water, tomatoes and bouillon. Cook in Radarange Oven on Full Power for 4 minutes, or until thickened. Stir halfway through cooking time.
3. Add potatoes. Stir lightly to coat. Cook in Radarange Oven, covered, on Full Power for 13 to 15 minutes, or until potatoes are tender. Sprinkle with Parmesan cheese, as desired.

Wax Bean Casserole

Yield: 4 to 6 servings

1 cup dry bread cubes
1 tablespoon butter or margarine, melted
1 (16 oz.) can wax beans, drained
1 (8 oz.) can stewed tomatoes
1/2 teaspoon instant minced onion
1/2 teaspoon salt
1/8 teaspoon pepper
1/2 cup shredded Cheddar cheese

1. Toss bread cubes and butter lightly in 1-1/2-quart casserole. Add beans, tomatoes, onion and seasonings. Stir to blend. Sprinkle cheese over top.
2. Cook in Radarange Oven on Cookmatic Level 5 for 6 to 7 minutes, or until heated through and cheese is melted.

Italian-Style Zucchini

Yield: 4 servings

1 lb. small fresh zucchini, thinly sliced
1 cup thinly sliced celery
1 (8 oz.) can tomato sauce
1/2 teaspoon salt
1/8 teaspoon pepper
1/8 teaspoon thyme
1/8 teaspoon basil
Dash garlic powder

1. Combine zucchini and celery in 1-1/2-quart casserole.
2. Combine remaining ingredients. Pour over vegetables.
3. Cook in Radarange Oven, covered, on Full Power for 8 to 10 minutes, or until heated through and vegetables are tender. Stir halfway through cooking time.

MICRO-TIP: After cooking, sprinkle with 1/2 cup shredded Mozzarella cheese. Cook in Radarange Oven, covered, on Full Power for 15 to 30 seconds, or until cheese is melted.

You will find sauces a real joy to make in your Radarange Oven. The double boiler, which often causes steam-burned hands, is gone forever. Scorching is also eliminated. In this chapter, you will find some basic French sauces, as well as dessert and meat sauces. Sauces can be made very easily in glass measuring cups and require only minimum amounts of stirring. Use the sauces in this chapter to accompany main dishes or desserts found in other chapters. Special sauces can be used to "dress up" otherwise plain foods. Make your own Radarange Oven salad dressings to complement fresh salads.

Jams and jellies are a delightful addition to any table! The Radarange Oven simplifies the usual long, drawnout process of jelly making. Surprise your family with flavorful jellies and jams made in your Radarange Oven. Original-gift-givers love these recipes. They are unique, yet always appreciated presents.

Pickles and other relishes can be easily made in the Radarange Oven. Make relishes ahead, and refrigerate them for future use.

Before preparing sauces, jams, and relishes in the Radarange Oven, be sure to read the general hints.

General Hints for Cooking Sauces, Jams and Relishes

1. Be sure to use the size container that is recommended in recipes to avoid boil-overs.
2. Sauces can be cooked directly in glass measures, for convenience. A glass measure should not be more than about half-filled to avoid boil-overs.
3. Cover sauces, jams or relishes as recommended in the recipes. Use a glass lid or heavy-duty plastic wrap. Remove these coverings away from you to avoid steam burns. You may wish to keep hot pads handy. Sugar mixtures can become quite hot during cooking.
4. Stir sauces during cooking, as recommended in the recipes. Stirring will prevent lumping. Less stirring is required in the microwave cooking of sauces than in conventional cooking.
5. When adding an ingredient such as pectin to a hot mixture, stir it in gradually.
6. Jams, jellies or preserves should be poured into sterilized jars and sealed with paraffin. If jars are not sterilized, the jams, jellies or preserves may be stored in airtight containers in the refrigerator.
7. Purchased syrups and ice cream toppings may be heated quickly and easily in the Radarange Oven. When syrups and toppings have been refrigerated, they can be quickly warmed or softened. Remove the syrups or toppings from glass jars. Pour syrups or toppings into glass dishes before heating. Heat for only a few seconds since syrups and toppings quickly become quite hot. Some of the jams and jellies in this chapter make good ice cream toppings when warmed in the Radarange Oven.
8. Many sauces, jams and relishes are cooked on Full Power. Items containing "special" or "delicate" ingredients, however, are cooked on lower Cookmatic Levels or settings. When preparing your own favorite recipes in the Radarange Oven, select a similar recipe in this chapter as a guide. Be sure to use a large enough utensil to avoid boil-overs. Use the same setting and approximately the same cooking time as the "guide" recipe. Make a note of the microwave cooking time on your recipe for future use.

CONVENIENCE SAUCE MIX COOKING CHART

TYPE	PKG. SIZE	ADDITIONAL INGREDIENTS*	SETTING	COOKING TIME
Au Jus Mix	3/4 oz.	2 cups water	Full Power	3 to 4 min.
Burgundy Wine Sauce Mix	1 oz.	1 cup water 1 tablespoon butter or margarine	Full Power	3 to 4 min.
Cheese Sauce Mix	1-1/4 oz.	1 cup milk	Cookmatic Level 8	2-1/2 to 3 min.
Gravy Mix (Chicken, Beef or Pork)	3/4 oz.	1 cup water	Full Power	3 to 4 min.
Hollandaise Sauce Mix	1-1/8 oz.	2/3 cup water	Full Power	1 to 1-1/2 min.
Sherry Wine Sauce Mix	1 oz.	1 cup milk 1 tablespoon butter or margarine	Cookmatic Level 8	3 to 4 min.
Spaghetti Sauce Mix	1-1/2 oz.	2 to 3 tablespoons butter or margarine 1-3/4 cups water 1 (6 oz.) can tomato paste	Full Power	7-1/2 to 8-1/2 min.

*May vary among different brands. Add extra ingredients as listed on package.

General Instructions for Cooking Convenience Sauce Mixes
1. Combine mix and additional ingredients in 1 or 1-1/2-quart casserole.
2. Cook in the Radarange Oven, according to the setting and cooking time on the chart, or until the sauce is boiling or thickened as recommended on the package instructions. Stir occasionally during the cooking time.

CANNED SAUCE HEATING CHART

SAUCE TYPE	CAN SIZE	UTENSIL	COOKING TIME ON FULL POWER
Gravy (Beef or Chicken)	10-1/2 oz.	2-cup glass measure or 1-quart casserole	1 to 2 min.
Spaghetti Sauce	15 oz.	1-quart casserole	2 to 3 min.

General Instructions for Heating Canned Sauces
1. Pour the sauce into the utensil listed on the chart.
2. Heat in the Radarange Oven on Full Power, according to the time on the chart. Stir before serving.

Bechemel Sauce
Yield: 1 cup

2 tablespoons butter or margarine
2 tablespoons all-purpose flour
1/4 teaspoon salt
1/2 teaspoon onion powder
1/8 teaspoon pepper
Dash thyme
1/2 cup chicken broth
1/4 cup light cream

1. Place butter in 1-quart casserole. Heat in Radarange Oven on Full Power for 20 to 30 seconds, or until melted.
2. Stir in flour and seasonings. Blend to smooth paste. Mix together chicken broth and cream. Stir in gradually.
3. Cook in Radarange Oven on Full Power for 1-1/2 to 3 minutes, or until bubbling and thickened. Stir occasionally during cooking time.

White Sauce and Variations

Yield: 1 cup

Thin White Sauce

Thick White Sauce

Cheese Sauce

Dill Sauce
Mustard Sauce

Newberg Sauce

2 tablespoons butter or margarine
2 tablespoons all-purpose flour
1/2 teaspoon salt
1 cup milk

VARIATIONS
1 tablespoon butter or margarine
1 tablespoon all-purpose flour

2 tablespoons butter or margarine
2 tablespoons all-purpose flour

3/4 cup shredded sharp Cheddar cheese
Dash cayenne pepper

1/2 teaspoon dill weed

1-1/2 to 2 tablespoons prepared mustard

1 egg yolk
1/4 cup heavy cream
1 tablespoon dry sherry
Dash cayenne pepper

1. Place butter in 1-quart casserole. Heat in Radarange Oven on Full Power for 30 to 45 seconds, or until melted.
2. Stir in flour and salt. Blend to smooth paste. Blend in milk gradually, stirring constantly.
3. Cook in Radarange Oven on Full Power for 2-1/2 to 3 minutes, or until thickened. Stir 3 to 4 times during cooking.

MICRO-TIP: This recipe makes a medium sauce.

Omit these amounts of butter and flour from original recipe.

Add these additional amounts with butter and flour in original recipe.

Stir cheese into cooked sauce in original recipe. Cook in Radarange Oven on Full Power for 1 to 1-1/2 minutes, or until cheese is melted. Add cayenne pepper.
Add to flour in original recipe.
Add to cooked sauce in original recipe.

Add cooked sauce from original recipe gradually to egg yolk. Stir in cream, sherry and cayenne pepper. Cook in Radarange Oven on Full Power for 2 minutes, or until heated through.

Sweet-Sour Sauce

Yield: 1-1/2 cups

1 (8-1/4 oz.) can pineapple chunks, with liquid
1-1/2 teaspoons cornstarch
3 tablespoons brown sugar
2 tablespoons vinegar
1 tablespoon soy sauce
1/2 green pepper, chopped

1. Drain pineapple juice into 1-quart glass casserole. Stir in cornstarch, brown sugar, vinegar and soy sauce. Cook in Radarange Oven on Full Power for 1 minute, or until mixture boils. Stir halfway through cooking time. Stir in green pepper and pineapple.
2. Cook in Radarange Oven, covered, on Full Power for about 2 minutes. Stir halfway through cooking time.

MICRO-TIP: May be served over meat balls, cocktail franks, pea pods other vegetables.

Sour Cream Dressing

Yield: 2 cups

1/2 cup sugar
3 tablespoons all-purpose flour
1 teaspoon dry mustard
1 teaspoon salt

1 cup milk
1 egg
1/2 cup vinegar
1 tablespoon butter or margarine
1 cup dairy sour cream

1. Combine sugar, flour, mustard and salt in 1-quart casserole.
2. Combine milk and egg. Stir into dry ingredients. Cook in Radarange Oven on Full Power for 1-1/2 to 3 minutes, or until thickened.
3. Stir in vinegar and butter. Cook in Radarange Oven on Full Power for to 1-1/2 minutes, or until heated through. Stir well and chill. When mixture is cold, fold in sour cream.

MICRO-TIP: May be served over fruit or vegetable salads.

Hollandaise Sauce

Yield: 1/2 cup

1/3 cup butter or margarine
1 to 2 tablespoons lemon juice
2 egg yolks
1/4 teaspoon salt
1/4 teaspoon dry mustard
Dash Tabasco sauce

1. Place butter in 1-quart casserole. Heat in Radarange Oven on Full Power for 40 to 60 seconds, or until melted.
2. Stir in remaining ingredients. Beat with spoon or whisk until well-mixed. Cook in Radarange Oven on Full Power for 1 to 1-1/2 minutes, or until thickened. Stir halfway through cooking time.
MICRO-TIP: Serve over vegetables or Eggs Benedict. (See recipe, page 69.)

Mornay Sauce

Yield: 1-3/4 cups

2 tablespoons butter or margarine
2 tablespoons all-purpose flour
1 teaspoon instant chicken bouillon
Dash pepper
1-1/4 cups milk
1/4 cup shredded Swiss cheese
2 tablespoons grated Parmesan cheese
1 teaspoon parsley flakes

1. Place butter in 1-quart casserole. Heat in Radarange Oven on Full Power for 20 to 30 seconds, or until melted. Blend in flour, bouillon, pepper and milk.
2. Cook in Radarange Oven on Full Power for 2 to 3 minutes, or until mixture boils. Stir ocasionally during cooking time. Mix in Swiss cheese. Sprinkle with Parmesan cheese and parsley.
3. Cook in Radarange Oven, covered, on Full Power for 30 seconds to 1 minute, or until heated through.
MICRO-TIP: May be served over meat, vegetables or spaghetti noodles.

Rich Mushroom Sauce

Yield: 1-1/2 cups

3 tablespoons butter or margarine
2 tablespoons all-purpose flour
1 teaspoon soy sauce
3/4 cup light cream
1/4 teaspoon salt
1 (4 oz.) can mushrooms, drained

1. Place butter in 1-quart glass measure or casserole. Heat in Radarange Oven on Full Power for 30 to 40 seconds, or until melted.
2. Blend in remaining ingredients. Cook in Radarange Oven on Full Power for 1-1/2 to 3 minutes. Stir halfway through cooking time.
MICRO-TIP: May be served over hamburger or steak.

Lemon Sauce For Fish

Yield: 1-1/2 cups

2 tablespoons butter or margarine
2 tablespoons all-purpose flour
1/2 teaspoon salt
1/2 cup light cream
1 egg yolk
1 cup chicken bouillon
1/4 cup lemon juice
1 tablespoon parsley flakes
Dash Tabasco sauce

1. Place butter in 1-quart casserole. Heat in Radarange Oven on Full Power for 20 to 30 seconds, or until melted. Blend in flour and salt.
2. Pour light cream into flour mixture, stirring constantly. Cook in Radarange Oven on Full Power for 45 seconds to 1 minute. Stir halfway through cooking time.
3. Blend egg yolk into bouillon. Stir mixture along with remaining ingredients into light cream mixture. Cook in Radarange Oven on Full Power for 1 to 2 minutes, or until heated through.

Bordelaise Sauce

Yield: 1-1/4 cups

3 tablespoons butter or margarine
1 tablespoon minced onion
3 tablespoons all-purpose flour
1 cup beef broth or bouillon
2 tablespoons red wine
1 tablespoon lemon juice
1/2 teaspoon tarragon
1 teaspoon finely chopped parsley
1/4 teaspoon bottled browning sauce

1. Combine butter and onion in 1-quart measure or casserole. Cook in Radarange Oven on Full Power for 1 minute, or until onion is tender.
2. Stir in flour. Blend to smooth paste. Pour in broth, wine, lemon juice, tarragon, parsley and browning sauce.
3. Cook in Radarange Oven on Full Power for 2-1/2 to 3 minutes, or until thickened. Stir halfway through cooking time.
MICRO-TIP: Serve with roast beef or steak.

Basic Tomato Sauce

Yield: 2 to 2-1/2 quarts

1 cup chopped onion
2 cloves garlic, minced
2 stalks celery, chopped
2 tablespoons vegetable oil
2 (28 oz. each) can whole tomatoes
1 (12 oz.) can tomato paste
1 teaspoon parsley flakes
1 tablespoon sugar
2 to 3 teaspoons salt
1/2 teaspoon leaf basil
1/2 teaspoon leaf oregano
1/4 teaspoon pepper
1 bay leaf
1/2 cup red wine (optional)

1. Combine onion, garlic, celery and oil in 3-quart casserole. Cook in Radarange Oven, covered, on Full Power for about 5 minutes, or until onion, garlic and celery are tender. Stir halfway through cooking time.
2. Stir in remaining ingredients. Cook in Radarange Oven, covered, on F Power for about 17 to 20 minutes, or until heated through. Stir halfwa through cooking time and break up tomatoes. Cool. Remove bay leaf.

MICRO-TIP: Sauce may be divided among 5, 1-pint freezer containers, covered, and frozen for later use.

Cooked Salad Dressing

Yield: Approx. 1-1/2 cups

2 tablespoons all-purpose flour
1 tablespoon sugar
1/2 teaspoon salt
1/2 teaspoon dry mustard
1 egg yolk
3/4 cup light cream
2 tablespoons vinegar
1 tablespoon butter or margarine
VARIATIONS

1. Stir together flour, sugar, salt and mustard in 1-quart casserole.
2. Combine egg yolk and light cream. Stir into flour mixture gradually. Cook in Radarange Oven on Full Power for 1 to 2 minutes, or until mixture boils and is thickened. Stir halfway through cooking time.
3. Stir in vinegar and butter with wire whip, until smooth. Cool and serv on salads.

Creamy French

1/2 teaspoon paprika
Dash cayenne pepper

Add to cooked dressing with vinegar and butter in step #3.

Creamy Italian

1/2 teaspoon celery salt
1/8 teaspoon garlic powder
Dash cayenne pepper

Add to cooked dressing with vinegar and butter in step #3.

Creamy Blue Cheese

1/3 cup crumbled blue cheese
Dash cayenne pepper

Add to cooked dressing, after cooling.

Fruit Dressing

Yield: 3 cups

1/2 cup sugar
1 tablespoon cornstarch
1 egg yolk
2 tablespoons lemon juice
3/4 cup unsweetened pineapple juice
2 cups whipped cream

1. Combine sugar, cornstarch and egg yolk in 1-quart casserole. Add jui
2. Cook in Radarange Oven on Full Power for 2 to 4 minutes, or until thickened. Stir halfway through cooking time. Cool and fold in whipp cream.

MICRO-TIP: May be served over fresh fruit.

Baked Rhubarb Sauce

Yield: 2 cups

2 cups chopped rhubarb
2 tablespoons water
Dash salt
1/2 cup sugar

1. Combine rhubarb and water in 2-quart glass casserole. Stir in salt. Cook in Radarange Oven, covered, on Full Power for about 3 to 4 minutes, or until rhubarb is tender. Stir halfway through cooking time. Mix in sugar.
2. Cook in Radarange Oven on Full Power for 1 minute, or until sugar is dissolved. Cool, covered.

MICRO-TIP: May be served warm or cold. Add few drops of red food coloring to sauce before cooking, if desired.

Apple-Raisin Sauce

Yield: 1-1/2 cups

2 tablespoons brown sugar
1 tablespoon cornstarch
1/8 teaspoon salt
1/8 teaspoon allspice
1 cup apple juice
1/4 cup seedless raisins
1/2 cup diced apples

1. Combine brown sugar, cornstarch, salt and allspice in 1-quart casserole. Blend in apple juice. Cook in Radarange Oven on Full Power for about 2 minutes, or until thickened. Stir halfway through cooking time.
2. Mix in raisins. Cook in Radarange Oven on Full Power for about 1 minute, or until warmed. Stir halfway through cooking. Add apples just before serving.

Applesauce

Yield: 3 to 4 cups

6 cups pared, cored and coarsely chopped apples (about 6 to 7 medium size apples)
2 tablespoons water
1 tablespoon lemon juice
1/2 cup brown sugar, firmly packed
1/4 cup sugar
1 teaspoon cinnamon
1/2 teaspoon nutmeg
1/2 teaspoon salt

1. Combine all ingredients in 1-1/2-quart casserole.
2. Cook in Radarange Oven, covered, on Full Power for 4 to 6 minutes, or until apples are tender. Mash or put through sieve, if desired.

MICRO-TIP: Lemon juice, brown sugar, cinnamon, nutmeg and salt can be omitted to make a simple sauce.

Dessert Lemon Sauce

Yield: 1 cup

1/2 cup sugar
1 tablespoon cornstarch
1 cup water
2 tablespoons butter or margarine
1/2 teaspoon grated lemon peel
1-1/2 tablespoons lemon juice
Dash salt

1. Combine sugar and cornstarch in 1-quart casserole. Stir in water.
2. Heat in Radarange Oven on Full Power for 1-1/2 to 2 minutes, or until thickened. Stir 2 or 3 times during cooking time.
3. Blend in butter, lemon peel, lemon juice and salt. Blend until smooth.

MICRO-TIP: May be served warm or cold.

Ruby-Strawberry Sauce

Yield: 4 to 5 cups

4 cups sliced, frozen rhubarb
3/4 cup sugar
2 tablespoons cornstarch
1 (10 oz.) pkg. frozen, sweetened strawberries, sliced

1. Combine all ingredients in 1-1/2-quart casserole.
2. Cook in Radarange Oven, covered, on Full Power for 12 to 14 minutes, or until mixture boils. Stir 3 to 4 times during cooking time.

MICRO-TIP: Fresh rhubarb and strawberries may be substituted for frozen. Decrease cooking time slightly.

Custard Sauce

Yield: 2-1/4 cups

4 egg yolks, beaten
1/3 cup sugar
1/4 teaspoon salt
1-1/2 cups milk
1/2 cup evaporated milk
1 teaspoon vanilla

1. Place eggs, sugar and salt in 4-cup glass measure. Mix until well-blend
2. Stir in milks and vanilla.
3. Cook in Radarange Oven on Cookmatic Level 8 for 5 to 7 minutes, or until back of spoon is coated. Stir once or twice during cooking time. Chill before serving.

Vanilla Sauce

Yield: 1 cup

3 tablespoons butter or margarine, softened
1/2 cup sugar
2 egg yolks, slightly-beaten
1/2 cup boiling water
Dash salt
1 teaspoon vanilla

1. Cream butter and sugar in 1-quart casserole.
2. Combine egg yolks with creamed mixture. Beat in water and salt. Hea Radarange Oven on Full Power for about 1 to 2 minutes, or until sauc is smooth and thickened. Stir well 2 or 3 times during cooking time. careful not to overcook. Stir in vanilla. Serve sauce hot.

Marshmallow-Caramel Sauce

Yield: 2 cups

1-1/2 cups brown sugar, firmly packed
2/3 cup light corn syrup
1/3 cup water
1/3 cup butter or margarine
1/2 cup milk
6 large marshmallows, diced

1. Combine sugar, corn syrup and water in 1-quart casserole. Cook in Radarange Oven on Full Power for 7 to 9 minutes, or until soft ball st is reached.* Stir occasionally during cooking.
2. Beat in remaining ingredients. Chill.
MICRO-TIPS:
• This sauce tastes great when served over ice cream.
* The soft ball stage is described on page 176.

Hot Fudge Sauce

Yield: 1 cup

1/2 cup sugar
3 tablespoons cocoa
1-1/2 tablespoons cornstarch
Dash salt
1/2 cup water, room temperature
2 tablespoons butter or margarine
1 teaspoon vanilla

1. Mix together dry ingredients in 1-quart casserole or 2-cup glass meas Stir in water.
2. Cook in Radarange Oven on Full Power for about 1-1/2 minutes. Stir halfway through cooking time. Blend in butter. Cook in Radarange O on Full Power for 30 seconds, or until butter is melted. Stir halfway through cooking time. Blend in vanilla. Stir thoroughly.

Blueberry Syrup

Yield: 1-3/4 cups

1/2 cup sugar
1 tablespoon cornstarch
1/4 cup water
1/4 cup light corn syrup
2 teaspoons lemon juice
2 cups blueberries

1. Combine sugar and cornstarch in 1-quart casserole. Add water, syrup and lemon juice. Stir in blueberries.
2. Cook in Radarange Oven on Full Power for 4-1/2 to 5 minutes, or un thickened.
MICRO-TIP: For a thicker sauce, add 1 additional teaspoon of cornsta

Golden Pancake Syrup

Yield: 2 cups

1 cup water
2-1/3 cups brown sugar, firmly packed
1/2 teaspoon maple flavor (optional)

1. Place water in 2-quart casserole. Heat in Radarange Oven on Full Pov for 1 to 2 minutes, or until boiling.
2. Stir in brown sugar. Heat in Radarange Oven on Full Power for 1 to 2 minutes, or until sugar is dissolved. Add maple flavor.
MICRO-TIP: Pour into syrup pitcher and serve warm. May be stored i refrigerator in covered jar.

Simple Strawberry Preserves

Yield: 3 cups

1 (16 oz.) pkg. frozen
  strawberries
3 tablespoons powdered fruit
  pectin
2 cups sugar
1 tablespoon lemon juice

1. Place strawberries in 2-quart casserole. Cook in Radarange Oven on Full Power for 2 minutes.
2. Stir in powdered fruit pectin. Cook in Radarange Oven on Full Power for about 2 minutes, or until few bubbles surface.
3. Stir in sugar and lemon juice. Cook in Radarange Oven on Full Power for 6 minutes. Stir 2 to 3 times during cooking time. Pour into glass jars. Cover and refrigerate.

MICRO-TIP: If sealed with paraffin, jars may be stored in the freezer for use when needed.

Apple Jelly

Yield: 2-1/2 to 3 cups

3-1/2 lbs. apples, washed, cored,
  and cut into eights
3-1/2 cups water
3 cups sugar, or 3/4 cup sugar
  for each 1 cup of juice
2 tablespoons lemon juice

1. Place apples and water in 3-1/2 to 4-quart casserole. Cook in Radarange Oven, covered, on Full Power for 10 to 15 minutes, or until apples are tender.
2. Strain apples and liquid through cheesecloth-lined strainer. (There should be 4 cups of juice.) Add sugar and lemon juice. Cook in Radarange Oven on Full Power for 30 to 35 minutes, or until jellying point is reached. Stir 3 to 4 times during cooking. Pour into jars and let cool. Refrigerate.

Peach-Cherry Conserve

Yield: 1-1/2 quarts

2 cups chopped peaches
1 (1 lb. 4 oz.) can crushed
  pineapple, drained
1 (8 oz.) bottle maraschino
  cherries, chopped, with liquid
7-1/2 cups sugar
1 (6 oz.) bottle liquid fruit
  pectin

1. Combine peaches, pineapple, cherries and cherry liquid in 4 to 5-quart casserole. Cook in Radarange Oven, covered, on Full Power for 5 minutes, or until peaches are tender.
2. Stir in sugar. Cook in Radarange Oven, uncovered, on Full Power for 12 to 15 minutes, or until mixture boils, and sugar is dissolved. Stir twice during cooking time.
3. Stir in liquid fruit pectin. Cook in Radarange Oven on Full Power for 3 to 5 minutes, or until mixture boils. Stir as needed during cooking time to avoid boiling over.
4. Allow to cool for 5 minutes. Stir occasionally during cooling time. Pour into jars or glasses. Seal with paraffin.

Cranberry Jelly

Yield: 4 cups

1 lb. cranberries, washed and
  drained
2 sticks cinnamon
6 whole cloves
1/4 cup water
2 cups sugar
1-3/4 cups water

1. Combine cranberries, cinnamon, cloves and 1/4 cup water in 2-quart casserole. Cook in Radarange Oven, covered, on Full Power for 4-1/2 to 5 minutes, or until cranberry skins open. Stir halfway through cooking time. Strain or put cranberries through food mill. Return to casserole.
2. Add sugar and 1-3/4 cups water. Blend well. Cook in Radarange Oven on Full Power for 7 to 9 minutes, or until mixture has boiled for 3 to 4 minutes. Stir once or twice during cooking time, to prevent boiling over. Chill until firm.

MICRO-TIP: May be poured directly into jars or into serving dish to be used as cranberry sauce.

Bread and Butter Pickles

Yield: 1-1/2 quarts

2 lbs. cucumbers, sliced
Cold water
1 cup vinegar
1 cup water
1 cup sugar
1 teaspoon salt
1 teaspoon celery seed
1 teaspoon mustard seed
1/2 teaspoon dill seed

1. Place cucumbers in 3-quart casserole. Cover with cold water. Soak un crisp. Cook in Radarange Oven, covered, on Full Power for 5 to 7 minutes, or until temperature of 110° F is reached.* Drain. Pack in ja
2. Mix together remaining ingredients in 1-1/2-quart casserole. Cook in Radarange Oven, covered, on Full Power for 7 to 8 minutes, or until mixture boils. Pour over cucumbers in jars. Seal.
   *MICRO-TIP: Use the Automatic Temperature Control System to cook 110° F, if your Radarange Oven has this feature.

Pickled Beet Relish

Yield: 2-1/2 cups

1 medium onion, chopped
1 tablespoon water
1 (1 lb.) can diced beets, drained
3/4 cup vinegar
1 cup sugar
1 cinnamon stick

1. Place the onion and water in 1-quart casserole. Cook in Radarange Ov covered, on Full Power for 2 minutes.
2. Add remaining ingredients. Cook in Radarange Oven, covered, on Full Power for about 4 to 5 minutes, or until mixture boils. Pour into jar. Refrigerate.

Fall Relish

Yield: Approx. 2 cups

1-1/2 cups finely chopped celery
1 cup finely chopped onion
3/4 cup finely chopped carrots
3/4 cup finely chopped green peppers
3/4 cup vinegar
1/2 cup sugar
1 teaspoon mustard seed
1 teaspoon salt

1. Combine all ingredients in 1-1/2-quart casserole.
2. Cook in Radarange Oven, covered, on Full Power for 10 to 15 minute or until vegetables are tender as desired. Ladle into containers and se

Spiced Apples

Yield: 4 to 6 servings

1-1/2 cups sugar
1 cup vinegar
1 cup water
1/2 cup red cinnamon hots candy
2 sticks cinnamon
1-1/2 teaspoons whole cloves
1-1/2 teaspoons whole allspice
1 lb. apples, cored and sliced into 1/4-inch slices

1. Combine all ingredients, except apples, in 2-quart casserole. Cook in Radarange Oven, covered, on Full Power for 10 minutes, or until mixt boils and candies are dissolved.
2. Add apples. Cook in Radarange Oven, covered, on Full Power for 3 minutes, or until apples are tender. Place apples in separate container Remove spices from syrup. Pour syrup over apples and refrigerate.

Spiced Pears

Yield: 1-1/2 quarts

2 cups water
2/3 cup white vinegar
2 cups sugar
2 (1 lb. 13 oz. each) cans Bartlett pears
Cinnamon sticks

1. Combine water, vinegar and sugar in 1 to 1-1/2-quart casserole. Cook Radarange Oven, covered, on Full Power for 7 to 9 minutes, or until mixture boils and sugar is dissolved.
2. Place pears in 1-1/2-quart casserole. Heat in Radarange Oven on Full Power for 2 minutes, or until warmed. Pack into jars. Add one stick cinnamon to each jar. Pour syrup over pears. Refrigerate one week before using.
   MICRO-TIP: Add red or green food coloring to syrup before pouring o fruit, if desired.

The Radarange Oven is a "natural" for the preparation of many desserts ranging from simple puddings to fruit crisps and custards.

Puddings will become popular desserts after you try them in the Radarange Oven. You'll find that they are fun to prepare in your glass measuring cups. Also, there is no scorching!

Custards can also be made with ease. Just remember not to overcook them. If overcooked, they will curdle and separate.

Fruits and fruit desserts are easily made in the Radarange Oven. Due to the short amount of cooking time fruits retain their fresh flavor.

In this chapter, you'll find recipes for the above mentioned desserts, as well as others, such as impressive cheesecakes. Many desserts can be prepared and cooked in minutes in the Radarange Oven! Cakes, cookies, candies and pies can be found in separate chapters in this cookbook. The "Radarange Oven Extras" chapter includes directions for rehydrating dried fruits, as well as for toasting nuts that can be used for dessert toppings.

Be sure to read the general hints before cooking desserts in the Radarange Oven.

General Hints for Cooking Desserts

1. Fruits
   Fruits are generally cooked covered. Follow the recipe instructions for the types of utensils and coverings recommended. Pierce the skins of fresh fruits or peel them before cooking. Cooking times are approximations, since the age, size and shape of fruits can affect the amount of cooking time. The amount of sugar and spices in fruit recipes can be adjusted, as desired.

   Canned fruits can be warmed in the Radarange Oven, if desired. Fruits can also be rehydrated easily in the Radarange Oven. For directions on how to rehydrate dried fruits, see the "Radarange Oven Extras" chapter, on page 182.

2. Puddings
   Puddings are easily prepared in the Radarange Oven. Avoid using non-fat-dry milk in the preparation of puddings. Puddings will not "set" properly if non-fat-dry milk is used. Skim milk can be used for making puddings and is often preferred by calorie-watchers. Stirring is required during cooking to avoid lumping.

   Puddings can be prepared directly in glass measures for convenience. Be sure to use a large enough utensil when preparing puddings to avoid spill-overs. A general rule to follow is: use a utensil which is about twice as large as the amount of pudding to be cooked. Prepare commercial packaged puddings, according to the directions on page 142. Canned puddings can be warmed on Full Power for a few seconds to give them a "freshly-made" taste.

3. Other Desserts
   Commercial ice cream can be softened in the Radarange Oven if it is frozen too solidly to easily scoop. It should be softened at a lower Cookmatic Level to avoid melting. Place the loosened carton (1/2 gallon) in the Radarange Oven and heat on Cookmatic Level 2 for 4 to 6 minutes, or until softened. Be careful not to melt.

   Frozen unbaked pastry-type desserts do not bake with good results in a microwave oven. The pastry tends to become soggy.

FROZEN FRUIT DEFROSTING CHART

PACKAGE SIZE	UTENSIL	DEFROSTING TIME ON DEFROST*
10 oz.	1-quart casserole	3-1/2 to 4-1/2 min.
20 oz.	1-1/2-quart casserole	8 to 10 min.

*On dial models, use Cookmatic Level 3 for defrosting.

General Instructions for Defrosting Fruit
1. Place the fruit in the utensil recommended on the chart. Cover the fruit with a glass lid or plastic wrap.
2. Defrost, according to the amount of time recommended on the chart. Stir the fruit halfway through the cooking time to break the fruit apart and rearrange.

Baked Grapefruit

Yield: 2 servings

1 grapefruit, cut in half
2 teaspoons brown sugar
1 teaspoon butter or margarine

1. Cut around each grapefruit section with sharp knife. Remove seeds. Sprinkle brown sugar over top. Dot with butter. Place grapefruit halve on paper plate or in 1-quart glass casserole.
2. Cook in Radarange Oven on Full Power for 1-1/2 to 2-1/2 minutes, or until heated through. Serve warm.
MICRO-TIP: Maraschino cherries may be placed in centers of grapefru halves for added color.

Baked Apples

Yield: 4 servings

4 medium apples, cored
1/4 cup sugar
Butter or margarine

1. Slice thin circle of peel from top of each apple. Arrange apples in 9 x 2-inch round dish. Spoon 1 tablespoon sugar into each apple cavity. Place small piece of butter on each apple, as desired. Cover with plast wrap.
2. Cook in Radarange Oven, covered, on Full Power for 3 to 4 minutes, c until apples are tender. Let apples stand few minutes before serving.
MICRO-TIP: Apples may be filled with mincemeat, whole cranberry sauce or raisins and nuts, if desired. Increase cooking time by 1 to 2 minutes.

Fruit-Flavor Gelatin

Yield: 4 servings

1 cup water
1 (3 oz.) pkg. fruit flavor gelatin
1 cup cold water

1. Place water in 1-quart casserole or glass measure. Heat in Radarange Oven on Full Power for 1-1/2 to 2 minutes, or until boiling.
2. Add gelatin. Stir until dissolved. Add cold water. Chill until set.
MICRO-TIP: For a 6 oz. pkg. of gelatin, double the amount of water an heating time.

Chilled Fruit Cup

Yield: 6 to 8 servings

1 cup water
2 tablespoons sugar
3 tablespoons quick-cooking tapioca
Dash salt
1 (6 oz.) can undiluted frozen orange juice concentrate
1-1/2 cups water
1 (10 oz.) pkg. frozen raspberries
1 tablespoon lemon juice
3 oranges, peeled and cubed
3 bananas, peeled and sliced

1. Mix together 1 cup water, sugar, tapioca and salt in 2-quart casserole. Cook in Radarange Oven, covered, on Full Power for 2 to 3 minutes, or until mixture boils. Stir halfway through cooking time.
2. Blend in orange juice concentrate and water. Chill for 1/2 hour.
3. Blend in raspberries and lemon juice. Refrigerate 6 hours or overnight. Add oranges and bananas when completely chilled.

Cheerleader Cheesecake

Yield: 12 to 15 servings

1/2 cup butter or margarine
2 cups graham cracker crumbs
1/2 cup sugar
1/2 teaspoon cinnamon
3 (8 oz. each) pkgs. cream cheese
5 eggs
1 cup sugar
1/2 teaspoon vanilla
2-1/2 cups dairy sour cream
1/3 cup sugar
1-1/2 teaspoons vanilla

1. Place butter in 2-quart utility dish. Heat in Radarange Oven on Full Power for 1 minute, or until melted. Blend in crumbs, sugar and cinnamon.
2. Press crumb mixture firmly against bottom and sides of dish. Cook in Radarange Oven on Full Power for 1-1/2 minutes, or until firm.
3. Beat cream cheese until smooth. Beat in eggs, one at a time. Mix in sugar and vanilla, until smooth and creamy. Pour over crust. Cook in Radarange Oven on Cookmatic Level 8 for 12 to 15 minutes, or until knife inserted near center comes out clean.*
4. Combine sour cream, sugar and vanilla. Blend well. Pour mixture over cheesecake. Cook in Radarange Oven on Full Power for 1-1/2 to 2-1/2 minutes, or until outer edge is set. Chill.

MICRO-TIPS:

• Glazed fresh fruit or fruit pie fillings such as strawberry, cherry or blueberry may be spread over top after chilled.

* You may want to turn dish halfway through cooking time.

Peachy Cheese Torte

Yield: 12 servings

1/2 cup butter or margarine, softened
1/3 cup brown sugar, firmly packed
1/2 teaspoon vanilla
3/4 cup all-purpose flour
2/3 cup finely chopped pecans
2 (8 oz. each) pkgs. cream cheese
2 eggs
1/2 cup sugar
1 teaspoon vanilla
1 teaspoon cinnamon
1 (29 oz.) can peach slices, drained
1 tablespoon brown sugar
1/2 teaspoon cinnamon

1. Beat butter, sugar and vanilla until well-blended. Gradually add flour and beat until well-blended. Stir in pecans. Press mixture firmly against bottom and sides of 2-quart utility dish. Cook in Radarange Oven on Cookmatic Level 7 for 3 to 4 minutes, or until firm.
2. Beat cream cheese until smooth. Beat in eggs, one at a time. Mix in sugar, vanilla and cinnamon until smooth and creamy. Pour over crust. Arrange peach slices on top of cheese mixture. Sprinkle with brown sugar and cinnamon.
3. Cook in Radarange Oven on Cookmatic Level 8 for 8 to 10 minutes, or until outer edge is set. Chill.

Marvelous Marble Cheesecake

Yield: 6 to 8 servings

1/4 cup butter or margarine
1 cup vanilla wafer crumbs
1/4 cup sugar
4 (3 oz. each) pkgs. cream cheese
2 eggs
1/2 cup sugar
1 teaspoon vanilla
1/3 cup semi-sweet chocolate
    morsels*
1 tablespoon milk

1. Place butter in 9 x 2-inch glass pie plate. Cook in Radarange Oven or Full Power for 30 to 40 seconds, or until melted. Stir in crumbs and cup sugar. Blend well.
2. Press crumb mixture firmly against bottom and sides of pie plate. Co in Radarange Oven on Full Power for 1 minute, or until bubbling near edges.
3. Beat cream cheese until smooth. Beat in eggs, one at a time. Beat in sugar and vanilla until smooth and creamy. Pour over crust.
4. Place chocolate morsels in 1-cup glass measure or small dish. Heat in Radarange Oven on Full Power for 1 to 2 minutes, or until melted. St halfway through cooking time. Stir in milk until well-blended. Spoon mixture over cream cheese filling. Use fork and lightly swirl chocolate into filling, using minimum number of strokes.
5. Cook in Radarange Oven on Cookmatic Level 8 for 3 to 4 minutes, or until outer edge is set.** Chill.
   MICRO-TIPS:
   *1/3 cup butterscotch morsels may be substituted for chocolate morsels.
   **You may want to turn dish halfway through cooking time.

Pineapple Bridge Dessert

Yield: 8 to 10 servings

2/3 cup butter or margarine
1-1/2 cups vanilla wafer crumbs
2-1/2 cups crushed pineapple,
    with liquid
1 (3 oz.) pkg. lemon flavor
    gelatin
1/2 cup sugar
3 eggs, separated
1/2 cup chopped nuts
1/4 cup sugar

1. Place half of butter in 8 x 8 x 2-inch dish. Heat in Radarange Oven on Full Power for 40 to 60 seconds, or until melted. Stir in crumbs. Blend well. Press 1 cup crumb mixture firmly against bottom of dish. Reserv remaining crumbs for topping.
2. Place pineapple syrup in 1-1/2-quart glass casserole. Heat in Radarang Oven on Full Power for 2 minutes, or until boiling. Stir in gelatin until dissolved. Cool to room temperature.
3. Cream remaining butter with 1/2 cup sugar. Mix in egg yolks, one at time, beating well. Add cooled gelatin mixture, pineapple and nuts.
4. Beat egg whites until they form soft peaks. Gradually mix in 1/4 cup sugar and continue to beat until stiff. Fold egg whites into pineapple mixture. Pour into crumb-lined dish. Top with reserved crumbs. Chill until firm.

Frozen Lemon Dessert

Yield: 9 to 12 servings

3 eggs, separated
1/2 cup sugar
Dash salt
1/4 cup fresh lemon juice
1/2 teaspoon grated lemon peel
1 cup whipped cream
3/4 to 1 cup vanilla wafer crumbs

1. Set egg whites aside. Combine egg yolks, sugar and salt in 1-quart casserole. Blend well. Stir in lemon juice and lemon peel. Cook in Radarange Oven on Full Power for 1-1/2 to 3 minutes, or until mixture thickened and coats spoon. Stir mixture once or twice during cooking time. Chill.
2. Beat egg whites until stiff. Fold in whipped cream and then lemon mixture.
3. Sprinkle half of crumbs in 8 x 8 x 2-inch dish. Pour in lemon mixture. Sprinkle remaining crumbs over top. Freeze until firm.

Desserts

141

Pistachio Ice Cream Dessert

Yield: 8 to 10 servings

1/3 cup butter or margarine
3/4 cup butter flavor cracker crumbs
1 (3-3/4 oz.) pkg. instant pistachio pudding mix
3/4 cup milk
1 pint softened vanilla ice cream
1 (4-1/2 oz.) container frozen non-dairy whipped topping
2 (1-1/4 oz. each) chocolate-covered English toffee bars, crushed*

1. Place butter in 8 x 8 x 2-inch dish. Heat in Radarange Oven on Full Power for 40 to 60 seconds, or until melted.
2. Blend in cracker crumbs. Press crumb mixture evenly against bottom of dish. Cook in Radarange Oven on Full Power for 2-1/2 minutes, or until bubbling over surface.
3. Combine pudding mix and milk in large mixing bowl. Beat at high speed with electric mixer until thick. Blend in ice cream. Pour over crust. Freeze for 2 hours.
4. Top with whipped topping and candy bars. Freeze 1 additional hour.
*MICRO-TIP: Toffee bars crush more easily when cold or frozen.

Ice Cream Sundae Dessert

Yield: 12 to 15 servings

1/3 cup butter or margarine
1 (15 oz.) pkg. chocolate sandwich cookies, crushed
1/2 gallon ice cream, any flavor
1 (12 oz.) jar chocolate fudge topping

1. Place butter in large mixing bowl. Cook in Radarange Oven on Full Power for 40 to 60 seconds, or until melted. Blend together cookie crumbs and butter. Press 3/4 of crumb mixture in bottom of 9 x 13 x 2-inch conventional metal pan.
2. Allow ice cream to soften at room temperature until soft enough to spread.* Spread evenly over crumbs.
3. Pour topping into small bowl or glass measure. Heat in Radarange Oven on Full Power for 30 to 60 seconds, or until topping has thinned. Drizzle over ice cream. Sprinkle top with remaining crumbs. Freeze.
MICRO-TIPS:
- Chocolate mint and peppermint ice cream are especially good flavors to use.
* For very hard ice cream, place loosened container in Radarange Oven. Heat in Radarange Oven on Cookmatic Level 2 for 7 to 9 minutes, or until softened. Do not completely melt.

Baked Custard

Yield: 4 servings

1-3/4 cups milk
1/4 cup sugar
1/8 teaspoon salt
3 eggs, slightly-beaten
1 teaspoon vanilla

1. Place milk in 2-cup glass measure. Heat in Radarange Oven on Full Power for 3 to 4 minutes, or until hot.
2. Stir sugar and salt into eggs. Blend well. Gradually stir in hot milk and vanilla, stirring constantly. Pour mixture into 4, 6-oz. custard cups or dessert dishes. Arrange custard cups in circle in Radarange Oven.
3. Cook in Radarange Oven on Cookmatic Level 4 for 9 to 12 minutes, or until custards are set but still quivery.* Cool at room temperature. Chill, if desired.
MICRO-TIPS:
- Custards may be topped with fruit, if desired.
* You may want to rearrange custard cups halfway through cooking time.

Mocha Bread Custard

Yield: 6 servings

1/2 cup semi-sweet chocolate morsels
1/2 cup strong coffee
1-1/2 cups milk
1 tablespoon butter or margarine, melted
3 eggs, beaten
6 tablespoons sugar
1/4 teaspoon salt
1/2 teaspoon vanilla
2 cups white bread cubes
1/4 teaspoon cinnamon (optional)

1. Place chocolate morsels in 1-quart casserole. Heat in Radarange Oven Full Power for 1-1/2 to 3 minutes, or until chocolate softens.
2. Add coffee, milk and butter. Heat in Radarange Oven on Cookmatic Level 8 for 3 to 4 minutes, or until mixture can be well-blended.
3. Mix together eggs, sugar, salt and vanilla in large mixing bowl. Stir chocolate mixture into egg mixture.
4. Place bread cubes in 1-1/2-quart casserole. Pour chocolate-egg mixtu on cubes. Sprinkle with cinnamon, as desired.
5. Cook in Radarange Oven on Cookmatic Level 4 for 10 to 11 minutes, until knife inserted near center comes out clean.
MICRO-TIP: May be served warm or cold with whipped cream.

Pudding From Prepared Mix

Yield: 4 servings

1 (3-1/2 oz.) pkg. prepared pudding mix
2 cups milk

1. Place pudding in 1-quart glass measure or casserole. Stir in enough m to dissolve pudding. Stir in remaining milk.
2. Cook in Radarange Oven on Cookmatic Level 8 for 5-1/2 to 7 minute or until smooth or thickened. Stir 2 or 3 times during cooking time.

Vanilla Cream Pudding

Yield: 4 servings

2 cups milk
1/4 cup cornstarch
2/3 cup sugar
1/2 teaspoon salt
2 eggs, slightly-beaten
2 tablespoons butter or margarine
1 teaspoon vanilla

1. Place milk in 2-cup glass measure. Heat in Radarange Oven on Cookmatic Level 8 for 2-1/2 to 3 minutes, or until heated through.
2. Blend together cornstarch, sugar and salt in 1-1/2-quart casserole. Gradually stir milk into cornstarch mixture with wire whip. Cook in Radarange Oven on Cookmatic Level 8 for 3 minutes, or until thicken and glossy. Stir halfway through cooking time.
3. Beat half of hot mixture into eggs. Return to hot mixture. Cook in Radarange Oven on Cookmatic Level 8 for 1 to 2 minutes, or until mixture begins to boil.
4. Mix well with wire whip, stirring in butter and vanilla. Pour into 4, 6 o custard cups or dessert dishes.

Fancy Bread Pudding

Yield: 6 to 8 servings

3 eggs, beaten
3/4 cup sugar
1 (13 oz.) can evaporated milk
1 cup milk
1/4 teaspoon nutmeg
1/4 teaspoon cinnamon
6 cups bread cubes
1 (1 lb. 4 oz.) can apple pie filling
1 cup raisins

1. Combine eggs, sugar, milks and spices in 3-quart casserole. Stir until blended.
2. Add bread cubes, apples and raisins. Let mixture stand until bread cub have become saturated.
3. Cook in Radarange Oven on Cookmatic Level 5 for 15 to 20 minutes, until knife inserted near center comes out clean.

Minute Tapioca Pudding

Yield: 6 servings

3 tablespoons quick-cooking tapioca
1/3 cup sugar
2 cups milk
1/8 teaspoon salt
1 egg, separated
1/2 teaspoon vanilla
1 tablespoon sugar

1. Mix together tapioca, sugar, milk, salt and egg yolk in 1-1/2-quart casserole. Let stand 5 minutes.
2. Cook in Radarange Oven on Cookmatic Level 8 for 7 to 8 minutes, or until mixture boils and is thickened. Stir in vanilla.
3. Beat egg white until foamy. Gradually add sugar, beating until mixture forms soft peaks. Fold into pudding mixture. Serve warm or chilled.

Light 'N' Fruity Tapioca

Yield: 6 servings

2 cups skim milk
1/4 cup sugar
1/4 cup quick-cooking tapioca
1/4 teaspoon salt
2 eggs, separated
2 tablespoons sugar
1 teaspoon vanilla
2 cups sliced, fresh or canned fruit

1. Place milk in 1-quart glass measure or casserole. Add 1/4 cup sugar, tapioca, salt and egg yolks. Blend well. Cook in Radarange Oven on Cookmatic Level 8 for 5-1/2 to 6 minutes, or until mixture begins to boil. Stir well after 4 minutes of cooking.
2. Beat egg whites until frothy. Gradually add sugar, beating until mixture forms soft peaks. Beat in vanilla. Fold into pudding mixture. Cool. Chill, if desired.
3. Spoon fruit into 6 serving dishes. Top with pudding.
   MICRO-TIPS:
   • This pudding has only 100 calories per serving.
   • Pudding servings may be topped with mandarin orange slices and maraschino cherries for colorful desserts.

Mocha Mousse

Yield: 5 to 6 servings

2 tablespoons water
1-1/2 teaspoons unflavored gelatin
1/2 cup evaporated milk
1/2 cup milk
2 (1 oz. each) squares unsweetened chocolate
3/4 cup sugar
1 teaspoon instant coffee
1/2 teaspoon salt
1 teaspoon vanilla
2 cups heavy cream

1. Soften gelatin in water.
2. Place milks and chocolate in 2-cup glass measure. Heat in Radarange Oven on Cookmatic Level 8 for 3 to 4 minutes, or until chocolate is melted. Blend in gelatin mixture, stirring until dissolved.
3. Blend in sugar, instant coffee and salt with wire whip, stirring until dissolved and smooth. Stir in vanilla. Cool.
4. Beat cream until it piles softly. Fold chocolate mixture into whipped cream. Pour mixture into freezer tray or mold. Freeze until firm, about 3 to 4 hours. Before serving, allow to soften slightly in refrigerator.

Pot de Creme

Yield: 6 to 8 servings

1-1/4 cups light cream
1 (6 oz.) pkg. semi-sweet chocolate morsels
1/4 cup sugar
3 eggs, separated
1 teaspoon vanilla
1/4 teaspoon salt
1/2 teaspoon vanilla
1/4 teaspoon cream of tartar
1/3 cup sugar

1. Combine light cream, chocolate morsels and sugar in 1-quart glass measure or casserole. Heat in Radarange Oven on Full Power for 2-1/2 to 4 minutes, or until chocolate is melted. Mix thoroughly. Stir once or twice during cooking time.
2. Beat together egg yolks, vanilla and salt until thick and lemon-colored. Beat chocolate mixture into egg yolks. Chill.
3. Beat egg whites, vanilla and cream of tartar until frothy. Gradually add sugar, beating until mixture forms stiff peaks. Fold into chocolate mixture. Chill in custard cups or dessert dishes.
   MICRO-TIP: 2 to 3 teaspoons of orange liqueur may be added to chocolate mixture, if desired.

Easy Rice Pudding

Yield: 4 to 6 servings

1 cup quick-cooking rice
1 (3-3/4 oz.) pkg. vanilla pudding mix
1/2 teaspoon cinnamon (optional)
1/4 teaspoon salt
3 cups milk
1/2 cup raisins (optional)
Nutmeg (optional)

1. Combine rice, pudding mix, cinnamon and salt in 2-1/2 to 3-quart casserole. Stir in milk gradually.
2. Cook in Radarange Oven, covered, on Cookmatic Level 8 for 7 to 9 minutes, or until mixture begins to boil. Stir halfway through cooking time with wire whip.
3. Stir in raisins. Sprinkle with nutmeg, as desired. Serve warm or chilled.
MICRO-TIP: Try French vanilla pudding for a richer flavor.

Butterscotch Pudding Parfait

Yield: 4 servings

3/4 cup brown sugar, firmly packed
2 tablespoons cornstarch
1/4 teaspoon salt
1 cup milk
1 cup evaporated milk
1 egg, slightly-beaten
2 tablespoons butter or margarine
1 teaspoon vanilla
3/4 cup crumbled macaroons

1. Combine sugar, cornstarch and salt in 1-quart glass measure or casserole. Gradually stir in milks. Cook in Radarange Oven on Cookmatic Level 8 for 5 to 6 minutes, or until thickened and bubbly.
2. Stir half of hot mixture into egg, stirring constantly. Return to hot mixture. Cook in Radarange Oven on Cookmatic Level 8 for 30 to 60 seconds, or until mixture begins to boil.
3. Stir in butter and vanilla. In 4 dessert dishes, alternate pudding and crumbled macaroons to make parfaits.

Pineapple-Banana Sundae

Yield: 6 servings

3 tablespoons butter or margarine
1/4 cup brown sugar, firmly packed
1 (20 oz.) can crushed pineapple in heavy syrup, undrained
1 teaspoon cinnamon
1/2 teaspoon mace
2 tablespoons water
1 tablespoon cornstarch
3 bananas, halved and sliced crosswise
1/4 cup chopped walnuts
Vanilla ice cream

1. Place butter and brown sugar in 1-1/2-quart dish. Heat in Radarange Oven on Full Power for 30 to 40 seconds, or until melted.
2. Add pineapple with syrup and spices to sugar mixture. Add cornstarch mixed with water. Heat in Radarange Oven on Full Power for 4 to 5 minutes, or until mixture boils. Stir once or twice during cooking time.
3. Place bananas in pineapple mixture and stir gently. Sprinkle with walnuts. Cook in Radarange Oven on Full Power for 2 minutes, or until heated through. Serve over vanilla ice cream, as desired.
MICRO-TIP: Sprinkle with additional nuts, if desired.

Heavenly Tarts

Yield: Filling for 6 tarts

6 (1-1/2 oz. each) filled chocolate almond bars, cut into small pieces
1/4 cup butter or margarine
1/4 cup milk
1 cup shredded coconut
6 baked tart shells
Whipped cream (optional)
Almonds (optional)

1. Place chocolate bars in 1-quart casserole. Add butter and milk. Heat in Radarange Oven, covered, on Cookmatic Level 6 for 4 to 5 minutes, or until chocolate bars are melted. Stir once during cooking time.
2. Add coconut. Mix well and spoon into tart shells. Chill before serving. Top each with whipped cream and almonds, if desired.

Fruit Crisp Topping

Yield: Topping for one fruit crisp recipe

2/3 cup all-purpose flour
1/2 cup quick-cooking rolled oats
1/4 cup chopped nuts
3 tablespoons brown sugar
1/2 teaspoon cinnamon
1/4 teaspoon nutmeg
1/4 cup butter or margarine

Combine flour, oats, nuts, brown sugar and spices in mixing bowl. Cut in butter with pastry blender. Cook on the following fruit crisp desserts.

Cherry Crisp

Yield: 6 servings

Fruit Crisp Topping*
1 (1 lb. 5 oz.) can prepared cherry pie filling
1/2 teaspoon almond extract

1. Press half of topping mixture into bottom of 8 x 8 x 2-inch dish.
2. Combine pie filling and almond extract. Spread evenly over crumb layer. Sprinkle remaining topping mixture over filling.
3. Cook in Radarange Oven on Full Power for 5 to 7 minutes, or until bubbling.

   *MICRO-TIP: See the "Fruit Crisp Topping" recipe on this page.

Strawberry-Rhubarb Crisp

Yield: 8 servings

4 cups rhubarb, cut in 1/2-inch pieces
1-1/2 cups sliced strawberries
1 cup sugar
1 tablespoon lemon juice
1 tablespoon quick-cooking tapioca
Fruit Crisp Topping*

1. Combine rhubarb, strawberries, sugar, lemon juice and tapioca in 8 x 8 x 2-inch dish. Sprinkle topping mixture over fruit.
2. Cook in Radarange Oven on Full Power for 10 to 12 minutes, or until rhubarb is tender.

   MICRO-TIPS:

   • May be served warm or cold with whipped cream or vanilla ice cream.

   * See the "Fruit Crisp Topping" recipe on this page.

Peach Crisp

Yield: 6 to 8 servings

1 (18 oz.) pkg. oatmeal cookie mix
1/2 cup shredded coconut
1/2 cup butter or margarine
6 medium peaches, peeled and sliced (4 cups)*
1 cup brown sugar, firmly packed
2 teaspoons lemon juice
2 tablespoons all-purpose flour
1/2 teaspoon cinnamon
2 tablespoons butter or margarine

1. Combine cookie mix and coconut in mixing bowl. Cut in butter with pastry blender. Press half of topping mixture into bottom of 2-quart utility dish. Set aside remaining topping mixture.
2. Combine peaches, brown sugar, lemon juice, flour and cinnamon in mixing bowl. Spread peach mixture over crust. Dot with butter. Sprinkle remaining topping mixture over filling.
3. Cook in Radarange Oven on Full Power for 6 to 8 minutes, or until peaches are tender.

   *MICRO-TIP: To make an "Easy Peach or Apple Crisp," 2 (21 oz. each) cans peach or apple pie filling can be substituted for the fresh peaches. Dot with only cinnamon and butter in step #2. Use "Fruit Crisp Topping," on this page instead of topping in step #1. Bake in Radarange Oven on Full Power for 4 to 6 minutes, or until bubbling.

Fruit Soup

Yield: 6 to 8 servings

1 (12 oz.) pkg. dried apricots
1/2 lemon, thinly sliced
1/2 cup raisins
2 quarts water
1 cup sugar
2 tablespoons quick-cooking tapioca
1/2 teaspoon salt
3 cinnamon sticks

1. Combine apricots, lemon slices, raisins and water in 3 to 4-quart casserole. Stir in sugar, tapioca, salt and cinnamon sticks. Cover with glass lid.
2. Cook in Radarange Oven, covered, on Full Power for 15 minutes. The cook on Cookmatic Level 5 for 20 to 25 minutes, or until fruit is tend Serve warm or chilled.

Peach-Pineapple Cobbler

Yield: 6 to 8 servings

1 (21 oz.) can peach pie filling
1 (8-1/2 oz.) can crushed pineapple, with liquid
1 cup all-purpose flour
2 tablespoons sugar
2 teaspoons baking powder
1/2 teaspoon grated orange peel
1/4 cup butter or margarine
1/4 cup milk
1 egg, slightly-beaten
Cinnamon

1. Combine pie filling and pineapple with liquid in 8 x 8 x 2-inch dish. C in Radarange Oven on Full Power for 6 to 8 minutes. Stir halfway through cooking time.
2. Combine flour, sugar, baking powder and orange peel in mixing bowl. Cut in butter with pastry blender.
3. Add milk and egg. Mix lightly with fork until just blended. Drop dough by tablespoons onto fruit. Sprinkle with cinnamon, as desired.
4. Cook in Radarange Oven on Full Power for 5 to 7 minutes, or until dough is fully cooked.

Apple Brown Betty

Yield: 6 to 8 servings

6 medium apples, pared, cored and sliced
1/2 cup raisins
1/2 cup chopped walnuts
1/3 cup honey
1/4 cup brown sugar, firmly packed
3 tablespoons all-purpose flour
2 tablespoons lemon juice
1 teaspoon cinnamon
1/4 teaspoon nutmeg
1/2 cup quick-cooking rolled oats
1/2 cup whole wheat flour
1/2 cup wheat germ
1/4 cup brown sugar, firmly packed
1 teaspoon cinnamon
1/4 cup butter or margarine

1. Combine apples, raisins, walnuts, honey, brown sugar, flour, lemon ju cinnamon and nutmeg in 8 x 8 x 2-inch dish.
2. Combine remaining dry ingredients in mixing bowl. Cut in butter with pastry blender. Sprinkle over top of apple mixture.
3. Cook in Radarange Oven on Full Power for 6 to 8 minutes, or until apples are tender.

Some-Mores

Yield: 1 serving

1 graham cracker
1 marshmallow
1/2 milk chocolate candy bar

1. Break graham cracker in half and place one half on paper plate. Top with chocolate and then marshmallow.
2. Heat in Radarange Oven on Full Power for 20 seconds, or until marshmallow and chocolate are melted. Top with second half of graha cracker.

You will be most pleased with cakes cooked in the Radarange Oven because they are very moist, light, and have a full volume. Undercook cakes rather than overcook them in order to prevent dehydration. The "carry-over" cooking of cakes is greater in microwave cooking than in conventional cooking. After cakes stand for several minutes, they will be ready to serve. Moisture which appears on the tops of cakes after cooking will disappear during the "carry-over cooking" time.

Cakes will not become brown when cooked in a microwave oven due to the short cooking time. Since most cakes are frosted or served with a topping, however, this lack of browning is generally not noticed.

Read the baking hints before cooking cakes in the Radarange Oven.

General Hints for Baking Cakes

1. **All testing for cakes in this chapter was done using glass utensils. When a plastic or ceramic utensil is used, cooking times may need to be shortened or lengthened respectively.**
2. Dish shapes can affect cake results. Circular dishes provide best cooking results. Arrange cupcakes in a circle, if baking them in custard cups. Use circular-shaped cupcake trays.
3. If you do not have a ceramic or plastic Bundt® dish, you can "create" one by placing a 2 to 3-inch diameter drinking glass in a 3 or 4-quart casserole. Pour the cake batter around the glass.

4. If you want to turn a cake out of the dish and onto a serving platter grease the dish or, for best results, line it with waxed paper before baking. This will allow easy removal of the cake. Do not use flour when greasing a dish since it will tend to lump in the bottom of the dish. Avoid using spray-on vegetable coating, as it makes cakes sticky.
5. You may wish to decrease the amount of batter slightly when cooking microwave oven cakes. Dishes should be about half-filled with batter. Excess batter can be used for baking cupcakes. See the chart, on page 149.
6. Cook cake layers separately, one at a time. The same dish may be used, if desired. Use a fresh piece of waxed paper when cooking the second layer.
7. Cakes should be cooked on Full Power for best results. You may want to turn some cakes halfway through cooking time.
8. You may wish to open the Radarange Oven door and turn cake dishes or rearrange cupcakes. Cakes will not "fall" when the Radarange Oven door is opened as they will if a conventional oven door is opened. Since microwave cooking is a "cool" type of cooking, there is no heat build-up within the Radarange Oven. The only heat is within the food itself. Since the air surrounding the cake inside the Radarange Oven remains cool, there is no air pressure change when the door is opened, as there is when the door of a conventional oven is opened. Therefore, cakes will not "fall."
9. Cakes are done when a toothpick inserted near the center comes out clean or when the top springs back when lightly pressed with a finger. Cakes may appear slightly moist after cooking. "Moisture" is not "raw" batter. This moisture will disappear when the cake stands for 3 to 5

minutes after cooking. Remember to allow for this "carry-over cooking" time.

10. Due to the short amount of cooking time microwave oven-cooked cakes will not brown. By using frosting or toppings, however, the lack of browning is not noticed, and cakes look very attractive. Try some of the frosting recipes in this chapter or one of your own favorites. Confectioners' sugar, a mixture of cinnamon and sugar, nuts or coconut may be sprinkled over the top of a cake. Sauces, fruit toppings and fresh or frozen fruit may be served over cake. Even pudding can be used as a topping for cake!

11. Cook frosting in a large enough utensil to avoid boil-overs. Glass measures may be used. Frosting will spread more evenly and easily after the cake's "carry-over cooking" time. The cake's surface should be slightly dry. Also, the cake can be cooled for a short time in the refrigerator before frosting. The cake's surface should be cool enough to prevent the frosting from melting.

12. Fruit cakes will require a longer cooking time than most cakes since the batter is dense.

13. Due to the short cooking time, angel food cakes or cakes leavened entirely with egg whites will not bake with good results in a microwave oven.

14. Cake batter from a mix may be stored in the refrigerator, if you wish to cook one layer first and cook the other later.

15. For coffee cake recipes, see the "Breads" chapter.

16. When cooking one of your own favorite cakes in the Radarange Oven, use one of the recipes in this chapter as a guide. You may get better results if the amount of liquid is decreased by about 1/4. Use the same setting and approximately the same amount of cooking time. Always slightly undercook a cake when first experimenting with your own recipe. Then, allow the cake to stand for 3 to 5 minutes. The moisture on the cake top should disappear during this "carry-over cooking" time. If necessary, the cake can be returned to the Radarange Oven for a few additional seconds (or minutes).

FROZEN CONVENIENCE CAKE DEFROSTING CHART

CAKE TYPE	SIZE	DEFROSTING TIME ON DEFROST*
Cake	10 to 11-1/2 oz.	1-1/2 to 2-1/2 min.
	12 to 14 oz.	2 to 3 min.
	16 to 18 oz.	2 to 3-1/2 min.
Pound Cake	10 to 11 oz.	2 to 3 min.

*On models having dial timers, use Cookmatic Level 3 for defrosting.

General Instructions for Defrosting Frozen Cakes

1. Remove the cake from the container, if metal. Place the cake on a plastic rack or a paper plate. Cover with a paper towel, if not frosted.

2. Defrost, according to the time on the chart. Do not melt the frosting.

Chocolate Icing Deluxe

Yield: Frosting for 3 dozen cupcakes or 1, 2-layer cake

1 large egg
2 cups confectioner's sugar
2 (1 oz. each) squares unsweetened chocolate
1/4 teaspoon salt
1/3 cup butter or margarine, softened
1 teaspoon vanilla

1. Beat egg with electric mixer until fluffy. Continue to beat while adding sugar gradually.

2. Place chocolate in 1-cup glass measure or small custard cup. Heat in Radarange Oven on Full Power for 2 to 3 minutes, or until melted.

3. Stir salt, butter and chocolate into egg and sugar mixture. Beat until smooth and creamy. Stir in vanilla.

CUPCAKE BAKING CHART*

QUANTITY OF CUPCAKES	BAKING TIME ON FULL POWER
1	10 to 15 sec.
2	20 to 30 sec.
4	35 to 45 sec.
6	50 sec. to 1 min., 10 sec.

*Any flavor or type of cupcake may be cooked according to the times on this chart.

General Instructions for Baking Cupcakes

1. Place the cupcake batter in glass custard cups or in compartments of a plastic muffin tray. Fill custard cups or tray compartments with 2 level tablespoons of batter. For trays having holes in the bottom, paper liners should be used. When using custard cups, arrange them in a circle, rather than in rows on the Radarange Oven glass tray. If a plastic tray is used, the cooking time may need to be shortened.
2. Cook in the Radarange Oven on Full Power according to the time on the chart. Remove the cupcakes from the custard cups or the plastic tray immediately after baking. If the cupcakes are not removed, a small amount of moisture will collect on the cupcake bottoms, causing the paper liners and cupcake bottoms to become soggy.
3. Be careful not to overcook cupcakes. Cupcakes will appear slightly moist when done. Allow cupcakes to set on a cooling rack for 2 to 3 minutes, after cooking.

White Mountain Frosting

Yield: Frosting for 3 dozen cupcakes, or 1, 2-layer cake

1/2 cup sugar
1/4 cup light corn syrup
2 tablespoons water
2 egg whites
1 teaspoon vanilla

1. Combine sugar, corn syrup and water in 1-quart casserole. Cook in Radarange Oven on Full Power for about 3 to 4 minutes, or until soft ball stage is reached.*
2. Beat egg whites until stiff peaks form. Pour hot syrup in thin stream and then vanilla into egg whites, while beating. Beat until stiff peaks form. Spread on cake.

   *MICRO-TIP: The soft ball stage is described on page 176.

Chocolate Cream Cheese Frosting

Yield: Frosting for 1, 8 x 12-inch cake

1 (6 oz.) pkg. semi-sweet chocolate morsels
1/4 cup butter or margarine
1 (3 oz.) pkg. cream cheese, softened
1 teaspoon vanilla
1/4 teaspoon salt
2-1/2 to 2-3/4 cups sifted confectioner's sugar

1. Place chocolate morsels and butter in 2-cup glass measure. Heat in Radarange Oven on Full Power for 1 minute, or until melted.
2. Beat cream cheese in small mixing bowl until smooth. Beat in melted chocolate. Add vanilla and salt.
3. Gradually beat in confectioners' sugar. Beat until frosting is smooth and of spreading consistency.

Cakes

CONVENIENCE CAKE MIX BAKING CHART

TYPE OF CAKE MIX	PKG. SIZE	DISH SIZE	COOKING TIME ON FULL POWER
Boston Cream Pie Cake Mix	15 to 16 ozs.	9-inch round	3 to 3-1/2 min.**
Bundt® Cake Mix	22 to 23 ozs.	12-cup Bundt® dish*	6-1/2 to 7-1/2 min.**
	26 to 28 ozs.	12-cup Bundt® dish*	7-1/2 to 8-1/2 min.**
Chocolate Cake Mix	9 ozs.	8 x 8 x 2-inch or 9-inch round	3 to 4 min.**
	18 to 20 ozs.	2 (8 x 8 x 2) or 2 (9-inch round)	3 to 3-1/2 min.** (one layer at a time)
Pineapple Upside Down Cake Mix	21 to 22 ozs.	8 x 8 x 2-inch or 9-inch round	5 to 6 min.**
Pound Cake Mix	16 ozs.	2 (8-1/2 x 4-1/2 x 2-1/2-inch) loaf dishes	2-1/2 to 3 min.** (one loaf at a time)
Pudding Cake Dessert Mix Chocolate	11 ozs.	8 x 8 x 2-inch or 9-inch round	4-1/2 to 5-1/2 min.**
Lemon	11 ozs.	8 x 8 x 2-inch or 9-inch round	4 to 5 min.**
Snack Cake Mix	13 to 15 ozs.	8 x 8 x 2-inch or 9-inch round	3 to 4-1/2 min.**
Stir and Frost Mix	11 to 13-1/2 ozs.	Use paperboard box provided with mix	2 to 3 min.**
Streusel Swirl Cake Mix	27 to 28 ozs.	10-cup Bundt® dish*	7-1/2 to 8-1/2 min.**
Yellow, White or Other	9 ozs.	8 x 8 x 2-inch or 9-inch round	3 to 3-1/2 min.**
Flavor Cake Mixes	18 to 20 ozs.	2 (8 x 8 x 2-inch) or 2 (9-inch round)	3 to 3-1/2 min.** (one layer at a time)
	18 to 20 ozs.	10-cup Bundt® dish*	6 to 7 min.**

*3-quart, round casserole with 2-inch diameter glass in center may also be used.

**With some cake mixes and with some cake dishes, you may want to turn dish halfway through cooking time.

General Instructions for Cooking Convenience Cake Mixes

1. Prepare the cake mix, according to the package instructions. For best results, use 1/4 less liquid than recommended on the package. Grease the dish, but do not flour. Line the bottom of the dish with waxed paper, if desired, for easy removal of the cake after cooking.

2. Cook, according to the instructions on the chart. The cake is done when a toothpick inserted in the center comes out clean or when the top springs back when lightly pressed with a finger.

Coconut-Pecan Frosting

Yield: Frosting for 1, 2-layer or 1, 3-layer cake

1/2 cup butter or margarine
1 cup evaporated milk
1 cup sugar
3 egg yolks
1 teaspoon vanilla
1-1/3 cups flaked coconut
1 cup chopped pecans

1. Place butter in 1-1/2-quart casserole. Heat in Radarange Oven on Full Power for 1 minute, or until melted.
2. Blend milk, sugar, egg yolks and vanilla into butter. Cook in Radarange Oven on Cookmatic Level 8 for 5 to 8 minutes, or until thickened. Stir occasionally during cooking.
3. Add coconut and pecans. Stir until cooled and of spreading consistency.
   MICRO-TIP: This is the traditional frosting for German Chocolate Cake. (See recipe, this page.)

German Chocolate Cake

Yield: 1, 3-layer cake

1 (4 oz.) pkg. German's sweet chocolate
1/2 cup hot water
1 cup butter or margarine
2 cups sugar
4 egg yolks
1 teaspoon vanilla
2-1/2 cups cake flour or 2-1/4 cups all-purpose flour
1 teaspoon baking soda
1/2 teaspoon salt
1 cup buttermilk
4 egg whites, stiffly-beaten

1. Place chocolate in 1-quart casserole. Heat in Radarange Oven on Cookmatic Level 6 for 4-1/2 to 5 minutes, or until melted. Stir in water. Blend well.
2. Cream butter and sugar in large mixing bowl. Add egg yolks, one at a time. Beat well after each addition. Blend in chocolate and then vanilla.
3. Sift together flour, soda and salt
4. Add sifted mixture alternately with buttermilk to chocolate mixture, beating after each addition. Fold in egg whites. Line bottoms of 3 9 x 2-inch round dishes with waxed paper. Evenly distribute batter among dishes. Cook each layer separately.
5. Cook in Radarange Oven on Full Power for 5 to 6 minutes, or until center springs back when lightly pressed with finger.* Repeat with remaining layers.
   MICRO-TIPS:
   • Use "Coconut-Pecan Frosting," on this page. Frost only top of each layer.
   * You may want to turn dish halfway through cooking time.

Carrot Cake

Yield: 1, 8 x 8 x 2-inch cake

1 cup sugar
1 cup all-purpose flour
1-1/4 teaspoons cinnamon
1 teaspoon baking soda
1 teaspoon baking powder
1/2 teaspoon salt
1/4 teaspoon ginger
1/4 teaspoon ground cloves
1/2 cup vegetable oil
2 eggs
1-1/2 cups grated carrots
1/4 cup dairy sour cream

CREAM CHEESE FROSTING
1 (3 (oz.) pkg. cream cheese
1/4 cup butter or margarine
1 teaspoon vanilla
2 cups confectioners' sugar
Milk (optional)

1. Blend together all dry ingredients in large mixing bowl.
2. Stir in oil. Add eggs, one at a time, mixing well after each addition. Blend in sour cream and carrots. Pour batter into greased 8 x 8 x 2-inch dish.
3. Cook in Radarange Oven on Full Power for 7 to 9 minutes, or until top springs back when lightly pressed with finger.* Cool.
4. For frosting, beat together cream cheese, butter and vanilla. Gradually add confectioners' sugar, beating until smooth. If too thick, add few drops milk, as desired.
   *MICRO-TIP: You may want to turn dish halfway through cooking time.

Oatmeal Cinnamon Cake

Yield: 1, 8 x 12-inch cake

1-1/2 cups boiling water
1 cup quick-cooking rolled oats
1/2 cup butter or margarine
1-1/2 cups all-purpose flour
1-1/2 teaspoons cinnamon
1 teaspoon baking soda
1 teaspoon salt
1 cup brown sugar, firmly packed
3/4 cup sugar
2 eggs, beaten

TOPPING
3/4 cup brown sugar, firmly packed
6 tablespoons butter or margarine
2 tablespoons milk
1 cup shredded coconut
1/2 cup chopped pecans

1. Pour water over oats in large mixing bowl. Break butter into chunks and drop over oats. Stir mixture until butter is melted.
2. Sift together flour, cinnamon, soda and salt. Stir into oat mixture. Mix well.
3. Stir in brown sugar and sugar. Stir in eggs. Mix thoroughly. Pour into 2-quart utility dish.
4. Cook in Radarange Oven on Full Power for 8 to 9 minutes, or until top springs back when lightly pressed with finger.*
5. For topping, combine brown sugar, butter and milk in 1-1/2-quart casserole. Heat in Radarange Oven on Full Power for 1 to 1-1/2 minutes or until mixture boils. Boil for 1 additional minute.
6. Blend in coconut and pecans. Spread on cooled cake.

   *MICRO-TIP: You may want to turn dish halfway through cooking time.

Pineapple Upside-Down Cake

Yield: 1, 8 x 8 x 2-inch cake

2 tablespoons butter or margarine
1/2 cup dark brown sugar, firmly packed
1 (15-1/4 oz.) can sliced pineapple, with liquid
1 (9 oz.) pkg. one layer yellow cake mix

1. Place butter in 8 x 8 x 2-inch dish. Heat in Radarange Oven on Full Power for 20 to 30 seconds, or until melted. Blend brown sugar with butter and pack evenly into bottom of dish.
2. Drain pineapple juice into glass measure. Arrange pineapple slices over butter-brown sugar mixture.
3. Prepare cake mix, as directed on package, substituting pineapple juice for water. Pour cake batter into dish, evenly distributing batter over entire surface.
4. Cook in Radarange Oven on Full Power for 5 to 7 minutes, or until top springs back when lightly pressed with finger. While hot, invert on serving platter.
   MICRO-TIPS:
   • Crushed pineapple may be substituted for sliced.
   • For added color, place maraschino cherry in center of each pineapple ring.

Fancy Pistachio Nut Cake

Yield: 1 cake

1 cup finely chopped pecans
3/4 cup sugar
2 tablespoons cinnamon
1 (1 lb., 2 oz.) pkg. yellow cake mix
1 (3-1/2 oz.) pkg. instant pistachio pudding mix
4 eggs
1 cup dairy sour cream
3/4 cup water or orange juice
1/4 cup vegetable oil
1 teaspoon vanilla

1. Mix together nuts, sugar and cinnamon in small bowl. Sprinkle 1/3 of mixture into generously greased 10-cup glass Bundt® dish, or place 2-inch diameter glass in center of generously greased 4-quart casserole to form ring mold. Cover sides and bottom of dish.
2. Blend together cake mix, pudding, eggs, sour cream, juice, oil and vanilla in large mixing bowl. Alternate layers of batter with remaining nut mixture in dish. Swirl batter with fork.
3. Cook in Radarange Oven on Full Power for 10 to 12 minutes, or until toothpick inserted in center comes out clean.* Let stand 10 minutes. Remove glass, and invert on serving platter.

   *MICRO-TIP: You may want to turn dish halfway through cooking time.

Triple Layer Coconut Cake

Yield: 1, 9-inch 3-layer cake

2-1/4 cups sugar
3/4 cup butter or margarine, softened
3 eggs
1-1/2 teaspoons vanilla
3-1/4 cups cake flour
4 teaspoons baking powder
1-1/2 teaspoons salt
1-1/2 cups milk
1 (3 oz.) lemon pudding mix
1/2 cup sugar
2 egg yolks
2-1/4 cups water

FROSTING
1-1/2 cups sugar
1/2 cup water
1/4 teaspoon cream of tartar
4 egg whites
1 teaspoon vanilla
1 cup shredded coconut

1. Gradually beat sugar into butter in large mixing bowl. Cream mixture. Mix in eggs and vanilla.
2. Sift together flour, baking powder and salt.
3. Alternately mix dry ingredients and milk into creamed mixture, beginning and ending with flour mixture. Beat after each addition. Line bottoms of 3, 9 x 2-inch round dishes with waxed paper. Evenly distribute batter among dishes. Cook each layer separately.
4. Cook in Radarange Oven on Full Power for 4 to 5 minutes, or until center springs back when lightly pressed with finger. Edges may appear slightly moist.** Cool. Repeat with remaining layers.
5. Blend together pudding mix, sugar, egg yolks and water, according to package instructions, in 1-quart casserole. Cook in Radarange Oven on Cookmatic Level 8 for 5-1/2 to 7 minutes, or until mixture boils and is thickened. Stir twice during cooking. Cool slightly. Spread between layers of cake.
6. For frosting, combine sugar, water and cream of tartar in 1-1/2-quart casserole. Cook in Radarange Oven on Full Power for 7 to 9 minutes, or until hard ball stage is reached.* Stir occasionally during cooking time.
7. Beat egg whites until stiff, but not dry. Gradually stir hot syrup and then vanilla into egg whites, beating constantly until stiff peaks form.
8. Frost cake. Sprinkle coconut on top and sides of cake.

MICRO-TIPS:

*The hard ball stage is described on page 176.

**You may want to turn dish halfway through cooking time.

Fudge Pudding Cake

Yield: 1, 8 x 8 x 2-inch cake

2 tablespoons butter or margarine
1/2 cup sugar
1 teaspoon vanilla
1 cup all-purpose flour
3 tablespoons cocoa
1 teaspoon baking powder
1/2 teaspoon salt
1/2 cup milk
1/2 cup chopped nuts
1-2/3 cups boiling water
1/2 cup sugar
5 tablespoons cocoa
1/4 teaspoon salt
Confectioners' sugar

1. Place butter in medium-size mixing bowl or 1-1/2-quart casserole. Heat in Radarange Oven on Full Power for 20 to 30 seconds, or until melted. Stir in 1/2 cup sugar and vanilla.
2. Mix together flour, 3 tablespoons cocoa, baking powder and 1/2 teaspoon salt. Stir into sugar mixture, alternately with milk. Stir in nuts.
3. Combine water with 1/2 cup sugar, cocoa and salt in 8 x 8 x 2-inch dish. Drop batter from Step #2 by rounded tablespoons onto this hot mixture.
4. Cook in Radarange Oven on Full Power for 4-1/2 to 5-1/2 minutes, or until top springs back when lightly pressed with finger.* Sprinkle with confectioners' sugar, as desired. While still warm, spoon out servings.

MICRO-TIPS:

• May be served with whipped cream or ice cream, if desired.
* You may want to turn dish halfway through cooking time.

Lime Gelatin Delight Cake

Yield: 1,
9-inch round cake

1 (9 oz.) pkg. white cake mix
1/2 cup water
1 egg white

1 (3 oz.) pkg. lime flavor gelatin
1 cup water
1 cup whipped topping
Green crystal sugar

1. Prepare cake mix, according to package directions. Pour batter into greased 9 x 2-inch round dish. Cook in Radarange Oven on Full Power for 3 to 3-1/2 minutes, or until top springs back when lightly pressed with finger.*
2. Place water in 2-cup glass measure. Heat in Radarange Oven on Full Power for 1-1/2 to 2 minutes, or until boiling. Stir in gelatin to dissolve.
3. Poke holes in cake with toothpick. Pour gelatin over cake. Refrigerate 1 hour.
4. Spread whipped topping over cake. Sprinkle with green crystal sugar, desired.

MICRO-TIPS:
- Undissolved lime flavor gelatin may be added to topping or 1 to 2 drops green food coloring may be added to tint green.
- 1 teaspoon reserved, undiluted gelatin may be sprinkled on top.
- This is a good dessert for St. Patrick's Day or for other holidays, use other flavors of gelatin and colors of sugar.

* You may want to turn dish halfway through cooking time.

Raspberry Preserves Cake

Yield: 1, 8 x 8 x
2-inch cake

1/2 cup butter or margarine
2/3 cup sugar
1/2 cup seedless raspberry preserves
1/4 cup dairy sour cream
2 eggs
1-1/2 cups cake flour
1/2 teaspoon baking soda
1/2 teaspoon cinnamon
1/4 teaspoon salt
1/2 cup seedless raspberry preserves

RASPBERRY FROSTING (OPTIONAL)
2 tablespoons butter or margarine, melted
2 cups confectioners' sugar
1 teaspoon vanilla
1/4 cup seedless raspberry preserves

1. Cream butter and sugar in large mixing bowl.
2. Mix in 1/2 cup preserves. Blend well. Add sour cream and then eggs. Beat well.
3. Blend together flour, baking soda, cinnamon and salt. Add gradually to first mixture, beating well. Pour batter into greased 8 x 8 x 2-inch dish.
4. Cook in Radarange Oven on Full Power for 4 to 5 minutes, or until top springs back when lightly pressed with finger.* Cool. Spread top with 1/2 cup preserves.

MICRO-TIPS:
- Good when served with whipped cream or frosted with "Raspberry Frosting," instead of preserves. (See directions below.)
- For frosting, combine butter, 1 cup sugar, vanilla and preserves. Blend well. Stir in remaining sugar until smooth. Spread on cooled cake.

* You may want to turn dish halfway through cooking time.

Chocolate Layer Cake

Yield: 1, 9-inch layer cake

1/2 cup butter or margarine
2 cups sugar
2 egg yolks
1 teaspoon vanilla
2 cups cake flour
3/4 cup cocoa
3/4 teaspoon salt
1 teaspoon baking soda
1-3/4 cups milk

1. Cream butter and sugar in large mixing bowl. Add egg yolks and vanilla. Beat well.
2. Combine dry ingredients.
3. Alternately add dry ingredients and milk to creamed mixture. Line bottoms of 2, 9 x 2-inch round dishes with waxed paper. Evenly distribute batter between dishes. Cook each layer separately.
4. Cook in Radarange Oven on Full Power for 5 to 6 minutes, or until top springs back when lightly pressed with finger.* Repeat with remaining layer.

*MICRO-TIP: You may want to turn dish halfway through cooking time.

Making pies can be a real art. With little effort, you'll find that pies are a real joy to make in the Radarange Oven. Radarange Oven pie crusts are very light and flaky. You'll enjoy preparing our crust recipes. If crusts are a threat to you, there are many ready-to-bake frozen crusts. Instructions for baking frozen unbaked crusts are included in this chapter. This chapter also contains a wide variety of pie fillings.

Read the general hints for cooking pie crusts and pies before baking pies in the Radarange Oven.

General Hints for Cooking Pie Crusts

1. When mixing pie crust pastry, remember proper mixing techniques in order to achieve a tender product. Too much liquid will give a soggy crust, so use water only as needed, according to the recipe. The use of too much flour can result in a tough pie crust. Too much shortening will make a pie crust greasy and too crumbly. For best results, use a pastry blender to cut in shortening. Stir with a fork.
2. Be certain that all pie crusts are rolled to an even thickness (approximately 1/8-inch thickness).
3. Always use a glass pie plate.
4. Pie crusts will not brown in a microwave oven due to the short amount of baking time. To achieve greater browning in a pie crust:
   a. Add yellow food coloring to the pie crust dough, as desired, when mixing.
   b. Brush the pie crust with vanilla and beaten egg white before baking.
   c. Crumb crusts, such as a graham cracker crust, will have a brown appearance due to dark-colored ingredients.
5. To minimize pie crust shrinkage during baking:
   a. Allow the pie crust dough to "rest" for 3 to 5 minutes before the final shaping.
   b. Place the pie crust dough gently into a glass pie plate being careful not to stretch the dough.
   c. Prick the bottom and sides of the pie crust dough using the tines of a fork.
   d. Cover the pie crust dough with a paper towel.
   e. Place an 8-inch pie plate inside of 9-inch pie plate over the pie crust, if desired, to prevent shrinkage. (This is optional).
   f. Cook in the Radarange Oven on Full Power according to the recipe. (Crumb crusts are also cooked on Full Power.) Remove the 8-inch pie plate, if used, before the final minute of cooking time to allow the pie crust to dry.
6. Do not overcook pie crusts. Allow pie crusts to stand for a few minutes, after cooking. Pie crusts will become crisper as they cool, during this standing time or "carry-over cooking" time. Allow pie crusts to cool before adding the fillings.

General Hints for Cooking Pies

1. Always cook the pie crust before adding the filling and cooking the pie. If an unbaked crust is used, the entire

crust may not cook and it will become soggy. Frozen pies with unbaked crusts will not cook in a microwave oven with good results. These pies can be baked conventionally, frozen and later defrosted and reheated in the Radarange Oven with good results. See the "Frozen Baked Pie Defrosting Chart," on this page.

2. Cook pies in glass pie plates.
3. Cut slits in top pie crust before cooking a 2-crust pie. Remember to pre-cook the bottom crust. When adding the top crust, moisten the edges of the cooked bottom crust and tuck the edges of the top crust under to seal.
4. Pies are cooked using a variety of settings, depending upon the type of ingredients in the filling. Fruit pies are generally cooked on Full Power, while pies containing milk, eggs and other "special" or "delicate" ingredients should be cooked on a lower Cookmatic Level or setting. Custard pies, for example, require a lower setting to prevent curdling and separation.
5. Pies should be allowed to cool on cooling racks or chilled before serving. If desired, cooked pies can be reheated. See the "Baked Pie Reheating Chart," on page 157.
6. When cooking your own favorite pie or pie crust, use a recipe in this chapter as a guide. Use the same setting and approximately the same amount of cooking time. Make a note of the Radarange Oven time required on your recipe for future use.

FROZEN BAKED PIE DEFROSTING CHART***

SIZE OF PIE	DEFROSTING TIME ON DEFROST*
8-inch (20 to 30 ozs.)	12 to 15 min.**
9-inch (30 to 40 ozs.)	18 to 22 min.**
10-inch (40 to 50 ozs.)	23 to 25 min.**

*On models having dial timers, use Cookmatic Level 3 for defrosting.

**To avoid overcooking, it may not be possible to completely thaw the center of the pie. Allow 15 to 20 minutes of standing time, after defrosting, if necessary.

***The times on this chart can also be used for defrosting unbaked pies in glass pie plates. Bake the pies conventionally.

General Instructions for Defrosting Frozen Baked Pies

1. Pies need to be cooked before freezing. In all recipes, the bottom crust needs to be cooked before the filling is added. This is necessary to achieve a completely cooked flaky bottom crust. Purchased frozen pies are usually **unbaked**. For good results, bake these pies conventionally and then freeze. Later the frozen pies can be transferred to glass pie plates and quickly defrosted in the Radarange Oven. When baking pies "from scratch" bake them in glass pie plates and then freeze. Or, bake two pies, eat one and freeze the other for later use.
2. Place cooked frozen pie in glass pie plate. Do not cover. Defrost in Radarange Oven on Defrost, or Cookmatic Level 3, according to the time on the chart. Allow the pie to stand for a few minutes after defrosting, if necessary.

Frozen Pie Crust

Yield: 1, 9-inch pie crust

1, 9-inch pie crust, frozen

1. Remove pie crust from metal tin and put into 9-inch glass pie plate. L stand 10 minutes, or until softened. Prick well with tines of fork. Cov with paper towel.
2. Cook in Radarange Oven, covered, on Full Power for 1-1/2 to 2 minu or until dough is cooked and no longer moist. Cool. Fill with desired filling.

BAKED PIE REHEATING CHART

TYPE OF PIE	AMOUNT OF PIE	COOKMATIC LEVEL	REHEATING TIME*	SPECIAL INSTRUCTIONS
Fruit Pie	1 piece**	Cookmatic Level 8	30 sec. to 1 min.	
	2 pieces**	Cookmatic Level 8	1 to 2 min.	————————
	Whole Pie	Cookmatic Level 8	3 to 4 min.	
Custard Pie	1 piece**	Cookmatic Level 6	30 sec. to 40 sec.	Turn during reheating to avoid melting.
	2 pieces**	Cookmatic Level 6	45 sec. to 1 min.	
	Whole Pie	Cookmatic Level 6	2-1/2 to 3-1/2 min.	

*The reheating time in this chart is based upon reheating pies of room-temperature. Increase the reheating time slightly when reheating refrigerator-temperature pies.

**A tart can be reheated by using the same reheat timings required for one piece of the same type of pie.

General Instructions for Reheating Baked Pies

1. Defrost the baked pie first, if necessary, according to the directions on the ''Frozen Baked Pie Defrosting Chart,'' on page 156.
2. Place the pie or piece of pie on a plate or heat in the glass pie plate. Cover with a paper towel.
3. Reheat in the Radarange Oven, covered, according to the setting and time recommended on the chart. Do not reheat pies for too long. The fillings become hot very quickly.

Pastry I*

Yield: 1, 8 or 9-inch pie shell

1 cup all-purpose flour
1/2 teaspoon salt
1/3 cup shortening
1-1/2 to 2 tablespoons cold water

1. Sift together flour and salt. Cut in shortening with pastry blender or fork.
2. Stir in water, one tablespoon at a time, with fork, until dough pulls away from sides of bowl.
3. Form into smooth ball and roll out on floured board or waxed paper until 1/8-inch thick. Place in 9-inch glass pie plate. Trim and flute edge. Prick bottom and sides well with tines of fork. Cover with paper towel.
4. Cook in Radarange Oven, covered, on Full Power for 3 to 4 minutes, or until dough is cooked and no longer moist. Cool. Fill with desired filling.
   MICRO-TIPS:
   • Shell may be cooked without pricking by covering with paper towel and placing an 8-inch pie plate on paper towel to keep crust flat and prevent shrinkage.
   * Double this recipe for pastry enough to cook 1, double-crust pie. Cook the bottom crust, according to the above recipe. Cook the top crust as recommended in the pie recipe you use.

Pastry II

Yield: Pastry for 1, double-crust pie

3 cups all-purpose flour
1/2 teaspoon salt
1 cup shortening
1 egg
2 teaspoons vinegar
5 teaspoons cold water

1. Sift together flour and salt. Cut in shortening with pastry blender or f
2. Combine egg and vinegar. Add to flour mixture, stirring with fork. Ad water, one teaspoon at a time, with fork, until dough pulls away from sides of bowl.
3. Divide dough into 2 equal portions. For bottom crust, roll one of the portions into smooth ball and roll out on floured board or waxed pape until 1/8-in. thick. Place in 9-inch glass pie plate. Trim and flute edge Prick bottom and sides well with tines of fork. Cover with paper towe
4. Cook in Radarange Oven, covered, on Full Power for 3 to 4 minutes, until dough is cooked and no longer moist. Cool. Fill with desired fillir Top with remaining pastry, sealing edges and slitting top. Cook pie, according to the amount of time in the recipe.

Baking Powder Crust

Yield: 1, 10-inch pie crust

1 cup all-purpose flour
1-1/2 teaspoons baking powder
1/8 teaspoon salt
1/4 cup solid shortening
4 to 5 tablespoons milk

1. Mix together flour, baking powder and salt in small mixing bowl. Cut shortening with pastry blender or fork.
2. Stir in milk, one tablespoon at a time, with fork, until dough pulls awa from sides of bowl.
3. Form into smooth ball and roll out on floured board or waxed paper u 1/8-inch thick. Place in 10-inch glass pie plate. Trim and flute edge. Prick bottom and sides well with tines of fork. Cover with paper towe
4. Cook in Radarange Oven, covered, on Full Power for 3 to 4 minutes, until dough is cooked but still moist. Cool. Fill with desired filling.

Graham Cracker Crust

Yield: 1, 9-inch pie crust

1-1/4 cups graham cracker crumbs
1/4 cup butter or margarine, melted
1/4 cup sugar

1. Mix together all ingredients until well-blended in 9-inch glass pie plate. Press crumb mixture firmly against bottom and sides of pie plate.
2. Cook in Radarange Oven on Full Power for 1 minute, 15 seconds. Coo Fill with desired filling.

MICRO-TIP: An easy way to press cracker crumbs against bottom of 9-inch glass pie plate is to press them with an 8-inch glass pie plate.

Chocolate Crumb Crust

Yield: 1, 9-inch pie crust

1-1/4 cups chocolate wafer crumbs
1/4 cup butter or margarine, melted

1. Mix together crumbs and butter in 9-inch glass pie plate. Press crumb mixture firmly against bottom and sides of pie plate.
2. Cook in Radarange Oven on Full Power for 1 minute, 15 seconds to 1 minute, 30 seconds. Cool. Fill with desired filling.

MICRO-TIP: An easy way to press wafer crumbs against bottom of 9-i glass pie plate is to press them with an 8-inch glass pie plate.

Gingersnap Crumb Crust

Yield: 1, 9-inch pie crust

1-1/3 cups gingersnap crumbs
6 tablespoons butter or margarine

1. Mix together crumbs and butter in 9-inch glass pie plate. Press crumb mixture firmly against bottom and sides of pie plate.
2. Cook in Radarange Oven on Full Power for 1 minute, 15 seconds to 1 minute, 30 seconds. Cool. Fill with desired filling.
   MICRO-TIP: An easy way to press gingersnap crumbs against bottom of 9-inch glass pie plate is to press them with an 8-inch glass pie plate.

Chocolate-Coconut Pie Shell

Yield: 1, 9-inch pie shell

2/3 cup chocolate stars or 1/2 cup semi-sweet chocolate morsels
2 tablespoons butter or margarine
2-2/3 cup flaked coconut
2/3 cup confectioners' sugar
2 tablespoons milk

1. Place chocolate and butter in 1-1/2-quart casserole. Heat in Radarange Oven on Full Power for 45 seconds to 1-1/2 minutes or until mixture is melted. Stir once or twice during melting.
2. Stir in remaining ingredients. Mix well. Press mixture firmly against bottom and sides of greased 9-inch pie plate. Chill until firm. Fill with desired filling.

Peanut Butter Crunch Crust

Yield: 1, 9-inch crust

Butter or margarine
1/3 cup chunky peanut butter
1/3 cup light corn syrup
2 cups toasted rice cereal

1. Grease 9-inch pie plate with butter, as desired. Set aside.
2. Combine peanut butter and corn syrup in 1-quart casserole. Heat in Radarange Oven on Full Power for 1 minute, or until peanut butter is softened.
3. Stir in cereal. Press mixture firmly against bottom and sides of pie plate. Chill.

Orange Mallow Pie

Yield: 1, 9-inch pie

1, 9-inch baked pie shell
32 large marshmallows or 3 cups miniature marshmallows
3/4 cup orange juice
2 tablespoons lemon juice
1 tablespoon grated orange peel
1-1/2 cups whipping cream*

1. Bake pie shell, as desired. Set aside.
2. Combine marshmallows, juices and orange peel in 1-quart casserole. Cook in Radarange Oven on Full Power for 2-1/2 to 4 minutes, or until marshmallows are melted. Stir 1 to 2 times during melting. Cool in refrigerator, until mixture begins to thicken.
3. Whip cream, until stiff, in small mixing bowl. Fold into marshmallow mixture. Pour filling into pie shell. Chill several hours before serving.

MICRO-TIPS:
• Chopped toasted almonds or grated orange peel may be sprinkled on top, if desired.
* Whipped topping mix may be used instead of whipping cream, if desired.

VARIATIONS

Lemon Mallow Pie

1/3 cup lemon juice
1/2 cup water
1 tablespoon grated lemon peel

Substitute these ingredients for orange juice, lemon juice and orange peel in original recipe.

Pineapple Mallow Pie

1 (8-3/4 oz.) can crushed pineapple
1 tablespoon lemon juice

Substitute these ingredients for orange juice, lemon juice and orange peel in original recipe.

Pumpkin Pie

Yield: 1, 9-inch pie

1, 9-inch baked pie shell
1 (16 oz.) can pumpkin
3/4 cup brown sugar, firmly packed
1/2 teaspoon cinnamon
1/4 teaspoon ground cloves
1/4 teaspoon ginger
1/4 teaspoon allspice
1/8 teaspoon nutmeg
2 eggs
1 cup evaporated milk

1. Bake pie shell, as desired. Set aside.
2. Mix together pumpkin, sugar and spices in large mixing bowl.
3. Beat eggs and milk together. Stir into pumpkin mixture. Pour filling i pie shell.
4. Cook in Radarange Oven on Cookmatic Level 6 for 18 to 20 minutes until filling is set and knife inserted near center comes out clean.

Cherry Pie

Yield: 1, 9-inch pie

Pastry for 2-crust, 9-inch pie
2 (16 oz. each) cans pitted, tart cherries, with 1/4 cup liquid
1/2 cup sugar
1/4 cup brown sugar, firmly packed
2 tablespoons cornstarch
1/2 teaspoon almond extract
1/2 teaspoon cinnamon
Dash nutmeg
2 tablespoons butter or margarine

1. Prepare pastry and cook bottom crust, according to directions on pa 158.
2. Combine remaining ingredients, except butter. Pour filling into pie sh Dot with butter. Top with remaining pastry. Seal edges and slit top.
3. Cook in Radarange Oven on Full Power for 8 to 10 minutes, or until crust is cooked and cherries are tender.
MICRO-TIP:
* A lattice design pastry top makes an attractive-looking pie.

Pecan Pie

Yield: 1, 10-inch pie

1, 10-inch baked pie shell
1-1/4 cups brown sugar, firmly packed
1 cup light corn syrup
1/4 cup water
4 eggs, well-beaten
1/4 cup butter or margarine, softened
1 teaspoon vanilla
1-1/2 cups (5 ozs.) pecan halves

1. Bake pie shell, as desired. Set aside.
2. Mix together sugar, corn syrup and water in 1-1/2-quart casserole. H in Radarange Oven on Full Power for 3 to 3-1/2 minutes, or until mixture boils. Boil for 2 minutes.
3. Gradually stir hot syrup into eggs. Stir in butter and vanilla. Pour filli into pie shell. Top with pecan halves.
4. Cook in Radarange Oven on Cookmatic Level 8 for 7 to 8 minutes, o until filling is set.

Cheesy Peach Pie

Yield: 1, 10-inch pie

1, 10-inch baked pie shell
1 (21 oz.) can peach pie filling*
1 teaspoon vanilla
1/8 teaspoon nutmeg
1 cup dairy sour cream
1 (3 oz.) pkg. cream cheese, softened
2 eggs, slightly-beaten
1/3 cup sugar
1 teaspoon vanilla
1/2 teaspoon cinnamon or nutmeg

1. Bake pie shell, as desired. Set aside.
2. Combine pie filling, vanilla and nutmeg. Turn into baked pie shell.
3. Beat together sour cream and cream cheese in small mixing bowl. B in remaining ingredients until smooth. Pour over peach mixture. Spri cinnamon on top.
4. Cook in Radarange Oven on Cookmatic Level 5 for 12 to 15 minutes until filling is set. Chill before serving.
* MICRO-TIP: Other fruit pie filling may be used, if desired.

Lemon Meringue Pie

Yield: 1, 9-inch pie

1, 9-inch baked pie shell
1 cup sugar
1/3 cup cornstarch
1 cup water
2/3 cup milk
4 eggs, separated
1/2 cup lemon juice
1 tablespoon butter or margarine
1 teaspoon grated lemon peel
MERINGUE
1/4 teaspoon cream of tartar
1/2 cup sugar

1. Bake pie shell, as desired. Set aside.
2. Combine sugar and cornstarch in 1-quart casserole. Slowly stir in water and milk. Cook in Radarange Oven on Full Power for 3 to 4 minutes, or until thickened. Stir twice during cooking time.
3. Mix part of hot mixture into slightly-beaten egg yolks. Return all to remaining hot mixture. Cook in Radarange Oven on Full Power for 2-1/2 to 4 minutes, or until mixture begins to boil. Stir once during cooking time.
4. Stir in lemon juice, butter and lemon peel, until butter is melted. Pour filling into pie shell.
5. For meringue, beat egg whites with cream of tartar, until foamy. Add sugar, 1 tablespoon at a time, beating until egg whites are stiff.
6. Spread meringue over filling. Seal edges. Cook in Radarange Oven on Cookmatic Level 9 for 2 to 4 minutes, or until meringue is set.

Apple Pie

Yield: 1, 9-inch pie

Pastry for 2-crust, 9-inch pie
6 to 8 medium apples, pared, cored and sliced
1/2 cup sugar
1/2 cup brown sugar, firmly packed
2 tablespoons all-purpose flour
1 tablespoon lemon juice
1 teaspoon cinnamon
Dash nutmeg
2 tablespoons butter or margarine

CRUMB TOPPING (OPTIONAL)
1/4 cup butter or margarine
1/4 cup all-purpose flour
1/4 cup quick-cooking rolled oats
1/4 cup brown sugar, firmly packed
1/4 cup chopped nuts
1/2 teaspoon cinnamon

1. Prepare pastry and cook bottom crust, according to directions on page 158.
2. Combine remaining ingredients, except butter. Pour filling into pie shell. Dot with butter. Top with remaining pastry. Seal edges and slit top.
3. Cook in Radarange Oven on Full Power for 8 to 10 minutes, or until top crust is cooked and apples are tender.

MICRO-TIP: For a delicious apple crumb pie, prepare same as above using 5 to 6 apples and sprinkle crumb topping over top.
1. Cut butter into dry ingredients. Sprinkle over apples.
2. Cook in Radarange Oven on Full Power for 8 to 10 minutes, or until apples are tender.

Peanut Butter Cream Pie

Yield: 1, 9-inch pie

1, 9-inch baked pie shell
1-1/2 cups brown sugar, firmly packed
1/3 cup all-purpose flour
1-1/2 cups light cream
1 egg, beaten
1/2 cup peanut butter

1. Bake pie shell, as desired. Set aside.
2. Combine sugar, flour and light cream in 1-1/2-quart casserole. Cook in Radarange Oven on Full Power for 4 to 5 minutes, or until thickened. Stir twice during cooking time with wire whip.
3. Add egg gradually, stirring with wire whip. Cook in Radarange Oven on Full Power for 1 to 2 minutes, or until boiling. Stir twice during cooking.
4. Add peanut butter, stirring until smooth. Cool. Turn into pie shell.
MICRO-TIPS:
• Top with whipped cream, if desired.
• Use "Peanut Butter Crunch Crust", page 159 for a double peanut butter flavor.

Strawberry Rhubarb Pie

Yield: 1, 9-inch pie

Pastry for 2-crust, 9-inch pie
3 cups rhubarb, sliced in 3/4-inch pieces*
3 cups sliced whole strawberries*
1 cup sugar
1/2 cup brown sugar, firmly packed
1/4 cup cornstarch
1/2 teaspoon cinnamon
Dash nutmeg
2 tablespoons butter or margarine

1. Prepare pastry and cook bottom crust, according to directions on page 158.
2. Combine remaining ingredients, except butter. Pour filling into pie shell. Dot with butter. Top with remaining pastry. Seal edges and slit top.
3. Cook in Radarange Oven on Full Power for 8 to 12 minutes, or until crust is cooked and fruit is tender.
   *MICRO-TIPS: Frozen rhubarb and frozen whole or sliced strawberries may be used, if desired.
   • A lattice design pastry top makes an attractive-looking pie.

Rhubarb Custard Pie

Yield: 1, 10-inch pie

1, 10-inch baked pie shell*
4 egg yolks
3/4 cup milk
1 teaspoon vanilla
1-1/2 cups sugar
3 tablespoons all-purpose flour
Dash salt
Dash nutmeg
3 cups diced rhubarb
MERINGUE
4 egg whites
1/4 teaspoon cream of tartar
1/2 cup sugar

1. Bake pie shell, as desired. Set aside.
2. Combine egg yolks, milk and vanilla.
3. Mix together sugar, flour, salt and nutmeg. Add to egg mixture.
4. Spread rhubarb evenly in pie shell. Pour filling into pie shell.
5. Cook in Radarange Oven on Cookmatic Level 8 for 10 to 12 minutes, until filling is almost set.
6. For meringue, beat egg whites with cream of tartar, until foamy. Add sugar, 1 tablespoon at a time, beating until egg whites are stiff.
7. Spread meringue over filling. Seal edges. Cook in Radarange Oven on Cookmatic Level 9 for 2 to 4 minutes, or until meringue is set.
   *MICRO-TIP: Use the "Baking Powder Crust", on page 158.

Custard Pie

Yield: 1, 9-inch pie

1, 9-inch baked pastry shell
2 cups milk
3 eggs, slightly-beaten
1/2 cup sugar
1/4 teaspoon salt
1/2 teaspoon vanilla
Nutmeg

1. Bake pie shell, as desired. Set aside.
2. Place milk in 4-cup glass measure. Heat in Radarange Oven on Cookmatic Level 8 for 5 to 6 minutes, or until almost boiling.
3. Blend together eggs, sugar, salt and vanilla. Gradually stir in hot milk. Pour filling into pie shell. Sprinkle with nutmeg, as desired.
4. Cook in Radarange Oven on Cookmatic Level 4 for 15 to 18 minutes, until knife inserted halfway between center and edge comes out clean and filling is almost set.

Chocolate Almond Pie

Yield: 1, 9-inch pie

1, 9-inch baked graham cracker crust pie shell
1 (3-3/4 oz.) milk chocolate bar with almonds*
16 large marshmallows, or 1-1/2 cups miniature marshmallows
1/2 cup milk
1 cup whipping cream

1. Prepare crust according to directions on page 158.
2. Break chocolate bars into pieces. Combine chocolate bars, marshmallows and milk in 1-quart casserole. Cook in Radarange Oven on Full Power for 1 to 2 minutes. Stir 2 or 3 times during cooking. Mix until smooth. Cool completely.
3. Whip cream until stiff in small mixing bowl. Fold into marshmallow mixture. Pour filling into crust. Chill several hours before serving.
   * MICRO-TIP: 7 (1/2 oz. each) milk chocolate bars with almonds may substituted.

Banana Cream Pie

Yield: 1, 9-inch pie

1, 9-inch baked pie shell*
1 (3-1/4 oz.) pkg. vanilla pudding mix
1-3/4 cups milk
16 large marshmallows or 1-1/2 cups miniature marshmallows
1/2 cup whipping cream
2 bananas, sliced

1. Bake pie shell, as desired. Set aside.
2. Place pudding mix in 1-quart casserole. Gradually stir in milk. Cook in Radarange Oven on Cookmatic Level 8 for 5-1/2 to 7 minutes, or until pudding boils and is thickened. Stir 2 to 3 times during cooking time.
3. Add marshmallows. Stir until marshmallows are melted. Cover with waxed paper. Chill.
4. Whip cream until stiff in small mixing bowl. Fold into cooled pudding mixture.
5. Slice bananas into pie shell. Pour filling over bananas. Chill several hours before serving.

*MICRO-TIP: This filling is especially good in the Chocolate-Coconut Pie Shell or the Graham Cracker Crust, pages 159 or 158.

Coconut Cream Pie

Yield: 1, 9-inch pie

1, 9-inch baked pie shell
3 cups milk
3/4 cup sugar
5 tablespoons cornstarch
1/2 teaspoon salt
3 egg yolks, beaten
1-1/2 cups shredded coconut
2 tablespoons butter or margarine
1-1/2 teaspoons vanilla

1. Bake pie shell, as desired. Set aside.
2. Place milk in 4-cup glass measure. Heat in Radarange Oven on Cookmatic Level 8 for 5 to 6 minutes, or until scalded.
3. Mix together sugar, cornstarch and salt in 2-quart casserole. Stir hot milk slowly into mixture.
4. Stir about 3/4 cup of hot mixture into egg yolks, stirring constantly. Return egg mixture to 2-quart casserole.
5. Cook in Radarange Oven on Cookmatic Level 8 for 3 to 4 minutes, or until thickened. Stir with wire whip often during cooking. Add coconut, butter and vanilla. Stir until butter is melted. Pour filling into pie shell. Chill several hours before serving.

MICRO-TIP: May be served topped with whipped cream and coconut, if desired.

Grasshopper Pie

Yield: 1, 9-inch pie

1, 9-inch baked chocolate crumb crust pie shell
2/3 cup milk
3 cups miniature marshmallows
1 cup whipping cream
1/4 cup green creme de menthe
2 tablespoons white creme de cacao

1. Prepare crust, according to directions on page 158. Reserve 2 tablespoons of crumbs for topping.
2. Place milk in 1-1/2-quart casserole. Heat in Radarange Oven on Full Power for 1-1/2 to 2-1/2 minutes, or until scalded.
3. Place marshmallows in milk. Cook in Radarange Oven on Full Power for 45 seconds to 1 minute, or until marshmallows are melted. Stir twice during melting. Chill until cooled and thickened.
4. Whip cream until stiff in large bowl. Gradually stir creme de menthe and creme de cacao into marshmallow mixture. Fold into whipped cream. Pour filling into pie shell. Sprinkle reserved crumbs on top. Freeze at least 2 to 3 hours before serving.

Lemon Chiffon Pie

Yield: 1, 9-inch pie

1, 9-inch baked pie shell
1 (3 oz.) pkg. lemon flavor gelatin*
1/2 cup sugar
1/2 teaspoon salt
4 eggs, separated
1 cup water
1 teaspoon grated lemon peel
1/2 cup whipping cream

1. Bake pie shell, as desired. Set aside.
2. Combine gelatin, sugar and salt in 1-1/2-quart casserole. Beat egg yo
   until thick and lemon-colored. Beat water and lemon peel into egg yo
   Stir into gelatin mixture.
3. Cook in Radarange Oven on Full Power for 3 to 4 minutes, or until
   mixture boils and gelatin is dissolved. Stir halfway through cooking t
   Chill until thickened.
4. Fold stiffly-beaten egg whites into gelatin mixture. Whip cream until
   in small mixing bowl. Fold into gelatin mixture.
5. Pour filling into pie shell. Chill several hours before serving.
   *MICRO-TIP: Other gelatin flavors may be used, if desired.

Coffee Cream Pie

Yield: 1, 9-inch pie

CRUST
3 eggs, separated
1/3 cup sugar
1 cup finely chopped nuts

FILLING
32 large marshmallows or 3 cups
   miniature marshmallows
1/4 cup water
1 tablespoon instant coffee
1 cup heavy cream

1. For crust, beat egg whites until soft peaks form. Gradually beat in su
   until stiff peaks form. Fold in nuts. Spread in greased 9-inch pie plate
   Prick bottom well with tines of fork.
2. Cook in Radarange Oven on Cookmatic Level 6 for 3 to 5 minutes, o
   until set. Crust will shrink slightly. Set aside.
3. Place marshmallows and water in 1-1/2-quart casserole. Cook in
   Radarange Oven on Cookmatic Level 8 for 45 seconds to 1 minute, o
   until marshmallows are melted. Stir twice during melting. Stir in insta
   coffee.
4. Stir about 3/4 cup of hot mixture into egg yolks, stirring constantly.
   Return egg mixture to 1-1/2-quart casserole. Cook in Radarange Ove
   Cookmatic Level 6 for 1 to 1-1/2 minutes, or until mixture just begin
   boil. Cool in refrigerator until mixture begins to thicken.
5. Whip cream until stiff in small mixing bowl. Fold into coffee mixture
   Pour filling into pie shell. Chill several hours before serving.
   MICRO-TIPS:
   • Whipped topping mix may be used instead of whipping cream.
   • May be served topped with whipped cream, if desired.

Sour Cream Raisin Pie

Yield: 1, 9-inch pie

1, 9-inch baked pie shell
1/2 cup sugar
1-1/2 tablespoons all-purpose flour
1 teaspoon cinnamon
1/8 teaspoon salt
2 egg yolks, beaten
1 cup dairy sour cream
1 cup finely chopped raisins

MERINGUE
2 eggs whites
1/8 teaspoon cream of tartar
1/4 cup sugar

1. Bake pie shell, as desired. Set aside.
2. Combine sugar, flour, cinnamon and salt in 1-quart casserole. Stir in
   yolks and sour cream. Stir in raisins. Cook in Radarange Oven on Fu
   Power for 3 to 5 minutes, or until mixture boils and is thickened. Pou
   filling into pie shell.
3. For meringue, beat egg whites with cream of tartar, until foamy. Add
   sugar, 1 tablespoon at a time, beating until egg whites are stiff.
4. Spread meringue over filling. Seal edges. Cook in Radarange Oven or
   Cookmatic Level 9 for 1 to 1-1/2 minutes, or until meringue is set.

Cookies are easily and quickly prepared in the Radarange Oven. Cook a dozen drop-type cookies quickly, when guests arrive unexpectedly. Children will also enjoy cooking Radarange Oven cookies.

Cookies can be made ahead and frozen. See the "Frozen Cookie Defrosting Chart", on page 166.

Read the general hints for baking drop cookies or refrigerator cookies and bar cookies, before baking in the Radarange Oven.

General Hints for Baking Drop Cookies or Refrigerator Cookies

1. Cookies will not brown in a microwave oven since the cooking time is so short. Many of the recipes in this chapter use dark colored sugars and spices to give cookies a browned appearance.
2. Cookies bake well on a high temperature plastic baking sheet lined with either waxed paper or parchment paper. Place cookies 2 inches apart on the paper. The waxed paper or parchment paper will then easily slide off of the sheet onto counter or table.
3. Cookies are done when they are set, but still moist. Allow

cookies to cool slightly, although not completely, before removing them from waxed paper. Cookies will become crisper as they cool.

4. When preparing your own favorite drop or refrigerator cookie recipes in the Radarange Oven, select a similar recipe in this chapter to use as a guide. Also, consider the following guides.

Conventionally prepared drop cookie and refrigerator cookie recipes can be converted to Radarange Oven recipes by following **three basic guidelines:**

1. A stiff dough is needed, so the amount of flour needs to be increased by approximately 20%.
2. The temperature of the cookie dough affects cooking times.
3. Cookies will not brown in a microwave oven like they brown in a conventional oven. Select cookie recipes that:
   a. Do not require browning (example: Sugar Cookies)
   b. Have dark brown sugar, spices, chocolate or other ingredients which add color. (Cookies may also be frosted or sprinkled with cinnamon and sugar, or colored sugar.)

General Hints for Cooking Bar Cookies

1. Bar cookies will not brown in a microwave oven due to the short cooking time. Use dark-colored sugars and spices to achieve a browned appearance. Many bar cookies can also be frosted so a lack of browning is not noticed.
2. The baking dish for bar cookies may be greased or ungreased, as desired. The dish should not be floured, since the flour will form a layer on the bottom of the cookies.
3. Bar cookies should generally be cooked on Full Power. Use the setting recommended in the recipe.
4. Bar cookies are done when they are set and a toothpick inserted near the center comes out clean or the top springs back when lightly pressed with a finger. Bar cookies may appear moist on top. Allow them to stand for a few minutes after cooking. Bar cookies will continue to "carry-over cook" during this time. If bar cookies are hard and tough, they have been over-cooked.
5. When preparing your own favorite bar cookie recipe in the Radarange Oven, select a similar recipe in this chapter as a guide. Then use the same setting and approximately the same amount of time. In general, cook bar cookies on Full Power for approximately 1/3 of the time required when baked in a conventional oven.

FROZEN COOKIE DEFROSTING CHART

COOKIE TYPE	QUANTITY OR PKG. SIZE	DEFROSTING TIME ON DEFROST*	SPECIAL INSTRUCTIONS
Frosted Brownies	1 (12 to 14 oz.) pkg.	2 to 3 min.	Remove from metal container to paper plate. Be careful not to melt frosting.
Cookies, Homemade or Purchased	1 dozen	1-1/2 to 2-1/2 min.	Place on paper plate or plastic rack. Cover with paper towel.

*On models having dial timers, use Cookmatic Level 3 for defrosting.

General Instructions for Defrosting Cookies
1. Read the "Special Instructions" in the chart before defrosting cookies.
2. Defrost, according to the recommended time and setting on the chart. If frosted, be careful not to melt the frosting.

REHEATING COOKIES CHART

QUANTITY OF COOKIES	TEMPERATURE	REHEATING TIME ON COOKMATIC LEVEL 8
1	Room temp.	15 sec.
1	Refrig. temp.	20 sec.

General Instructions for Reheating Cookies
1. Wrap the cookie in a napkin or place it on a cooking grill or plate. Cover with a paper towel.
2. Reheat in the Radarange Oven, covered, on Cookmatic Level 8 according to the time on the chart. Increase the amount of reheating time when reheating more than 1 cookie. Reheated cookies will give you that "freshly-baked" cookie flavor.

COOKIE MIX BAKING CHART

TYPE OF MIX	PKG. SIZE	UTENSILS AND/OR NUMBER OF COOKIES	EXTRA INGREDIENTS	COOKING TIME ON FULL POWER
Brownie Mix	8 ozs.	9 x 5 x 2-inch loaf dish	—	3 to 4 min.
	22 to 24 ozs.	8 x 8 x 2-inch dish	—	7 to 8 min.
	22 to 24 ozs.	2-quart utility dish	—	7 to 8 min.
Chocolate Chip Cookie Mix	14 to 15 ozs.	12 (3/4-inch diameter) balls on waxed paper	—	1 min., 15 sec. to 1 min., 45 sec.
Date Bar Mix	14 to 15 ozs.	8 x 8 x 2-inch dish	—	4 to 5 min.
Oatmeal Cookie Mix	14 to 18 ozs.	12 (3/4-inch diameter) balls on waxed paper	3 tablespoons all-purpose flour	1 min., 15 sec. to 1 min., 45 sec.
Peanut Butter Cookie Mix	14 to 15 ozs.	12 (3/4-inch diameter) balls on waxed paper	1/4 cup all-purpose flour	1 min., 15 sec. to 1 min., 45 sec.
Sugar Cookie Mix	15 to 17 ozs.	12 (3/4-inch diameter) balls on waxed paper	1/3 cup all-purpose flour	1 min., 15 sec. to 1 min., 45 sec.

General Instructions for Cooking Cookies from Mixes

1. Prepare the cookie mix, according to the package instructions. In some cases, additional flour is required as indicated in the chart.
2. Cook the cookies on Full Power, according to the time given in the chart, or until the cookies are firm but still moist. When only 12 cookies are cooked at one time, repeat the process with the remaining cookies.
3. Brownies should be moist when removed from the Radarange Oven. Brownie mixes may vary in their formulation of ingredients. Because of this, some mixes may require slightly shorter or longer cooking times. Check brownies frequently during cooking the first time a particular brand is prepared. Note any variations in timing.

CONVENTIONAL DROP COOKIE CONVERSION CHART

QUANTITY OF COOKIES	TEMPERATURE	COOKING TIME ON FULL POWER
*12 cookies on waxed paper	Room Temp.	1 to 2 min.
*12 cookies on waxed paper	Refrig. Temp.	1 to 2 min.

*Times and quantities can be adjusted as needed.

General Instructions for Cooking Conventional Drop Cookies in the Radarange Oven

1. Prepare the cookie dough, according to the **3 basic guidelines,** on page 165.
2. Drop cookies on a high temperature plastic baking sheet lined with waxed paper. Cook a dozen at a time. You may want to turn sheet halfway through cooking time.
3. Cook in the Radarange Oven on Full Power, according to the time on the chart. Allow the cookies to cool slightly before removing them from the waxed paper.

Easy Oatmeal Cookies

Yield: 4 dozen cookies

1 (9 oz.) pkg. spice cake mix
1-1/4 cups quick-cooking or old-fashioned rolled oats
1/2 cup all-purpose flour
1/4 cup vegetable oil, or 1/4 cup shortening, melted
1/4 cup milk
1 egg
2 tablespoons dark brown sugar
1 cup raisins
1/2 cup chopped nuts (optional)

1. Mix together all ingredients, except raisins and nuts, in large mixing bowl.
2. Stir in raisins and nuts. Drop by teaspoons onto high temperature pla baking sheet lined with waxed paper. Cook dozen at a time.
3. Cook dozen in Radarange Oven on Full Power for 1 minute, 10 secor to 1 minute, 20 seconds, or until firm but slightly moist.* Allow cook to cool slightly before removing from waxed paper. Repeat with remaining cookies.

*MICRO-TIP: You may want to turn sheet halfway through cooking ti

Ginger Cream Cookies

Yield: 4 to 5 dozen

3/4 cup butter or margarine
1 cup sugar
1 egg
1/4 cup molasses
3 cups all-purpose flour
2-1/2 teaspoons baking soda
1-1/4 teaspoons cinnamon
1-1/4 teaspoons ginger
1-1/4 teaspoons ground cloves
Sugar

1. Cream butter and sugar in large mixing bowl. Beat in egg and molas
2. Blend together flour, soda and spices. Add to liquid ingredients. Mix Chill. Shape dough into 3/4-inch diameter balls. Roll in sugar, as des Place 12 balls on high temperature plastic baking sheet lined with wa paper.
3. Cook dozen in Radarange Oven on Full Power for 1-1/2 to 2 minutes until firm but slightly moist.* Allow cookies to cool slightly before removing from waxed paper. Repeat with remaining cookies.

*MICRO-TIP: You may want to turn sheet halfway through cooking ti

Thumbprint Cookies

Yield: 3 dozen

2/3 cup butter or margarine
1/3 cup sugar
2 eggs, separated
1 teaspoon vanilla
1/2 teaspoon salt
1-3/4 cups sifted all-purpose flour
3/4 cup finely chopped pecans
1/2 cup preserves

1. Cream butter and sugar until fluffy in large mixing bowl.
2. Stir in egg yolks, vanilla and salt, beating well. Gradually stir in flour Mix well.
3. Shape dough into 3/4-inch diameter balls. Dip in slightly-beaten egg whites and then roll in pecans. Place 12 balls on high temperature plastic baking sheet lined with waxed paper. Make thumbprint in eac
4. Cook dozen in Radarange Oven on Full Power for 1 to 1-1/2 minutes until firm but slightly moist.* Allow cookies to cool slightly before removing from waxed paper. Fill "thumbprints" with preserves just before serving. Repeat with remaining cookies.

MICRO-TIPS:

• Cookies may also be filled with pie filling rather than preserves.

* You may want to turn sheet halfway through cooking time.

Peanut Butter and Jelly Cookie-Wiches

Yield: 4 to 4-1/2 dozen

1/2 cup butter or margarine
1/2 cup chunky-style peanut butter
1/2 cup sugar
1/2 cup brown sugar, firmly packed
1 egg
1-1/2 cups all-purpose flour
3/4 teaspoon baking soda
1/2 teaspoon baking powder
1/4 teaspoon salt
Jelly or jam

1. Mix together butter, peanut butter, sugars and egg thoroughly in larg mixing bowl. Blend in remaining ingredients, except jelly. Cover and chill.
2. Shape dough into 3/4-inch diameter balls. Place 12 balls on high temperature plastic baking sheet lined with waxed paper.
3. Cook dozen in Radarange Oven on Full Power for 1 minute, 30 secor to 1 minute, 45 seconds, or until set but still slightly moist.* Allow cookies to cool slightly before removing from waxed paper. When co "sandwich" cookies together with jelly or jam filling, as desired. Rep with remaining cookies.

MICRO-TIPS:

• Chocolate syrup makes a good filling, too.

* You may want to turn sheet halfway through cooking time.

Snicker Doodle Cookies

Yield: 3 dozen

1/2 cup butter or margarine
1/2 cup sugar
1/4 cup dark brown sugar, firmly packed
1 egg
1/2 teaspoon vanilla
1-3/4 cups all-purpose flour
1 teaspoon cream of tartar
1/2 teaspoon baking soda
1/4 teaspoon salt
2 tablespoon sugar
1-1/4 teaspoons cinnamon

1. Cream butter and sugars in large mixing bowl. Beat in egg and vanilla.
2. Combine flour, cream of tartar, baking soda and salt. Blend into creamed mixture. Chill.
3. Shape dough into 3/4-inch diameter balls. Roll in mixture of sugar and cinnamon. Place 12 balls on high temperature plastic baking sheet lined with waxed paper.
4. Cook dozen in Radarange Oven on Full Power for 1 minute, 30 seconds to 2 minutes, or until cookies are set, but still slightly moist around edges.* Allow cookies to cool slightly before removing from waxed paper. Repeat with remaining cookies.

*MICRO-TIP: You may want to turn sheet halfway through cooking time.

Honey Pecan Balls

Yield: 2-1/2 dozen

1/2 cup butter or margarine, softened
2 tablespoons honey
1 teaspoon vanilla
1-1/2 cups all-purpose flour
1/4 teaspoon salt
1/2 cup chopped pecans
Confectioners' sugar

1. Cream butter and honey in small mixing bowl. Stir in vanilla. Add remaining ingredients, except confectioners' sugar. Mix thoroughly. Refrigerate dough for at least 2 hours.
2. Shape dough into 1-inch diameter balls. Dough will be crumbly. Place 12 balls on high temperature plastic baking sheet lined with waxed paper.
3. Cook dozen in Radarange Oven on Full Power for 1 minute, 15 seconds to 1 minute, 45 seconds, or until no longer moist on outside.* Be careful not to overcook. Allow cookies to cool slightly before removing from waxed paper. Roll in confectioners' sugar, as desired, while still warm. Repeat with remaining cookies.

*MICRO-TIP: You may want to turn sheet halfway through cooking time.

Chocolate Nut Cookies

Yield: 4 to 5 dozen

1/2 cup butter or margarine
3/4 cup semi-sweet chocolate morsels
2 cups sugar
2 teaspoons vanilla
1 egg
1/2 teaspoon salt
2 cups all-purpose flour
1/2 cup chopped walnuts
Confectioners' sugar

1. Combine butter and chocolate morsels in large mixing bowl. Heat in Radarange Oven on Cookmatic Level 6 for 1-1/2 to 2 minutes, or until mixture is melted. Stir well halfway through cooking time.
2. Beat in sugar, vanilla and egg. Mix in salt and flour until well-blended. Stir in walnuts. Shape dough into 3/4-inch diameter balls. Roll in confectioners' sugar, as desired. Place 12 balls on high temperature plastic baking sheet lined with waxed paper.
3. Cook dozen in Radarange Oven on Full Power for 1 minute, 15 seconds to 1 minute, 45 seconds, or until firm but slightly moist.* Allow cookies to cool slightly before removing from waxed paper. Repeat with remaining cookies.

*MICRO-TIP: You may want to turn sheet halfway through cooking time.

Shortbread

Yield: 1, 8 x 8 x 2-inch dish

1 cup butter or margarine
1/2 cup dark brown sugar, firmly packed
1/4 teaspoon vanilla
2-1/2 cups all-purpose flour

1. Cream butter, sugar and vanilla in large mixing bowl, until light and fluffy.
2. Gradually add flour, beating until smooth. Pat mixture into ungreased 8 x 8 x 2-inch dish. Prick with tines of fork evenly over surface to eliminate air bubbles.
3. Cook in Radarange Oven on Full Power for 3 to 3-1/2 mintues, or until evenly raised and set. Cut into bars while warm.

Chocolate Drops

Yield: 2-1/2 dozen

1/4 cup butter or margarine
1 (9 oz.) pkg. chocolate cake mix
1/3 cup all-purpose flour
1 egg
1/2 cup chopped nuts or 1/2 cup shredded coconut (optional)
Pecan halves

1. Place butter in large mixing bowl. Heat in Radarange Oven on Full Power for 30 to 40 seconds, or until melted.
2. Stir cake mix, flour, egg and nuts into butter. Blend well.
3. Shape dough into 3/4-inch diameter balls. Place 12 balls on high temperature plastic baking sheet lined with waxed paper. Top each ball with pecan half.
4. Cook dozen in Radarange Oven on Full Power for 1 minute, 45 seconds to 2 minutes, or until firm but slightly moist.* Allow cookies to cool slightly before removing from waxed paper. Repeat with remaining cookies.

MICRO-TIPS:
• Balls may be rolled in additional coconut before baking, if desired.
* You may want to turn sheet halfway through cooking time.

Coconut Oatmeal Cookies

Yield: 3 dozen

1/3 cup butter or margarine
1 cup dark brown sugar, firmly packed
1 egg
1/2 teaspoon vanilla
1/2 teaspoon almond extract
1-1/2 cups all-purpose flour
1 cup quick-cooking rolled oats
3/4 cup shredded coconut
3/4 teaspoon baking soda
3/4 teaspoon baking powder

1. Cream butter and brown sugar in large mixing bowl.
2. Add egg, vanilla and almond extract. Beat well.
3. Combine remaining ingredients. Blend into creamed mixture. Shape dough into 3/4-inch diameter balls. Place 12 balls on high temperature plastic baking sheet lined with waxed paper.
4. Cook dozen in Radarange Oven on Full Power for 1 minute, 15 seconds to 1 minute, 45 seconds, or until firm but slightly moist.* Allow cookies to cool slightly before removing from waxed paper. Repeat with remaining cookies.

*MICRO-TIP: You may want to turn sheet halfway through cooking time.

Chocolate Chip Cookies

Yield: 3 to 4 dozen cookies

1/2 cup shortening, softened
1/2 cup dark brown sugar, firmly packed
1/4 cup sugar
1 (1 oz.) pkg. instant cocoa mix
1 egg
1/2 teaspoon vanilla
1-1/4 cups all-purpose flour
1/2 teaspoon baking soda
1/2 teaspoon salt
1 (6 oz.) pkg. chocolate morsels
1/2 cup chopped nuts (optional)

1. Beat together shortening, sugars, cocoa mix, egg and vanilla in large mixing bowl.
2. Combine flour, baking soda and salt. Stir into creamed mixture. Mix well. Stir in chocolate morsels and nuts. Drop by teaspoons onto high temperature plastic baking sheet lined with waxed paper. Cook dozen at a time.
3. Cook dozen in Radarange Oven on Full Power for 1 minute, 45 seconds to 2 minutes, or until firm but slightly moist.* Allow cookies to cool slightly before removing from waxed paper. Repeat with remaining cookies.

*MICRO-TIP: You may want to turn sheet halfway through cooking time.

Marshmallow Treats

Yield: 1-1/2 dozen, 2 x 2-inch squares

1/4 cup butter or margarine
4 cups miniature marshmallows
5 cups toasted rice cereal

1. Place butter in 2-quart utility dish. Heat in Radarange Oven on Full Power for 45 to 60 seconds, or until melted.
2. Stir in marshmallows, coating with butter. Cook in Radarange Oven on Full Power for 2 to 2-1/2 minutes, or until marshmallows are melted. halfway through cooking time.
3. Stir in cereal. Mix until well-coated. Pat evenly into dish. Let stand until cool and set. Cut into squares.

MICRO-TIP: If large marshmallows are used, slightly more time may be needed for melting.

Refrigerator Filled Cookies

Yield: 2-1/2 dozen

1/2 cup butter or margarine, softened
1/2 cup brown sugar, firmly packed
1 egg
2 cups all-purpose flour
1/2 teaspoon salt
1/4 teaspoon baking soda
Jam or pie filling

1. Cream butter and brown sugar in large mixing bowl. Add egg. Combine remaining ingredients, except for jam or pie filling. Stir into creamed mixture.
2. Shape dough into 1-1/2-inch diameter rolls. Wrap in waxed paper. Chill 2 to 3 hours.
3. Cut rolls into 1/2-inch slices. Place 12 slices on high temperature plastic baking sheet lined with waxed paper. Top each with 1/4 teaspoon jam or pie filling, as desired. Top each with another cookie slice. Seal edges.
4. Cook dozen in Radarange Oven on Full Power for 1 minute, 15 seconds to 1 minute, 45 seconds, or until set.* Allow cookies to cool slightly before removing from waxed paper. Repeat with remaining cookies.

*MICRO-TIP: You may want to turn sheet halfway through cooking time.

Lemon Drops

Yield: 5-1/2 to 6 dozen

1/2 cup butter or margarine
1-1/2 teaspoons grated lemon peel
1-1/2 tablespoons lemon juice
1 cup brown sugar, firmly packed
1 egg
2-1/2 cups all-purpose flour
1/2 teaspoon salt
1/2 teaspoon baking soda
Non-pareils (decorative candies)

1. Cream together butter, lemon peel and lemon juice in large mixing bowl. Beat in brown sugar and egg.
2. Combine flour, salt and baking soda. Blend into creamed mixture. Mix well.
3. Shape dough into 1-inch diameter rolls. Chill dough, if necessary, for easier handling. Roll in non-pareils, as desired. Refrigerate for at least 3 hours.
4. Cut rolls in 1/4-inch slices. Place 12 slices on high temperature plastic baking sheet lined with waxed paper.
5. Cook dozen in Radarange Oven on Full Power for 1 minute, 15 seconds to 1 minute, 45 seconds, or until cookies are set but still slightly moist around edges.* Allow cookies to cool slightly before removing from waxed paper. Repeat with remaining dough.

*MICRO-TIP: You may want to turn sheet halfway through cooking time.

Five Layer Bars

Yield: 1 dozen bars

1/3 cup butter or margarine
1 cup graham cracker crumbs
3/4 cup milk chocolate morsels
3/4 cup shredded coconut
2/3 cup chopped walnuts
2/3 cup sweetened condensed milk

1. Place butter in 8 x 8 x 2-inch dish. Heat in Radarange Oven on Full Power for 45 seconds to 1 minute, or until melted.
2. Blend in cracker crumbs. Press evenly against bottom of dish. Cook in Radarange Oven on Full Power for 1 to 1-1/2 minutes.
3. Sprinkle on chocolate morsels, coconut and nuts in layers in listed order. Pour condensed milk over all. Cook in Radarange Oven on Full Power for 3 to 4 minutes, or until bubbling all over surface. Cool. Cut into bars.

Scotch Toffee Bars

Yield: 12 bars

1/2 cup butter or margarine, melted
2 cups quick-cooking rolled oats
1/2 cup brown sugar, firmly packed
1/4 cup dark corn syrup
1-1/2 teaspoons vanilla
1/2 teaspoon salt
1 (6 oz.) pkg. chocolate morsels
1/4 cup chopped nuts

1. Combine butter, oats, brown sugar, corn syrup, vanilla and salt in 2-quart utility dish. Press firmly against bottom of dish.
2. Cook in Radarange Oven on Full Power for 2 to 3 minutes, or until bubbling all over.* Smooth surface. Top with chocolate morsels.
3. Heat in Radarange Oven on Cookmatic Level 6 for 1 minute, or until chocolate morsels are melted. Spread chocolate evenly over bottom crust. Sprinkle with nuts. Chill. Cut into bars. Store in airtight container in refrigerator.

*MICRO-TIP: You may want to turn dish halfway through cooking time.

Marbled Butterscotch Bars

Yield: 2-1/2 to 3 dozen bars

1/2 cup butter or margarine
3/4 cup brown sugar, firmly packed
1 egg
1 teaspoon vanilla
1 cup all-purpose flour
1/2 teaspoon baking powder
1/8 teaspoon baking soda
1/8 teaspoon salt
1/2 cup semi-sweet chocolate morsels, melted

1. Cream butter and brown sugar in large mixing bowl. Beat in egg and vanilla.
2. Stir together flour, baking powder, soda and salt. Beat into creamed mixture. Spread batter in 2-quart utility dish. Swirl melted chocolate o top with knife.
3. Cook in Radarange Oven on Full Power for 4-1/2 to 5-1/2 minutes, or until top springs back when lightly pressed with finger. Cool. Cut into squares.

Chewy Peanut Butter Bars

Yield: 1 to 1-1/2 dozen bars

1/3 cup butter or margarine
1/2 cup peanut butter
1 cup sugar
1/4 cup dark brown sugar, firmly packed
2 eggs
1 teaspoon vanilla
1 cup all-purpose flour
1 teaspoon baking powder
1/4 teaspoon salt
1 (3-1/2 oz.) can flaked coconut (about 1-1/2 cups)

1. Cream together butter, peanut butter and sugars until light and fluffy large mixing bowl. Add eggs and vanilla. Beat well.
2. Mix in flour, baking powder and salt, stirring until thoroughly blended. Stir in coconut.* Spread evenly in greased 2-quart utility dish.
3. Cook in Radarange Oven on Full Power for 6 to 7 minutes, or until top springs back when lightly pressed with finger.** Cool. Cut into squares
MICRO-TIPS:
   *Reserve 1/4 cup coconut to sprinkle over bars as a topping before cooking, if desired.
   **You may want to turn dish halfway through cooking time.

Applesauce Coconut Bars

Yield: 1 dozen bars

1-1/2 cups applesauce
1/4 cup dark brown sugar, firmly packed
2 tablespoons all-purpose flour
1 tablespoon lemon juice
1/2 cup butter or margarine
1/2 cup dark brown sugar, firmly packed
1/2 cup all-purpose flour
1 cup quick-cooking rolled oats
1/2 teaspoon cinnamon
1/2 cup shredded coconut

1. Combine applesauce, 1/4 cup dark brown sugar, 2 tablespoons flour a lemon juice in 1-quart casserole. Cook in Radarange Oven on Full Pow for 2-1/2 to 3 minutes, or until thick and bubbly. Cool.
2. Cream butter and brown sugar. Blend in flour and oats. Press mixture against bottom of 8 x 8 x 2-inch dish. Cook in Radarange Oven on Ful Power for 2-1/2 minutes. Let cool 5 minutes.
3. Spread cooled applesauce mixture over bottom layer. Mix cinnamon a coconut. Sprinkle over applesauce. Cook in Radarange Oven on Full Power for 5 to 6 minutes, or until filling is bubbly and begins to pull away from sides of dish. Chill. Cut into bars.

Banana Bars

Yield: 1 dozen bars

1/4 cup butter or margarine
3/4 cup dark brown sugar, firmly packed
1 egg, slightly-beaten
1/2 cup dairy sour cream
1/2 cup mashed bananas
1/2 teaspoon vanilla
1 cup all-purpose flour
1/2 teaspoon salt
1/2 teaspoon baking soda

1. Cream butter and sugar in large mixing bowl. Blend in egg.
2. Add sour cream, bananas and vanilla. Stir well.
3. Combine flour, salt and baking soda. Blend into banana mixture. Sprea in greased 8 x 8 x 2-inch dish.
4. Cook in Radarange Oven on Full Power for 5 to 6 minutes, or until top springs back when lightly pressed with finger. Cool. Cut into bars.
MICRO-TIP: Frost with a confectioners' sugar frosting.

Date Bars

Yield: 1 dozen bars

1/3 cup butter or margarine
1 cup dark brown sugar, firmly packed
2 eggs
1 teaspoon grated orange peel
1 teaspoon vanilla
1 cup all-purpose flour
1/2 teaspoon baking powder
1/4 teaspoon salt
1 (8 oz.) pkg. coarsely chopped, pitted dates
1/2 cup chopped walnuts
Confectioners' sugar

1. Cream butter and brown sugar in large mixing bowl. Beat in eggs, orange peel and vanilla.
2. Mix together flour, baking powder and salt. Stir into liquid ingredients. Stir in dates and nuts. Spread evenly in 8 x 8 x 2-inch dish.
3. Cook in Radarange Oven on Full Power for 6 to 7 minutes, or until toothpick inserted in center comes out clean.* Sprinkle with confectioners' sugar, as desired. Chill. Cut into bars.

   *MICRO TIP: You may want to turn dish halfway through cooking time.

Applesauce Squares

Yield: 1 to 1-1/2 dozen squares

1/2 cup butter or margarine, softened
1 cup dark brown sugar, firmly packed
1/2 cup applesauce
1 egg
1 teaspoon grated lemon peel
1-1/2 cups all-purpose flour
1 teaspoon cinnamon
1/2 teaspoon ground cloves
1/2 teaspoon baking soda
3/4 cup raisins or
   3/4 cup chopped walnuts
ICING (Optional)
1/2 cup brown sugar, firmly packed
1/4 cup butter or margarine
2 tablespoons milk
1/2 cup confectioners' sugar

1. Cream butter and brown sugar in large mixing bowl. Beat in applesauce, egg and lemon peel.
2. Combine flour, spices and baking soda. Stir into creamed mixture. Stir in raisins. Spread evenly in ungreased 8 x 8 x 2-inch dish.
3. Cook in Radarange Oven on Full Power for 5 to 6 minutes, or until top springs back when lightly pressed with finger. Cool. Cut into bars.
4. For icing, combine brown sugar, butter and milk in 1-quart casserole. Cook in Radarange Oven on Full Power for 1 to 1-1/2 minutes, or until mixture boils. Boil 1 minute.
5. Blend in confectioners' sugar. Cool slightly. Spread on cool bars.

Cinnamon Bars

Yield: 2-1/2 to 3 dozen bars

1/2 cup butter or margarine
1/2 cup brown sugar, firmly packed
1 egg yolk
1-1/2 teaspoons cinnamon
Dash salt
1 cup all-purpose flour
1 egg white
1/4 cup confectioners' sugar
1/4 cup chopped pecans

1. Cream together butter, brown sugar, egg yolk, cinnamon and salt in large mixing bowl. Stir in flour. Spread dough in 2-quart utility dish.
2. Beat egg white until foamy. Stir in confectioners' sugar. Spread this mixture over batter. Sprinkle with pecans.
3. Cook in Radarange Oven on Full Power for 4 to 6 minutes, or until toothpick inserted in center comes out clean.* Cool slightly. Cut into squares.

   *MICRO TIP: You may want to turn dish halfway through cooking time.

Fudge Brownies

Yield: 1 dozen brownies

2 (1 oz. each) squares semi-sweet chocolate
1/2 cup butter or margarine
1/2 cup milk
1 cup sugar
2 eggs, slightly-beaten
1 teaspoon vanilla
2/3 cup all-purpose flour
1/2 teaspoon baking powder
Dash salt
3/4 cup chopped walnuts (optional)

1. Combine chocolate and butter in 8 x 8 x 2-inch dish. Heat in Radarange Oven on Cookmatic Level 6 for 3 minutes, or until mixture is melted. Stir occasionally during melting.
2. Blend in milk. Cool.
3. Stir in sugar, eggs and vanilla with fork until well-blended. Combine flour, baking powder and salt. Stir into chocolate mixture. Stir in nuts.
4. Cook in Radarange Oven on Full Power for 5 to 7 minutes, or until top springs back when lightly pressed with finger. May look slightly moist top when done. Cool. Cut into bars.

MICRO-TIP: These moist, cake-type brownies may be sprinkled with confectioners' sugar or spread with your favorite chocolate icing, if desired.

Double-Decker Crunchies

Yield: 1 to 1-1/2 dozen squares

1 (6 oz.) pkg. semi-sweet chocolate morsels
1/2 cup confectioners' sugar, sifted
2 tablespoons butter or margarine
2 tablespoons milk
4 cups toasted rice cereal
1 (6 oz.) pkg. butterscotch morsels
1/2 cup chunky-style peanut butter

1. Place chocolate morsels, confectioners' sugar, butter and milk in 3-quart casserole. Heat in Radarange Oven on Full Power for 1-1/2 to 2-1/2 minutes, or until chocolate morsels are melted. Stir in cereal. Coat well.
2. Place butterscotch morsels and peanut butter in 1-quart casserole. Heat in Radarange Oven on Full Power for 1-1/2 to 2-1/2 minutes, or until butterscotch morsels are melted.
3. Spread half of chocolate mixture in greased 8 x 8 x 2-inch dish. Spread butterscotch mixture over chocolate layer. Top with remaining chocolate mixture. Chill slightly. Cut into bars.

Triple Treats

Yield: 1-1/2 dozen bars

1/2 cup butter or margarine
1/2 cup dark brown sugar, firmly packed
1 egg
1/2 teaspoon vanilla
1 cup all-purpose flour
1-1/4 cups confectioners' sugar
2 tablespoons evaporated milk
1 tablespoon butter or margarine, softened
1/2 teaspoon vanilla
1/4 teaspoon almond extract
2/3 cup confectioners' sugar
1/2 cup butter or margarine, softened
1/2 cup semi-sweet chocolate morsels
1 egg
1/4 cup slivered almonds or 1/4 cup chopped walnuts

1. Cream 1/2 cup butter and brown sugar in large mixing bowl. Add 1 egg, 1/2 teaspoon vanilla and flour. Beat until fluffy. Spread evenly in ungreased 8 x 8 x 2-inch dish. Cook in Radarange Oven on Full Power for 3 to 4 minutes, or until firm to touch.* Cool.
2. Beat together 1-1/4 cups confectioners' sugar, evaporated milk, 1 tablespoon butter, vanilla and almond extract, until creamy. Spread on cooled bottom layer. Allow to stand and become firm.
3. Cream 2/3 cup confectioners' sugar and 1/2 cup butter in small bowl. Place chocolate morsels in 1-cup glass measure or small dish. Heat in Radarange Oven on Cookmatic Level 6 for 2-1/2 minutes, or until melted. Stir well. Add to creamed mixture with egg. Beat until fluffy. Spread on white layer. Sprinkle with nuts. Refrigerate. Cut into bars before serving.

*MICRO-TIP: You may want to turn dish halfway through cooking time.

Cherry Bars

Yield: 1 dozen bars

1/2 cup butter or margarine
1/2 cup dark brown sugar, firmly packed
2 eggs
1-1/2 cups all-purpose flour
3/4 teaspoon baking powder
1/8 teaspoon almond extract
1 (21 oz.) can cherry pie filling
Cinnamon

1. Cream butter and brown sugar in large mixing bowl.
2. Blend in eggs. Add flour, baking powder and almond extract. Spread 1/2 mixture in 8 x 8 x 2-inch dish.
3. Cook in Radarange Oven on Full Power for 2 to 2-1/2 minutes, or until top springs back when lightly pressed with finger.
4. Spread cherries evenly over top. Drop remaining dough over cherries by tablespoons. Sprinkle with cinnamon, as desired.
5. Cook in Radarange Oven on Full Power for 6 to 8 minutes, or until top of dough springs back when lightly pressed with finger.* Cool. Cut into bars.

MICRO-TIPS:

• Any flavor fruit pie filling may be substituted.

* You may want to turn dish halfway through cooking time.

Pumpkin Squares

Yield: 1 dozen bars

2 eggs, slightly-beaten
1 cup canned pumpkin
1/2 cup vegetable oil
1 cup all-purpose flour
1 cup dark brown sugar, firmly packed
1/2 cup walnuts (optional)
1-1/2 teaspoons cinnamon
1 teaspoon baking powder
1/2 teaspoon baking soda
1/2 teaspoon ground cloves
1/4 teaspoon salt
ICING (Optional)
1-1/2 cups confectioners' sugar
3 teaspoons milk or light cream
4 teaspoons undiluted, frozen orange juice concentrate

1. Combine and blend eggs, pumpkin and oil in large mixing bowl.
2. Combine remaining ingredients and blend into pumpkin mixture. Pour batter into greased 2-quart utility dish.
3. Cook in Radarange Oven on Full Power for 6 to 7 minutes, or until top springs back when lightly pressed with finger.* Cool. Cut into bars.
4. For icing, blend together all ingredients until smooth. Drizzle icing over bars before serving.

*MICRO-TIP: You may want to turn dish halfway through cooking time.

Granola Chewies

Yield: 3 dozen

1/2 cup butter or margarine
2/3 cup dark brown sugar, firmly packed
1/3 cup honey
1-1/2 cups quick-cooking or old-fashioned rolled oats
1 cup finely chopped, dried apricots
1/2 cup shredded coconut
1/2 cup chopped almonds
1/2 cup toasted wheat germ

1. Place butter in 2-quart glass utility dish. Heat in Radarange Oven on Full Power for 1 minute, or until melted. Stir in brown sugar and honey, stirring until smooth.
2. Gradually stir in oats, apricots, coconut, almonds and wheat germ. Stir until all ingredients are well-mixed. Spread mixture evenly in utility dish.
3. Cook in Radarange Oven on Cookmatic Level 6 for 12 minutes, or until firm but slightly moist. Stir halfway through cooking time. Allow mixture to cool slightly and then shape into 1-inch diameter balls. Store in tightly-covered container.

Candies are easily prepared in the Radarange Oven. In fact, some of the Radarange Oven candies, such as Quickie Fudge and Peanut Clusters are so easily made that children will want to prepare them.

Candies can be made ahead and stored in airtight containers. Or, you can quickly prepare candies for a spur-of-the-moment party or snack.

Read the general hints for cooking candies before making candies in the Radarange Oven.

General Hints for Cooking Candies

1. Candy becomes very hot during cooking. Select a cooking utensil which will withstand hot temperatures. Select a utensil which is large enough to hold the candy during cooking to avoid boil-overs. Use the recommended utensil in the recipe. Generally candy is cooked uncovered for easy stirring.

2. Candies are prepared using a variety of settings. Some candies are quickly cooked on Full Power, while others require a lower Cookmatic Level or setting due to "delicate" or "special" ingredients.

3. You may wish to use a candy thermometer when preparing candies. Do not leave the candy thermometer in the candy while the microwave oven is in operation. The Automatic Temperature Control System should not be used for candy making, since the temperature range of the control ends at 190° F.

4. In this cookbook, candies are described as being completely done when the following stages are reached:

Soft Ball: The candy syrup, when dropped into very cold water, forms a soft ball which flattens on removal from water.

Firm Ball: The candy syrup, when dropped into very cold water, forms a firm ball which does not flatten on removal from water.

Hard Ball: The candy syrup, when dropped into very cold water, forms a hard ball which is hard enough to hold its shape, yet elastic.

Soft Crack: The candy syrup, when dropped into very cold water, separates into threads which are hard but not brittle.

Hard Crack: The candy syrup, when dropped into very cold water, separates into threads which are hard and brittle.

5. Since candies do become quite hot during cooking, be careful when removing them from the Radarange Oven. You may wish to keep hot pads handy.

6. When preparing your own favorite candy recipes, select a recipe in this chapter to use as a guide. Then use the same setting, and approximately the same amount of cooking time. Record the amount of Radarange Oven time on your recipe for later use.

Peanut Clusters

Yield: 3-1/2 to 4 dozen

1 (6 oz.) pkg. chocolate morsels
1 (12 oz.) pkg. butterscotch morsels
1 (12 oz.) pkg. salted peanuts

1. Combine chocolate and butterscotch morsels in 2-quart casserole. Heat in Radarange Oven on Cookmatic Level 6 for 5 to 6 minutes, or until melted. Stir once during melting.
2. Stir in peanuts. Drop by teaspoons onto waxed paper. Let set until firm. Store in airtight container.

MICRO-TIP: If mixture hardens before dropped on waxed paper, return to Radarange Oven on Cookmatic Level 6 for 1 to 2 minutes, or until softened.

Chinese Clusters

Yield: 3-1/2 to 4 dozen

1 (6 oz.) pkg. chocolate morsels
1 (6 oz.) pkg. butterscotch morsels
1 (3 oz.) can chow mein noodles
1 (6-1/2 oz.) can cocktail peanuts

1. Place chocolate and butterscotch morsels in 1-1/2 to 2-quart casserole. Heat in Radarange Oven on Cookmatic Level 6 for 3 to 3-1/2 minutes, or until melted. Stir until smooth.
2. Stir in chow mein noodles and peanuts. Drop by teaspoons onto waxed paper. Let set until firm.

Peanut Brittle

Yield: about 2 lbs.

2 cups sugar
1 cup light corn syrup
1/3 cup water
1 (16 oz.) pkg. salted peanuts
1 tablespoon butter or margarine
1 tablespoon baking soda

1. Grease 2, 15-1/2 x 12-inch baking sheets. Keep warm.
2. Place sugar, corn syrup and water in 3-quart casserole. Cook in Radarange Oven on Full Power for 8 to 10 minutes, or until soft ball stage is reached.* Stir occasionally during cooking time.
3. Stir in peanuts. Cook in Radarange Oven on Cookmatic Level 8 for 10 to 12 minutes, or until hard crack stage is reached.**
4. Stir in butter and baking soda. Pour half of candy onto each sheet, spreading to 1/4-inch thickness. Cool. Break into pieces.

MICRO-TIPS:

*The soft ball stage is described on page 176.
**The hard crack stage is described on page 176.

Turtles

Yield: 2 to 2-1/2 dozen

1 (14 oz.) pkg. caramels
2 tablespoons evaporated milk
1 tablespoon butter or margarine
1 (5 oz.) pkg. pecan halves
1 (6 oz.) pkg. semi-sweet chocolate morsels
1, 1-inch square paraffin, grated

1. Place caramels, milk and butter in 1-quart glass measure or casserole. Heat in Radarange Oven on Full Power for 2 to 3 minutes, or until caramels are melted.
2. Arrange pecan halves in groups of 3 on buttered baking sheet. Spoon about 1 tablespoon warm caramel mixture over each group of pecans. Refrigerate, uncovered, for 30 minutes.
3. Place chocolate morsels and paraffin in 2-cup glass measure. Heat in Radarange Oven on Full Power for 2 to 4 minutes, or until chocolate morsels and paraffin are melted. Stir halfway through cooking time. Spoon enough chocolate mixture over each caramel to cover. Allow to cool. Remove from baking sheet.

MICRO-TIP: May be stored in single layer in tightly covered container in refrigerator for as long as 3 weeks.

Divinity

Yield: 6 to 7 dozen pieces

4 cups sugar
1 cup light corn syrup
3/4 cup water
1/4 teaspoon salt
3 egg whites
1 teaspoon vanilla
1/2 cup chopped nuts (optional)

1. Mix together sugar, corn syrup, water and salt in 1-1/2-quart casserol. Cook in Radarange Oven on Full Power for 20 to 22 minutes, or until hard ball stage is reached.* Stir once or twice during cooking.
2. While syrup cooks, beat egg whites until stiff peaks form in large mix bowl. Gradually pour hot syrup over egg whites while beating at high speed until mixture is thickened and candy starts to lose its gloss. Beating may require about 12 minutes.
3. Add vanilla and nuts to beaten mixture. Drop by teaspoons onto wax paper.

MICRO-TIPS:
• Candy may be tinted with food coloring for special occasions.
* The hard ball stage is described on page 176.

Old-Fashioned Taffy

Yield: 1 lb.

2 cups sugar
1/4 cup vinegar
1/4 cup water
1 teaspoon vanilla

1. Combine sugar, vinegar and water in 1-1/2-quart casserole. Cook in Radarange Oven on Full Power for 8 to 10 minutes, or until soft crac stage is reached.* Add vanilla.
2. Divide mixture into 3 equal amounts and pour onto three well-greased dinner plates. Allow to cool until taffy feels warm to hand, but not h
3. Grease hands well. Pull taffy until it turns shiny white color and is qu stiff to handle. Twist as rope and snip strand into bite-size pieces.

MICRO-TIPS:
• If batches become too hard to pull, heat in Radarange Oven on Full Power for 30 seconds to 1 minute, or until softened. Allow to cool, pull the same as above.
* The soft crack stage is described on page 176.

Quickie Fudge

Yield: 4 to 5 dozen pieces

1 lb. confectioners' sugar
1/2 cup cocoa
1/4 cup milk
1/2 cup butter or margarine
1 teaspoon vanilla
1/2 cup chopped nuts

1. Blend together confectioners' sugar and cocoa in 8 x 8 x 2-inch dish. Pour in milk. Place butter on top. Heat in Radarange Oven on Full Po for 2 minutes, or until butter is melted. Stir well to mix ingredients.
2. Add vanilla and nuts. Stir until blended. Place in freezer for 20 minute or in refrigerator for 1 hour. Chill. Cut into 1-inch squares. Store in airtight container.

Marshmallow Creme Fudge

Yield: 5 to 6 dozen pieces

1/2 cup butter or margarine
2 cups sugar
1 (5.3 oz.) can evaporated milk (2/3 cup)
1 (12 oz.) pkg. semi-sweet chocolate morsels*
1 (7 oz.) jar marshmallow creme
1 teaspoon vanilla
1 cup chopped nuts (optional)

1. Place butter in 9 x 9 x 2-inch dish. Heat in Radarange Oven on Full Power for 1 minute, or until melted.
2. Blend in sugar and evaporated milk. Mix well.
3. Cook in Radarange Oven on Cookmatic Level 8 for 8 to 10 minutes, until soft ball stage is reached.** Stir mixture frequently during cooki time.
4. Blend in chocolate morsels, marshmallow creme, vanilla and nuts. St until smooth. Chill until firm. Cut into 1-inch squares. Store in airtigh container.

MICRO-TIPS:
*Two cups milk chocolate morsels may be substituted for 1 (12 oz. pkg. semi-sweet chocolate morsels.
**The soft ball stage is described on page 176.

Almond Bark

Yield: 1 pound

3/4 lb. white or dark chocolate*
2/3 cup roasted almonds**

1. Place chocolate in 2-cup glass measure or mixing bowl. Heat in Radarange Oven on Cookmatic Level 6 for 3 to 3-1/2 minutes, or until melted.
2. Stir in almonds. Pour immediately onto waxed paper or aluminum foil. Spread thinly. Cool for approximately 1 hour and then break into pieces for serving.

MICRO-TIPS:

 *1 (12 oz.) pkg. semi-sweet chocolate morsels may be substituted for 3/4 lb. chocolate, if desired.
 **Pecans may be substituted for almonds.

Vanilla Caramels

Yield: 2-1/2 lbs.

1 cup butter or margarine
2 cups sugar
2 cups dark corn syrup
2 cups light cream

1. Place butter in 3-quart casserole. Heat in Radarange Oven on Full Power for 1 to 1-1/2 minutes, or until melted.
2. Blend in sugar, corn syrup and 1 cup light cream. Heat in Radarange Oven on Full Power for 20 to 25 minutes, or until firm ball stage is reached.* Stir occasionally during cooking time to avoid boil-overs.
3. Gradually blend in remaining light cream. Cook in Radarange Oven on Full Power for 10 to 15 minutes, or until firm ball stage is reached.
4. Pour mixture into greased 2-quart utility dish. Cool for 3 hours, or until firm. Turn out on cutting board. Cut into squares. Wrap squares individually in small pieces of waxed paper, if desired.

*MICRO-TIP: The firm ball stage is described on page 176.

Chocolate Creams

Yield: 2 dozen

2 tablespoons extra-strong coffee
4 (1 oz. each) squares semi-sweet chocolate, melted
1/4 cup light cream, scalded
2 egg yolks, slightly-beaten
1/2 cup butter or margarine
1 teaspoon vanilla
1/2 cup confectioners' sugar
1/2 cup chopped salted peanuts
Shredded coconut

1. Stir coffee into melted chocolate. Set aside.
2. Blend hot cream into egg yolks, stirring constantly. Cook in Radarange Oven on Full Power for 30 seconds. Stir with wire whip.
3. Cream butter, vanilla and confectioners' sugar. Add chocolate and egg mixtures, gradually. Mix well. Stir in peanuts. Refrigerate until stiffened. Spoon by heaping teaspoons into bon-bon cups. Sprinkle with coconut, as desired. Refrigerate.

Chocolate-Gumdrop Squares

Yield: 24 squares

1 (12 oz.) pkg. semi-sweet chocolate morsels
2 cups halved miniature marshmallows
2/3 cup small gumdrops
1/2 cup chopped walnuts

1. Place chocolate morsels in 1-quart casserole. Heat in Radarange Oven on Full Power for 2-1/2 to 3-1/2 minutes, or until melted. Stir halfway through cooking time.
2. Spread three-fourths of chocolate on waxed paper in 9 x 6-inch rectangle. Top with marshmallows, gumdrops and nuts. Drizzle remaining chocolate over top. Chill. Cut into squares.

MICRO-TIP: This is a candy that children will like to prepare.

Cathedral Window Candy

Yield: 40 to 50 slices

1/2 cup butter or margarine
1 (12 oz.) pkg. semi-sweet chocolate morsels
1 (10 oz.) pkg. colored miniature marshmallows
1 cup chopped nuts
2 to 2-1/2 cups shredded coconut

1. Place butter in 3-quart casserole. Heat in Radarange Oven on Full Power for 1 minute, or until melted. Add chocolate morsels. Heat in Radarange Oven on Cookmatic Level 6 for 3 to 3-1/2 minutes, or until chocolate is melted.
2. Cool chocolate enough so that marshmallows won't melt when stirred in. Add marshmallows and nuts. Allow to stand until stiff enough to form into rolls.
3. Spread coconut on 2, 1-1/2 feet each, sheets of waxed paper. Divide marshmallow mixture in half. Form in long rolls on coconut. Coat all sides of rolls evenly with coconut. Store in refrigerator until firm. Cut in 1/4 to 1/2-inch slices.

MICRO-TIP: If the chocolate mixture hardens too much to roll out, heat in Radarange Oven on Cookmatic Level 6 for 1 to 1-1/2 minutes, or until softened.

Candy Cookies

Yield: 3-1/2 to 4 dozen

2 cups sugar
1/2 cup milk
1/2 cup butter or margarine, melted
3 tablespoons cocoa
1 tablespoon vanilla
3 cups quick-cooking rolled oats
1 cup shredded coconut
1 cup chopped nuts

1. Combine sugar, milk, butter and cocoa in 1-quart glass measure or casserole. Heat in Radarange Oven on Full Power for 1-1/2 to 2-1/2 minutes, or until mixture boils. Boil 1 minute. Add vanilla.
2. Pour sauce over oats, coconut and nuts in large mixing bowl. Mix well. Drop by teaspoons onto waxed paper. Allow to cool until set.

Caramel Peanut Puffs

Yield: 30 pieces

1 (14 oz.) pkg. caramels
3 tablespoons water
30 large marshmallows
1-1/2 cups chopped salted Spanish peanuts

1. Place caramels and water in 1-quart glass measure or casserole. Heat in Radarange Oven on Full Power for 2-1/2 to 4 minutes, or until melted. Stir halfway through melting.
2. Dip marshmallows into caramel syrup using toothpicks and roll to coat completely. Roll in peanuts. Place on waxed paper. Let dry at room temperature.

MICRO-TIP: If syrup gets thick, stir in 1/2 teaspoon water and reheat Radarange Oven on Cookmatic Level 8 for 30 seconds, or until soften.

Chocolate Crispies

Yield: 1-1/2 to 2 dozen

2 ozs. semi-sweet chocolate
1/2 cup sugar
3 tablespoons light corn syrup
1 tablespoon water
2 cups crisp rice cereal

1. Place chocolate in 2-quart casserole. Heat in Radarange Oven on Full Power for 2-1/2 to 3-1/2 minutes, or until melted.
2. Stir in sugar, corn syrup and water. Cook in Radarange Oven on Full Power for 1 to 2 minutes, or until sauce is heated.
3. Add cereal. Stir until cereal is well-coated. Drop by tablespoons onto waxed paper. Allow to cool until set.

Peanut-Butterscotch Mash

Yield: 2 lbs.

2 cups sugar
1-1/2 cups miniature marshmallows, or 32 large marshmallows
1 (5.3 oz.) can evaporated milk (2/3 cup)
1 (12 oz.) pkg. butterscotch morsels
1 teaspoon vanilla
1 (12 oz.) pkg. chocolate morsels
2/3 cup chunky-style peanut butter
1 cup chopped salted peanuts

1. Combine sugar, marshmallows and milk in 1-1/2-quart casserole. Cook in Radarange Oven on Full Power for 3 to 4 minutes, or until marshmallows are melted. Stir once or twice during cooking time.
2. Stir in butterscotch morsels and vanilla. Stir until melted and well-blended. Spread in greased 2-quart utility dish. Cool slightly.
3. Combine chocolate morsels and peanut butter in 1-quart glass measure or casserole. Heat in Radarange Oven on Full Power for 1-1/2 to 2-1/2 minutes, or until melted. Stir halfway through cooking time. Blend in nuts. Spread over butterscotch layer. Cut before too hard.

MICRO-TIP: For Cherry Chip Mash, use 10 to 12 ounces of cherry morsels instead of butterscotch morsels.

Coconut Almond Balls

Yield: 5 dozen

3/4 cup mashed potatoes
1 lb. confectioners' sugar
4 cups flaked coconut
1 teaspoon almond extract
5 tablespoons water
2 tablespoons corn syrup
2 tablespoons butter or margarine, softened
1 (15.4 oz.) pkg. chocolate fudge frosting mix
Toasted almonds (optional)

1. Combine potatoes, confectioners' sugar, coconut and almond extract in large mixing bowl. Mix well. Drop by teaspoons onto waxed paper. For easier shaping, chill for 1/2 hour, and then roll into balls. Chill balls for 45 to 60 minutes, or until very firm.
2. Place water, corn syrup and butter in 1-1/2-quart casserole. Cook in Radarange Oven on Full Power for 1 to 2 minutes, or until heated through. Stir in frosting mix. Cook in Radarange Oven on Full Power for 2 to 3 minutes, or until smooth and creamy.* Dip balls in chocolate, and place on waxed paper. Top each ball with almond, if desired.

MICRO-TIPS:
• If chocolate mixture hardens, return to Radarange Oven on Cookmatic Level 6 until softened.
* Additional water may be added, if necessary.

Chocolate Sandwiches

Yield: 4 dozen

1/4 cup butter or margarine, melted
1/4 cup cocoa
1/2 cup confectioners' sugar
1 egg
1 teaspoon vanilla
1-1/2 cups graham cracker crumbs
1/2 cup chopped walnuts
1/2 cup shredded coconut
1/4 cup butter or margarine, melted
2 tablespoons milk
1 teaspoon vanilla
2 teaspoons dry vanilla pudding mix (not instant)
2 cups confectioners' sugar
1 (6 oz.) pkg. semi-sweet chocolate morsels
1/4 cup chopped walnuts

1. Combine butter, cocoa, 1/2 cup confectioners' sugar, egg and vanilla in 2-quart utility dish. Stir in cracker crumbs, nuts and coconut. Press mixture firmly against bottom of dish. Chill.
2. Combine butter, milk, vanilla and pudding mix in 1-cup glass measure. Cook in Radarange Oven on Full Power for 45 to 60 seconds, or until mixture boils and is thickened.
3. Beat above mixture into confectioners' sugar, until smooth. Spread over first layer.
4. Place chocolate morsels in 1-cup glass measure. Heat in Radarange Oven on Full Power for 1 to 1-1/2 minutes, or until melted. Spread over vanilla layer. Sprinkle nuts over top. Chill. Cut into small squares.

The Radarange Oven is well-known as a great cooking device, but it can also be used for a wide variety of other uses. Some of these uses involve food, such as toasting nuts or rehydrating dried fruit. Try making your own dried bread crumbs, croutons and yogurt, quickly and economically, in the Radarange Oven.

Do you have a baby in the house? Quickly heat your child's food in the Radarange Oven. Better still, make your own homemade baby food and heat it quickly to the temperature desired, in the Radarange Oven.

The Radarange Oven is also a time-saver when it is used for non-food related tasks, such as drying flowers. Make your own Radarange Oven-dried flower arrangements for gifts.

Also, when the holiday season arrives, your Christmas tree can be extra-special by decorating it with your very own handmade Christmas ornaments. Dough ornaments are quickly and easily made in the Radarange Oven and can be designed for other holidays, as well.

You can see that the Radarange Oven will save you time and energy in many "extra" ways. Enjoy using your creative talents with your Radarange Microwave Oven.

Note: Do not leave the microwave oven unattended when drying **anything**. Foods or other items being dried can become too dry and can ignite. If anything does ignite, press the Stop switch and open the oven door only after the ignition ceases.

Cinnamon Toasted Pecans

Yield: 1 cup nuts

1 tablespoon butter or margarine
1 (3 to 4 oz.) pkg. pecan halves
  (about 1 cup)
1/4 cup sugar
1/2 teaspoon cinnamon
1/4 teaspoon nutmeg (optional)

1. Place butter in small dish or glass measure. Heat in Radarange Oven Full Power for 20 seconds, or until melted.
2. Place pecan halves in plastic bag. Pour melted butter over nuts and t in bag.
3. Mix together sugar, cinnamon and nutmeg. Pour over pecans in bag. Shake to coat evenly. Spread pecans on paper plate.
4. Cook in Radarange Oven on Full Power for 1 to 1-1/2 minutes, or unt hot.

Toasted Almonds

Yield: 1 cup nuts

1 cup almonds (or other nuts)

Place almonds on paper plate. Cook in Radarange Oven on Full Powe for 1-1/2 to 2 minutes, or until hot.

Spicy Walnuts

Yield: 1 cup nuts

1 tablespoon butter or margarine, melted
1 teaspoon soy sauce
1/2 teaspoon paprika
1/4 teaspoon ginger
1/8 teaspoon garlic salt
1 cup walnut halves

1. Combine all ingredients, stirring to coat each nut with other ingredients. Spread walnuts in single layer in 2-quart utility dish.
2. Cook in Radarange Oven on Full Power for 1-1/2 to 2-1/2 minutes, or until nuts are light brown. Stir twice during cooking time.

Croutons

Yield: 1-1/2 cups

2 cups bread cubes, with crusts removed
2 tablespoons butter or margarine, melted
1/2 teaspoon paprika
1/2 teaspoon onion salt

1. Mix together all ingredients in 2-quart utility dish, stirring to coat bread cubes with other ingredients.
2. Heat in Radarange Oven on Full Power for 2 to 2-1/2 minutes, or until croutons are dry. Stir halfway through heating. Croutons will become crisper as they cool.

MICRO-TIPS:

- Serve on salads or casseroles.
- If croutons become soggy, reheat in Radarange Oven on Full Power for 1 minute, or until crisp.
- For cheese-flavor croutons, substitute 1/2 teaspoon of cheese flavor salt for the onion salt.

Dough Ornaments

Yield: 7 to 9 ornaments

3 cups all-purpose flour
1 cup salt
1-1/4 cups water
Food coloring (optional)
Instant tea (optional)

1. Combine all ingredients. Food coloring for added color or instant tea for browning may be added to the water, as desired. Knead dough for 5 to 7 minutes, or until smooth.
2. Roll portion of dough to 1/8 to 1/4-inch thick on waxed paper sheet cut to fit high temperature plastic baking sheet. Cut out 7 to 9 designs with cookie cutter. Remove excess dough and save to use later. Decorate and then pierce surface of each ornament evenly all over with toothpick or straight pin to eliminate air bubbles. Make small hole at top of each ornament for hanging. Slide waxed paper onto high temperature plastic baking sheet.
3. Cook in Radarange Oven on Full Power for 2 to 3 minutes, or until ornaments are dry and firm. Remove from waxed paper before completely cool.

MICRO-TIPS:

- Roll out long strands of dough and use them to make added detail such as bows and facial features.
- Ornaments may be decorated with colored crystal sugar or nonpareils. When cooled, you may varnish or paint each ornament to seal out moisture.

Dried Bread Crumbs

Yield: 1/2 cup crumbs

2 slices of bread

1. Place bread slices on plastic rack. Heat in Radarange Oven on Full Power for 1 to 1-1/2 minutes, or until dry. Cool.
2. Break each slice into several pieces. Grate in blender or crush into crumbs with rolling pin. Store in airtight container.

DRYING FLOWERS IN THE RADARANGE OVEN

Drying flowers in the Radarange Oven is another wonderful use of this labor-saving appliance. As in any craft, it is important to follow the directions carefully and accurately.

Brightly colored flowers dry best. Flowers, such as roses,

carnations, violets and zinnias work well with this process. For flower drying, you will need silica gel, which is available in most hobby shops and, of course, fresh flowers.

For best results, flowers should be only partially opened. Avoid using flowers with thick centers. Use the chart as a guide for drying other flowers.

FLOWER DRYING CHART

FLOWER TYPE	HEATING TIME ON FULL POWER	MINIMUM AMOUNT OF STANDING TIME***
*Carnation	2-1/2 to 3 min.	5 to 10 min.
Daffodil	1-1/2 to 2 min.	5 to 10 min.
Pansy — 1st drying	45 sec.	5 min.
2nd drying	1 to 1-1/2 min.	10 min.
Rose	1-1/2 min.	2 to 5 min.
Sunflower	1-3/4 min.	1-1/2 days**
Violet	1-1/2 to 2 min.	5 to 10 min.
Zinnia	2 to 2-1/2 min.	5 to 10 min.

*For best results dry three carnations at one time.
**Sunflowers should stand covered with a plastic bag during standing time.
***You may wish to increase the standing time for some flowers.

General Instructions for Drying Flowers
1. Partially fill a large glass or jar with silica gel. Place a flower stem-down into the silica gel. Slowly fill the remaining portion of the jar with gel. Be careful to place the silica gel between all petals of each flower. Use a toothpick to separate the petals. Cover the flower completely with silica gel.
2. Place the jar in the Radarange Oven. Place 1 cup of water in the rear left corner of the Radarange Oven. Heat in Radarange Oven on Full Power for 1 to 3 minutes, depending upon the general size of the flower. Longer heating times are required for larger flowers. Check the chart for specific times.
3. Use a separate jar for each flower. Silica gel may be reused only after it is completely cooled. Remove the flower from the jar when it is cooled. See the chart for the recommended amount of standing time.
4. After the standing time, slowly pour the silica gel from the jar. Carefully remove the flower. Gently brush any excess grains of gel from the petals or stem. Allow the silica gel to cool before reusing.
5. Floral wire may be used to support the stems. Artificial coloring may be added to the flowers when the flowers are completely dry, if desired. Leaves should be dried separately and then added to the stems.

DRIED FRUIT REHYDRATING CHART

FRUIT TYPE	AMOUNT	AMOUNT OF WATER	UTENSIL	1ST COOKING TIME ON FULL POWER	2ND COOKING TIME ON COOKMATIC LEVEL 3
Apples	8 ozs.	2-1/2 cups	2-quart casserole	8 to 12 min.	—
Apricots	6 ozs.	1-1/2 cups	1-1/2-quart casserole	4 to 6 min.	—
Mixed, Dried Fruit	8 ozs.	2 cups	1-1/2-quart casserole	6 min.	3 to 5 min.
Mixed, Dried Fruit	11 ozs.	2 cups	2-quart casserole	6 min.	5 to 7 min.
Peaches	11 ozs.	2 cups	1-1/2-quart casserole	6 min.	4 to 6 min.
Prunes	16 ozs.	2 cups	1-1/2-quart casserole	6 min.	4 to 6 min.

General Instructions for Rehydrating Dried Fruit

1. Place dried fruit and water in utensil recommended on the chart. Cover with a glass lid.
2. Cook in Radarange Oven, covered, according to the instructions on the chart, or until the fruit is plump and tender, as desired. Stir 1 or 2 times during cooking, to separate fruit pieces.

BABY FOOD HEATING CHART*

JAR SIZE	HEATING TIME ON FULL POWER
1/2 (4-1/2 to 4-3/4 oz.) jar	10 to 15 sec.
1 (4-1/2 to 4-3/4 oz.) jar	15 to 30 sec.

*The heating times on this chart include main dishes, vegetables, fruits or fruit desserts. Use this chart as a guide for heating your own homemade baby foods.

General Instructions for Heating Baby Food

1. Place the baby food in a custard cup or on a serving plate. Baby food should not be heated in jars. Avoid using jars or bottles having restricted openings in a microwave oven.
2. Heat in the Radarange Oven on Full Power according to the time on the chart, or until warmed to desired temperature.
3. A plate of baby foods, including half of the contents of each of 3 jars (such as a main dish, vegetable and dessert) may be heated. Heat in the Radarange Oven on Full Power for 45 seconds to 1 minute, 15 seconds, or until warmed to desired temperature.

a

Accessories (Utensils) . . . 6
Acorn Squash . . . 119
Adapting Conventional Recipes . . . 15
All-At-Once Spaghetti . . . 61
Almond Bark . . . 179
Appetizers and Snacks . . . 25-31
   Appetizers and Snacks Frozen Convenience
     Food Chart . . . 26
   Calico Crackers . . . 29
   Caramel Popcorn Balls . . . 29
   Chinese Hors D'Oeuvres . . . 27
   Clams-in-the-Shell . . . 28
   Coquilles . . . 28
   Escargot . . . 28
   Frank Kabobs . . . 31
   Frozen Pizza Chart . . . 27
   Glazed Bacon . . . 26
   Hot Cheesy Clam Dip . . 31
   Hot Crab Meat Canapes . . . 29
   Nachos . . . 27
   Nibbles Snack . . . 30
   Oyster Cracker Snax . . . 31
   Pizza Fondue . . . 31
   Prepare-Ahead Crab Balls . . . 29
   Savory Sausage Canapes . . . 29
   Stuffed Mushrooms . . . 30
   Sweet-Sour Meat Balls . . . 30
   Teriyaki Strips . . . 26
Appetizers and Snacks Frozen Convenience
   Food Chart . . . 26
Apple Brown Betty . . . 146
Apple Jelly . . . 135
Apple 'N' Rice Casserole . . . 53
Apple Pie . . . 161
Apple-Raisin Sauce . . . 133
Applesauce . . . 133
Applesauce Coconut Bars . . . 172
Applesauce Squares . . . 173
Apricot-Baked Chicken . . . 110
Arcing . . . 4
Arranging . . . 4
Artichoke . . . 121
Asparagus Royale . . . 122
Asparagus Sea Shore Style . . . 123
Automatic Temperature Control System . . . 13

b

Baby Food Heating Chart . . . 185
Bacon Cooking Chart . . . 94
Baked Apples . . . 138
Baked Canadian Bacon . . . 103
Baked Custard . . . 141
Baked Grapefruit . . . 138
Baked Pie Reheating Chart . . . 138

Baked Potatoes . . . 126
Baked Rhubarb Sauce . . . 133
Baked Stuffed Whole Fish . . . 79
Baking Powder Crust . . . 158
Banana Bars . . . 172
Banana Cream Pie . . . 163
Banana Nut Bread . . . 47
Barbecued Chicken Thighs . . . 114
Barbecued Hamburgers . . . 63
Basic Meat Balls . . . 101
Basic Tomato Sauce . . . 132
Bechemel Sauce . . . 129
Beef Cooking Chart . . . 90
Beef Corkscrew Bake . . . 60
Beef 'N' Tater Casserole . . . 101
Beef-Noodle Casserole . . . 60
Beef Strips with Tomatoes . . . 100
Beef Stroganoff . . . 101
Beverages . . . 32-36
   Cocoa . . . 33
   Easy Spiced Tea . . . 36
   Egg Coffee . . . 35
   French Chocolate . . . 34
   Hot Egg Nog . . . 35
   Hot Rum Lemonade . . . 36
   Instant Hot Chocolate Mix . . . 33
   Irish Coffee . . . 35
   Mexican Coffee . . . 35
   Moroccan Mint Tea . . . 35
   Mulled Wine Punch . . . 36
   Raspberry Cooler . . . 36
   Russian Tea . . . 36
   Variations for Hot Chocolate Chart . . . 34
Biscuit Breakfast Ring . . . 47
Blanching Vegetables Chart . . . 116-117
Blueberry Muffins . . . 48
Blueberry Syrup . . . 134
Bordelaise Sauce . . . 131
Bran-Oatmeal . . . 55
Bread and Butter Pickles . . . 136
Breads . . . 43-49
   Banana Nut Bread . . . 47
   Biscuit Breakfast Ring . . . 47
   Blueberry Muffins . . . 48
   Cheese Spoon Bread . . . 47
   Cherry Crumb Coffee Cake . . . 46
   Convenience Bread Mix Baking
     Chart . . . 46
   Cranberry Muffins . . . 48
   Frozen Convenience Breads Defrost
     Chart . . . 45
   Perpetual Muffins . . . 48
   Pumpkin Bread Ring . . . 45
   Quick Corn Bread Ring . . . 45
   Quick Sweet Rolls . . . 49
   Rye Bread . . . 49

Toffee Coffee Cake . . . 47
Broccoli-Onion Casserole . . . 124
Browning . . . 14
Browning Skillets . . . 4, 14
Bursting . . . 4
Butter, melting . . . 192
Butterscotch Pudding Parfait . . . 144

c

Cakes . . . 147-154
   Carrot Cake . . . 151
   Chocolate Cream Cheese Frosting . . . 149
   Chocolate Icing Deluxe . . . 148
   Chocolate Layer Cake . . . 154
   Coconut-Pecan Frosting . . . 151
   Convenience Cake Mix Baking
     Chart . . . 150
   Cupcake Baking Chart . . . 149
   Fancy Pistachio Nut Cake . . . 152
   Frozen Convenience Cake Defrosting
     Chart . . . 148
   Fudge Pudding Cake . . . 153
   German Chocolate Cake . . . 151
   Lime Gelatin Delight Cake . . . 154
   Oatmeal Cinnamon Cake . . . 152
   Pineapple Upside-Down Cake . . . 152
   Raspberry Preserves Cake . . . 154
   Triple Layer Coconut Cake . . . 153
   White Mountain Frosting . . . 149
Calico Bean Pot . . . 123
Calico Crackers . . . 29
Candies . . . 176-181
   Almond Bark . . . 179
   Candy Cookies . . . 180
   Caramel Peanut Puffs . . . 180
   Cathedral Window Candy . . . 180
   Chinese Clusters . . . 177
   Chocolate Creams . . . 179
   Chocolate Crispies . . . 180
   Chocolate-Gumdrop Squares . . . 179
   Chocolate Sandwiches . . . 181
   Coconut Almond Balls . . . 181
   Divinity . . . 178
   Marshmallow Creme Fudge . . . 178
   Old-Fashioned Taffy . . . 178
   Peanut Brittle . . . 177
   Peanut-Butterscotch Mash . . . 181
   Peanut Clusters . . . 177
   Quickie Fudge . . . 178
   Turtles . . . 177
   Vanilla Caramels . . . 179
Candy Cookies . . . 180
Canned Sauce Heating Chart . . . 129
Canned Soups and Stews Heating Chart . . . 38
Canning . . . 17

ntonese Ribs . . . 104
ramel Peanut Puffs . . . 180
ramel Popcorn Balls . . . 29
rrot Cake . . . 151
rry-Over Cooking Time . . . 4
thedral Window Candy . . . 180
uliflower Oriental . . . 125
ntura® Dinnerware . . . 6,7
real Cooking Chart . . . 54-55
eerleader Cheesecake . . . 139
eese Sauce (White Sauce) . . . 130
eese Soufflé . . . 73
eese Spoon Bread . . . 47
eesy Peach Pie . . . 160
erry Bars . . . 175
erry Crisp . . . 145
erry Crumb Coffee Cake . . . 46
erry Pie . . . 160
ewy Peanut Butter Bars . . . 172
icken Cacciatore . . . 112
icken Liver Stroganoff . . . 113
icken Livers Chablis . . . 113
icken 'N' Dumplings . . . 112
icken 'N' Rice . . . 111
icken Parmesan . . . 112
icken Teriyaki . . . 111
ili Con Carne . . . 40
lled Fruit Cup . . . 139
nese Clusters . . . 177
nese Hors D'Oeuvres . . . 27
ocolate Almond Pie . . . 162
ocolate Chip Cookies . . . 170
ocolate-Coconut Pie Shell . . . 159
ocolate Cream Cheese Frosting . . . 149
ocolate Creams . . . 179
ocolate Crispies . . . 180
ocolate Crumb Crust . . . 158
ocolate Drops . . . 170
ocolate-Gumdrop Squares . . . 179
ocolate Icing Deluxe . . 148
ocolate Layer Cake . . . 154
ocolate Morsels, Melting . . . 192
ocolate Nut Cookies . . . 169
ocolate Sandwiches . . . 181
namon Bars . . . 173
namon Toasted Pecans . . . 182
ms-in-the-Shell . . . 28
ssic Green Bean Treat . . . 126
ssic Meat Loaf . . . 102
coa . . . 33
conut Almond Balls . . . 181
conut Cream Pie . . . 163
conut Oatmeal Cookies . . . 170
conut-Pecan Frosting . . . 151
ffee Cream Pie . . . 164
orful Fillets . . . 77
nvenience Bread Mix Baking Chart . . . 46
nvenience Cake Mix Baking Chart . . . 150

Convenience Main Dish Mix Cooking Chart . . . 99
Convenience Sandwich Filling Seasoning Mix
   Cooking Chart . . . 63
Convenience Sauce Mix Cooking Chart . . . 129
Conventional Drop Cookie Conversion Chart . . . 167
Converting Conventional Recipes
   (See Adapting Conventional Recipes)
Convenience Foods Charts (See specific food,
   such as Cakes, Breads, etc.)
Cooked Salad Dressing . . . 132
Cooked Shrimp . . . 79
Cookie Mix Baking Chart . . . 167

Cookies . . . 165-175

   Applesauce Coconut Bars . . . 172
   Applesauce Squares . . . 173
   Banana Bars . . . 172
   Cherry Bars . . . 175
   Chewy Peanut Butter Bars . . . 172
   Chocolate Chip Cookies . . . 170
   Chocolate Drops . . . 170
   Chocolate Nut Cookies . . . 169
   Cinnamon Bars . . . 173
   Coconut Oatmeal Cookies . . . 170
   Conventional Drop Cookie Conversion
      Chart . . . 167
   Cookie Mix Baking Chart . . . 167
   Date Bars . . . 173
   Double-Decker Crunchies . . . 174
   Easy Oatmeal Cookies . . . 168
   Five Layer Bars . . . 171
   Frozen Cookie Defrosting Chart . . . 166
   Fudge Brownies . . . 174
   Ginger Cream Cookies . . . 168
   Granola Chewies . . . 175
   Honey Pecan Balls . . . 169
   Lemon Drops . . . 171
   Marbled Butterscotch Bars . . . 172
   Marshmallow Treats . . . 170
   Peanut Butter and Jelly
      Cookie-Wiches . . . 168
   Pumpkin Squares . . . 175
   Refrigerator Filled Cookies . . . 171
   Reheating Cookies Chart . . . 166
   Scotch Toffee Bars . . . 171
   Shortbread . . . 169
   Snicker Doodle Cookies . . . 169
   Thumbprint Cookies . . . 168
   Triple Treats . . . 174

Cooking Grill . . . 5,10
Cooking Variables . . . 11
Cookmatic Power Levels . . . 3, 5, 12
Coquilles . . . 28
Corelle® Livingware . . . 6,7
Corn and Potato Chowder . . . 41
Corn-in-the-Husk . . . 125
Covering (Wrapping) . . . 5
Cranberry Jelly . . . 135

Cranberry Muffins . . . 48
Cranberry Squash . . . 119
Cream of Tomato and Rice Soup . . . 39
Creamy Blue Cheese Salad Dressing
   (Cooked Salad Dressing) . . . 132
Creamy French Salad Dressing
   (Cooked Salad Dressing) . . . 132
Creamy Italian Dressing
   (Cooked Salad Dressing) . . . 132
Creole Halibut . . . 78
Croutons . . . 183
Crunchy Crab Bake . . . 76
Crustless Quiche Lorraine . . . 72
Cupcake Baking Chart . . . 149
Cured Breakfast Meats Cooking Chart . . . 93
Curried Scallops . . . 79
Curried Shrimp and Broccoli . . . 80
Custard Pie . . . 162
Custard Sauce . . . 134

d

Date Bars . . . 173
Defrosting . . . 13
Delicate Ingredients . . . 5
Dessert Lemon Sauce . . . 133

Desserts . . . 137-146

   Apple Brown Betty . . . 146
   Baked Apples . . . 138
   Baked Custard . . . 141
   Baked Grapefruit . . . 138
   Butterscotch Pudding Parfait . . . 144
   Cheerleader Cheesecake . . . 139
   Cherry Crisp . . . 145
   Chilled Fruit Cup . . . 139
   Easy Rice Pudding . . . 144
   Fancy Bread Pudding . . . 142
   Frozen Fruit Defrosting Chart . . . 138
   Frozen Lemon Dessert . . . 140
   Fruit Crisp Topping . . . 145
   Fruit-Flavor Gelatin . . . 138
   Fruit Soup . . . 146
   Heavenly Tarts . . . 144
   Ice Cream Sundae Dessert . . . 141
   Light 'N' Fruity Tapioca . . . 143
   Marvelous Marble Cheesecake . . . 140
   Minute Tapioca Pudding . . . 143
   Mocha Bread Custard . . . 142
   Mocha Mousse . . . 143
   Peach Crisp . . . 145
   Peach-Pineapple Cobbler . . . 146
   Peachy Cheese Torte . . . 139
   Pineapple-Banana Sundae . . . 144
   Pineapple Bridge Dessert . . . 140
   Pistachio Ice Cream Dessert . . . 141
   Pot de Creme . . . 143
   Pudding from Prepared Mix . . . 142
   Some-Mores . . . 146

Strawberry-Rhubarb Crisp . . . 145
Vanilla Cream Pudding . . . 142

Dill Sauce (White Sauce) . . . 130
Dishes (See Utensils)
Divinity . . . 178
Double-Decker Crunchies . . . 174
Dough Ornaments . . . 183
Dried Bread Crumbs . . . 183
Dried Fruit Rehydrating Chart . . 185
Dried Legume Cooking Chart . . . 122
Duckling Bordeaux . . . 114

e

Easy Barbecued Chicken . . . 110
Easy New England Clam Chowder . . . 40
Easy Oatmeal Cookies . . . 168
Easy Rice Pudding . . . 144
Easy Spiced Tea . . . 36
Egg and Sausage Scramble . . . 70
Egg Coffee . . . 35
Egg Salad Sandwiches . . . 66
Eggs and Cheese . . . 67-73
Cheese Soufflé . . . 73
Crustless Quiche Lorraine . . . 72
Egg and Sausage Scramble . . . 70
Eggs Benedict . . . 69
Eggs Delicious . . . 73
Fancy Scrambled Eggs . . . 71
Fried Eggs Chart . . . 69
Hash 'N' Egg Nests . . . 73
Poached Eggs Chart . . . 70
Puffy Omelet . . . 72
Savory Bacon Omelet . . . 72
Scrambled Eggs Chart . . . 68
Toast-Framed Egg . . . 71
Wake-Up Special . . . 71
Wheat Crusted Quiche . . . 71
Eggs and Hamwich . . . 66
Eggs Benedict . . . 69
Eggs Delicious . . . 73
Erupting (See Bursting)
Escargot . . . 28
Everyday Foods Heating and Reheating
Chart . . . 192

f

Fall Relish . . . 136
Fancy Bread Pudding . . . 142
Fancy Pistachio Nut Cake . . . 152
Fancy Scrambled Eggs . . . 71
Fiesta Rice . . . 56
Fillet of Sole with Oyster Sauce . . 77
Fish and Seafood . . . 74-81
Baked Stuffed Whole Fish . . . 79
Colorful Fillets . . . 77

Cooked Shrimp . . . 79
Creole Halibut . . . 78
Crunchy Crab Bake . . . 76
Curried Scallops . . . 79
Curried Shrimp and Broccoli . . . 80
Fillet of Sole with Oyster Sauce . . . 77
Fish and Seafood Convenience Food
Chart . . . 76
Fish and Seafood Defrosting Chart . . . 75
Fish for One . . . 77
French Fish Fillets . . . 77
Fresh Crab Claws . . . 76
Halibut Teriyaki . . . 78
Salmon Quiche . . . 78
Savory Salmon Steaks . . . 78
Scalloped Oysters . . . 80
Shoestring Tuna Casserole . . . 81
Shrimp Creole . . . 80
Springtime Sole . . . 77
Stuffed Red Snapper . . . 79
Tuna Divan . . . 81
Tuna Stroganoff . . . 81
Tuna Tot Casserole . . . 81

Fish and Seafood Convenience Food Chart . . . 76
Fish and Seafood Defrosting Chart . . . 75
Fish for One . . . 77
500-Watt Microwave Oven Meat Cooking
Chart . . . 90
Five Layer Bars . . . 171
Flounder Stew . . . 41
Flower Drying Chart . . . 184
Foil and Metal Utensils . . . 6
Frank Kabobs . . . 31
Frankfurter Cooking Chart . . . 94
Freezer to Radarange Oven . . . 14
French Chocolate . . . 34
French Dip Sandwiches . . . 62
French Fish Fillets . . . 77
French Onion Soup . . . 38
Fresh Crab Claws . . . 76
Fresh Vegetable Cooking Chart . . . 118-119
Fried Eggs Chart . . . 69
Frozen Baked Pie Defrosting Chart . . . 156
Frozen Convenience Breads Defrosting
Chart . . . 45
Frozen Convenience Cake Defrosting
Chart . . . 148
Frozen Convenience Meat and Main Dish
Chart . . . 98
Frozen Cookie Defrosting Chart . . . 166
Frozen Fried Chicken Cooking Chart . . . 109
Frozen Fruit Defrosting Chart . . . 138
Frozen Lemon Dessert . . . 140
Frozen Main Dish Defrosting Chart . . . 97
Frozen Pie Crust . . . 156
Frozen Pizza Chart . . . 27
Frozen Turkey Roast Cooking Chart . . . 110

Fruit Crisp Topping . . . 145
Fruit Dressing . . . 132
Fruit-Flavor Gelatin . . . 138
Fruit Soup . . . 146
Fudge Brownies . . . 174
Fudge Pudding Cake . . . 153

g

German Chocolate Cake . . . 151
Ginger Cream Cookies . . . 168
Gingersnap Crumb Crust . . . 159
Glass Ceramic Utensils . . . 7
Glass Utensils . . . 7
Glazed Bacon . . . 26
Glossary . . . 4
Golden Pancake Syrup . . . 134
Goulash . . . 60
Graham Cracker Crust . . . 158
Granola . . . 55
Granola Chewies . . . 175
Grasshopper Pie . . . 163
Ground Beef, Lamb and Veal Patty
Cooking Chart . . . 96

h

Halibut Teriyaki . . . 78
Ham Salad Sandwiches . . . 65
Hamburger Stroganoff . . . 102
Hard-Cooked Eggs . . . 17, 67
Hash 'N' Egg Nests . . . 73
Hearty Hamburger Soup . . . 39
Heavenly Tarts . . . 144
Herbed Broccoli . . . 124
Holding Time . . . 5
Hollandaise Sauce . . . 131
Honey Pecan Balls . . . 169
Honeyed Beets . . . 123
Hot Cheesy Clam Dip . . . 31
Hot Crab Meat Canapes . . . 29
Hot Crab Meat Sandwiches . . . 65
Hot Dogs (See Frankfurters)
Hot Egg Nog . . . 35
Hot Fudge Sauce . . . 134
Hot Rum Lemonade . . . 36
Hot Swiss Chicken Salad Sandwiches . . . 64

i

Ice Cream Sundae Dessert . . . 141
Instant Hot Chocolate Mix . . . 33
Irish Coffee . . . 35
Irish Lamb Stew . . . 41
Italian Spaghetti . . . 61
Italian-Style Zucchini . . . 127

j

Jambalaya . . . 56

l

Lamb and Veal Shoulder Steaks . . . 94
Lamb Cooking Chart . . . 91
Lasagna . . . 59
"Left-Over" Turkey in Buns . . . 66
Lemon Chiffon Pie . . . 164
Lemon Drops . . . 171
Lemon Mallow Pie (Orange Mallow Pie) . . . 159
Lemon Meringue Pie . . . 161
Lemon Sauce for Fish . . . 131
Light 'N' Fruity Tapioca . . . 143
Lime Gelatin Delight Cake . . . 154
Low Calorie Cooking . . . 17

m

Macaroni and Cheese . . . 58
Made-Right Mushroom Burgers . . . 64
Mandarin Carrots . . . 124
Marbled Butterscotch Bars . . . 172
Marshmallow-Caramel Sauce . . . 134
Marshmallow Creme Fudge . . . 178
Marshmallow Treats . . . 170
Marvelous Marble Cheesecake . . . 140
Meal Planning . . . 20-24
Meat Ball Stew . . . 42
Meat Cooking Methods: Summary Chart . . . 89
Meats and Main Dishes . . . 82-105
  Bacon Cooking Chart . . . 94
  Baked Canadian Bacon . . . 103
  Basic Meat Balls . . . 101
  Beef Cooking Chart . . . 90
  Beef 'N' Tater Casserole . . . 101
  Beef Strips with Tomatoes . . . 100
  Beef Stroganoff . . . 101
  Cantonese Ribs . . . 104
  Classic Meat Loaf . . . 102
  Convenience Main Dish Mix Cooking Chart . . . 99
  Cured Breakfast Meats Cooking Chart . . . 93
  500-Watt Microwave Oven Meat Cooking Chart . . . 90
  Frankfurter Cooking Chart . . . 94
  Frozen Convenience Meat and Main Dish Chart . . . 98
  Frozen Main Dish Defrosting Chart . . . 97
  Ground Beef, Lamb and Veal Patty Cooking Chart . . . 96
  Hamburger Stroganoff . . . 102
  Lamb and Veal Shoulder Steaks . . . 94
  Lamb Cooking Chart . . . 91
  Meat Cooking Methods: Summary Chart . . . 89
  Methods for Cooking Meats . . . 84-88
  Oriental Pork . . . 105
  Pork Chop Maui . . . 104
  Pork Cooking Chart . . . 91

  Pork, Lamb, and Veal Chops . . . 94
  Pork-Vegetable Roast . . . 104
  Pre-Cooked Ham Chart . . . 92
  Recommended End Temperature Chart . . . 90
  Roast Defrosting Chart . . . 83
  Salisbury Steak . . . 102
  Sauces for Meats . . . 88
  Sausage Cooking Chart . . . 93
  Slow Cook Pot Roast . . . 100
  Small Size Meats Defrosting Chart . . . 83
  Spanish Lamb Chops . . . 105
  Spiced Cider Baked Ham . . . 103
  Steak Teriyaki . . . 100
  Stuffed Peppers . . . 101
  Stuffed Pork Chops . . . 104
  Sukiyaki . . . 100
  Sweet-Sour Pork . . . 105
  Taco Casserole . . . 102
  Tangy Ham Loaf . . . 105
  Tender Beef Steak Cooking Chart . . . 95
  Veal Cooking Chart . . . 91
  Veal Parmigiana . . . 103
  Veal Scallopini . . . 103
Methods for Cooking Meats . . . 84-88
Mexican Coffee . . . 35
Minestrone Soup . . . 40
Minute Tapioca Pudding . . . 143
Mocha Bread Custard . . . 142
Mocha Mousse . . . 143
Mornay Sauce . . . 131
Moroccan Mint Tea . . . 35
Mulled Wine Punch . . . 36
Mustard Sauce (White Sauce) . . . 130

n

Nachos . . . 27
Newburg Sauce (White Sauce) . . . 130
Newspapers . . . 7
Nibbles Snack . . . 30

o

Oatmeal Cinnamon Cake . . . 152
Old-Fashioned Beef Stew . . . 42
Old-Fashioned Taffy . . . 178
Orange Mallow Pie . . . 159
Orange Rice . . . 51
Oriental Pork . . . 105
Oyster Cracker Snax . . . 31

p

Paper Utensils . . . 7
Parsley Buttered Carrots . . . 124
Party Potatoes . . . 126
Pasta Convenience Foods Chart . . . 58-59
Pasta Cooking Chart . . . 57

Pasta Yield Chart . . . 57
Pastry I . . . 157
Pastry II . . . 158
Peach-Cherry Conserve . . . 135
Peach Crisp . . . 145
Peach-Pineapple Cobbler . . . 146
Peachy Cheese Torte . . . 139
Peanut Brittle . . . 177
Peanut Butter and Jelly Cookie-Wiches . . . 168
Peanut Butter Cream Pie . . . 161
Peanut Butter Crunch Crust . . . 159
Peanut-Butterscotch Mash . . . 181
Peanut Clusters . . . 177
Pecan Pie . . . 160
Perpetual Muffins . . . 48
Pickled Beet Relish . . . 136
Piercing . . . 5

Pies . . . 155-164

  Apple Pie . . . 161
  Baked Pie Reheating Chart . . . 157
  Baking Powder Crust . . . 158
  Banana Cream Pie . . . 163
  Cheesy Peach Pie . . . 160
  Cherry Pie . . . 160
  Chocolate Almond Pie . . . 162
  Chocolate-Coconut Pie Shell . . . 159
  Chocolate Crumb Crust . . . 158
  Coconut Cream Pie . . . 163
  Coffee Cream Pie . . . 164
  Custard Pie . . . 162
  Frozen Baked Pie Defrosting Chart . . . 156
  Frozen Pie Crust . . . 156
  Gingersnap Crumb Crust . . . 159
  Graham Cracker Crust . . . 158
  Grasshopper Pie . . . 163
  Lemon Chiffon Pie . . . 164
  Lemon Mallow Pie (Orange Mallow Pie) . . . 159
  Lemon Meringue Pie . . . 161
  Orange Mallow Pie . . . 159
  Pastry I . . . 157
  Pastry II . . . 158
  Peanut Butter Cream Pie . . . 161
  Peanut Butter Crunch Crust . . . 159
  Pecan Pie . . . 160
  Pineapple Mallow Pie (Orange Mallow Pie) . . . 159
  Pumpkin Pie . . . 160
  Rhubarb Custard Pie . . . 162
  Sour Cream Raisin Pie . . . 164
  Strawberry Rhubarb Pie . . . 162
Pineapple-Banana Sundae . . . 144
Pineapple Bridge Dessert . . . 140
Pineapple Mallow Pie (Orange Mallow Pie) . . . 159
Pineapple Upside-Down Cake . . . 152
Pistachio Ice Cream Dessert . . . 141

Pizza Fondue . . . 31
Pizzawiches . . . 64
Plastic Rack . . . 5
Plastic Utensils . . . 8
Poached Eggs Chart . . . 70
Popcorn . . . 17
Pork Chops Maui . . . 104
Pork Cooking Chart . . . 91
Pork, Lamb and Veal Chops . . . 94
Pork-Vegetable Roast . . . 104
Pot de Creme . . . 143

Poultry . . . 106-114
Apricot-Baked Chicken . . . 110
Barbecued Chicken Thighs . . . 114
Chicken Cacciatore . . . 112
Chicken Liver Stroganoff . . . 113
Chicken Livers Chablis . . . 113
Chicken 'N' Dumplings . . . 112
Chicken 'N' Rice . . . 111
Chicken Parmesan . . . 112
Chicken Teriyaki . . . 111
Duckling Bordeaux . . . 114
Easy Barbecued Chicken . . . 110
Frozen Fried Chicken Cooking Chart . . . 109
Frozen Turkey Roast Cooking Chart . . . 110
Poultry Defrosting Chart . . . 109
Poultry Dressing . . . 108
Roasting Directions for Whole
    Poultry . . . 107-108
Shake and Bake Chicken . . . 111
Speedy Baked Chicken . . . 111
Stuffed Duckling L'Orange . . . 114
Swiss Turkey and Ham Bake . . . 113

Poultry Defrosting Chart . . . 109
Poultry Dressing . . . 108
Power Levels . . . 3, 12-13
Precautions . . . 17 (Also see
    Use and Care Manual)
Pre-Cooked Ham Chart . . . 92
Preheating . . . 5, 14
Prepare-Ahead Crab Balls . . . 29
Pudding from Prepared Mix . . . 142
Puffy Omelet . . . 72
Pumpkin Bread Ring . . . 45
Pumpkin Pie . . . 160
Pumpkin Squares . . . 175
Puncturing (See Piercing)

q

Quick Corn Bread Ring . . . 45
Quick Fried Rice . . . 51
Quick Sweet Rolls . . . 49
Quickie Fudge . . . 178

r

Radarange Oven Cooking Techniques . . . 10

Radarange Oven "Extras" . . . 182-185
Baby Food Heating Chart . . . 185
Cinnamon Toasted Pecans . . . 182
Croutons . . . 183
Dough Ornaments . . . 183
Dried Bread Crumbs . . . 183
Dried Fruit Rehydrating Chart . . . 185
Flower Drying Chart . . . 184
Spicy Walnuts . . . 183
Toasted Almonds . . . 182

Raspberry Cooler . . . 36
Raspberry Preserves Cake . . . 154
Ratatouille . . . 125
Rearranging . . . 12
Recommended End Temperature Chart . . . 90
Refrigerator Filled Cookies . . . 171
Reheating . . . 16, 192
Reheating Cookies Chart . . . 166
Reheating Liquids . . . 16, 17
Reuben Sandwich . . . 65
Rhubarb Custard Pie . . . 162
Rice and Spinach Deluxe . . . 51

Rice, Cereals and Pastas . . . 50-61
All-At-Once Spaghetti . . . 61
Apple 'N' Rice Casserole . . . 53
Beef Corkscrew Bake . . . 60
Beef-Noodle Casserole . . . 60
Bran-Oatmeal . . . 55
Cereal Cooking Chart . . . 54-55
Fiesta Rice . . . 56
Goulash . . . 60
Granola . . . 55
Italian Spaghetti . . . 61
Jambalaya . . . 56
Lasagna . . . 59
Macaroni and Cheese . . . 58
Orange Rice . . . 51
Pasta Convenience Foods Chart . . . 58-59
Pasta Cooking Chart . . . 57
Pasta Yield Chart . . . 57
Quick Fried Rice . . . 51
Rice and Spinach Deluxe . . . 51
Rice Cooking and Convenience Food
    Chart . . . 52-53
Rice Yield Chart . . . 50
Roman Noodles . . . 61
Saucy Chops and Rice . . . 56
Swedish Rice Pudding . . . 56
Wild Rice and Mushrooms . . . 51

Rice Cooking and Convenience Food
    Chart . . . 52-53
Rice Yield Chart . . . 50
Rich Mushroom Sauce . . . 131
Roast Defrosting Chart . . . 83
Roasting Directions for Whole Poultry
    . . . 107-108

Roman Noodles . . . 61
Rotating (See Turning)
Ruby-Strawberry Sauce . . . 133
Russian Borscht . . . 42
Russian Tea . . . 36
Rye Bread . . . 49

s

Salisbury Steak . . . 102
Salmon Quiche . . . 78

Sandwiches . . . 62-66
Barbecued Hamburgers . . . 63
Convenience Sandwich Filling Seasoning
    Mix Cooking Chart . . . 63
Egg Salad Sandwiches . . . 66
Eggs and Hamwich . . . 66
French Dip Sandwiches . . . 62
Ham Salad Sandwiches . . . 65
Hot Crab Meat Sandwiches . . . 65
Hot Swiss Chicken Salad Sandwiches . . . 64
"Left-Over" Turkey in Buns . . . 66
Made-Right Mushroom Burgers . . . 64
Pizzawiches . . . 64
Reuben Sandwich . . . 65
Surf and Turfwiches . . . 63
Taco Heroes . . . 65
Turkey, Bacon and Tomato
    Sandwiches . . . 66

Sauces for Meats . . . 88

Sauces, Jams and Relishes . . . 128-136
Apple Jelly . . . 135
Apple-Raisin Sauce . . . 133
Applesauce . . . 133
Baked Rhubarb Sauce . . . 133
Basic Tomato Sauce . . . 132
Bechemel Sauce . . . 129
Blueberry Syrup . . . 134
Bordelaise Sauce . . . 131
Bread and Butter Pickles . . . 136
Canned Sauce Heating Chart . . . 129
Cheese Sauce (White Sauce) . . . 130
Convenience Sauce Mix Cooking
    Chart . . . 129
Cooked Salad Dressing . . . 132
Cranberry Jelly . . . 135
Creamy Blue Cheese Dressing
    (Cooked Salad Dressing) . . . 132
Creamy French Salad Dressing
    (Cooked Salad Dressing) . . . 132
Creamy Italian Dressing
    (Cooked Salad Dressing) . . . 132
Custard Sauce . . . 134
Dessert Lemon Sauce . . . 133
Dill Sauce (White Sauce) . . . 130
Fall Relish . . . 136

Fruit Dressing . . . 132
Golden Pancake Syrup . . . 134
Hollandaise Sauce . . . 131
Hot Fudge Sauce . . . 134
Lemon Sauce for Fish . . . 131
Marshmallow-Caramel Sauce . . . 134
Mornay Sauce . . . 131
Mustard Sauce (White Sauce) . . . 130
Newburg Sauce (White Sauce) . . . 130
Peach-Cherry Conserve . . . 135
Pickled Beet Relish . . . 136
Rich Mushroom Sauce . . . 131
Ruby-Strawberry Sauce . . . 133
Simple Strawberry Preserves . . . 135
Sour Cream Dressing . . . 130
Spiced Apples . . . 136
Spiced Pears . . . 136
Sweet-Sour Sauce . . . 130
Vanilla Sauce . . . 134
White Sauce (and Variations) . . . 130
Saucy Chops and Rice . . . 56
Sausage Cooking Chart . . . 93
Savory Bacon Omelet . . . 72
Savory Salmon Steaks . . . 78
Savory Sausage Canapes . . . 29
Scalloped Corn . . . 125
Scalloped Oysters . . . 80
Scalloped Tomato Potatoes . . . 127
Scotch Toffee Bars . . . 171
Scrambled Eggs Chart . . . 68
Seafood (See Fish)
Shake and Bake Chicken . . . 111
Shells . . . 8
Shielding . . . 5
Shoestring Tuna Casserole . . . 81
Shortbread . . . 169
Shrimp and Crab Gumbo . . . 39
Shrimp Creole . . . 80
Simple Strawberry Preserves . . . 135
Slow Cook Pot Roast . . . 100
Small Size Meats Defrosting Chart . . . 83
Snicker Doodle Cookies . . . 169
Some-Mores . . . 146

Soups and Stews . . . 37-42
Canned Soups and Stews Heating Chart . . . 38
Chili Con Carne . . . 40
Corn and Potato Chowder . . . 41
Cream of Tomato and Rice Soup . . . 39
Easy New England Clam Chowder . . . 40
Flounder Stew . . . 41
French Onion Soup . . . 38
Hearty Hamburger Soup . . . 39
Irish Lamb Stew . . . 41
Meat Ball Stew . . . 42
Minestrone Soup . . . 40
Old-Fashioned Beef Stew . . . 42
Russian Borscht . . . 42

Shrimp and Crab Gumbo . . . 39
Sour Cream Dressing . . . 130
Sour Cream Raisin Pie . . . 164
Spanish Lamb Chops . . . 105
Speedy Baked Chicken . . . 111
Spiced Apples . . . 136
Spiced Cider Baked Ham . . . 103
Spiced Pears . . . 136
Spicy Walnuts . . . 183
Springtime Sole . . . 77
Standing Time (See Holding Time)
Steak Teriyaki . . . 100
Straw Utensils . . . 8
Strawberry-Rhubarb Crisp . . . 145
Strawberry Rhubarb Pie . . . 162
Stuffed Duckling L'Orange . . . 114
Stuffed Mushrooms . . . 30
Stuffed Peppers . . . 101
Stuffed Pork Chops . . . 104
Stuffed Red Snapper . . . 79
Sukiyaki . . . 100
Surf and Turfwiches . . . 63
Swedish Rice Pudding . . . 56
Sweet-Sour Meat Balls . . . 30
Sweet-Sour Pork . . . 105
Sweet-Sour Red Cabbage . . . 124
Sweet-Sour Sauce . . . 130
Swiss Turkey and Ham Bake . . . 113

t
Taco Casserole . . . 102
Taco Heroes . . . 65
Tangy Ham Loaf . . . 105
Tender Beef Steak Cooking Chart . . . 95
Teriyaki Strips . . . 26
Temperature Probe (See Automatic Temperature Control System)
Thawing (See Defrosting)
Thermometers . . . 10
Thumbprint Cookies . . . 168
Toast-Framed Egg . . . 71
Toasted Almonds . . . 182
Toffee Coffee Cake . . . 47
Toll House Baked Beans . . . 123
Triple Layer Coconut Cake . . . 153
Triple Treats . . . 174
Tuna Divan . . . 81
Tuna Stroganoff . . . 81
Tuna Tot Casserole . . . 81
Turkey, Bacon and Tomato Sandwiches . . . 66
Turning . . . 6, 12
Turtles . . . 177
T.V. Dinners . . . 6, 98
Twice-Baked Potatoes . . . 127

u
Utensil Test . . . 7

Utensils and Accessories . . . 6
Metals . . . 6
Newspapers . . . 7
Use of Bottles . . 185

V
Vanilla Caramels . . . 179
Vanilla Cream Pudding . . . 142
Vanilla Sauce . . . 134
Variations for Hot Chocolate Chart . . . 34
Veal Cooking Chart . . . 91
Veal Parmigiana . . . 103
Veal Scallopini . . . 103

Vegetables . . . 115-127
Acorn Squash . . . 119
Artichoke . . . 121
Asparagus Royale . . . 122
Asparagus Sea Shore Style . . . 123
Baked Potatoes . . . 126
Blanching Vegetables Chart . . . 116-117
Broccoli-Onion Casserole . . . 124
Calico Bean Pot . . . 123
Cauliflower Oriental . . . 125
Classic Green Bean Treat . . . 126
Corn-in-the-Husk . . . 125
Cranberry Squash . . . 119
Dried Legume Cooking Chart . . . 122
Fresh Vegetable Cooking Chart . . . 118-119
Frozen Vegetable Cooking Chart . . . 120-121
Herbed Broccoli . . . 124
Honeyed Beets . . . 123
Italian-Style Zucchini . . . 127
Mandarin Carrots . . . 124
Parsley Buttered Carrots . . . 124
Party Potatoes . . . 126
Ratatouille . . . 125
Scalloped Corn . . . 125
Scalloped Tomato Potatoes . . . 127
Sweet-Sour Red Cabbage . . . 124
Toll House Baked Beans . . . 123
Twice-Baked Potatoes . . . 127
Wax Bean Casserole . . . 127

W
Wake-Up Special . . . 71
Warnings and Precautions . . . 17 (Also see Use and Care Manual)
Water, Boiling . . . 192
Wax Bean Casserole . . . 127
Wheat Crusted Quiche . . . 71
White Mountain Frosting . . . 149
White Sauce (and Variations) . . . 130
Wieners (See Frankfurters)
Wild Rice and Mushrooms . . . 51
Wooden Utensils . . . 8
Wrapping (See Covering)

EVERYDAY FOODS HEATING AND REHEATING CHART

FOOD	AMOUNT	HEATING TIME	COOKMATIC LEVEL OR SETTING	SPECIAL INSTRUCTIONS
Butter (melting)	1 tablespoon or less	20 sec.	Full Power	—
	1/2 cup	40 to 60 sec.	Full Power	—
(softening)	1/2 cup	1 to 1-1/2 min.	Cookmatic Level 3	—
Cheese (softening)	1 (5 oz.) jar	2 to 3 min.	Cookmatic Level 3	—
Chicken, cooked (2 pieces)	6-1/2 to 7 ozs.	1 to 2 min.	Full Power	Cover with plastic wrap.
Chocolate, morsels (melting)	6 ozs.	1-1/2 to 2-1/2 min.	Cookmatic Level 5	Stir occasionally during heating time.
	12 ozs.	2-1/2 to 3-1/2 min.	Cookmatic Level 5	Stir occasionally during heating time.
squares (melting)	1 oz.	1-1/2 to 3 min.	Cookmatic Level 5	—
Coffee or Tea	1 cup	1 to 1-1/2 min.	Full Power	—
Coffee Cake (2-inch squares)	1 to 2	15 to 20 sec.	Full Power	Wrap with napkin or plastic wrap.
Cream Cheese (softening)	3 ozs.	1 to 2 min.	Cookmatic Level 3	—
	8 ozs.	2 to 3 min.	Cookmatic Level 3	—
Dinner plate, with meat, potato and vegetable (reheating)	1 plate	1-1/2 to 2 min.	Full Power	Cover with waxed paper or plastic wrap.
Frankfurter, in bun	1 sandwich	20 to 30 sec.	Full Power	Wrap with napkin or plastic wrap.
Meat Patty	1 (4 oz.)	30 to 40 sec.	Full Power	—
Milk (hot)	1 cup	1-1/2 to 2 min.	Cookmatic Level 8	—
Pie, fruit (4-inch)	1 slice	20 to 30 sec.	Full Power	Cover with napkin or plastic wrap.
Pizza	1 slice	30 to 45 sec.	Full Power	Heat on plastic rack.
Roll, dinner	1 roll	15 to 20 sec.	Full Power	Cover with napkin.
Sandwich	1 sandwich	45 to 60 sec.	Full Power	Cover with napkin or plastic wrap.
Soup	1 (8 oz.) serving	1-1/2 to 2 min.	Full Power	—
Water (hot)	1 cup	1 to 2 min.	Full Power	—
(boiling)	1 cup	2 to 3 min.	Full Power	—